The Censors as Guardians of Public and Family Life in the Roman Republic

This volume explores the effects of the Roman censorial mark (*nota censoria*) and the influence of censorial regulations on the development of written law in ancient Rome.

The censor was one of the most fascinating legal institutions of Republican Rome. One of the most colourful and anecdotal areas of censorial activities was in the upkeep of public morals (*regimen morum*) through which censors controlled private, even intimate, aspects of Roman life. Although the office of the censor has been studied by various scholars from prosopographical, historical, and social perspectives, there has been no comprehensive study of its impact on the development of written law. This book aims to fill the gap by providing an overview of the applications of the *nota censoria* to demonstrate its impact on the development of numerous regulations in both private and public laws during the Republican and Imperial periods. This book explores the relationship between magistrate law (*ius honorarium*) and *regimen morum*, and how the activities of the censors in this area influenced the formation of praetorian edicts and later legislation during the Principate period, most notably the marriage laws of Augustus. By examining the influence of the censor and the censorial *nota* in these spheres, readers will gain a new understanding of the overall significance of the censor's office in shaping the Roman legal order.

The Censors as Guardians of Public and Family Life in the Roman Republic will be of interest to students and scholars of Roman law in both the Republican and Imperial periods, as well as to those interested in Roman moral attitudes and society more broadly.

Anna Tarwacka is Professor of Social Sciences in the field of law, classical philologist, and head of the Roman Law Department at Cardinal Stefan Wyszyński University in Warsaw. She is the author of five monographs and numerous articles, and co-author of the textbook *Roman Public Law* (2021). She specialises in Roman public and private laws. Tarwacka conducts research on piracy in ancient Rome, the office of the censor, and the legal aspects of the collection of ancient jokes known as *Philogelos*. She is a populariser of antiquity; she runs the blog 'Rzymianie i prawo' ('Romans and the Law') and a YouTube channel of the same name. She is also the author of a children's book on Roman law.

The Censors as Guardians of Public and Family Life in the Roman Republic

Anna Tarwacka

Routledge
Taylor & Francis Group
LONDON AND NEW YORK

First published 2025
by Routledge
4 Park Square, Milton Park, Abingdon, Oxon OX14 4RN

and by Routledge
605 Third Avenue, New York, NY 10158

Routledge is an imprint of the Taylor & Francis Group, an informa business

The present study is a result of the project 2018/29/B/HS5/00949 financed by the National Science Centre, Poland.

British Library Cataloguing-in-Publication Data
A catalogue record for this book is available from the British Library

ISBN: 978-1-032-78199-0 (hbk)
ISBN: 978-1-032-78195-2 (pbk)
ISBN: 978-1-003-48666-4 (ebk)

DOI: 10.4324/9781003486664

Typeset in Times New Roman
by codeMantra

To Professor Jan Zabłocki,
my teacher, my inspiration, my friend

Contents

Abbreviations

AAH	*Acta Antiqua Academiae Scientiarum Hungaricae*
AFDUDC	*Anuario da Facultade de Dereito da Universidade da Coruña*
AJP	*American Journal of Philology*
ANRW	*Aufstieg und Niedergang der römischen Welt. Geschichte und Kultur im Spiegel der neueren Forschung*, red. H. Temporini, Berlin–New York
Arctos	*Acta Philologica Fennica*
Athenaeum	*Studi di Letteratura e Storia dell'Antichità*
AUPA	*Annali del Seminario Giuridico dell'Università degli Studi di Palermo*
BIDR	*Bulletino dell'Istituto di Diritto Romano*
CJ	*Classical Journal*
CP	*Classical Philology*
CQ	*Classical Quarterly*
Diritto@Storia	*Rivista internazionale di Scienze Giuridiche e Tradizione Romana*, http://www.dirittoestoria.it/
Emerita	*Revista de Linguistica y Filologia Clasica*
FIRA	*Fontes iuris romani anteiustiniani in usum scholarum ediderunt* S. Riccobono, J. Baviera, C. Ferrini, J. Furlani, V. Arangio-Ruiz, I–III, Florentiae 1940–1943
Historia	*Zeitschrift für Alte Geschichte*
HSCP	*Harvard Studies in Classical Philology*
Index	*Quaderni camerti di studi romanistici. International Survey of Roman Law*
Iura	*Rivista internazionale di diritto romano e antico*
Ius Antiquum	*Древнее Право*
JRS	*Journal of Roman Studies*
Klio	*Beiträge zur alten Geschichte*
Labeo	*Rassegna di diritto romano*
MEFRA	*Mélange d'archéologie et d'histoire de l'Ecole française de Rome*
Mnemosyne	*A Journal of Classical Studies*
NNDI	*Novissimo Digesto Italiano, Torino*

ORF	*Oratorum Romanorum Fragmenta Liberae Rei Publicae*[2], ed. H. Malcovati, Torino 1953
RE	*Paulys Realencyclopädie der classischen Altertumswissenschaft, Stuttgart*
PBSR	*Papers of the British School at Rome*
Philologus	*Zeitschrift für antike Literatur und ihre Rezeption*
RGDR	*Revista General de Derecho Romano*, http://www.iustel.com/v2/revistas/detalle_revista.asp?id=11
RhM	*Rheinisches Museum für Philologie*
RIDA	*Revue Internationale des Droits de l'Antiquité*
RIDROM	*Revista Internacional de Derecho Romano*, http://www.ridrom.uclm.es/
SDHI	*Studia et documenta historiae et iuris*
TAPA	*Transactions and Proceedings of the American Philological Association*
TLL	*Thesaurus Linguae Latinae, München*
TR	*The Legal History Review / Tijdschrift voor Rechtsgeschiedenis / Revue d'Histoire du Droit*
ZSS	*Zeitschrift der Savigny-Stiftung für Rechtsgeschichte. Romanistische Abteilung*

Introduction

To the modern reader, the term 'censorship' is primarily associated with the restriction of freedom of speech and the control over the expression of political and moral perspectives. However, the Latin term *censura* has only gradually evolved towards such an understanding. Initially, it designated only the office of the censor, an official whose primary powers included taking a census of the population, leasing public revenues and expenditures, and – with time – guarding morality (*regimen morum*) regulated by the customs of the forefathers (*mores maiorum*).

The issue of the censorial mark (*nota censoria*) is a continuation of my research on the office of the censor.[1] It is a broadly encompassing problem, linked to both public and private laws. The use of the *nota* is the most colourful aspect of censorial activity. Sources describe various cases where citizens were punished for violating customs. Some of them concern public life such as the activities of officials, military affairs, bribery, or false testimony, while others pertain to family matters and social life in the broadest sense, including certain professions. It is worth noting here that in ancient times, the intervention of officials in the private lives of citizens was viewed with astonishment by foreigners. Modern scholars tend to view this sphere of censorial activity as anecdotal and devoid of legal significance. However, the political importance of the Roman family and, in particular, the legal position of its head – the *pater familias* – were so important that they decided to subject it to strict control.

The term *mores maiorum* is not just a general term denoting vague rules introduced by the ancestors: rather, it is the quintessence of 'Romanness,' the foundation of society's identity, and the guarantee of state stability. These rules were guarded by censors, and the instrument of protection was precisely the censorial mark. Therefore, we can define censorship in two ways: from the public law perspective, it was a controlling element of the Republican system, while in private law, it was an intermediate stage in the formation of legal protection based on principles of equity.

The extent of the influence of the censors on the public and private lives of the Romans, and hence on public and private laws, is therefore the subject of this research. The actions of censors shaped the attitudes of citizens and led to the creation of legal protection. The censorial *nota* imposed by officials in charge of morality (*regimen morum*) was a repressive instrument, but its primary function was to

DOI: 10.4324/9781003486664-1

prevent socially undesirable behaviour. Of course, it is possible to find examples of censors' decisions that were random in nature, but in general, their activities formed a coherent programme for the development of society's consciousness.

The censorial mark was an instrument used in the censorial practice of the Republican period. Therefore, literary texts from this period or historical works describing Republican history and the early Principate, as well as the works of antiquarians, form the source base. The works of Cato, Varro, Cicero, Livy, Valerius Maximus, Pliny the Elder, Festus, Aulus Gellius, Suetonius, and Tacitus, as well as Polybius, Dionysius of Halicarnassus, Plutarch, and Cassius Dio, were of key importance for this research. Late texts by Lydus and Zonaras were also helpful.

Among texts of a legal nature, some provisions of the *leges regiae* and the Law of the Twelve Tables, excerpts from edicts and censorial speeches quoted in various sources, and commentaries by jurists preserved in the *Digest* were relevant.

Rhetorical texts, particularly declamations erroneously attributed to Quintilian, also proved to be significant. These exercises usually revolve around fictitious themes and often have a dubious legal basis. However, many of them contain references to *mores maiorum*, which were foundational to the censors' activities in overseeing morality. The authors of these texts may have drawn precisely on censorial practice. Therefore, it is possible that the content of the declamations reflects the practice of the *nota censoria*.

The office of the censor has long been a subject of interest for researchers dealing with various aspects of the ancient world, including Roman law scholars. Of primary importance are the studies by Theodor Mommsen,[2] as well as Wolfgang Kunkel and Roland Wittmann,[3] in which the powers of censors are described in general terms. These issues were also addressed by the authors of monumental histories of Rome, its systems, and its laws.[4] Encyclopaedic studies on censors[5] are also worth mentioning.

In older literature, monographs on particular aspects of censorship have been dedicated by Carl Ernst Jarcke,[6] Franz Gerlach,[7] Georg Hahn,[8] Oskar Leuze,[9] and Angiola Lotti Faravelli.[10] Among the later authors of monographic studies, Filippo Cancelli,[11] Jaakko Suolahti,[12] Georges Pieri,[13] Eduardo Reigadas Lavandero,[14] and Gema Polo Toribio[15] must be mentioned. Numerous articles on the censors have been written by Alan Astin,[16] who is also the author of a biography of Cato the Elder, Michel Humm,[17] who also wrote a book on Appius Claudius, Elio Lo Cascio,[18] and Yaroslav V. Melničuk.[19] Recently, studies on the census have been undertaken by Giovanbattista Greco[20] and Lorenzo Gagliardi,[21] while Noémie Lemmenais wrote about censorship in the context of Republican ethos.[22] There is also a forthcoming monograph concerning censorship with studies on various topics.[23]

Several works have been devoted to specific issues closely related to the activities of censors but discussed in a broader context. Mention should be made of studies on public contracts,[24] as well as various aspects of activities of officials.[25] The *fasti censorii*,[26] a source of great importance, has also been the subject of research.

In the literature on censorship, the question of the *nota censoria* has been addressed many times. It has appeared in studies of the censors' office, but it has been discussed from a 'procedural' rather than a 'material' perspective.

The *regimen morum* itself has also been the subject of numerous studies. A catalogue of reasons for the application of the censorial *nota* was created by Theodor Mommsen.[27] Censorial control of morals was addressed by Max Nowak,[28] Eberhard Schmähling,[29] Ewoud Slob,[30] Alan Astin,[31] Ernst Baltrusch,[32] Michel Humm,[33] and Nadja el Beheiri.[34] The issue of infamy has also often been of great interest to scholars. The classic work on infamy was written by A.H.J. Greenidge,[35] and the terms *infamia* and *ignominia* were compared by Max Kaser[36] and Joseph Georg Wolf.[37] More recently, an extremely interesting monograph on the evolution of infamy has been written by Clément Bur.[38] A great deal of space has also been devoted by scholars to the broader problem of customs and limitations of luxury.[39]

However, the issue of the influence of censors on lawmaking seems to require in-depth research. Adopting the view that censorial mark was incidental disregards the significance of the *regimen morum* for law in the Republican period, as well as for the development of many later institutions. The problem of interference by censors in the public and private lives of citizens is most often addressed only in anecdotal convention and dismissed as insignificant. Therefore, it seems justified to undertake such research.

The subject of the research is the issue of the use of the censorial mark and the influence of censorial regulations in this area on the development of law. It can be assumed that the censors, through their actions resulting from their control over society, contributed to the development of numerous regulations in the field of both private and public laws in both the Republican and Imperial periods. Such influence could be discernible in at least two spheres that will become the subject of analysis. The first sphere is the praetorian edicts, which provided protection in certain situations that were also subject to censorship. The questions posed should concern the relationship between the *ius honorarium* and the *regimen morum*: did the solutions introduced by the praetors precede censorial action, or were the censors the forerunners of certain regulations? Did the censorial mark coexist with the sanctions applied by the praetors, or were they mutually exclusive? Which was more widely applicable? The second area of analysis will be the issue of the continued application of censorial norms arising from *mores maiorum* during the Principate. It seems particularly relevant to examine the question of the possible impact of the censor's actions on Augustus' marriage legislation. Finally, all these threads are intended to provide an answer to the question of the overall significance of the office of censor in the formation of the Roman legal order.

Notes

1 The present study includes research presented in two of my books published in Polish: *Prawne aspekty urzędu cenzora w starożytnym Rzymie*, Warszawa 2012, and *Cenzor w sypialni. Urzędnicza kontrola moralności w życiu rodzinnym Rzymian okresu republiki*, Warszawa 2021. Apart from these Polish studies, my other works on censorship include: *The Censors and Their Duties in the Comedies of Plautus*, "RGDR" 23/2014, http://www.iustel.com/v2/revistas/detalle_revista.asp?id_noticia=415488; *The Roman Censors as Protectors of Public Places*, "Diritto@Storia" 12/2014, http://www.dirittoestoria.it/12/tradizione-romana/Tarwacka-Roman-Censors-Protectors-Public-Places.htm;

Come vendicarsi dei censori? Scontri politici e responsabilità penale dei guardiani della morale, "Diritto@Storia" 14/2016, http://www.dirittoestoria.it/14/tradizione/Tarwacka-Come-vendicarsi-dei-censori.htm; *The Censors' Influence on Marriage in Republican Rome*, "Zeszyty Prawnicze" 18.1/2018, pp. 173–191; *The Censorial Mark in Ancient Roman Marital Matters*, "Zeszyty Prawnicze" 19.1/2019, pp. 241–255; *A Censor and a Woman. Censorial Reproach of Clodia in Cicero's 'Pro Caelio'*, [in:] *Women, Society and Law. From Roman Law to Digital Age*, eds. M. Eysymontt, C. Lázaro Guillamón, Warsaw 2022, pp. 171–182; *Adoption under the Scrutiny of the Censors in Republican Rome*, [in:] *Family, Law, and Society: From Roman Law to the Present Day*, eds. E. Dawidziuk, P. Panero, A. Tarwacka, Berlin–Lausanne–Bruxelles–Chennai–New York–Oxford 2023, pp. 77–91.

2 T. Mommsen, *Römisches Staatsrecht*[3], II.1, Graz 1952 (reprint), pp. 331–469.

3 W. Kunkel, R. Wittmann, *Staatsordnung und Staatspraxis der römischen Republik. Zweiter Abschnitt. Die Magistratur*, München 1995, pp. 391–471.

4 L. Lange, *Römische Alterthümer*[2], Berlin 1863; O. Karlowa, *Römische Rechtsgeschichte. I. Staatsrecht und Rechtsquellen*, Leipzig 1885; K.J. Beloch, *Römische Geschichte bis zum Beginn der punischen Kriege*, Berlin–Leipzig 1926; P. De Francisci, *Arcana imperii*, III.1, Milano 1948; Idem, *Primordia civitatis*, Roma 1959; H. Siber, *Römisches Verfassungsrecht in geschichtlicher Entwicklung*, Lahr 1952; F. De Martino, *Storia della costituzione romana*[2], Napoli 1973; F. Cassola, L. Labruna, *Linee di una storia delle istituzioni repubblicane*[2], Napoli 1979; A.W. Lintott, *The Constitution of the Roman Republic*, Oxford 1999; A. Ziolkowski, *Storia di Roma*, Milano 2010.

5 E. De Ruggiero, *Dizionario epigrafico di antichità romane*, Roma 1900, s.v. *censor*; W. Kubitschek, *Censores*, "RE" 3/1899, pp. 1902–1908; F. Guizzi, *Censores*, "NNDI" 3/1964, pp. 101–104.

6 C.E. Jarcke, *Versuch einer Darstellung des censorischen Strafrechts der Römer: ein Beytrag zur Geschichte des Criminalrechts*, Bonn 1824.

7 F.D. Gerlach, *Die römische Censur in ihrem Verhältniß zur Verfassung. Eine historische Untersuchung*, Basel 1842.

8 G. Hahn, *De censorum locationibus*, Lipsiae 1879.

9 O. Leuze, *Zur Geschichte der römischen Censur*, Halle 1912.

10 A. Lotti Faravelli, *Origine della censura romana*, Como 1937.

11 F. Cancelli, *Studi sui censores e sull'arbitratus della lex contractus*, Milano 1960.

12 J. Suolahti, *The Roman Censors. A Study on Social Structure*, Helsinki 1963 with a review of A.H. McDonald, *The Censorship*, "CR" 15.1/1965, pp. 89–91.

13 G. Pieri, *L'histoire du cens jusqu'à la fin de la République romaine*, Paris 1968 with a review by P.A. Brunt, "TR" 37/1969, pp. 263–267.

14 E. Reigadas Lavandero, *Censura y res publica: aportación constitucional y protagonismo político*, Madrid 2000.

15 G. de las Heras Sánchez, G. Polo Toribio, *Plus quam annua ac semestris*, "AFDUDC", 11/2007, pp. 169–175; G. Polo Toribio, *Algunas puntualizaciones entorno a la figura jurídica del incensus*, "RGDR" 12/2009, https://www.iustel.com/v2/revistas/detalle_revista.asp?id_noticia=408008&d=1; Eadem, *La prorogatio en la magistratura censoria*, "RGDR" 13/2009, https://www.iustel.com/v2/revistas/detalle_revista.asp?id_noticia=408537&d=1; G. Polo, *Idoneidad de las tabulae censoriae como instrumentos de publicidad de los miembros de la comunidad*, "RIDROM" 5/2010, pp. 126–177, http://www.ridrom.uclm.es/documentos5/Polo_pub.pdf; G. Polo Toribio, *Finalidad probatoria de la professio censualis*, "RIDROM" 8/2012, pp. 118–142; Eadem, *Lex de censoribus creandis*, [in:] *Homenaje al Profesor Armando Torrent*, eds. A. Murillo Villar, M. Aránzazu Calzada González, S.C. Pérez-Gómez, A.J. Torrent Ruiz, Madrid 2016, pp. 717–730; Eadem, *Manumissio. Libertas. Census. Civis. Incensus*, Madrid 2023.

16 A.E. Astin, *Augustus and Censoria Potestas*, "Latomus" 22.2/1963, pp. 226–235; Idem, *Cato the Censor*, Oxford 1978; Idem, *The Censorship of the Roman Republic: Frequency and Regularity*, "Historia" 31/1982, pp. 174–187; Idem, *Censorships in the Late*

Republic, "Historia" 34.2/1985, pp. 175–190; Idem, *Cicero and the Censorship*, 'CP' 80.3/1985, pp. 233–239; Idem, *Livy and the Censors of 214-169 B.C.*, [in:] *Studies in Latin Literature and Roman History*, ed. C. Deroux, IV, Bruxelles 1986, pp. 122–134; Idem, *Livy's Report of the lectio senatus and the recognitio equitum in the Censorship of 169-8 BC*, "Historia" 37.4/1988, pp. 487–490; Idem, *Regimen morum*, "JRS" 78/1988, pp. 14–34; Idem, *The Role of Censors in Roman Economic Life*, "Latomus" 49.1/1990, pp. 20–36.

17 M. Humm, *L'image de la censure chez Valère Maxime: formation et évolution d'un paradigme*, [in:] *Valeurs et mémoire à Rome: Valère Maxime ou la vertu recomposée*, ed. J.-M. David, Paris 1998, pp. 73–93; Idem, *La figure d'Appius Claudius Caecus chez Tite-Live*, [in:] *Le censeur et les Samnites sur Tite-Live, livre IX*, eds. D. Briquel, J.-P. Thuillier, Paris 2001, pp. 65–96; Idem, *Servius Tullius et la censure: élaboration d'un modèle institutionnel*, [in:] *Invention des grands hommes de la Rome antique*, eds. M. Coudry, T. Späth, Paris 2001, pp. 221–247; Idem, *Appius Claudius Caecus. La république accomplie*, Rome 2005; Idem, *Il 'regimen morum' dei censori e le identità dei cittadini*, [in:] *'Homo, caput, persona'. La costruzione giuridica dell' identità nell'esperienza romana*, eds. A. Corbino, M. Humbert, G. Negri, Pavia 2010, pp. 283–314.

18 E. Lo Cascio, *The Size of the Roman Population: Beloch and the Meaning of the Augustan Census Figures*, "JRS" 84/1994, pp. 23–40; Idem, *Le procedure di recensus dalla tarda repubblica al tardo antico e il calcolo della popolazione di Roma*, [in:] *La Rome impériale: démographie et logistique*, ed. C. Virlouvet, Roma 1997, pp. 3–76; Idem, *Il census a Roma e la sua evoluzione dall'età "serviana" alla prima età imperiale*, "MEFRA" 113.2/2001, pp. 565–603; Idem, *La popolazione*, [in:] *Roma imperiale. Una metropoli antica*, ed. E. Lo Cascio, Roma 2010, pp. 17–69.

19 J.V. Melničuk, Римские цензоры и характер государственных подрядов *('cura operum locandarum')*, "Ius Antiquum" 1.6/2000, pp. 32–42; Idem, Законодательное оформление института цензуры *(V-IV* вв. до н.э.*)*, "Ius Antiquum" 1.8/2001, pp. 62–65; Idem, Ответственность цензоров перед *'civitas'* в середине *V* - середине *II* вв. до н.э., "Ius Antiquum" 1.9/2002, pp. 113–125; Idem, Некоторые аспекты римского сакрального ритуала *'lustrum'*, "Ius Antiquum" 1.11/2003, pp. 54–64; Idem, *'Lustrum' en su aspecto marcial*, "Diritto@Storia" 4/2005, http://www.dirittoestoria.it/4/Tradizione-Romana/Melniciuk-Lustrum.htm.

20 G. Greco, *Census. Profili storico-giuridici delle attività di censimento a Roma*, Torino 2022.

21 L. Gagliardi, *I censimenti romani della tarda repubblica e il caso dei 'proletarii'*, "BIDR" 117/2023, pp. 81–89. Cf. Idem, *'Romam commigrare'. I Romani, I Latini e l'immigrazione*, Milano 2023.

22 N. Lemmenais, *Censeurs et mos maiorum dans la construction de l'ethos républicain*, "Revue historique" 706.2/2023, pp. 259–279.

23 *The Roman Censorship: Perceptions and Realities*, eds. K. Webb, T. Smith, A. Antoniou, forthcoming.

24 E. Badian, *Publicans and Sinners. Private Enterprise in the Service of the Roman Republic*, Oxford 1972; M.R. Cimma, *Ricerche sulle società di publicani*, Milano 1981; F. Milazzo, *La realizzazione delle opere pubbliche in Roma arcaica e repubblicana. Munera e ultro tributa*, Napoli 1993; C. Nicolet, *Censeurs et publicains. Économie et fiscalité dans la Rome antique*, Paris 2000; A. Trisciuoglio, *Sarta tecta, ultrotributa, opus publicum faciendum locare. Sugli appalti relativi alle opere pubbliche nell' età repubblicana e augustea*, Napoli 1998; M.E. Fernández Baquero, *La actividad de los censores en la Administración de la República romana*, "e-Legal History Review" 15/2013, https://www.iustel.com/v2/revistas/detalle_revista.asp?id_noticia=412967.

25 J. Bleicken, *Zum Begriff der römischen Amtsgewalt. Auspicium – potestas – imperium*, Göttingen 1981; O. Licandro, *In magistratu damnari. Ricerche sulla responsabilità dei magistrati romani durante l'esercizio delle funzioni*, Torino 1999; G. Urso, *Cassio*

Dione e i magistrati. Le origini della repubblica nei frammenti della 'Storia romana', Milano 2005; N. Rampazzo, *Quasi praetor non fuerit. Studi sulle elezioni magistratuali in Roma repubblicana tra regola ed eccezione*, Napoli 2008.

26 C. De Boor, *Fasti censorii*, Berolini 1873; F. Münzer, *Zu den Fasti censorii*, "RhM" 61/1906, pp. 19–27; R.V. Cram, *The Roman Censors*, "HSCP" 51/1940, pp. 71–110; A. Degrassi, *Fasti Capitolini*, Torino 1954; cf. also T.R.S. Broughton, *The Magistrates of the Roman Republic*, I, Atlanta, GA 1951 (reprint 1986); II, New York 1952.

27 T. Mommsen, *Römisches Staatsrecht...*, II.1, pp. 377–382.

28 M. Nowak, *Die Strafverhängungen der Censoren*, Breslau 1909.

29 E. Schmähling, *Die Sittenaufsicht der Censoren. Ein Beitrag zur Sittengeschichte der römischen Republik*, Stuttgart 1938.

30 E. Slob, *Luxuria. Regelgeving en maatregelen van censoren ten tijde van de Romeinse Republiek*, Utrecht 1986.

31 A.E. Astin, *Regimen morum...*, pp. 14–34.

32 E. Baltrusch, *Regimen morum. Die Reglamentierung des Privatlebens der Senatoren und Ritter in der römischen Republik und frühen Kaiserzeit*, München 1989.

33 M. Humm, *Il regimen morum...*, pp. 283–314.

34 N. El Beheiri, *Das regimen morum der Zensoren. Die Konstruktion des römischen Gemeinwesens*, Berlin 2012; Eadem, *Das regimen morum zwischen Institution und Geschichte*, [in:] *Ad geographiam historico-iuridicam ope iuris Romani colendam. Studia in honorem Gábor Hamza*, eds. A. Földi, I. Sándor, I. Siklósi, Budapest 2015, pp. 149–160.

35 A.H.J. Greenidge, *Infamia. Its Place in Roman Public and Private Law*, Oxford 1894.

36 M. Kaser, *Infamia und ignominia in den römischen Rechtsquellen*, "ZSS" 73/1956, pp. 220–278.

37 J.G. Wolf, *Das Stigma ignominia*, "ZSS" 126/2009, pp. 55–113; Idem, *Lo stigma dell'ignominia*, [in:] *Homo, caput, persona. La costruzione giuridica dell' identità nell'esperienza romana*, eds. A. Corbino, M. Humbert, G. Negri, Pavia 2010, pp. 491–550.

38 C. Bur, *La citoyenneté dégradée. Une histoire de l'infamie à Rome (312 av. J.-C.-96 apr. J.-C.)*, Rome 2018. This author has also created a database of *infames Romani*: https://poolcorpus.univ-jfc.fr/infames-romani. Cf. also C. Bur, *Les censeurs privaient-ils du droit de vote? Retour sur l'aerarium facere et le tribu mouere*, "MEFRA" 128.2/2016, pp. 419–437; Idem, *Le spectacle du cens. Relecture du déroulement de la professio sous la République romaine*, "Athenaeum" 105.2/2017, pp. 520–550; Idem, *'Auctoritas' et 'mos maiorum'*, [in:] *L'auctoritas à Rome. Une notion constitutive de la culture politique*, eds. J.-M. David, F. Hurlet, Bordeaux 2020, pp. 65–90.

39 A. Bottiglieri, *La legislazione sul lusso nella Roma repubblicana*, Napoli 2002; E. Zanda, *Fighting Hydra-like Luxury. Sumptuary Regulation in the Roman Republic*, London–New Delhi–New York–Sydney 2013 (reprint); F.J. Casinos Mora, *La restricción del lujo en la Roma Republicana. El lujo indumentario*, Madrid 2015.

I The office of censor in Republican Rome

1. Preliminary remarks

The office of censor was of significant importance in Republican Rome from the perspective of the state policy. Perhaps their most interesting role was the supervision of morality (*regimen morum*). They had the right to punish citizens with a censorial mark for behaviour contrary to ancestral customs (*mores maiorum*). The effect of the mark was the loss of reputation (*ignominia*) and degradation in the social hierarchy, including removal from the Senate, from the equestrian *centuria*, transfer from a rural to an urban *tribus*, and inclusion in the group of *aerarii*. The source texts on the imposition of the mark are anecdotal in nature, usually dealing with individual cases, and were often seen as of little use in studying Roman law. The study of private law in the Republican period has so far focused on the *ius civile* and *ius honorarium*. However, a careful analysis of the source texts leads to the conclusion that the actions of the censors often influenced private law in such a way that they made it possible to hold someone liable even without corresponding regulation of positive law. Adopting such a research perspective allows us to look at the development of private law in a different way and to draw new conclusions concerning many of its institutions, especially in the area of family law. In public law, the role of censors was also crucial: it was their actions that constituted one of the controlling elements of the Republican system, making it possible to socially degrade citizens who broke the rules of public life. It should be remembered that for a long time, systemic issues were regulated only in the area of *mores maiorum* and not in positive law. Therefore, it was the censors who guarded them.

Censors were higher, curule, ordinary officials. Holding this office was considered the culmination of a political career, although formally censorship was not included in the *cursus honorum*. Most often, former consuls were chosen as censors, i.e. people who were experienced and respected in society. During the elections held every five years at the *comitia centuriata*, two officials were appointed, whose term of office lasted eighteen months. The same assembly also voted on the *lex de potestate censoria*, confirming the election. The office of censor could only be held once; re-election was prohibited.

The powers of the censors were gradually extended.[1] In addition to the basic task of taking a census of all citizens by property class, *centuria* and *tribus* every

DOI: 10.4324/9781003486664-2

five years, and celebrating the purification ceremony called *lustrum condere*, they were also given the competence to determine the composition of the elite equestrian centuries (*recognitio equitum*), as well as the list of senators (*lectio senatus*). Over time, censors began to exercise guardianship over morality (*regimen morum*), applying the sanction of a censorial mark for breaches of moral norms. The censors also had the task of leasing public revenues and expenditures on behalf of the state in the form of public lease contracts (*locationes censoriae*) concluded with private entities, most often companies of the publicans (*societates publicanorum*). These contracts covered the construction and repair of public buildings, such as roads, aqueducts, or temples, the exploitation of mines and salt works, and the collection of various taxes and public tributes. The censors were also responsible for public places and exercised control to ensure that private individuals would not erect buildings on public land. They also issued permissions for leading water from aqueducts to private buildings.

The censors' magisterial powers were called *potestas*; they could summon the people for *contiones* and also for the lustration. In terms of their duties to protect public places, they had the power of coercion, including the imposition of fines and the seizure as pledge as well as ordering demolitions. They also had the right to issue edicts, which was particularly important in the context of the *regimen morum*. The edicts of the censors, promulgated at the beginning of the term, included an announcement of the policy related to the imposition of the mark. The officials informed the public about what acts might meet with their disapproval and result in the imposition of sanctions (*edicta de moribus*).[2] This indicates that the censors had far-reaching discretion regarding the catalogue of behaviours that, in their view, violated *mores maiorum*.

The censors were assisted in their tasks by auxiliary officials: heralds (*praecones*), those who received citizens' declarations during the census (*iuratores*), scribes (*scribae*), architects, as well as clerks (*accensi*), secretaries (*nomenclatores*), and probably also messengers (*viatores*).

The power of the censors was discretionary. There was no appeal against their decisions, and the control mechanism was exceptionally strong application of the principle of collegiality.[3] Both censors were elected at the same time, ensuring no conflicts ensued between them. The death of one censor resulted in his colleague having to resign from office.[4] Collegiality was also expressed in the right to apply *intercessio* against the official decision of the other censor, particularly in matters relating to the movement of citizens down the social hierarchy as a result of the application of a censorial mark. The most desirable state of affairs seems to have been the unanimity of the censors. *Intercessions* were, of course, not uncommon, but a serious conflict dividing the censors could lead to a complete blocking of their ability to perform their official functions.

2. Terminological issues

The term *censor*[5] derives from the verb *censere*, meaning 'to estimate' – *aestimare*. The term *τιμητής*, used in Greek, has a similar etymology.

According to Festus,[6] censors were called so because the citizens valued their property at what the officials determined, thereby emphasising their function in property valuation. However, the verb *censere* also meant 'to express an opinion, to decide.' Iavolenus,[7] commenting on the work of Cassius, derived the term *censor* from this very meaning of *censere*. These authors emphasised the most important duty of the censors, which included performing the census and registering the citizens.

According to Varro,[8] a censor is someone on whose *arbitrium*, i.e. opinion or judgement, the people were registered during the census. There is a significant shift in meaning in the definition, which was probably intended to support the declining powers of the censors, who were fundamental in upholding the values of the Roman *nobilitas*. This view was later mirrored by Isidore of Seville, who considered[9] censors as judges of estates, translating the term *censere* as 'to judge' – *iudicare*, adding that they were called so from the valuation of bronze. Additionally, Placidus,[10] Plautus' scholiast, called the censors judges of estates and customs. These authors underline an important aspect of censorship, which was the arbitrariness of the censors' decisions.

A deeper meaning of the activity of the censors was sought by the French researcher Georges Dumézil,[11] who argued convincingly that *censere* should be understood as defining an individual's place in society. The task of censors was not only to prepare a list of the population but also to determine a person's position. The key concept associated with the census is therefore the merit of a citizen (*dignitas*), which the censor can decide upon.

3. The origins of the office of the censor

Conducting the census – according to the sources introduced in Rome by King Servius Tullius[12] – was a competence of the consuls from the beginning of the Republican period.[13] The census was supposed to take place every five years, but due to the decemvirate period and subsequent turmoil, this was not possible. In 444 BC, for the first time, the *fasti consulares* recorded a college of three rather than two top officials in the state.[14] This year marked the beginning of the period of the military tribunate,[15] only ended by the agreement reached under the *leges Liciniae Sextiae* in 367 BC. During this time, the state was headed by two, three, four, and sometimes six officials. Sources refer to them as military tribunes with consular powers (*tribuni militum consulari potestate*), but sometimes also as consuls, especially when there were only two of them. The tribunes' power was less extensive than that of the consuls, but it is not known whether they could perform auspices. If not, it would have to be assumed that during the period in question, consuls were elected annually and, if necessary, tribunes with lesser powers (*minore imperio*) were co-opted to their college.[16] The reasons for the appointment of tribunes can be traced to the plebeians' desire to achieve consulship. By allowing them to hold the office of tribune, the patricians would avoid such a far-reaching concession.[17] For the first time, however, a plebeian was elected tribune only in 400 BC, which falsifies this thesis. Another explanation was that the consuls were unable to cope with the numerous war campaigns of the period, which were fought on many fronts and required commanders. However, the years of the military tribunate were not particularly turbulent, so this thesis is also untenable.[18]

After years of decemviral rule, the Romans certainly revived their hatred of the monarchical system (*odium regni*) with renewed vigour: they feared usurpation and did not want to give too much power to officials. One remedy was to affirm the right of citizens to appeal against the magistrate's judgement (*ius provocationis*) and to forbid the creation of offices *sine provocatione*. Another way was to limit the scope of power of the highest officials, which was initially achieved by increasing the number of people in the college. It was only later that new, specialised magistrates were introduced: praetors or curule aediles. Arguably, within the college, officials divided functions between themselves. One, for example, remained in Rome, while the others went on war campaigns.[19]

Under these political conditions, censorship was established according to the sources. This event was depicted by Livy.[20] First, the historian stated with pathos that the censorship – an office that had very humble beginnings – later acquired such importance that those holding it could exercise control over the customs and way of life of the Romans; the censors could decide on the fame and infamy of senators, knights, and members of the *centuriae*, watch over the law of private and public places, as well as the taxes of the Roman people. According to the historian, in 443 BC, during the second consulship of M. Geganius Macerinus and the fifth of T. Quinctius Capitolinus,[21] a problem was posed in the Senate concerning the conduct of the census – a task very absorbing and inappropriate for consuls.[22] For years,[23] the census had not been carried out because of the wars threatening Rome. It was argued that a new magistracy was needed to watch over the scribes, guard the tables, and make decisions on the conduct of the census. The senators approved of this idea, even though it concerned a minor matter, as they were pleased that there would be more patrician officials in the state. The question of relieving the consuls and military tribunes was also raised. For the new office, the people elected Papirius and Sempronius, who may have held the office of *consules suffecti* the year before, but Livy himself had doubts about this matter.[24] They were called censors from the office they held. Similar reasons for the appointment of censors[25] were given by Pomponius in the *Enchiridion*.[26] The jurist wrote that when the census had not been carried out for a long time and the consuls could not cope with this task either, censors were appointed.

Sources on the origins of censorship are sometimes considered unreliable by some scholars.[27] Theodor Mommsen argued that the names of the first censors, Papirius and Sempronius, are forgeries, as is the mention of their alleged consulship in 444 BC, and he postponed the beginning of censorship to the year 434 BC.[28] Karl Beloch, on the other hand, argued that the names of the censors of this period often coincide with those of the military tribunes.[29] Hence, he inferred that it was the tribunes who carried out the census, and that calling them censors was a later falsification. He considered the census carried out by Papirius and Sempronius to have been performed the year before, when they were consuls, and postponed the date of the creation of the office of censor until 366 BC. Heinrich Siber was also of the opinion that the censorship as an ordinary office dated only from 366 BC onwards and that before this, either extraordinary officials – *(duoviri) censui agendo* – had been appointed or the task of carrying out the census had been entrusted to a pair of military tribunes with consular powers.[30]

Filippo Cássola and Luigi Labruna[31] have also argued that the link between the censorship and the military tribunate was initially very strong.[32] It is possible that the duty to carry out the census was first placed on the tribunes, and only in time was it transferred to the new officials – the censors.[33] The tribunes were obliged to carry out the census, and therefore, according to the authors, no new office was created, but only members were co-opted to the college and assigned special functions. On the other hand, Alfred Klotz[34] and Jaakko Suolahti[35] have expressed the belief that the year 443 BC should be considered authentic for the establishment of the censorship and thus be placed this year.

A very important factor that may somewhat illuminate the problem at hand was the enactment of the *lex Canuleia* in 445 BC,[36] which gave plebeians *conubium*, i.e. the possibility to marry patricians.[37] This law effectively opened the way for plebeians to the highest offices by indirectly granting them the right to perform auspices. Indeed, the only argument put forward by the patricians against it was that auspices could be disrupted by uncertain offspring because they came from mixed marriages (*ne incerta prole auspicia turbarentur*).[38] The introduction of the military tribunate was a countermeasure against the admission of plebeians to the consulship: even if, in practice, the office remained in the hands of patricians for many years, there was a theoretical possibility of electing a plebeian. Conducting the census was – despite Livy's dismissive tone – of colossal military importance: it enabled the proper allocation of citizens to *centuriae*.[39] In these circumstances, it is hardly surprising that the patricians welcomed the creation of a specialised office set up for the purpose of conducting the census, which was only available to them.[40] It seems unlikely to me that the census was to be conducted by military tribunes, who may have been drawn from among the plebeians, especially as the census was crowned by the performance of a sacred lustration ceremony.[41]

Wolfgang Kunkel and Roland Wittmann[42] linked the appointment of censors in this period to an increase in revenue to the treasury, which had then become permanent. Quaestors were appointed to manage it and censors to increase the efficiency of tax collection. This was due to the increased complexity of the census procedures, which until then had essentially a military purpose.

It can therefore be assumed that, in 443 BC, the competence to conduct the census of citizens was transferred to new officials subsequently called censors. Initially, they were treated as members of a college of military tribunes with consular powers, but the novelty of their appointment was probably connected to the necessity to extend their powers in order for them to be able to finish the time-consuming task of conducting the census. Only patricians were eligible for that magistracy. The question remains on what basis this was done. In Livy's account, the body that dealt with the question of their election was the senate. However, the historian supplemented this information in another book of his work.[43] This mention is related to the *lex Aemilia*, to which, however – crucially – the law under which the censors were first appointed is compared. It is usually called *lex de censoribus creandis*.[44] It was most likely enacted at the *comitia centuriata* after the Senate had passed a relevant resolution.

The key year for further consideration is 434 BC, when the *lex Aemilia*[45] was enacted, fundamentally changing the rules of censorship. The proposer of this law was the dictator M. Aemilius Mamercus.[46] Livy wrote that when it appeared the threat for which the dictator had been appointed had passed, he nevertheless decided to commemorate his dictatorship and change the rules of censorship, considering either that it involved too much power or that it had been exercised for too long. He therefore convened a *contio*, during which he announced that the security of the Republic was ensured by the gods, and that he must advise them on what should be done for the freedom of the Roman people within the walls, i.e. in the city. He expressed concern that great powers should not be too long-lasting and that those which could not be limited by law should be restricted in time. While other offices were annual, censorship lasted five years, making it difficult to be subject to the same people for such an extended period. He went on to announce that he was introducing a bill whereby censorship would not last longer than eighteen months. The next day, the bill was passed, and M. Aemilius Mamercus resigned from office to demonstrate his opposition to remain in power for too long. Praised by the assembled people, he returned home.[47] Meanwhile, during the time, the censors were C. Furius and M. Geganius,[48] who, embittered by the diminution of their office, punished Mamercus[49] by transferring him to another *tribus* and inflating the value of his property eightfold,[50] thus placing him among the *aerarii*.[51] Mamercus endured this valiantly and later even defended the censors.[52]

On the basis of Livy's words concerning the diminution of censorship, the law in question was named *lex Aemilia de censura minuenda*. The historian's account shows that its objective was to reduce the term of office for censors from five years to one and a half years. This information was further confirmed by Livy when he wrote about the censorship of Appius Claudius.[53] The passage confirms that the aim of *lex Aemilia* was to reduce the term of office for censors from five years to eighteen months. However, it is worth examining the context in which this information was presented.

In 312 BC, the censors were Appius Claudius and C. Plautius Venox.[54] After eighteen months, Plautius resigned from office, while Appius refused to step down.[55] Frontinus' account[56] further demonstrates that Appius deceived Plautius by suggesting that he was also going to resign from his office. This deception resulted in the buildings that were already completed when Appius himself held the office, and which had been commissioned by both censors, being solely attributed to Appius and named after him: the Via Appia[57] and the Aqua Appia.

Returning to Livy's account: the plebeian tribune P. Sempronius spoke against Appius.[58] He quoted the contents of the *lex Aemilia* and praised its proposer, who had reduced the duration of censorship from five years to one and a half years. He then asked Appius what he would have done if he had been censor when this law was passed. According to Appius, this had nothing to do with his case because – even if the *lex Aemilia* was binding on those censors during whose term it was passed, since the people enacted it after their election and the last thing the people decides becomes law – it could not bind him or other censors elected later. The provision of the Twelve Tables[59] was therefore used as an argument.

The reasoning of Appius Claudius was further subjected to crushing criticism and the decemviral provision was submitted to a completely different interpretation.[60] Tribune Sempronius referred directly to the law by asking whether, since the dictatorship of Aemilius, none of the censors had read the Twelve Tables and knew that the law was what the people had recently decided. He argued that, on the contrary, all the censors knew this provision and obeyed the *lex Aemilia* rather than the former law under which the censors were first appointed. The tribune also invoked a kind of Kollisionsregel, according to which, when two laws conflict, the new one always supersedes the old one.

The cited provision of the Twelve Tables is the subject of dispute. According to Antonio Guarino,[61] it should be considered inauthentic. An opposing view has been expressed by Bernardo Albanese,[62] as well as by Cosimo Cascione.[63] In order to take a position, it is necessary to examine the context carefully.

The case of Appius Claudius, according to Livy, is an expression of the dispute over the interpretation of this provision. Patrician officials tried to prove that the term *iussum* meant all decisions of the assemblies, not only *leges*. Appius himself argued that the *lex Aemilia* bound only those censors during whose term of office it was enacted. Subsequent elections, which also constituted a *iussum populi*, abrogated it.

The plebeian tribune Sempronius, on the other hand, argued that only the *lex* could be regarded as the *iussum populi*, and consequently, since no laws regulating censorship were passed after the *lex Aemilia*, it was this *lex* that should be regarded as binding.

This interpretive dispute was undoubtedly politically motivated. The conflict between patricians and plebeians continued, with patricians apparently trying to offset the effects of certain concessions they were forced to make.[64] The case of Appius Claudius was special because of his individual characteristics. Besides, the Claudii family was viewed rather negatively.[65] However, it can be considered that the interpretation of the rule found in the provision 12,5 of the Twelve Tables adopted by Appius was sometimes applied by patricians wishing to weaken the power of certain provisions.

Since this provision appears twice in Livy's account within the context of a major political dispute, it should be considered authentic.[66] The Appius Claudius affair caused a social storm and was certainly well-known, so it is difficult to assume that Livy falsified the course of events. In addition, he probably also had several sources on the subject, which makes his account seem all the more trustworthy.

Also noteworthy is the rule stating that, in the event of a conflict between two laws, the later always overrules the earlier: *ubi duae contrariae leges sunt, semper antiquae obrogat nova*. This rule originated from the interpretation of Tab. 12,5 assuming that only a law in the strict sense (*lex*) can be regarded as a decision of the people (*iussum populi*). *Obrogatio* means the weakening of the force of a law by its successor.[67] It can therefore be assumed that it is a modification of a part of a law, that part of a law which is obviously in conflict with the new norms.[68] During the Republican period, *obrogatio* could be performed by the Senate[69] as well as by the assembly by passing another law.

It is worth returning to the case of Appius Claudius.[70] After delivering his speech, the tribune Sempronius ordered the censor to be captured and imprisoned.[71] Six of the other tribunes agreed with his decision, but three assisted Appius (*auxilium*), resulting in his release. He then exercised the censorship himself, despite facing hostility from the people.

Other ancient authors also mentioned the *lex Aemilia*. Valerius Maximus,[72] in describing the case of the reappointed censor Rutilus,[73] reported that Rutilus himself rebuked the people for re-electing him to an office that their ancestors had decided should be limited because of the excessive powers attached to it. The text thus shows that, at least in the Roman's perception, the term of office of the censors had been shortened.

According to Zonaras,[74] censors originally held office for five years, then for eighteen months, and then again for five years. A Byzantine author drawing from the work of Cassius Dio therefore confirms that there was a shortening of the term of office.[75] The information concerning the five-year censorship at the end of this term probably refers to the time of Augustus, to whom the people wanted to grant censorial powers (*censoria potestas*) and guardianship of laws and morals (*cura legum et morum*) precisely for a period of five years. It appears from the text of Cassius Dio that Augustus was indeed granted such power, but it seems that he rejected the function offered to him.[76]

The sources quoted give every reason to believe that the object of the *lex Aemilia* was to fix the term of office of censors for eighteen months. Problems of interpretation, however, are posed by the apparent inconsistency in Livy's account, who first states that the origins of censorship were very modest and then that the law of Aemilius constituted its limitation.

An attempt to solve this problem is to assume that, while at least until the *lex Aemilia*, the task of performing the census rested with the military tribunes with consular powers. It can therefore be seen that they compiled the lists of citizens during a term of one year. The setting of the duration of the censorship at one and a half years thus represented an extension of the time allowed for the census.[77] It is also possible to assume that the duration of the censorship was not initially fixed; the censors only stepped down from office after completing their assigned tasks.[78] It may be assumed that the extension of the duration of office was associated at the same time with the loss of *imperium*, which, after all, military tribunes were entitled to. However, this is in complete contradiction with the sources.

Determining the object of the *lex Aemilia* is not the only contentious issue among scholars. Some, as mentioned above, have postponed the origin of the censorship to 366 BC, the moment a compromise was reached between patricians and plebeians within the *leges Liciniae Sextiae*. Beloch[79] put forward the thesis that the placement of the *lex Aemilia* in 434 BC is a historian's error. Instead, he identifies the consul of the year 366 BC, L. Aemilius Mamercinus,[80] the namesake of the official described by Livy, as the proposer of the law.

Beloch's thesis, however, cannot be reconciled with the fact that the emergence of censorship is nevertheless linked to the conflict between patricians and plebeians. The traditional date of the enactment of the *lex Aemilia* seems to fit much better with the political situation. It should be stressed that the powers of the censors were quite extraordinary, not only politically but also religiously.[81] Livy pointed out that it was not possible for the censors to have a limitation on their powers (*iuris modum imponere*), and therefore, a time limit (*modus temporis*) was needed. It can be assumed that the restraint of the duration of the office was a guarantee to keep it within certain limits.[82] Therefore, the traditional interpretation of the content of the *lex Aemilia* seems most convincing.

The relationship between the censorship and the consulship, on the other hand, raises the question of *imperium*. It is commonly assumed that *the lex curiata* conferred *imperium* on higher officials (consuls, praetors, as well as the dictator and *magister equitum*), while the *lex centuriata* conferred only *potestas*. This view was challenged by Filippo Cancelli,[83] who argued that the powers of the censors included *imperium* and were distinguished from those of other senior officials only by their lack of military functions. A very controversial hypothesis was presented by Wilhelm Soltau,[84] according to whom the *lex centuriata* gave the censors *imperium*, but only for the time needed to carry out the *lustrum*. According to the researcher, the *lex centuriata* was not enacted until after the completion of the census, just before the sacrificial ceremony. In support of this view, Soltau cited a passage from Varro's *De lingua Latina*[85] concerning the *contio* convened by the censors and the drawing of lots to determine which of them would conduct the purification ceremony. However, it appears that these activities took place at the beginning of their term and aimed to establish the distribution of responsibilities among colleagues. In contrast, André Magdelain[86] argued that on the day of the *lustrum*, the censor, endowed with the authority to perform the *auspicia maxima*,[87] received supreme military power (*imperium militare*) from Jupiter himself.

The whole dispute, however, rests on the belief that the Romans themselves, when thinking about officials, reasoned in terms of *cum imperio* and *sine imperio*. And yet this is not the source division. Censors did possess the right to perform *auspicia maxima*, but their relationship with the army was mainly externalised during the census when they assigned citizens to their centuries and during the lustration.[88] The censor's task was to sacrifice a boar, a ram, and a bull (*suovetaurilia*), leading the army into the city, which was certainly a demonstration of power. Indeed, the *lustrum* in this aspect resembles a triumph, during which the ban on the entry of armed men into Rome was also lifted. All of this highlights strongly the significant role of censorship but does not constitute an argument related to the *imperium* itself.

4. Public perception of the office of censor

In order to understand the functioning of the censor's office, it is useful to examine the perception of this magistracy by the ancients themselves. Both the perception of the Romans and the opinions expressed by foreigners describing the history of the Republic are important.

In the surviving sources, there are a few very general passages on censorship, from which – apart from a catalogue of the powers themselves – it is possible to glean how the office was perceived. Livy emphasised the growing importance of the censorship, which he described as having humble beginnings (*res a parva origine orta*). From his work also comes information about the authority (*auctoritas*) enjoyed by censors. In this case, the message is negative. The censor Q. Fulvius Flaccus,[89] wishing to decorate the temple of Fortuna Equestris in Rome, plundered marble tiles from the temple of Juno Lacinia in Croton, against which the inhabitants did not protest, intimidated by the censor's *auctoritas*.[90] This clearly indicates the high esteem the censors enjoyed, since even in such a blatant case the people did not dare to prevent the sacrilege. Flaccus' action, however, stirred indignation in the Senate, which passed a resolution to return the roof tiles and make propitiatory offerings (*piacula*) to Juno. A contract of lease (*locatio*) was concluded for the repair of the roof at the expense of the state.[91] Cicero also mentioned censorial *auctoritas* in his *Pro Cluentio* speech, opposing the court's judgment and *res iudicata*. The speaker attempted to play down the role of censorial decisions for pragmatic reasons – he needed this to defend his client. However, the term *auctoritas* itself was invoked in the context of the censorial mark: *animadversio atque auctoritas censoria*. This clearly indicates the esteemed position of censors and the binding nature of their decisions. It was only in the late Republican period that their authority began to be contested. The question arises, however, to what extent the term *auctoritas*, as applied to censors, may have had a technical nature, similar to its usage in relation to the Senate. It does not seem to refer exclusively to a censorial mark but rather had a broader meaning and referred to the constitutional position of censors, whose decisions were not subject to appeal.

Beginning his chapter on the censorial mark, Valerius Maximus compared its importance to military discipline and likened the effects of the censors' efforts to the glory of war.[92] In his view, Rome's power consisted not only of the virtues of the military commanders but also of the care of customs in peacetime. Conquests are futile if one lives improperly within the state, not prioritising above everything else in the forum and the Senate the duties and customs that provide a solid foundation for society. Therefore, he saw fit to chronicle the actions of the censors. His opinion gives us a proof of the importance of the magistracy.

A strong connotation of severity with censorship seems to have established itself in Latin. The semantic families of the terms *severitas*[93] – meaning 'severity' or 'seriousness' – and *acerbitas*[94] – meaning 'sternness' – were the most commonly used. This connection is confirmed by the anecdotal account of Valerius Maximus, who stated that a censor, who is in addition Cato, represents a double example of severity.[95] Cato's character, his intransigence, obstinacy, sternness, and unwillingness to compromise earned him the nickname of *Censorius*.[96]

Writing about sumptuous meals as a measurable indicator of social standing in his time, Juvenal recalled the Republican era when the austere customs of censors caused concern even among their colleagues in office and ensured modesty.[97] No one thought of exquisite turtle dishes then. It is noteworthy that the poet mentioned the traditionally censorial families[98] and Cato, who was a *homo novus*, and further endowed him with the epithet *durus* – 'tough', wishing to emphasise his exceptional severity.[99]

Censors were generally feared. It was said of Tiberius Gracchus that when he returned home in the evening, citizens would turn off the lights lest he suspect them of excessive luxury.[100]

There were also some common metaphors associated with censorship. Describing Cato's efforts to become a censor,[101] Plutarch reported that while other candidates[102] tried to please the voters, Cato argued that the people needed a doctor and a great cleansing.[103] Therefore, he chose not the most pleasing but the most demanding candidates. Because of these words, he was elected by all.[104]

Caelius used a similar metaphor in a letter to Cicero.[105] He mocked the censor Appius Claudius,[106] writing that he had allowed himself to be persuaded that censorship was a cleansing agent. He adds that he was probably mistaken because he wanted to wash away the filth and, in doing so, open his veins. Ordinarily, it was the censor who was supposed to take care of the customs of his fellow citizens. Caelius jokes that Appius wanted to cleanse himself by holding this office and, in doing so unwittingly, exposed himself to accusations.[107]

Another conclusion can be drawn from this source: the mere election as censor may, at least in theory, have been proof of the chosen one's irreproachable character. The reality was, of course, different, but Caelius' irony seems to testify to just such a public perception of the office of censor, where at the beginning of their term, they enjoyed a huge mandate of trust from the citizens. Practice repeatedly verified this belief negatively, but nevertheless, the censor remained in the minds of the average Roman as a man without blemish.

In a surviving excerpt from Varro's *Menippean Satires*, one can find a witty remark about how great it was to be a censor and not attempt to move many people into the ranks of the *aerarii*.[108] The use of a censorial mark against enemies or at least political opponents occurred more than once in the history of censorship. The legal mechanisms that offered the chance to limit such a practice were the collegiality of the office and the necessity to take an oath of impartiality.[109]

However, since censors were tasked with guarding morality in others, they themselves were required to have a crystal-clear character and lifestyle. It seems that, usually placed on a pedestal, the office must have been an extremely tempting target for derision in the event of any slip-ups.

Sometimes the behaviour of a censor, his habits or inclinations provided the impetus for jokes, especially if they deviated even slightly from accepted patterns. Macrobius quoted an anecdote related to the censorship of Crassus and Domitius[110]: dressed in black mourning robes, Crassus mourned the dead moray eel he had raised in the pool of his house like a daughter, which his colleague accused him of in the Senate as a crime (*deforme crimen*).[111] However, Crassus did not deny it at all and even took credit for it. The story was spiced up by Aelian,[112] who noted that Crassus gave his moray eel a funeral, and recounted how he responded to Domitius in a cutting manner, claiming that Domitius had not mourned any of his three wives.

During his election campaign for the office of consul, Cicero – famous for his prickly wit – joked that the current censor, L. Cotta,[113] with a taste for wine, would treat him harshly for drinking water.[114] This was an allusion to the censorial *regimen morum*, under which excessive luxury was stigmatised. However, since the censor himself was an amateur wine drinker, he would certainly not have condemned this in others.

Interestingly, the office of censor does not appear in any surviving comedy texts.[115] It seems, however, that Roman audiences must have recognised an allusion to this magistracy while watching Megaronides from Plautus' comedy *Trinummus*, who is described as a *castigator*[116] and an authority on morals.[117] It is conceivable that such themes carried in comedy must nevertheless have had a wider application in plays that unfortunately did not survive till our times.[118]

The texts by Greek authors cited so far have been anecdotal in nature. However, it is worth examining passages authored by them that describe the office of the censor and its powers. Indeed, their perspectives should shed an interesting light on this institution due to their external viewpoint.[119]

The first author from whom we might expect some information is obviously Polybius. Unfortunately, however, he only briefly mentions censors: in an economic context, concerning public contracts (*locationes censoriae*),[120] when discussing the equestrian *centuriae*,[121] and when describing the funerals of the most eminent citizens.[122] This is rather surprising, since censorship was certainly one of the mechanisms necessary to preserve the Republic's systemic balance so praised by Polybius. Apparently, however, he did not regard its role as essential.[123]

Key information, however, was provided by Dionysius of Halicarnassus,[124] who described censorship in comparison with Athenian and Spartan institutions. This is the view of a man who examined the birth of the Principate along with the Augustan ideology of a return to ancestral customs and analysed the history of the office of the censor through this prism. According to the historian,[125] the Athenians were known to punish idlers who did not take part in the affairs of state,[126] while the Lacedaemonians allowed old men to beat citizens who misbehaved in public with canes.[127] The Romans, on the other hand, by opening up every house and extending the power of the censors down to the bedroom, made these officials the guardians of everything that went on in their homes.

In the passage, there is a clear juxtaposition between the control known to the Greeks in the public sphere and the typically Roman intrusion into the private sphere, which was difficult for foreigners to comprehend. For the Greeks, the home was a boundary that basically no one could cross,[128] and breaking this taboo certainly seemed strange to them. Dionysius also emphasised,[129] that it was the job of censors to control the lives of all Romans and to punish those who deviated from the customs of their forefathers.

Plutarch wrote about censors on more than one occasion. While creating a biography of a protagonist who achieved censorship, he also explained the specifics of this office.[130] Writing about Cato's censorship,[131] Plutarch devoted much space to the characteristics of this office. He emphasised that it towered above others in terms of honours and represented the pinnacle of a political career. The powers of those holding it included insight into life and customs. The Romans believed that neither marriage, the upbringing of children, daily life, nor feasts should be beyond their control and judgement. For all these showed a person's true character better than public life and politics. For this reason, officials were appointed to be the watchdogs, the controllers, and those who meted out punishments to ensure that no one indulged in pleasure or deviated from accepted customs.

It should be marked that both authors placed emphasis on only one of the censorial powers – the control of customs (*regimen morum*).[132] It seems, therefore, that this may have constituted a novelty that needed to be explained for the non-Roman reader.

Censorship was also addressed by Cassius Dio,[133] for whom the office in question was already of historical interest only. However, this fragment of his work is preserved only in an abridged form in Zonaras' *Epitome historiarum*.[134] The text describes the origins of censorship and lists its powers, but there are hardly any evaluative elements. There is only a reference to the fact that the censors began to surpass the consuls in power.

Interestingly, however, *regimen morum* as the special competence of censors was singled out by much later authors. The antiquarian Lydus, who lived in the time of Justinian, described the office of censor in the context of excess in his book *De magistratibus*. He first gave general information about the appointment of the office to inventory the estates of citizens because of the costs of wars, then introduced a passus on theatre and luxury, and finally wrote about the control of customs. He reported[135] that the censors were stern, unemotional and hard-hearted towards those they accused of excess, paying no attention to anyone's wealth or dignity. He also went on to write that censors could investigate the customs of all citizens and apply penalties, from which there were no exceptions. The author's belief in the omnipotence of the censors rings out from the text. The definition of a censor in Suidas' lexicon is also significant[136]: according to the lexicographer, the task of the censors was to ensure that citizens led a moderate life, in accordance with the old customs.[137]

One can therefore conclude that censorship was synonymous with severity for the Romans. The citizens were made aware of the limits, crossing which exposed them to sanctions and the loss of their good name in society. The censors themselves were seen as people of exceptional dignity, which at the same time put them in a rather difficult position: they had to be beyond reproach in order not to expose themselves to ridicule.

From a systemic point of view, censorship had the character of a controlling element. The censors – elected by the people – determined a person's place in society, being able to promote or demote them. It was one of those Republican institutions that ensured the balance of the system.

The Greeks, on the other hand, saw the office of the censor as a kind of curiosity. To them, such far-reaching interference in the private lives of citizens, extending all the way to the bedroom, seemed unusual. At the same time, they emphasised the prominent position of censors in the social hierarchy. They also did not shy away from quoting anecdotes, noting the comic potential of such an unusual magistracy.

5. External indications of the office of censor

As officials at the top of their careers, censors had to stand out from their fellow citizens. The lack of lictors meant that they did not present themselves as dignified as consuls, yet an elusive mist of dignity surrounded them.[138] They were given due respect, even from other officials.

Suetonius, commenting on the uncouthness of Domitius, Nero's grandfather, reported that the latter, being only an aedile, forced a censor to give way to him.[139] Under normal circumstances, therefore, it was the censor who took precedence. This hierarchy was of immense importance to the Romans. When two citizens met in a narrow street, it depended on their dignity which one should give way to the other. The consul or praetor could have recourse to the lictors in case of trouble[140]; the censor, in most cases, did not have to do so, as the tone of Suetonius indicates. The historian regarded the behaviour of the aedile as downright implausible.

According to Zonaras,[141] censors were entitled to the same external indications of holding office as higher magistrates, except for the assistance of lictors. Certainly, these distinctions included the right to sit in the curule chair (*sella curulis*)[142] as well as certain elements of dress. High magistrates[143] had the right to wear the purple-bordered toga (*toga praetexta*) and be cremated in it after death.[144] Therefore, it may be assumed that the censors also had this privilege.

Athenaeus,[145] however, reported that they were treated even more specially: he wrote that among the Romans, censors – the highest officials – killed sacrificial animals with an axe dressed in a purple toga and with a wreath on their heads. The Greek author seems to have had in mind here a lustration ceremony in which the censor sacrificed a boar, a ram, and a bull (*suovetaurilia*). A very interesting iconographic source that can confirm this account is a relief from an altar attributed to Domitius Ahenobarbus, dated to around 100 BC.[146] It depicts a census and a *lustratio*. The censor about to perform the sacrifice stands beside the altar dressed in a toga, wearing a wreath on his head. The purple toga was probably worn by the censors during the purification ceremony, and a purple-bordered one on other occasions.

It is worth investigating whether other elements of dress distinguished the censors. Festus provided[147] information on a special type of footwear, the *mullei* – leather tall boots dyed red – which were used by the kings of Alba Longa and later by patricians in Rome. He also cited a statement by Cato in *Origines* indicating that such boots were worn by curule magistrates.[148] Therefore, it can be inferred that censors, as *magistratus curules*, also had the right to wear *mullei*.

It is also worth referring at this point to the term *viri censorii* used in the sources. A definition of the term *censorius*[149] can be found in Placidus' scholia[150]: he stated that the word *censorius* was used to describe someone worthy of the office of censor or one who had already held that office. It should be added that even if someone later held a lower office, the title still applied to him.[151]

The title *vir censorius*[152] apparently provided certain privileges. Polybius, describing Roman funeral customs, reported that – when actors imitating famous members of the family and wearing their masks walked in the procession – each of them also wore the attire corresponding to the office held by the ancestor in question.[153] In the case of the censors, this was a purple toga, not just purple-bordered.[154] The question arises as to whether those who attained the dignity of censor were buried in a *toga praetexta* or *purpurea*.

Sources from the Principate used the term 'censorial funeral' (*funus censorium*).[155] For instance, Tacitus reported that the Senate enacted a censorial funeral for the emperor Claudius.[156] In the case of this particular *princeps*, the Senate's decision may also have been dictated by his holding the office of censor alongside Vitellius. *Funus censorium* denoted a type of public funeral[157] more grandiose than consular funerals. Since consuls were known to be buried in purple-bordered togas, it can be assumed that censors were probably honoured with a purple toga.[158] During the Principate, this privilege was granted to emperors performing censorial functions, as well as others. However, the term *funus censorium* did not necessarily have a technical meaning. It may have referred to the funerals of persons considered worthy of censorship, corresponding with Placidus' definition mentioned earlier. Initially reserved for emperors precisely because of their censorial powers, it later came to be granted even to women, which may mean associating with *funus sollemne* or 'solemn funeral' rather than with the office of censor.

There are doubts as to whether the *viri censorii* were given special treatment in the Senate hierarchy.[159] Gellius cited Varro's advice to Pompey when he assumed his first consulship regarding the sessions of the Senate.[160] It is clear from the text that the consuls were asked for their opinion first.[161] Initially, the *princeps senatus* was the first among senators of that rank to speak, but later the president of the session was allowed to ask first whoever he wished, as long as that person was from among the *viri consulares*.[162]

For a long time, it was thought that the oldest former patrician censor was customarily nominated *princeps senatus*.[163] However, the accounts available to us show that it was much more common for the position to be held by the incumbent patrician censor.[164] It seems, therefore, that this choice was rather political[165] and not determined by any binding rules for the censors performing *lectio senatus*. However, it is clear from the phrase *ex quo (scil. consulari) gradu* that the *princeps senatus* must have originated from among the consulars.

It seems, therefore, that formally the highest rank in the Senate hierarchy was that of *vir consularis*.[166] There is no evidence that *censorii* were particularly privileged. However, it can be assumed that they were generally held in high esteem, which may have led to their actual distinction. Nonetheless, the decision depended on the official who convened and presided over the session of the Senate.

6. Censorial records and their storage

The censors did an enormous amount of work and produced numerous documents.[167] Therefore, they had to be provided with a place to store them. It is important to consider both the content and types of these documents, as well as where the censors held office and where their archives were located.

The *tabulae censoriae* are repeatedly mentioned in the sources. Varro even quoted excerpts from them.[168] According to the grammarian, one of the censors would conduct auspices during the night and then order the usher to convene the people, using the traditional formula. The usher called first in the temple and then from the walls. At dawn, in the presence of the officials and the people,[169] the censors drew lots as to which of them was to conduct the *lustrum*, and this one presided over the *contio*. The *tabulae* thus contained a description of the rituals, as well as the formulas to be used on the occasion.[170]

Censorial documentation contained information on citizens.[171] Every new pair of censors had access to the previous lists and compiled new ones using the criteria they decided to apply. They thus created a hierarchy of the Roman population. Additional information is provided by other source texts. Opposing Rullus's agrarian plebiscite, Cicero mentioned[172] that the tribune looked through the *tabulae censoriae* so as not to miss any buildings or public land in Sicily. Therefore, these documents certainly contained a register of such properties. The censors also kept an accurate list of the public lands of Italy.[173]

In another speech, Cicero accused Clodius[174] of taking over the house of the equestrian Q. Seius, whom he had murdered, where an altar and a chapel were located.[175] The orator claimed that he could prove this based on the *tabulae censoriae* and the testimony of witnesses. This reference indicates that information about sacred places (*loca sacra*) was also in the censorial archives. In addition, it can be inferred that these *tabulae* constituted strong evidence in the case.[176] From the construction of the sentence, it appears that they were treated at least as seriously as the testimony of witnesses, although placing them first could indicate that they held even greater weight.

The jurist Marcellus, on the other hand, provided information on a resolution of the Senate which ranked documents produced at the time of the census and other public documents higher in the hierarchy of evidence than the testimony of witnesses.[177] However, it is not known when this *senatus consultum* was passed, nor is there any other mention of it. The importance of *tabulae censoriae* as a means of evidence probably grew gradually. During the Republican period, they were considered at least equivalent to witness testimony, while a clear rule regarding their greater importance might have appeared later.

According to Pliny the Elder, everything from which the state profited was called *pascua* in the *tabulae censoriae*, because initially the only tax (*vectigal*) was paid for the use of public pastures.[178] This shows the very conservative and traditional nature of this documentation, in which not even new terminology or grammar was introduced.[179] As a result, there were problems of interpretation. For example, Gellius quoted excerpts from the correspondence between Servius Sulpicius and Varro.[180] The jurist asked for an explanation of an unfamiliar term that appeared *in censoris libris*, which is probably in *tabulae censoriae*.[181] The doubt concerned the phrase *favisae Capitolinae*,[182] which, according to Varro, meant the cellars beneath the Capitol where sacred things no longer in use were stored.

Tabulae censoriae were subject to legal protection. In Cicero's description of Oppianicus' crimes during the trial of Cluentius, one of the accusations was that the decurions of Larinum had ruled that Oppianicus had destroyed the municipal censorial documents.[183] The verb *corrumpere* is to be understood here as any interference with the text recorded on the plates with the aim of falsifying the data. The decurions here were most likely the judges in the tribunal that convicted Oppianicus.[184] The municipal law concerning the destruction of *tabulae censoriae* was probably modelled on the one in force in Rome.[185] However, it is uncertain which procedure was followed: whether a criminal tribunal proceeding (*quaestio*)[186] or a trial for a fine tried by *recuperatores*.[187] The phrase *universi decuriones* is rather indicative of a numerous jury. Cicero seems to have had a serious criminal trial in mind here.

Dionysius of Halicarnassus provided interesting information on censorial documents.[188] The Greek historian used the home archives of the censorial families, which he calls *τιμητικὰ ὑπομνήματα*, that is 'censorial notes'. This passage indicates that after his term of office the censor kept a copy of the basic documents relating to the census.[189] This copy remained in the family and was treated in the same way as the family sacra. This should not come as a surprise, as an ancestor who was honoured with the position of censor added splendour to the whole family.[190]

Several buildings related to the activity of the censors can be mentioned.[191] According to Livy, in 435 BC, a second pair of censors, Furius and Geganius,[192] made an acceptation (*probatio*) of a new building on the Field of Mars, the *Villa Publica*, which also immediately housed a census.[193] It was an extensive complex of buildings and gardens.[194]

A censorial building within the boundaries of the *pomerium* was called *Atrium Libertatis*,[195] which Nicholas Purcell[196] identified with the building in the forum known as the *Tabularium*. However, his thesis is impossible to prove definitively, so the exact location of the Atrium has not been conclusively identified.[197] Livy reported that in 169 BC, the censors, accused of treason (*perduellio*),[198] immediately went to the *Atrium Libertatis*. There, they sealed public documents, closed the *tabularium* and sent back the public slaves, claiming that they would take no official action before the verdict of the popular assembly.[199] This excerpt provides valuable information. Firstly, in the *Atrium Libertatis*, there was an archive where the *tabulae publicae* were stored. These documents were certainly related not only to the census but also to public lease contracts. Slaves owned by the state were employed to operate the archive.

From the account of Granius Licinianus,[200] it can additionally be inferred that various plaques, such as maps, related to public land were also placed in the *Atrium*, apparently intended to facilitate the censors' work. In 167 BC, in the *Atrium Libertatis*, the censors held a drawing of lots for the *tribus to* which the freedmen were to be enrolled.[201] The lot fell on the *tribus Esquilina*,[202] as announced by the censor Tiberius Gracchus. This building probably served as the censors' primary headquarters, where they made their decisions.

The censorial records were also stored in the Temple of the Nymphs. In a speech in defence of Milo, Cicero accused Clodius of deliberately setting fire to this Temple in order to destroy the documents archived there.[203] These may have been the lists of citizens entitled to benefit from distributions of grain (*frumentationes*).[204] This suggests that Cicero aimed to convince his audience of Clodius' disreputable intentions. The destruction of the lists could make it difficult for many to prove their civic status.

It can be inferred from Livy's account that, at the end of their term of office, the censors submitted to the *aerarium*[205] located in the temple of Saturn lists of those whom they had punished with a censorial mark, with the sanction of being transferred to the *aerarii*,[206] and whose names should therefore be known to the quaestors.[207]

Furthermore, there was a need to keep records of local censuses. There is epigraphic evidence of a building called the *Censorium*, which was probably used for this purpose.[208]

Thus, censorial documentation was stored in various locations, which certainly had the advantage that, in the event of a fire, it would not be lost in its entirety.

7. The crisis of the office of censor and the assimilation of powers by the *princeps*

Censorship took shape as an atypical office. On the one hand, it was associated with extremely broad powers, even when detached from military matters, but on the other hand, it is impossible to overlook certain shortcomings which must have ultimately weakened it. First and foremost, the censors held their posts for only eighteen months, followed by a further three and a half years out of office. This meant they were not always able to see certain projects through to completion, especially renovation and construction projects. Of course, it was possible to apply for an extension of their term of office (*prorogatio*)[209] by the Senate if necessary, but this was an ad hoc measure. Interruptions in the activity of the magistracy led to certain functions having to be taken over by other officials, particularly the aediles. This applied, for example, to the granting of concessions for water supply.[210] The lack of continuity in office was not a positive feature and certainly had a negative impact on the consistency of censorship policies across various levels. It is conceivable, for example, that the end of their term and the prospect of a gap of more than three years before the next censors were elected could have led to a general loosening of customs or problems with completing construction projects. This shortcoming may have contributed to the crisis of censorship that coincided with the decline of the Republican period.

Sulla carried out a thorough reform of the state's political system, seeking to secure Senate's supremacy, while reducing the powers of the plebeian tribunes. During his dictatorship, censorship certainly faced a profound crisis. However, it is uncertain to what extent the dictator formally intervened in the office. It is clear that censors were not elected during this period, but whether this was due to the abolition of the magistracy or for other reasons is difficult to determine.

Sources report that the dictator increased the composition of the Senate to 600 members and introduced the principle of admitting former quaestors.[211] Since Sulla himself compiled the lists of the Senate,[212] there was apparently no need to elect censors. Certainly, some of their tasks could have been performed by other officials, often by the dictator himself, as in the case of public contracts.[213] On the other hand, a conspicuous shortcoming must have been the failure to conduct a census and the abandonment of the *regimen morum*, which may have started to be perceived as a relic by this time but was nevertheless still a deeply ingrained institution in the public mind. The state could do without the census, as two of its most important reasons had already become obsolete: in 167 BC, the poll-tax (*tributum*) was abolished in Italy, and the property value necessary for military service was gradually lowered, eventually allowing even the proletarians to enlist.

In 70 BC, Sulla's reforms began to disintegrate. The consuls Pompey and Crassus ensured the restoration of the former powers to the plebeian tribunes. This was also the period when Cicero delivered his *Divinatio in Caecilium*. Speaking of irregularities in the judiciary, the orator expressed the desire of the people to allow others besides senators to serve as judges. He also emphasised that due to the shame and guilt of the judges, the people wanted censorship, which had previously seemed oppressive but was now seen as desirable once again.[214]

Thes text could be an indication that censorship, like the plebeian tribunate, needed to be reactivated. Sulla reduced the tribunes' powers to such an extent that the office became a mere image without substance (*imago sine re*).[215] Cicero was drawing a clear parallel with censorship, which may also have lost some of its attributes. However, the passage cited does not provide definite information: the orator could have been referring to the necessity of electing new censors rather than restoring the office to its earlier form.[216]

Commenting on this passage of Cicero's speech, Pseudo-Asconius wrote that the Roman people so hated this sad and harsh office that it remained abandoned for many years.[217] Based on this account, however, it cannot be assumed that the non-appointment of censors was due to any normative act but rather to public resentment.

Scholars look for arguments for the abolition of censorship in a scholiast's commentary on the same passage. The anonymous author wrote that Sulla abolished the censors acting in the interests of *nobilitas*.[218] It is markworthy that the commentator here wrote about both tribunes and censors, suggesting that both offices had suffered the same fate. However, this text does not provide compelling evidence.[219] The scholiast may have misunderstood Cicero's statement, and there is no reason to believe that he had any other source to support such an interpretation.

Did Sulla therefore abolish the office of censor? It is difficult to find a clear answer to this question. Rather, it seems that censorship did not fit into the political order introduced by the dictator,[220] and since there was no need for it, he himself did not order elections. On the other hand, abolishing the office by law would not have been in line with the political beliefs of the optimates,[221] whose representative the dictator was. It was one thing to minimise the influence of the tribunes, quite another to become the proposer of a law[222] abolishing an office that guarded the *mores maiorum* and had a strong sacral connotation in the *lustrum* ceremony.[223] This is something Sulla, who was reportedly very superstitious, would be unlikely to do.

Sulla's biography, on the other hand, seems to indicate that he had something to fear from the censors. He did not shy away from luxury or from socially unacceptable relationships; he surrounded himself with actors.[224] Possibly, that is why, without publicity, he brought about a situation in which this magistracy somewhat lost its right to exist. Certainly, the factor that made it easier was a kind of re-evaluation of the principles accepted in society,[225] which no longer looked to the customs of the ancestors as the only possible standard of behaviour. This interpretation also seems to be indicated by Cicero, quoted above, who claimed that censorship was seen as too harsh. On the other hand, the turmoil of the post-Sullan years, the escalation of violence, and the powerlessness of the judiciary, led to a rise in the popularity of the office, making its reactivation possible. Since the judges in the permanent criminal tribunals (*quaestiones perpetuae*) were senators, there was a demand for strict *lectiones senatus* that would eliminate individuals who did not meet moral requirements for the Senate, and the same applied to the equestrians.

Although censorship regained its full powers after the dictator's resignation, there was an increasing shift away from the old rules, and the *mores maiorum* were slowly becoming a relic. This is why the office of the censor became the subject of a reform carried out based on the *lex Clodia de censoria notione*, which led to a complete paralysis of its functions,[226] as censors were obliged to accept all accusations and conduct a full trial ending in a verdict. The abrogation of the plebiscite of Clodius did nothing to restore the former splendour of this magistracy. Despite the apparent crisis, however, censorship was still seen as the pinnacle of a political career and an important office for the Republic.

Caesar was the first politician who decided to accept the office of dictator after Sulla, in an attempt to remove the *odium* from this office. He also received many other dignities and honours,[227] but never crowned his *cursus honorum* with censorship. Cassius Dio reported[228] that Caesar was elected guardian of the customs[229] of his fellow citizens for three years and dictator for ten years in 46 BC. He added that it was as if the title of censor was not worth it. The historian further noted[230] that in 44 BC, the Senate passed a resolution to make Caesar sole censor for life.[231] This resolution, along with others conferring honours on him, was inscribed in golden letters on a silver tablet and deposited at the foot of the statue of Jupiter Capitolinus.[232] It should be marked, however, that Cassius Dio reported that Caesar accepted almost all the honours offered to him.[233] *A contrario*, there must have been something he declined; perhaps censorship was one of them.

Two opinions are presented among scholars on this competence of Caesar. Theodor Mommsen[234] considered that the censorial functions were within the scope of the dictator's authority, and therefore sources that speak of the conferral of any special prerogatives in this regard are unreliable. However, it seems that a dictator was by definition appointed to tasks less time-consuming than censorship,[235] most often military. Caesar's dictatorship was characterised by many irregularities, but it is difficult to write censorial powers into it, contrary to source accounts.

Pietro De Francisci[236] considered that the *praefectura morum* was a function that allowed Caesar to concentrate the powers of the censors, presumably to avoid collegiality. Heinrich Siber[237] argued that the *praefectura morum* was only mistakenly treated as censorship by Suetonius and Cassius Dio. In his view, Caesar was only given the ability to regulate matters of morality without having to obtain the approval of the people, i.e. not in the form of *leges rogatae* but *leges datae*, and that his *leges sumptuariae* fell into this category.[238] On the other hand, before his death, Caesar adopted, in his opinion, the *potestas censoria* for life, although he did not hold the office of censor, which, however, is in complete contradiction with the source accounts.

Francesco De Martino[239] argued that, although Caesar did not assume the official title of *praefectus morum*, he was given separate powers allowing him, for example, to carry out *lectio senatus*.[240] He also believed that Caesar – being ahead of Augustus in this – did not want to hold the office itself, being content with the powers associated with it.

It must therefore be recognised that – in principle – Caesar did not want to exercise censorship. He obtained the necessary powers in other ways. There is no reason to think that the *praefectura morum* constituted a new office, but rather merely a power all the more so since the sources do not title Caesar *praefectus*.[241] From Cassius Dio's account, it can be inferred that Caesar considered the censorship unworthy, which may have been due to the crisis the office was undergoing since Sulla's time. The *praefectura morum* may have been an expression of entrusting the sphere of morals to the control of Caesar by his fellow citizens.

On the other hand, it cannot be entirely ruled out that towards the end of his life Caesar got a little carried away with his mania for grandeur and planned to take on the title of sole censor for life – *censor sine collega*. However, it is unlikely that he managed to do so, as this is contradicted by Cassius Dio's remark on Domitian as the first one to have obtained such a dignity.[242]

After the fall of the Republic, the extent of the power of the first *princeps* took shape slowly, with Octavian gradually acquiring powers that allowed him to control virtually all the activities of the state. The two crucial stages of this process were 27 and 23 BC. In 27 BC, Octavian resigned the office of triumvir and announced the restoration of the Republican system. The Senate gave him the honorific title *Augustus*. Four years later, the *princeps* resigned his consulship. He retained, however, the *imperium* resulting from his management of the provinces – a vast one comprising Syria, Egypt, Further Spain, and Transalpine Gaul – which the Senate modified so that it would not expire when he crossed the *pomerium*. This gave him *imperium maius* compared to the power of all other governors.[243]

The *Res gestae Divi Augusti*[244] show that Augustus conducted the census and the lustration ceremony three times. However, it is uncertain whether the competence that allowed him to do this was the *censoria potestas* or perhaps the *imperium* he had as consul. Augustus also conducted *lectiones senatus*, always placing himself at the head of the list as *princeps senatus*. This also seems to indicate his activity as a censor.

His actions as guardian of customs are also significant, which, after all, fell within the remit of the Republican censors. Augustus' marriage legislation aimed – at least as far as declarations were concerned – at a return to *mores maiorum*. Interestingly, as transmitted by Livy's epitomator in justifying his motion *de maritandis ordinibus* in the Senate,[245] Augustus quoted a speech by the censor Q. Metellus[246] *De uxoribus ducendis* (also titled *De prole augenda*) delivered in 131 BC, in which

Metellus encouraged Romans to marry and have offspring.[247] Invoking the words of the censor lent dignity to his own idea. Augustus could also argue that he was not the first to mandate marriage.[248] Although the censor's speech was not a source of law, failure to comply with its demands resulted in a censorial mark. It should also be marked that Augustus – by quoting Metellus' speech – was apparently putting himself in the position of censor, which may also provide valuable information when considering his competence.

Moreover, the speech was published as an edict. Suetonius stated that this was to disseminate it to the citizens and to convince them that their ancestors had already dealt with the issue.[249] However, it is difficult to suppose that the edict was merely informative; it may have foreshadowed the criteria used within the *regimen morum*.

According to Suetonius, the *princeps* also read in the Senate and proclaimed by edict the speech of P. Rutilius Rufus[250] concerning the erection of buildings.[251] This was to support his draft plebiscite *de modo aedificiorum urbis* or the more general *lex sumptuaria*.[252] The restrictions consisted of setting a permitted maximum wall thickness and, indirectly, the height of buildings.[253] This bill was voted on in 18 BC. It was passed – like the *lex Iulia de maritandis ordinibus* – through a *concilia plebis*, as Augustus made the proposal using his tribunician powers. This project, too, was part of a policy associated with a return to ancestral customs. Construction issues were one element of the censors' activities during the Republic.

The exercise of the duty of guarding morality was one of the key elements of Augustus' policy and must have been associated by his contemporaries with censorship. Macrobius, for example, mentioned the case of an equestrian who, accused of negligence and proving his innocence, called the emperor outright a censor.[254]

It is therefore necessary to try to answer the question of whether, and possibly during what period, Augustus acted as a censor, whether he had a *censoria potestas*, or whether perhaps his *imperium* was sufficient.

An interesting clue may be that the inept censorship of Plancus and Paulus[255] in 22 BC was mentioned by Suetonius[256] as the last before the reign of Claudius. Therefore, it appears that in the years 22 BC–47 AD, there were no censors. This could indicate that at least after 22 BC, Augustus did not exercise censorship, or at most, only had certain powers associated with this office.

The *princeps* himself never mentions censorship in the *Res gestae*,[257] although he does describe the three censuses[258] and lustrations he carried out. When writing about them, he always adds information about his consulship or *imperium consulare*. He conducted the censuses alone or with a colleague: the first time with M. Agrippa, the third time with Tiberius.[259] In addition to this, it is known that the emperor regularly conducted reviews of the equestrian centuries with the help of ten elected senators.[260]

A passage found in the Greek version of the *Res gestae* concerns the control over morality.[261] Augustus proclaimed that when the people and the Senate entrusted him with the position of guardian of laws and customs with supreme authority and without a colleague, he accepted no office contrary to the customs of his ancestors. The proposed Latin version reads: *ut curator legum et morum summa potestate solus crearer, nullum magistratum contra morem maiorum delatum recepi*. He did, however, discharge the tasks incumbent upon him with the *tribunicia potestas*. In addition, the Emperor stressed that he had selected a colleague five times.

This text is the subject of dispute because it seems to contradict information given by historians. Suetonius reported[262] that Augustus was given the *tribunicia potestas* for life,[263] which he held collegially. Augustus could not, of course, become a plebeian tribune because he was a patrician.[264] According to the historian, he also accepted the lifetime guardianship of customs and statutes (*regimen morum legumque*), and it was based on this – although without the honour of censorship – that he conducted the census three times. Cassius Dio, on the other hand, recorded that in 19 BC Augustus accepted the position of guardian of good manners and the power of censorship for five years.[265] These honours were conferred on him by the popular assembly.

At first glance, therefore, the texts in question contradict each other. It is necessary to provide a chronology of the emperor's actions, which may have been of a censorial nature. It is first essential to establish when the censuses in question took place.[266] Between 29 and 28 BC, Octavian – holding the office of consul – conducted the *lectio senatus* and the census together with Marcus Agrippa, then *consul designatus*. While Octavian then had *imperium* attached to the consulship, Agrippa had not yet taken office. This may indicate an action performed *censoria potestate*.[267] This is confirmed by the inscription Fasti Venusini[268] discovered around AD 1470 in Venusia (Apulia).

> CIL IX,422: *Imp. Caes. VI, M. Agrippa II cos., idem censoria potestate lustrum fecerunt.*
>
> *The Emperor Caesar in his sixth and Marcus Agrippa in his second consulate performed lustrum by virtue of censorial power.*
>
> (transl. AT)

The inscription shows that Octavian and Agrippa carried out the *lustrum*, exercising the power of censorship.

A similar conclusion can be drawn from a passage in the work of Cassius Dio.[269] According to the historian, Octavian along with Agrippa carried out the census and performed the *lectio senatus*. The participle *τιμητεύσας* is most often translated as 'exercising censorship.'[270] Such a translation leads scholars to accuse Cassius of an obvious error, since Augustus was certainly not a censor *sensu stricto*. Georges Pieri – stretching somewhat to acquit Dio – translates it as 'exercising censorial power.'[271] Meanwhile, grammatically, it is an aorist participle from the verb *τιμάω*, which means 'to estimate' and also 'to carry out census.' So, the translation should rather read 'having carried out the census.' Cassius Dio, therefore, wrote that Augustus and Agrippa first conducted the census and then enacted other reforms and performed the *lectio senatus*. In these circumstances, the historian's text must be considered correct, although the order of events may be somewhat questionable: usually the *lectio senatus* took place first and then the census. However, since Octavian considered the selection of senators a rather thankless task,[272] he could have reversed the sequence of events.

According to Mario Attilio Levi,[273] the ability to exercise censorial functions was granted to Octavian by the *lex Saenia*,[274] proposed by the *consul suffectus* of late 30 BC, L. Saenius. This law, however, according to Levi, did not confer *censoria potestas*, but only allowed a consul to perform acts normally reserved for censors. Levi does not take Agrippa into account, who despite not being a consul, wielded powers similar to those of Octavian. However, it is important to consider the subject matter of the *lex Saenia* concerned and its relationship to censorial powers. The source accounts[275] unambiguously link this law to the admission of plebeian families to the patriciate. Therefore, it seems difficult to link the introduction of broad censorship powers to the *lex Saenia*. Instead, it concerned only the question of admission to the patriciate (*adlectio in numerum patriciorum*).

It should be marked that Augustus himself wrote in his *Res gestae* that he conducted the census during his sixth consulship, whereas on other occasions he emphasised that he did so *consulari cum imperio*. Here he did not specify the authority he used. It can therefore be assumed that both he and Agrippa were granted the extraordinary power of *censoria potestas*.[276] However, it was a temporary authority. The question therefore arises as to whether Augustus received it on other occasions.

In 22 AD, the election of the aforementioned censors Plancus and Paulus took place. This was one of the political manifestations intended to convince the people of Augustus' Republican views and to prepare the ground for the soon-to-be-held Jubilee Games (*ludi saeculares*).[277] Velleius Paterculus reported[278] that their censorship was characterised by dissent. It brought no honour to the officials themselves and no good to the state. Paulus was unable to fulfil his duties, while Plancus himself was characterised by all the vices that he could accuse others of as a censor.

The circumstances of the appointment of these officials were characteristic: the emperor was offered a lifetime censorship, which he did not accept, and instead appointed Plancus and Paulus.[279] Augustus himself did not list the census done at this time among his achievements, but – according to Cassius Dio[280] – he performed some of the censorial tasks personally.

Cassius Dio also relayed that in 19 BC, Augustus accepted the *cura morum* and *censoria potestas* for five years, which were then extended to another five years. Two more *lectiones senatus* took place in 18 and 11 BC. Perhaps after this second *lectio*, the census began, which was completed with the *lustrum* in 8 BC.[281] Special officials were then elected, called *triumviri legendi senatus*,[282] who carried out the *lectio* in 4 AD. The last recorded census in the *Res gestae*, which Augustus conducted with Tiberius, took place in 14 AD.

Prior to the creation of the office of censor, the authority to conduct the census belonged first to the king and then to the consuls. Perhaps, therefore, over time Augustus considered that the *imperium consulare* was sufficient for him to carry out the census. At the time of the first census, Agrippa was not a consul, so the *censoria potestas* was essential. Subsequent ones could already be conducted *consulari cum imperio*.

Regarding the issue of Augustus' exercise of the *regimen morum (legumque)*, several observations must be made. The excerpt quoted above, *Res gestae* 1,6, known only from the Greek version of the text, has become a subject of debate among scholars. Some[283] believe that it testifies to the emperor's non-acceptance of the function of *curator legum et morum*, while others[284] maintain the view that Augustus nevertheless accepted it, but only resigned to exercise it within an extraordinarily extended framework, i.e. *maxima potestate*. The latter theory seems to harmonise better with the accounts of Suetonius and Cassius Dio.

In literature, the first *princeps* was very often portrayed as a guardian of customs. Horace wrote *moribus ornes, legibus emendes*.[285] Ovid had Jupiter prophesy the apotheosis of Augustus and praise his achievements.

> Ovid., *Met*. 15,832–834: *Pace data terris animum ad civilia vertet*
> *iura suum legesque feret iustissimus auctor*
> *exemploque suo mores reget...*
> *When peace has been bestowed upon all lands he shall turn his mind to the rights of citizens, and as a most righteous jurist promote the laws. By his own good example shall he direct the ways of men.*
> (Transl. G.P. Goold)

According to the poet, having made peace, the emperor turned people's minds to civic affairs, introduced laws and statutes, and upheld customs by setting an example. Even if Ovid was not entirely sincere, the passage reflects a common belief.

From the passages quoted from *Res gestae*, Suetonius, and Cassius Dio, it appears that – even if Augustus ultimately refused – the Roman people and the Senate were unanimous in granting him *regimen morum*, which may indicate the existence of a Senate resolution and a law,[286] although the powers were declined. This leads us to believe that calling the emperor *curator morum* had its justification and, although legally inaccurate, was probably common.[287]

All this, however, seems very surprising in the final analysis. Why was Augustus so reluctant to embrace censorship? Why did he avoid assuming the powers associated with it when he was actually exercising them?

It was a very thankless function for Augustus to have the task of compiling a list of senators. Of course, it was of colossal political importance, and the emperor wanted to have a monopoly on it, but he nevertheless resorted to various ploys to take the *odium* off himself. Suetonius, for example, reported that one of the *lectiones* took place by the senators' decision, where each chose the other (*ipsorum arbitratu quo vir virum legit*).[288] This refers to the first *lectio* in 28 BC. Octavian managed to persuade some senators to resign voluntarily, thus sparing him the trouble of removing them. This also explains the reversal of the order of tasks[289]: Octavian first had the Senate lionised on its own, conducted a census with Agrippa and only then carried out the *lectio* proper.

As for overseeing customs, Augustus claimed to undertake this using his *tribunicia potestas*. This may have been due to his knowledge of the political realities of the Republican period. The task of the censors was to guard the *mores maiorum*. The instrument that allowed them to fulfil this duty was the censorial mark. They often announced in the edicts they issued which behaviours they did not approve of, thus informing citizens what could lead to censor's *ignominia*. On numerous occasions, the censors attempted to restrain luxury or encourage Romans to have offspring. However, the means at their disposal were not always sufficient. Often, the figure of the censor himself – usually a distinguished man at the height of his political career – provided an incentive to comply with certain norms, but not always. Therefore, it sometimes became necessary to back up the censors' efforts with appropriate legislative measures. A censorial edict could anticipate the content of a later law or plebiscite. The mere possibility of proposing motions was therefore sufficient to introduce restrictions on luxury or to popularise marriages. Augustus benefitted from the *ius agendi cum plebe* vested in him by virtue of his possession of the *tribunicia potestas*. It is also worth noting the difference between the heyday of the Republic, when ancestral customs were still regarded as the natural way of doing things, and its decline, when they were increasingly becoming a thing of the past. Where once the threat of a censorial mark sufficed, harsher sanctions became necessary.[290]

Further illumination of the issue requires a reminder of certain basic tenets of Augustan policy. Imperial propaganda sought at all costs to maintain the semblance of the Republic,[291] portraying the *princeps* as one among equal citizens. In his *Res gestae*, the emperor described the moment when the Republican system was restored in 27 BC, and he received the honourable title *Augustus* from the Senate. He stressed that from then on, he was superior to everyone only in his *auctoritas* and that he had no more power than his colleagues in office.[292]

The basic rules for holding office during the Republican period were: tenure, collegiality, incompatibility, gratuitousness, and the prohibition against holding office again (*iteratio*) before a certain time. The first two rules were repeatedly violated during the decline of the Republic: Sulla and Caesar held the dictatorship for more than the stipulated six months, and Pompey became sole consul (*consul sine collega*). The last rule was most spectacularly broken by Marius, who held the consulship seven times, including five consecutive terms. Augustus, on the other hand, tried – at least on the surface – to adhere to these rules. Above all, he often selected his colleagues for various offices. If he wished to remain in power longer than the term of a particular magistracy, he would accept the *potestas* without assuming the office itself, such as when he took on the tribunician power. This mere possession of *potestas* without taking office also created the impression of preserving the principle of incompatibility. Sometimes, when declining to accept an office, he would also appoint someone else to it instead, as in the case of Plancus and Paulus. This gave the impression of legalism and a desire to maintain the Republican *status quo*, although it should be noted that appointing officials did not prevent the *princeps* from relieving them of certain duties. Until 23 BC, Augustus continuously served as consul, but thereafter he abandoned this practice, perhaps precisely because he did not want to further violate the prohibition of *iteratio*.

Censorship was one of the most prestigious offices of Republican Rome, typically assumed at the culmination of a political career. This authority of the censors often sufficed to ensure that the norms they established were respected. The sanction they applied was a mark with far-reaching consequences in the sphere of public law. The office began to decline, in fact, from the time of Sulla, but for Cicero, it remained one of the pillars of the Republic: he even suggested fixing the term of office of censors at a full five years.[293]

Augustus, however, was a sophisticated politician. Assuming the *censoria potestas* for life would certainly have constituted a breach of the rules.[294] Moreover, since he could carry out the censorial tasks using his other powers, the formal adoption of the *censoria potestas* would have seemed superfluous. The *princeps* only did so in 29 BC so that he could conduct the census jointly with Agrippa. When he realised that, prior to the creation of the office of censor, the census had been conducted by the consuls, he considered the *imperium* sufficient authority.

It should be, however, noted that – despite all the coquetry – Augustus was clearly creating himself as a censor and was perceived as such overall. Above all, one of the fundamental elements of his policy was the restoration of ancestral customs. Laws and plebiscites enacted at the request of the *princeps* himself or officials implementing his intentions,[295] the suppression of manifestations of excessive luxury,[296] and even the arts – above all poetry, but also sculpture, for example[297] – served this purpose.

The publication of Metellus' speech in the form of an edict should also be recalled. The publication of a censorial edict was usually accompanied by the delivery of a speech justifying the new regulations.[298] It therefore seems that here too, Augustus indirectly implied that he was a censor. A similar effect was probably also intended by the publication in the edict of a speech by Rutilius which, although not originally delivered by a censor, referred to issues within the competence of these officials.

It seems, therefore, that the first *princeps* never exercised censorship. Probably in 29 BC, he adopted the *censoria potestas* to conduct a census. He carried out the following censuses using his *imperium,* referring to the time when censuses were conducted by consuls even before the censor's office was established. The other tasks of the censors, above all the *cura morum*, were carried out by him under other powers, mainly the *tribunicia potestas*. The *princeps* – knowing the principles of the Republican system – was aware that his ability to bring plebiscite projects was sufficient. This is probably why he never accepted the position of *curator morum* entrusted to him by the Senate and the people in the form of *senatus consultum* and *lex*. Such decisions stemmed from a desire to maintain the appearance of the continued existence of the Republic. It was for this reason that he limited the range of dignities he accepted and, if he did not have to hold a magistracy, rejected it in a false impulse of nobility.

The emperor who tried to reactivate the censorship in its traditional form was Claudius, an avid antiquarian and lover of antiquity, a Republican by conviction.[299] According to Suetonius, this was the first censorship since 22 BC, when Plancus and Paulus held the office.[300] The tradition-bound *princeps* retained the standard eighteen-month term as censor and selected a colleague, L. Vitellius.[301] They took office in 47 AD (800 a.U.c.), a year in which Claudius also prepared the Jubilee Games (*ludi saeculares*). It was a special year by all means.[302] Pliny recorded that in that year a phoenix was brought into the city and taken to the *comitium*.

However, the author himself believed this story was a fabrication. Probably, the emperor wanted as many memorable events as possible to honour the year of his censorship.

Unfortunately, no sources provide information on how Claudius and Vitellius were appointed as censors.[303] Certainly, they both tried to carry out all the tasks traditionally incumbent on censors. They conducted the census[304] and the *recognitio equitum*,[305] took away public places from private citizens,[306] and issued numerous edicts.[307] Regarding the composition of the Senate,[308] the emperor admitted the Gallic elite to it, which he convinced the Senate to do in a speech[309] preserved on a bronze tablet exhibited in Lyon.

> CIL XIII,1668: *quid ergo non Italicus senator provinciali potior est iam vobis cum hanc partem censurae meae adprobare coepero quid / de ea re sentiam rebus ostendam sed ne provinciales quidem / si modo ornare curiam poterint reiciendos puto.*
>
> *But, you may say, is an Italian senator not better than a provincial one for all that? When I come to deal with this part of my censorship, I shall then show you by my actions what I feel on this matter. No, I think that not even provincials should be excluded, if they can ornament the Senate House at all.*
>
> (Transl. D.C. Braund)

The emperor argued that during his censorship he would try to show the values of these senators and that they should not be rejected when there was a possibility that they would grace the senatorial curia.[310]

However, the censorship of Claudius and Vitellius was only an episode that did not lead to the permanent restoration of the office. Twenty-five years later, in April 73 AD, Vespasian, aware of the decline of many senatorial and equestrian families and the increasing demoralisation of society,[311] took office as censor with his son Titus.[312] They too held office for eighteen months,[313] carrying out the *lectio senatus*,[314] the *recognitio equitum*, and the census, ending their tenure with a purification ceremony.[315]

A fundamental change related to censorship was later made by Domitian, who in 84 AD assumed the office of *censor perpetuus*, i.e. lifelong censor,[316] without choosing a colleague. The epitomator of Cassius Dio's work noted that Domitian was the first and only among citizens and rulers to assume the office of *censor perpetuus*.[317]

Domitian's programme was to return to the customs of the forefathers and restore morality.[318] Paradoxically, the emperor himself fell far short of the standards introduced, which did not escape the attention of his contemporaries.[319] Juvenal presented his viewpoint particularly emphatically in the Second *Satire*.

> Iuv., *Sat.* 2,29–31: *qualis erat nuper tragico pollutus adulter*
> *concubitu, qui tunc leges revocabat amaras*
> *omnibus atque ipsis Veneri Martique timendas...*

Exactly so was that adulterer of more recent times, defiled by a union worthy of tragedy, who tried to revive bitter laws to terrify everyone, even Venus and Mars.

(Transl. S. Morton Braund)

The poet ironically remarked that Domitian – himself an adulterer[320] – restored the old laws that even Venus and Mars should fear. This is an allusion to the reinstatement of the *lex Iulia de adulteriis*,[321] and perhaps also the *lex Scantinia*,[322] in the form of edicts.[323] The poet also commented,

Iuv., *Sat.* 2,63: *dat veniam corvis, vexat censura columbas.*
That's a judgment that acquits the ravens and condemns the doves.

(Transl. S. Morton Braund)

This passage has acquired a proverbial significance. It is translated as follows: "Censorship forgives the ravens and harasses the pigeons." Its interpretation, however, is much more complex. Laronia, speaking here, resents Domitian because punishments for sexual offences affect women and not men. It seems, therefore, that *corvi* are men, while *columbae* are women, as indicated by the grammatical genders of these nouns. However, it is worth taking a closer look at the symbolism of these birds. The raven[324] was considered a symbol of denunciation, and the pigeon[325] a symbol of marital fidelity. Therefore, it can also be assumed that Domitian allowed denunciations, which resulted in punishments falling on the innocent.

His censorship was thus a degeneration both on formal grounds, due to the lack of a colleague and the unlimited duration of its exercise, and on factual grounds, due to its dishonest exercise. Domitian completely discredited the office of censor. This is why it was never assumed by Trajan, even though he too sought to rectify customs.[326] Pliny the Younger praised Trajan in the *Panegyric* for assuming neither censorship nor *praefectura morum*, because he preferred to assess characters through privileges rather than punishments.[327] He further wrote that the life of a *princeps* is one of perpetual censorship, emphasising that the emperor must maintain his own morals to be set an example for his fellow citizens, who value this more than the power of the office. After Trajan, reference to censorship in connection with the person of the *princeps* became rare, more as a reflection of the Pliny's ideal than as a connection with the office itself.[328]

The possibility of the censor restoring morality was still believed in by Decius, who requested the Senate to elect a worthy person in 251 AD.[329] The choice fell on the future emperor Valerian. The resolution was passed unanimously because the senators believed that Valerian had conducted himself like a censor throughout his life.[330] He, however, refused to accept office. In justifying his decision, he stated that the powers of a censor were inherent in the dignity of the emperor and could not be exercised by a private person.[331] Valerian's decision was probably dictated by a pragmatic view of the situation. He was aware of the danger hanging over him. He was a favourite of the emperor, who had high hopes for him. The censorship would have had to end in disaster, as the restoration of old customs was no longer possible and holding office would have had to end in disgrace. Edward Gibbon commented very accurately on the situation: *A censor may maintain, he can never restore the morals of the state.*[332]

The overview of competences contained in the speech by Decius seems very interesting.

> SHA, *Valer.* 6,2–6: *suscipe censuram, quam tibi detulit Romana res publica, quam solus mereris, iudicaturus de moribus omnium, iudicaturus de moribus nostris. tu aestimabis qui manere in Curia debeant, tu equestrem ordinem in antiquum statum rediges, tu censibus modum pones, tu vectigalia firmabis divides statues, tu res publicas recensebis; tibi legum scribendarum auctoritas dabitur...*
>
> *Receive the censorship, which the Roman Republic has offered you and which you alone deserve, you who are now about to pass judgment on the character of all men, on our character as well. You will decide who are worthy to remain in the senate house, you will restore the equestrian order to its ancient status, you will determine the amount of our property, you will safeguard, apportion, and order our revenues, you will administer the properties of the state, the authority of writing laws will be granted to you.*
>
> (Transl. D. Magie)

Valerius would judge the customs of all, determine who was to remain in the Senate, restore the equestrian state to its former splendour, determine the values of the census, confirm, distribute, and determine taxes, and keep an inventory of public things. The jurisdiction of the censor was not to be exercised over the prefect of the city, the *consules ordinarii*, the *rex sacrorum*, and *the virgo Vestalis maxima*, provided, however, that she remained in chastity.[333] Further on, the authority to write laws,[334] which is puzzling in the context of censorship, appears. It seems, however, that the *leges* referred to here are *leges locationis*, i.e. public contracts, not legal acts.

The term censor was still used to refer to the emperor Carus.[335] Then, in 333 AD, the title of censor was borne by the emperor's nephew Dalmatius.[336] It was, however, only a title of honour or even a nickname.

In contrast, an attempt to restore the office of censor may have been made as late as the end of the fourth century AD, probably in 397 or 398 AD. On this matter, Q. Aurelius Symmachus delivered a speech *De censura non restituenda.*[337] In a letter to the praetorian prefect Theodore, Symmachus mentioned two speeches, one of which was based on a discussion in the Senate against censorship.[338] In this speech, Symmachus made serious arguments[339] against the reinstatement of the office. The Senate was apparently afraid of censorship, presumably because of the need to place its fate in someone else's hands.

The history of censorship from the time of Augustus, and even Caesar, shows two trends. Firstly, it gradually disappeared as an independent office, and secondly, its powers were increasingly assimilated by the *princeps*. The reason for this process was the specific nature of the censorial prerogatives, which could no longer be entrusted to independent officials as this would have threatened the emperor's position. This primarily concerned control over the composition of the two highest orders: the equestrian and senatorial. Censorial functions that were less important to the sole ruler began to be entrusted to specially appointed officials, mainly *curatores*.[340]

A remarkably interesting source text illustrating this point is the statement by Agrippa (quoted by Cassius Dio)[341] who advised Octavian on how to behave and what kind of regime to establish in the state. The conversation is said to have taken place in 29 BC, at a crucial moment for the fate of the state. It appears from the text that Agrippa advised Octavian to take full control of the Senate and the equites, and to admit people to these orders by his own decisions.[342] He also advised Octavian to personally conduct censuses.[343] Agrippa proposed[344] the creation of a new office, to which a senator could be appointed for life, tasked with overseeing the families, property, and morals of those in the senatorial and equestrian orders. This official would himself handle such behaviour which did not deserve punishment, but for more serious matters he would to refer to Octavian. Agrippa proposed calling him *ὑποτιμητής* – 'subcensor,' emphasising the ruler's superior position over him. At the same time, Agrippa added that – since this role did not involve commanding an army – it could be held for life, unless the official's own behaviour or illness interfered, giving Octavian the right to dismiss him.

A new idea seems to have taken shape: the *princeps* was perceived as a 'super-censor' with full control over the Senate and the equestrian order, from which new officials, above all the prefects, were drawn. This power could not be assumed by anyone else, as it would have monumentally threatened the emperor's position. Augustus still experimented, although he retained exclusive influence over the *lectiones senatus* and *recognitiones equitum*. Subsequent emperors, even if they reinstated censorship, exercised it themselves, selecting only their colleagues. Late attempts to reactive the office of censor were doomed to failure due to the impossibility of excluding key prerogatives from the ruler's range of powers.

8. Summary

The creation of the office of censor was part of the political struggle between patricians and plebeians at the dawn of the Republican period. The prospect of allowing plebeians to hold the consulship led to the creation of a patrician magistracy, endowed with the powers to conduct a census of the population and the sacred ceremony of *lustrum condere*. Over time, the powers of the censors also began to include the conclusion of contracts for the lease of public revenues and expenditures, and the custody of public places. They also reviewed the equestrian *centuriae* and arranged the list of senators. Simultaneously, a *regimen morum*, or censorial control over the observance of ancestral customs, developed, enabling officials to punish citizens with a censorial mark.

The introduction of the office of censor was one of the stages in the formation of the Republican system. The census was originally performed by the king and later taken over by the consuls. When the plebeians began to plead effectively to hold office, the patricians guarded the sacral aspects of their political monopoly particularly jealously. For this reason, powers comparable to those of consuls were granted to military tribunes with consular power, and censors elected from among the patricians were appointed with the duty of performing purification ceremonies. Although their powers were considered modest, it was the sacral aspect of the power that made it a significant office, which is probably why its term was limited to eighteen months by the *lex Aemilia*.

Censors enjoyed great authority and public trust, which meant that the demands placed on them were high. Romans considered them stern, and foreigners looked on with surprise, especially at their prerogatives related to the control of morals, which allowed censors to interfere in the private affairs of fellow citizens.

The activities of the censors were meticulously documented on *tabulae censoriae*, kept in places associated with this office, such as the *Villa Publica* complex used for the census, the *Atrium Libertatis*, and the Temple of the Nymphs. The censors kept copies of these documents and included them into their personal archives.

The decline of the Republic brought a crisis of censorship, probably resulting primarily from shifts in the socially accepted hierarchy of values. It was also influenced by the interests of prominent politicians who feared the censorial mark. The advent of the Principate brought further changes. The censorship as a separate office gradually began to disappear, and its powers of *regimen morum* were largely assimilated by the *princeps*. This demonstrates the immense importance of this magistracy, which, with its extensive powers of control, could pose a threat to the ruler.

Notes

1 Their scope was summarised, as it were, by Cicero in his treatise *On the Laws*. Although the subject under consideration here is the ideal system, one can see the actual state of affairs in the following catalogue. Cic., *De leg.* 3,7: 'Censors shall make a list of the citizens, recording their ages, families, and slaves, and other property. They shall have charge of the temples, streets, and aqueducts within the city, and of the public treasury and the revenues. They shall make a division of the citizens into tribes and other divisions according to wealth, age, and rank. They shall enrol the recruits for the cavalry and infantry; they shall prohibit celibacy; they shall regulate the morals of the people; they shall allow no one guilty of dishonourable conduct to remain in the Senate' (transl. C.W. Keyes).

2 Cf. E. Baltrusch, *Regimen morum. Die Reglamentierung des Privatlebens der Senatoren und Ritter in der römischen Republik und frühen Kaiserzeit*, München 1989, pp. 25–27.

3 Cic., *De leg.* 3,7: They shall be two in number... (transl. C.W. Keyes). Cf. H. Siber, *Zur Kollegialität der römischen Zensoren*, [in:] *Festschrift Fritz Schulz*, I, ed. W. Flume, Weimar 1951, pp. 466–474; F. De Martino, *Storia della costituzione romana*², II, Napoli 1973, pp. 266–267; W. Kunkel, R. Wittmann, *Staatsordnung und Staatspraxis der römischen Republik. Zweiter Abschnitt. Die Magistratur*, München 1995, s. 199–201; R. Bunse, *Die frühe Zensur und die Entstehung der Kollegialität*, "Historia" 50.2/2001, pp. 145–162; N. El Beheiri, *Das regimen morum der Zensoren. Die Konstruktion des römischen Gemeinwesens*, Berlin 2012, pp. 127–131; C. Bur, *La citoyenneté dégradée. Une histoire de l'infamie à Rome (312 av. J.-C.-96 apr. J.-C.)*, Rome 2018, pp. 65–70.

4 See Liv. 6,27; 9,34; 24,43; 27,6. Cf. O. Karlowa, *Römische Rechtsgeschichte. I. Staatsrecht und Rechtsquellen*, Leipzig 1885, p. 229; J. Suolahti, *The Roman Censors. A Study on Social Structure*, Helsinki 1963, pp. 78–79; A. Manzo, *'Lustratio' e divieto del 'suffectus': due aspetti sacerdotali del censore?*, "Teoria e Storia del Diritto Privato" 12/2019, pp. 1–22.
5 Cf. TLL, s.v. *censor*; A. Forcellini (ed.), *Totius Latinitatis Lexicon*, Patavii 1805, s.v. *censor*; A. Ernout, A. Meillet, *Dictionnaire étymologique de la langue latine*, Paris 1951, s.v. *censeo*; M. de Vaan, *Etymological Dictionary of Latin and the Other Italic Languages*, Leiden–Boston, MA 2008, s.v. *censeo*.
6 Fest. (Paul.) 51 L., s.v. *censores*: Censores dicti, quod rem suam quisque tanti aestimare solitus est, quantum illi censuerint. [The censors were so called because everyone used to estimate his property according to what they decided – transl. AT].
7 D. 50,16,111 (Iavol. 6 *ex Cass.*): 'Censere' est constituere et praecipere. unde etiam dicere solemus 'censeo hoc facias' et 'semet aliquid censuisse.' inde censoris nomen videtur esse tractum [The expression, "To be of the opinion," means to determine and direct; hence, we are accustomed to say, "I am of the opinion that you should do this," and "The Senate directed that such-and-such a thing should be done." It is from this verb that the word "censor" is derived – transl. S.P. Scott].
8 Varr., *L.L.* 5,81: The Censor was so named as the one at whose censio 'rating,' that is, arbitrium 'judgement,' the people should be rated (transl. R.G. Kent). Cf. Varr. apud Non. 519,29: Itaque quod hos arbitros instituerunt populi, censores appellarunt: idem valet censere et arbitrari. [And because they appointed them judges of the people they called them censors: for to assess and to judge means the same – transl. AT]. Cf. Varr. apud Non. 519,21; A. Cenderelli, *Varroniana. Istituti e terminologia giuridica nelle opere di M. Terenzio Varrone*, Milano 1973, p. 93.
9 Isid., *Etym.* 9,4,13: Censores apud veteres Romanos erant. Est enim nomen censoris dignitas iudicialis. Censere enim iudicare est. Item censores sunt patrimoniorum iudices, a censu aeris appellati. [There were censors among the ancient Romans. The name of the censor is a judicial dignity. Because to assess is to judge. Similarly, the censors are judges of patrimonies, called from the assessment of crude metal – transl. AT].
10 Placidus p. 23: The censors are the judges of patrimonies and customs (transl. AT). Cf. Placidus p. 17 (ed. Deuerling): A 'censorius' is one who is worthy to become a censor, or one who has been a censor. The name and dignity of the censor, a judge of morals and customs, was great to the ancient Romans. Indeed, "censere" means "to judge" (transl. AT). On Placidus, cf. M. Schanz, C. Hosius, *Geschichte der römischen Literatur bis zum Gesetzgebungswerk des Kaisers Justinian*, IV.2, München 1971, pp. 257–260.
11 Cf. G. Dumézil, *Servius et Essaila Fortune. sur la fonction sociale de Louange et de Blâme et sur les élément indo-européens du cens romain*, Paris 1943, pp. 173–188.
12 Cf. below.
13 Cf. W. Kubitschek, *Censores*, "RE" 3/1899, pp. 1902; J. Suolahti, *The Roman Censors…*, pp. 143–165; F. Guizzi, *Censores*, "NNDI" 3/1964, p. 102.
14 Cf. Liv. 4,7.
15 However, it should be noted that the first military tribunes had to lay down their powers due to the protest of the augurs; then consuls were appointed. In the following years, tribunes were often elected, but there were also consuls.
16 Cf. F. Cássola, L. Labruna, *Linee di una storia delle istituzioni repubblicane*[2], Napoli 1979, pp. 90–91.
17 This is what Pomponius suggested in the *Enchiridion* (D. 1,2,2,25).
18 Cf. A. Ziółkowski, *Storia di Roma*, Milano 2010, pp. 116–118.
19 In the sources he is sometimes referred to as *praefectus urbis* (e.g. Liv. 4,36). Cf. F. Cássola, L. Labruna, *Linee…*, p. 92.
20 Liv. 4,8,1–7.

21 Cf. C. De Boor, *Fasti censorii,* Berolini 1873, p. 3; T.R.S. Broughton, *The Magistrates of the Roman Republic*, I, Atlanta, GA 1951 (reprint 1986), p. 53. See also Cic., *Ad fam.* 9,21,2.
22 Cf. a further passage from Livy's account – Liv. 4,8,3–7.
23 According to Dionysius of Halicarnassus (11,63), from 457 BC.
24 Cf. C. De Boor, *op. cit.*, p. 3; T.R.S. Broughton, *op. cit.*, I, pp. 53–54; J. Suolahti, *The Roman Censors…*, pp.168–171.
25 Cf. also Dion. Hal., *Ant. Rom.* 11,63; Zon. 7,19 is a summary of the relevant (unpreserved) passages of Cassius Dion; cf. G. Urso, *Cassio Dione e i magistrati. Le origini della repubblica nei frammenti della 'Storia romana,'* Milano 2005, pp. 136–142.
26 D. 1,2,2,17 (Pomp. l. sing. *ench.*): Subsequently, when the census occupied much time, and the consuls were not able to discharge this duty, censors were appointed (transl. S.P. Scott).
27 G. Sabbatucci, *La censura: istituzione rivoluzionaria dell'antica Roma*, "Index" 3/1972, pp. 192–202, wrote about the 'myth of the rise of censorship.'
28 T. Mommsen, *Römisches Staatsrecht*, II.1, Leipzig 1899, pp. 335–336; cf. R.V. Cram, *The Roman Censors*, "HSCP" 51/1940, pp. 73–77.
29 K.J. Beloch, *Römische Geschichte bis zum Beginn der punischen Kriege*, Berlin–Leipzig 1926, pp. 77–86; Contra F. De Martino, *Storia della costituzione romana*[2], I, Napoli 1973, pp. 326–328; M.V. Giangrieco Pessi, *Dalla 'lex Aemilia' al plebiscito Ovinio: Problemi e riflessioni*, [in:] *Leggi e società nella repubblica romana*, ed. F. Serrao, II, Napoli 2000, pp. 299–307; Eadem, *Brevi riflessioni sul ruolo della censura nella dialettica costituzionale della prima repubblica*, [in:] *'Societas – ius.' 'Munuscula' di allievi a Feliciano Serrao*, Napoli 1999, pp. 159–170.
30 H. Siber, *Römisches Verfassungsrecht in geschichtlicher Entwicklung*, Lahr 1952, pp. 100–101. Cf. O. Leuze, *Zur Geschichte der römischen Censur*, Halle 1912, p. 142, who regarded the first censors as extraordinary officials, while the subsequent ones as ordinary.
31 Cf. F. Cássola, L. Labruna, *Linee…*, pp. 92 ff.
32 Opposing such an interpretation was F. De Martino, *Storia…*, I, pp. 326–330, who argued that the introduction of censorship did not consist in the exclusion of part of the competence from the power of the highest officials. In his view, the roots of the office of the censor were sacred (*lustrum*), and it was only with time that it acquired political prerogatives.
33 Cf. also D. Flach, *Die Gesetze der frühen römischen Republik. Text und Kommentar*, Darmstadt 1994, pp. 236–237.
34 A. Klotz, *Zur Geschichte der römischen Zensur*, "RhM" 88/1939, pp. 27–36.
35 J. Suolahti, *The Roman Censors…*, pp. 21–25. cf. M.P. Nilsson, *The Introduction of Hoplite Tactics at Rome: Its Date and Its Consequences*, "JRS" 19/1929, pp. 1–11, who believes that the establishment of the censors at this point was related to the need to relieve the consuls (or tribunes) dealing with the introduction of hoplite formation battle tactics in the army, and also to the need to accurately assess the fortunes of the citizens in order to determine which of them were to serve as hoplites.
36 Cf. G. Rotondi, *'Leges publicae populi Romani.' Elenco cronologico con una introduzione sull'attività legislativa dei comizi romani*, Milano 1912, pp. 207–208; D. Flach, *op. cit.*, pp. 230–231.
37 Cf. E. Fantham, *Censorship. Roman Style*, "Echos du Monde Classique" 21/1977, p. 45.
38 Liv. 4,6.
39 Cf. E.S. Staveley, *The Significance of the Consular Tribunate*, "JRS" 43/1953, p. 30.
40 Differently, G. Sabbatucci, *op. cit.*, pp. 192–202, who regarded censorship as the plebeians' 'ticket' to the patrician order.
41 The sacral aspect of censorship was emphasised by C.E. Jarcke, *Versuch einer Darstellung des censorischen Strafrechts der Römer: ein Beytrag zur Geschichte des Criminalrechts*, Bonn 1824, pp. 10–14; F. De Martino, *Storia…*, I, pp. 32 ff.

42 Cf. W. Kunkel, R. Wittmann, *op. cit.*, pp. 391–394.
43 Liv. 9,37,7: and they obeyed the Aemilian law in preference to that ancient ordinance which governed the first elections of censors, precisely because it was the latest which the people had enacted, and because in a conflict of two laws the old is ever superseded by the new (transl. B.O. Foster).
44 Cf. G. Rotondi, *op. cit.*, p. 209; D. Flach, *op. cit.*, pp. 234–237; J.V. Melničuk, *Законодательное оформление института цензуры (V-IV вв. до н.э.)*, "Ius Antiquum" 1.8/2001, pp. 62–65; cf. however M. Ducos, *Les Romains et la loi. Recherches sur les rapports de la philosophie grecque et de la tradition romaine à la fin de la République*, Paris 1984, pp. 174–177.
45 Liv. 4,24,3–6: Cf. G. Rotondi, *op. cit.*, p. 211; D. Flach, *op. cit.*, pp. 245–246.
46 Cf. T.R.S. Broughton, *op. cit.*, I, p. 62.
47 Cf. a further passage from Livy's text – Liv. 4,24,6–9.
48 Cf. C. De Boor, *op. cit.*, p. 3; T.R.S. Broughton, *op. cit.*, I, p. 61; J. Suolahti, *The Roman Censors…*, pp. 171–174.
49 This episode was considered inauthentic by M. Humm, *Il 'regimen morum' dei censori e le identità dei cittadini*, [in:] *'Homo, caput, persona.' La costruzione giuridica dell' identità nell'esperienza romana*, eds. A. Corbino, M. Humbert, G. Negri, Pavia 2010, pp. 287 and 302. A.E. Astin, *'Regimen morum,'* "JRS" 78/1988, p. 16, n. 12 only recommended caution in interpretation and does not question the reliability of Livy's account. On the other hand, J.F. Keseberg, *De censoribus Romanorum commentatio*, Quedlinburg 1829, pp. 7–8, argued that the *regimen morum* was in the hands of the censors from the time of their appointment in 443 BC and considered Livy's account to be faithful. Cf. F.D. Gerlach, *Die römische Censur in ihrem Verhältniß zur Verfassung. Eine historische Untersuchung*, Basel 1842, p. 214. Livy seems to be anticipating while mentioning that Mamercus was transferred to the ranks of the *aerarii* (cf. below), since at that time everyone still paid a fixed tax (*tributum*). The use of this phrase was intended to clarify for readers the financial nature of the applied sanction.
50 This was in order to collect the appropriate tax from the former dictator. The censors seemed to want to increase the size of the tax and therefore entered a higher value of the property. In contrast, M. Humm, *Il 'regimen morum'…*, p. 302, found that the census of the first class was eight times the census of the lowest class, so that the censors multiplied the value of the *aerarius'* property eightfold in order for Mamercus to pay the appropriate tax. The problem of interpretation may arise from the fact that Livy used the terms *tribu movere* and *aerarium facere*, which were not yet likely to be in use at the time. The decision of the censors was probably to charge Mamercus a high tax and to record a false value of his property.
51 This does not seem to have been a case of acting within the *regimen morum*, which at the time was not yet a specified function of the censors, although Livy did use the term *aerarium facere*. The action of the censors was, in my view, rather an expression of revenge, which they could afford to take, since their decisions were discretionary. Therefore, despite the doubts, the event can be considered authentic.
52 Cf. G. Greco, *Census. Profili storico-giuridici delle attività di censimento a Roma*, Torino 2022, pp. 134 ff.
53 Liv. 9,33,4–9.
54 Cf. C. De Boor, *op. cit.*, p. 8; T.R.S. Broughton, *op. cit.*, I, p. 160; J. Suolahti, *The Roman Censors…*, pp. 220–225; H. Beck, *Karriere und Hierarchie. Die römische Aristokratie und die Anfänge des 'cursus honorum' in der mittleren Republik*, Berlin 2005, pp. 159–187.
55 G.C. Fiske, *The Politics of the Patrician Claudii*, "HSCP" 13/1902, p. 35, suggested that Appius' decision was due to the enormity of the undertakings he had embarked upon and which he had failed to complete within eighteen months.
56 Frontin., *De aquaed.* 1,5: As colleague in the censorship Appius had Gaius Plautius, to whom was given the name of "the Hunter" for having discovered the springs of this water. But since Plautius resigned the censorship within a year and six months, under

the mistaken impression that his colleague would do the same, the honour of giving his name to the aqueduct fell to Appius alone, who, by various subterfuges, is reported to have extended the term of his censorship, until he should complete both the Way and this aqueduct (transl. C.E. Bennett).

57 Cf. B. Macbain, *Appius Claudius and the Via Appia*, "CQ" 30.2/1980, pp. 356–372; M. Humm, *Appius Claudius Caecus et la construction de la via Appia*, "MEFRA" 108.2/1996, pp. 693–746.

58 This refers to P. Sempronius of the nickname Sofon, whom Pomponius mentioned in the *Enchiridion* (D. 1,2,2,37). Cf. B. Albanese, *Brevi studi di diritto romano (III). V. Publio Sempronio Sofo, giurista, ed il regime della censura*, "AUPA" 47/2002, s. 55–67.

59 Tab. 12,5 = Liv. 7,17,12: The interrex Fabius stated that in the Twelve Tables there was a law which enacted that whatsoever the people had last ordained should be held as binding by law (transl. E.H. Warmington). Cf. M. Zabłocka, *Le XII Tavole – fonte dei principi del diritto contemporaneo*, "Iura" 53/2002, pp. 1–16.

60 Liv. 9,34,6–7.

61 A. Guarino, *Il dubbio contenuto pubblicistico delle XII tavole*, "Labeo" 34/1988, pp. 323–335.

62 B. Albanese, *'Privilegia', 'maximus comitiatus', 'iussum populi' (XII Tab. 9,1–2,12–15)*, "Labeo" 36/1990, pp. 19–35.

63 C. Cascione, *'Quodcumque postremum populus iussisset, id ius ratumque esset': spunti per un'interpretazione politica del versetto*, [in:] *Scritti in onore di Michele Scudiero*, I, Napoli 2008, pp. 421–425.

64 Livy (7,17) also described a case of a similar dispute concerning the consular election held in 352 BC by the *interrex* M. Fabius Ambustus, who wanted two patrician consuls to be elected. When it was alleged that such an election would be contrary to the *lex Licinia Sextia de consule plebeio*, he argued precisely that the decision of the electoral commissions was also an *iussum populi*: *aiebat in duodecim tabulis legem esse ut quodcumque postremum populus iussisset, id ius ratumque esset.*

65 Liv. 9,34,1–5: It is a name that is far more hostile to your liberty than that of the Tarquinii (transl. B.O. Foster). Cf. M. Humm, *La figure d'Appius Claudius Caecus chez Tite-Live*, [in:] *Le censeur et les Samnites sur Tite-Live, livre IX*, eds. D. Briquel, J.-P. Thuillier, Paris 2001, pp. 67–96; Idem, *Appius Claudius Caecus. La république accomplie*, Rome 2005, pp. 77–93.

66 Only the word *ratumque* may be a later interpolation. Cf. C. Cascione, *'Quodcumque postremum'*..., pp. 421–425.

67 Fest. (Paul.) 203 L., s.v. *obrogare*: Obrogare est legis prioris infirmandae causa legem aliam ferre. [To obrogate means to pass another law in order to weaken the former one – transl. AT]; Ulp. 1,3: Lex aut 'rogatur', id est fertur; aut 'abrogatur', id est prior lex tollitur; aut 'derogatur', id est pars primae legis tollitur; aut 'subrogatur', id est adicitur aliquid primae legi; aut 'obrogatur', id est mutatur aliquid ex prima lege [A law is either passed, that is, enacted; or abrogated, that is, a former law is repealed; or modified, that is, a part of the original law is annulled; or subrogated, that is, something is added to the first law; or opposed by another, that is to say some part of the first law is changed – transl. S.P. Scott]. Cf. *Rhet. Her.* 2,10,15; Cic., *Phil.* 1,23; F. Reduzzi Merola, *'Abrogare, derogare, obrogare' in Cicerone*, [in:] *Au-delà des frontierès. Mélanges de droit romain offers à Witold Wołodkiewicz*, II, eds. M. Zabłocka, J. Krzynówek, J. Urbanik, Z. Służewska, Varsovie 2000, pp. 739–742; Eadem, *'Aliquid de legibus statuere'. Poteri del senato e sovranità del popolo nella Roma tardorepubblicana*, Napoli 2007, pp. 11–14.

68 In my view, Paulus Deacon's definition taken from Festus does not exclude the fact that the new law partially amended the previous one, rather than merely weakening it.

69 Cf. F. Reduzzi Merola, *'Abrogare, derogare, obrogare'*..., pp. 735–742; Eadem, *'Aliquid de legibus statuere'*..., pp. 7–15.

70 Liv. 9,34,26.
71 Plebeian tribunes had the right of detention called *ius prendendi* (cf. Gell. 13,12) over citizens and therefore had among their auxiliaries messengers called *viatores* who helped them to exercise this power. However, a tribune's decision could always be blocked by his colleague in office, allowing the imprisoned citizen to exercise the *ius auxilii*.
72 Val. Max. 4,1,3: ... he summoned the people to assembly and rebuked them in a speech as stern as he could make it for presenting him twice with a power which their ancestors had thought proper to limit in duration because it seemed too great (transl. D.R. Shackleton Bailey).
73 Cf. below.
74 Zonar. 7,19: They held office at first and at the last for five-year periods, but in between for a year and a half (transl. E. Cary).
75 Cf. G. Urso, *op. cit.*, pp. 140–141.
76 Dio Cass. 54,10,5; see also below.
77 Cf. F. Cassola, L. Labruna, *I censori*, [in:] *Lineamenti di storia del dirtto romano*^{2}, ed. M. Talamanca, Milano 1989, pp. 168–169; D. Flach, *op. cit.*, pp. 245–246.
78 Cf. G. Urso, *op. cit.*, p. 141.
79 K.J. Beloch, *op. cit.*, p. 83; cf. H. Siber, *Römisches Verfassungsrecht…*, p. 101.
80 Cf. T.R.S. Broughton, *op. cit.*, I, p. 114.
81 Cf. M.V. Giangrieco Pessi, *Dalla 'lex Aemilia'…*, pp. 309–311; Eadem, *Brevi riflessioni…*, pp. 159–170.
82 Cf. U. Coli, *Sui limiti di durata delle magistrature romane*, [in:] *Studi in onore di Vincenzo Arangio-Ruiz nel XLV anno del suo insegnamento*, ed. M. Lauria, Napoli 1953, pp. 395–418; G. de las Heras Sánchez, G. Polo Toribio, *Plus quam annua ac semestris*, "AFDUDC", 11/2007, pp. 169–175.
83 F. Cancelli, *Studi sui censores e sull' arbitratus della lex contractus*, Milano 1960, pp. 1–57. Contra G. Greco, *op. cit.*, pp. 163–167.
84 W. Soltau, *Zur römischen Verfassungsgeschichte. Zur 'lex centuriata de imperio'*, "Philologus" 75/1918, pp. 232–237.
85 Varr., *L.L.* 6,87.
86 A. Magdelain, *Recherches sur l'imperium. La loi curiate et les auspices d'investiture*, Paris 1968, pp. 49–51.
87 Cf. Gell. 13,15,4; see also below.
88 Cf. W.F. Otto, *Lustrum*, "RhM" 71/1916, pp. 17–40; R.M. Ogilvie, *Lustrum Condere*, "JRS" 51.1–2/1961, pp. 31–39; D. Baudy, *Römische Umgangsriten. Eine ethologische Untersuchung der Funktion von Wiederholung für religiöses Verhalten*, Berlin–New York 1998, pp. 223–261.
89 Cf. C. De Boor, *op. cit.*, p. 13; T.R.S. Broughton, *op. cit.*, I, p. 404; J. Suolahti, *The Roman Censors…*, pp. 366–367; E. Reigadas Lavandero, *Censura y 'res publica'. Aportación constitucional y protagonismo político*, Madrid 2000, pp. 324–330.
90 Liv. 42,3,3: ...auctoritate censoria sociis deterritis id sacrilegium prohibere [... the inhabitants being prevented by the censor's high office from forbidding the sacrilege – transl. E.T. Sage, A.C. Schlesinger]. Cf. Val. Max. 1,1,20; M.P. Fronda, *Privata hospica, beneficia publica? Consul(ar)s, Local Elite and Roman Rule in Italy*, [in:] *Consuls and Res Publica. Holding High Office in the Roman Republic*, eds. H. Beck, A. Duplá, M. Jehne, F. Pina Polo, Cambridge 2011, pp. 235–236.
91 Liv. 42,3,1–11.
92 Val. Max. 2,9 init. Cf. M. Humm, *L'image de la censure chez Valère Maxime: formation et évolution d'un paradigme*, [in:] *Valeurs et mémoire à Rome: Valère Maxime ou la vertu recomposée*, ed. J.-M. David, Paris 1998, pp. 73–93.
93 Cic., *De rep.* 4,6 apud Non. 423 M: The community is said to have feared their severity at first (transl AT). Cf. Gell. 4,20; Val. Max. 2,9,8; Nep. *Cat. Mai.* 2,3. In the negative sense of Ps.-Ascon., *In Cic. Div. in Caec.* p. 103 ed. Orelli.

94 Cf. Liv. 4,24,8; 39,44,9.
95 Val. Max. 2,9,3: ... Censor and Cato, a twofold pattern of severity (transl. D.R. Shackleton Bailey). Cf. F. della Corte, *Catone Censore. La vita e la fortuna*, Torino 1949, pp. 27–28.
96 Cf. Amm. Marc. 16,5,2.
97 Iuv., *Sat.* 11,90–92: Back when people quaked at the Fabii and at stern Cato and at the Scauri and Fabricius, and when the strict censor's rigid morality scared even his colleague (transl. S. Morton Braund). Cf. C.S. Razzini, *Il diritto romano nelle satire di Giovenale*, Torino 1913, p. 99.
98 On the *gentes censoriae* cf. J. Suolahti, *The Roman Censors...*, pp. 97–137 and 706–717.
99 Plutarch (*Cat. Mai.* 19,3) expressed surprise that the citizens applauded Cato's severe censure, erected a monument to him in the temple of Salus and commemorated him with the following inscription: "that when the Roman state was tottering to its fall, he was made censor, and by helpful guidance, wise restraints, and sound teachings, restored it again" (transl. B. Perrin).
100 Plut., *Tib. Gracch.* 14,3.
101 Plut., *Mor.* 199 b. This was the second attempt. The first time Cato ran unsuccessfully as a candidate was in 189 BC. During that campaign, the candidate M. Acilius Glabrio was accused of failing to show in triumph some of the spoils gained in the war with Antioch and appropriating them to himself. Cato testified against him. Glabrio, despite having a good chance of victory, withdrew his candidature. Cf. A. Barzanò, *Catone il Vecchio e il processo contro Manio Acilio Glabrione candidato alla censura (189 a.C.)*, [in:] *Processi e politica nel mondo antico*, ed. M. Sordi, Milano 1996, pp. 129–144.
102 Liv. 39,40,2–3: For the censorship there was fierce rivalry among the candidates – the patricians being Lucius Valerius Flaccus, Publius and Lucius Scipio, Gnaeus Manlius Vulso and Lucius Furius Purpureo, and the plebeians Marcus Porcius Cato, Marcus Fulvius Nobilior, Tiberius Sempronius Longus and Marcus Sempronius Tuditanus. Although these were patricians and plebeians from the most eminent families, Marcus Porcius stood head and shoulders above them all (transl. J.C. Yardley). Cato faced opposition in this election from a united nobilitas determined to prevent him from reaching office. Cf. A.E. Astin, *Cato the Censor*, Oxford 1978, pp. 59–77; D.F. Epstein, *Personal Enmity in Roman Politics 218-43 B.C.*, London–New York 1987 (reprint 1989), pp. 72–73.
103 The term *καθαρμός* means purification in the sense of expiation. Perhaps it is here synonymous with *lustratio*. For the opinion of the censors, the auspiciousness of the *lustrum* was significant. Cato even gave a speech *De lustri sui felicitate*. Surely, however, *καθαρμός* can also be understood here as purification in the moral sense.
104 Cf. Plut., *Cat. Mai.* 16,4–6.
105 Cic., *Ad fam.* 8,14,4: He is convinced that the Censorship is face cream or washing soda, but I fancy he is making a mistake; in trying to scrub out the stains he is laying open all his veins and vitals (transl. D.R. Shackleton Bailey).
106 Cf. C. De Boor, *op. cit.*, p. 29; T.R.S. Broughton, *op. cit.*, II, p. 247; J. Suolahti, *The Roman Censors...*, pp. 483–486; E. Reigadas Lavandero, *op. cit.*, pp. 478–485.
107 Appius was charged with *lex Scantinia*, and it was also alleged that he had appropriated some works of art while acting as governor. Cf. Cic., *Ad fam.* 8,12. It is worth adding that Appius' censure was political in nature. As a partisan of Pompey, he sought to remove supporters of Caesar from the Senate.
108 Varr. apud Non. 190,34 = Varr., *Sat. Menipp.* 196 (ed. Astbury): This is great: to be a censor and try not to turn many people into 'aerarii' (transl. AT).
109 Cf. below.
110 Macrob., *Sat.* 3,15,4–5: Although Crassus, a former censor – he was the colleague of Gnaius Domitius – was considered the most eloquent of all and had pride of place

among the men of greatest distinction, he nonetheless put on mourning when a moray of his died in a fishpond at his home and grieved for it like a daughter. It was no secret: indeed, his colleague Domitius upbraided him for it in the senate, as though it were an ugly crime. Nor was Crassus ashamed to admit it – far from it, the censor actually boasted of it – if the gods be pleased! – and took credit for acting with affectionate devotion (transl. R.A. Kaster). Cf. C. De Boor, *op. cit.*, p. 25; T.R.S. Broughton, *op. cit.*, II, p. 17; J. Suolahti, *The Roman Censors…*, pp. 440–445; E. Reigadas Lavandero, *op. cit.*, pp. 427–432.

111 The two censors were at odds with each other and accused each other of excessive luxury. Cf. Cic., *De or.* 2,45; 227; 230; 242; *Brut.* 162–165; Val. Max. 9,1,4; Plin. Mai. 17,6.

112 Aelian., *De nat. anim.* 8,4.

113 Cf. Cic., *De dom.* 84; C. De Boor, *op. cit.*, pp. 27–28; T.R.S. Broughton, *op. cit.*, II, p. 161; J. Suolahti, *The Roman Censors…*, pp. 472–474; E. Reigadas Lavandero, *op. cit.*, pp. 461–464.

114 Plut., *Cic.* 27,3.

115 However, an interesting observation was made by F. della Corte, *op. cit.*, p. 28, who considered that Plautus' atypical comedy, *Captivi*, which featured no female characters and lacked obscene humour, was a response to Cato's censorship, calling for a return to ancestral customs.

116 Cf. Hor., *Ars poet.* 174: castigator censorque minorum [chastiser and censor of the young – transl. AT].

117 Cf. Plaut., *Trin.* 734–746; C.F. Amunátegui Perelló, *Origen de los poderes del paterfamilias. El pater familias y la patria potestas*, Madrid 2009, pp. 128–129.

118 For a broader discussion of allusions to censorial tasks in Plautus' comedies, cf. A. Tarwacka, *The Censors and Their Duties in the Comedies of Plautus*, RGDR 23/2014, http://www.iustel.com/v2/revistas/detalle_revista.asp?id_noticia=415488.

119 The Greeks were familiar with the institution of the census. Cf. Plat., *Rep.* 550 c; Arist., *Pol.* 1266a 13; M. Coudry, *Denys d'Halicarnasse, Plutarque, Dion Cassius: trois visions grecques de la censure?*, [in] *Visions grecques de Rome. Griechische Blicke auf Rom*, eds. M.L. Freyburger, D. Meyer, Paris 2007, pp. 32–34.

120 Polyb. 6,13; 6,17; cf. A.E. Astin, *The Role of Censors in Roman Economic Life*, "Latomus" 49.1/1990, pp. 20–36.

121 Polyb. 6,19.

122 Polyb. 6,53; see also below.

123 Cf. M. Coudry, *op. cit.*, pp. 31–32.

124 Cf. M. Coudry, *op. cit.*, pp. 36–46.

125 Dion. Hal., *Ant. Rom.* 20,13,1–3; cf. Liv., *Per.* 14; Val. Max. 2,9,4; Gell. 17,21,39; C. De Boor, *op. cit.*, p. 11; T.R.S. Broughton, *op. cit.*, I, p. 196; J. Suolahti, *The Roman Censors…*, pp. 256–259; E. Reigadas Lavandero, *op. cit.*, pp. 191–196.

126 Cf. Thuc. 2,40; Plut., *Sol.* 31,2.

127 Cf. E. Schmähling, *Die Sittenaufsicht der Censoren. Ein Beitrag zur Sittengeschichte der römischen Republik*, Stuttgart 1938, pp. 9–10.

128 Although there were some exceptions to this rule as well, such as the Athenian institution of the *δοκιμασία*, a procedure for controlling those who were to hold public office, or the office of the *γυναικονόμοι*, controlling the behaviour of women; cf. below.

129 Dion. Hal., *Ant. Rom.* 19,16,5.

130 Cf. M. Coudry, *op. cit.*, pp. 46–50.

131 Plut., *Cat. Mai.* 16.

132 It should be mentioned, however, that the 20th book of the work of Dionysius of Halicarnassus has not survived in its entirety, so we do not know whether there was more information about the censors there. The overall context, however, seems to point to the centrality of the *regimen morum* as a topic of consideration.

133 Cf. M. Coudry, *op. cit.*, pp. 50–62.
134 Zon. 7,19. This work covers the history of the world from creation to the death of Emperor Alexios I Komnenos in 1118. In the section on Roman history up to the 3rd century, Zonaras modelled his work on Cassius Dio. Cf. L. Wenger, *Die Quellen des römischen Rechts*, Wien 1953, p. 205; G. Urso, *op. cit.*, pp. 136–155; M.O. Lindholmer, *Digressions and the Fall of the Republic in Cassius Dio*, [in:] *Digressions in Classical Historiography*, eds. M. Baumann, V. Liotsakis, Berlin–Boston, MA 2024, pp. 258–264.
135 Lyd., *De mag.* 1,43.
136 Sud. s.v. *κήνσωρ*.
137 Cf. F.D. Gerlach, *op. cit.*, p. 214.
138 An interesting comparison was made by Valerius Maximus (2,10 praef.), who, writing about the dignity of famous people (*maiestas clarorum virorum*), called it *quasi privata censura*. A famous man does not need courts or auxiliary officials to maintain his dignity, and the same was true of censors. Even without lictors, they presented themselves magnificently.
139 Suet., *Ner.* 4: he was haughty, extravagant, and cruel, and when he was only an aedile, forced the censor Lucius Plancus to make way for him on the street (transl. J.C. Rolfe).
140 Cf. Val. Max. 2,2,4b.
141 Zon. 7,19: …employed all the insignia of the greater offices save lictors (transl. E. Cary).
142 Cf. Liv. 40,45,8; K. Tuori, *Breaking Chairs. Sella Curulis in Roman Law, Identity and Memory*, "Arctos" 54/2020, pp. 271–272.
143 This right seems to be linked to the ability to perform *aspicia maxima*. See Gell. 13,15.
144 Cf. Macrob., *Sat.* 1,6,9.
145 Athen. 14,660c: And among the Romans, the Censors, which was the highest office in the whole state, clad in a purple robe, and wearing crowns, used to strike down the victims with an axe (transl. C.D. Yonge).
146 M. Torelli, *Typology & Structure of Roman Historical Reliefs*, Ann Arbor, MI 1982, pp. 8–20. More on the Altar in Chapter II. See Figure 2.
147 Fest. 128 L., s.v. *mulleos*: mullei ["red high-soled shoes"] are a type of shoe, they say; these were used first by the Alban kings, then by the patricians. M. Cato [says] in Book 7 of the Origines: "someone who had obtained a curule magistracy [wore] red high-soled shoes … [perhaps: fastened by a leather strap?], others thick boots" (transl. G. Manuwald).
148 Cf. F.X. Ryan, *Rank and Participation in the Republican Senate*, Stuttgart 1998, pp. 57–58.
149 Cf. *TLL*, s.v. *censorius*; J. Suolahti, *The Roman Censors…*, pp. 83–84.
150 Placidus p. 17 (ed. Deuerling).
151 Zon. 9,17: …for if one descended from a higher office to a lower one, he still retained the rank of his former position undiminished (transl. E. Cary).
152 The term *vir censorius* to describe a former censor appears in Gellius (5,6,15), Macrobius (*Sat.* 2,11).
153 Polyb. 6,53,7: These representatives wear togas, with a purple border if the deceased was a consul or praetor, whole purple if he was a censor, and embroidered with gold if he had celebrated a triumph or achieved anything similar (transl. W.R. Paton).
154 A purple-bordered toga was worn by actors imitating consuls and praetors, while if an ancestor held a triumph, a toga embroidered with gold was worn.
155 Tac., *Ann.* 4,15: The same year brought still another bereavement to the emperor, by removing one of the twin children of Drusus, and an equal affliction in the death of a friend. This was Lucilius Longus, his comrade in evil days and good, and the one member of the senate to share his isolation at Rhodes. Hence, in spite of his modest antecedents, a censorian funeral and a statue erected in the Forum of Augustus at the

public expense were decreed to him by the Fathers, before whom, at that time, all questions were still dealt with (transl. J. Jackson). Cf. Tac., *Ann.* 6,27; *Hist.* 4,47; SHA, *Pert.* 15,1; *Sept. Sev.* 7,8; F. Vollmer, *De funere publico Romanorum*, Leipzig 1892, pp. 343–345 with a review by W.A. Merrill, *Vollmer on Public Funerals at Rome*, "CR", 8.6/1894, pp. 264–265; J.M.C. Toynbee, *Death and Burial in the Roman World*, London 1971 (reprint 1996), pp. 56–57; G. Wesch-Klein, *'Funus publicum'. Eine Studie zur öffentlichen Beisetzung und Gewährung von Ehrengräbern in Rom und den Westprovinzen*, Stuttgart 1993, pp. 38–40.

156 Tac., *Ann.* 13,2: By decree of the Senate (...) Claudius was granted a censorial funeral and soon afterwards a consecration (transl. AT).

157 F. Vollmer, *op. cit.*, p. 344, considers the term *funus censorium* to be of republican origin.

158 According to J. Gagé, *Les rites anciens de lustration du Populus et les attributs "triomphaux" des censeurs*, "MEFRA" 82.1/1970, pp. 43–49, the attributes of the censor were triumphal attributes. However, G. Wesch-Klein, *op. cit.*, p. 39, expressed the opinion that – since *funus censorium* was also granted to women – the term could not refer to the censor's funeral and burial in a purple toga. She is convinced that the type of funeral in question signifies an exceptionally grand celebration, which was authorised during the republican period by the censors by virtue of the *regimen morum* they exercised. In the following discussion, however, the researcher allows for the possibility that women were also buried in purple togas.

159 Lange wrote about the lack of privileging of *censorii*. This conclusion was also reached by F.X. Ryan, *Rank and Participation...*, pp. 96–102. The primacy of the *censorii*, on the other hand, is argued by P. Willems, *Le sénat de la république romaine*, I, 1878 (reprint Aalen 1968), pp. 249–259; T. Mommsen, *Römisches Staatsrecht...*, III, pp. 969–970; J. Suolahti, *The Roman Censors...*, pp. 18–19; Idem, *'Princeps senatus'*, "Arctos" 7/1972, p. 207.

160 Gell. 14,7,9: furthermore, the senators ought to be asked their opinions in order, beginning with the grade of consul. And in that grade in former times the one to be called upon first was always the one who had first been enrolled in the senate; but at the time when he was writing he said that a new custom had become current, through partiality and a desire to curry favour, of asking first for the opinion of the one whom the presiding officer wished to call upon, provided however that he was of consular rank (transl. J.C. Rolfe). Cf. Gell. 14,7,1–3; A. Cenderelli, *op. cit.*, pp. 72–74.

161 Since Varro wrote in 71 BC, it has been assumed that the *censorii* could have been deprived of their privileged position by Sulla, who would also have abolished the position of *princeps senatus*. Cf. T. Mommsen, *Römisches Staatsrecht...*, III, pp. 969–970; J. Suolahti, *'Princeps senatus'*, "Arctos" 7/1972, p. 209. However, there is no evidence for this, and in addition it should be noted that there is a reference to an earlier practice in the text (*antea*). Cf. F.X. Ryan, *Rank and Participation...*, p. 101; P. Tansey, *The 'Princeps Senatus' in the Last Decades of the Republic*, "Chiron" 30/2000, pp. 15–30.

162 Gell. 4,10,1–4: Before the passage of the law which is now observed in the proceedings of the senate, the order in calling for opinions varied. Sometimes the man was first called upon whom the censors had first enrolled in the senate, sometimes the consuls elect; some of the consuls, influenced by friendship or some personal relationship, used to call first upon anyone they pleased, as a compliment, contrary to the regular order. However, when the usual order was not followed, the rule was observed of not calling first upon any but a man of consular rank (transl. J.C. Rolfe). Gellius further added that, in addition to the *princeps senatus*, the *consules designati* were sometimes the first to speak. If someone else was asked first, care was taken that it was a *vir consularis*.

163 He should be descended from the so-called *gentes maiores* (*gens Aemilia, Claudia, Cornelia, Fabia, Valeria* and perhaps *Manlia*). Cf. T. Mommsen, *Römisches*

Staatsrecht..., II.1, pp. 966–967; P. De Francisci, '*Arcana imperii*', III.1, Milano 1948, p. 94; J. Suolahti, '*Princeps senatus*'..., p. 208; M. Bonnefond-Coudry, *Le 'princeps senatus': vie et mort d'une institution républicaine*, "MEFRA" 105/1993, p. 112.
164 Cf. F. Mora, *La scelta del 'princeps senatus'*, "Historia" 52.4/2003, pp. 502–504.
165 Cf. J. Suolahti, '*Princeps senatus*'..., pp. 208–210.
166 On the importance of consuls, cf. recently M. Jehne, *The Rise of the Consular as a Social Type*, [in:] *Consuls and 'Res Publica'. Holding High Office in the Roman Republic*, eds. H. Beck, A. Duplá, M. Jehne, F. Pina Polo, Cambridge 2011, pp. 211–231.
167 Cf. E. Posner, *Archives in the Ancient World*, Cambridge, MA 1972 (reprint 2003), pp. 170–171. On the importance of the census data see C. Ando, *Census, Censor, Citizenship. Republican Subjectivity in Advance of Monarchy*, [in:] *Citizenship in Antiquity*, eds. J. Filonik, C. Plastow, R. Zelnick-Abramovitz, London 2023, pp. 616–626.
168 Varr., *L.L.* 6,87: Now first I shall put down some extracts from the Censors' Records: When by night the censor has gone into the sacred precinct to take the auspices, and a message has come from the sky, he shall thus command the herald to call the men: "May this be good, fortunate, happy, and salutary to the Roman people – the Quirites – and to the government of the Roman people – the Quirites – and to me and my colleague, to our honesty and our office: All the citizen soldiers under arms and private citizens as spokesmen of all the tribes, call hither to me with an inlicium 'invitation,' in case anyone for himself or for another wishes a reckoning to be given." The herald calls them first in the sacred precinct, afterwards he calls them likewise from the walls. When it is dawn, the censors, the clerks, and the magistrates are anointed with myrrh and ointments. When the praetors and the tribunes of the people and those who have been called to the invitation meeting have come, the censors cast lots with each other, as to which one of them shall conduct the ceremony of purification. When the sacred precinct has been determined, then after that he who is to perform the purification conducts the assembly (transl. R.G. Kent). Cf. W. Kunkel, R. Wittmann, *op. cit.*, pp. 422–423; B. Albanese, *Brevi studi di diritto romano (II). III. Sui frammenti di 'censoriae tabulae' in Varr., 'De L. Lat.' 6,86–87*, "AUPA" 43/1995, s. 67–102. See also below.
169 The phrase *quique inlicium vocati sunt* means those who are called to *contio*; cf. Fest. (Paul.) 100 L.
170 Also, the *precatio* formula used at the time of the *lustrum*, similar to the one used here, was found in the *tabulae censoriae*. Cf. Val. Max. 4,1,10; see also below.
171 Cf. E.A. Meyer, *Legitimacy and Law in the Roman World. 'Tabulae' in Roman Belief and Practice*, Cambridge 2004, pp. 92–95; C. Bur, *La citoyenneté dégradée. Une histoire de l'infamie à Rome (312 av. J.-C.-96 apr. J.-C.)*, Rome 2018, pp. 75 ff.
172 Cic., *De leg. agr.* 1,4: He searches through the whole of Sicily in the censors' registers; he leaves no building, no lands unnoticed (transl. J.H. Freese).
173 Cf. E. Deniaux, *Rome, de la Cité - État à l'Empire. Institutions et vie politique aux Iie et ie siècle av. J.-C.*, Paris 2001, p. 68.
174 Cic., *Har. resp.* 30: I will demonstrate this beyond all doubt by reference to the registers of the censors and the recollection of many persons (transl. N.H. Watts).
175 On the obligation to demolish them, cf. below.
176 Cf. E.A. Meyer, *op. cit.*, p. 220. Some authors also attribute to them an informative function. Cf. G. Polo, *Idoneidad de las tabulae censoriae como instrumentos de publicidad de los miembros de la comunidad*, "RIDROM" 5/2010, pp. 126–177.
177 D. 22,3,10 (Marc. 3 *dig.*): The Senate decreed that the registers of the Censor and the public records are better evidence than that of witnesses (transl. S.P. Scott).
178 Plin. Mai. 18,11: even now in the censor's accounts all the sources of national revenue are termed 'pastures', because rent of pasture-land was for a long time the only source of public income H. Rackham).
179 Cf. Cic., *Or.* 156: as I would to say centuria fabrum et procum, using the language of the census records, rather than fabrorum et procorum (transl. G.L. Hendrickson, H.M. Hubbell). E.A. Meyer, *op. cit.*, p. 60.

180 Gell. 2,10,1: Servius Sulpicius, an authority on civil law and a man well versed in letters, wrote to Marcus Varro and asked him to explain the meaning of a term which was used in the records of the censors; the term in question was favisae Capitolinae (transl. J.C. Rolfe). Cf. M. Schanz, C. Hosius, *op. cit.*, I, München 1979, p. 595; A. Cenderelli, *op. cit.*, pp. 71–72.

181 Cf. Dion. Hal., *Ant. Rom.* 4,22,2; M. Schanz, C. Hosius, *op. cit.*, I, p. 27.

182 Gell. 2,10,3–4: These, he said, were certain underground chambers and cisterns in the area, in which it was the custom to store ancient statues that had fallen from the temple, and some other consecrated objects from among the votive offerings. And then Varro goes on to say in the same letter, that he had never found any explanation of the term favisae in literature, but that Quintus Valerius Soranus used to assert that what we called by their Greek name thesauri (treasuries) the early Latins termed flavisae, their reason being that there was deposited in them, not uncoined copper and silver, but stamped and minted money. His theory therefore was, he said, that the second letter had dropped out of the word flavisae, and that certain chambers and pits, which the attendants of the Capitol used for the preservation of old and sacred objects, were called favisae (transl. J.C. Rolfe).

183 Cic., *Pro Cluent.* 41: He it was whom the Town Council of Larinum adjudged by a unanimous finding to have falsified the public records of their censors (transl. H. Grose Hodge). Cf. Cic., *Pro Cluent.* 125: But so long as it is an established fact that 125 Oppianicus was the man who was convicted of falsifying with his own hand the public records of his town... (transl. H. Grose Hodge).

184 Two of them were punished by the censors with a mark for corruption. Cf. Cic., *Pro Cluent.* 127.

185 The penalty for falsification of *tabulae publicae* was applied from the *lex Cornelia de falsis*; D. 48,10,16,2 (Paul. 3 *resp.*): And also others who have made false entries in registers, public documents, or anything else of the kind, without sealing them, or, in order to prevent the truth from being known, have concealed or stolen anything, or made a substitution, or unsealed a paper, there is no doubt that it is customary for them to be punished with the same penalty (transl. S.P. Scott). However, this arose from the interpretation of the jurists, specifically the responsum of Paulus, rather than from the law itself, and was therefore probably introduced as early as the Principate. Erasing or adding something to the *tabulae*, on the other hand, was punishable by the *lex Iulia peculatus*; D. 48,13,10,1 (Venon. 3 *iudic. publ.*): He who erases anything from the public registers, or inserts anything therein, is liable under this law (transl. S.P. Scott). Both of these solutions, however, were probably later than the process of Cluentius. B. Santalucia, *Osservazioni sulla giustizia penale nei 'municipia'*, [in:] B. Santalucia, *Altri studi di diritto penale romano*, Padova 2009, pp. 337–339, considers the case of *crimen peculatus*.

186 Cf. U. Laffi, *Le funzioni giudiziarie dei senati locali nel mondo romano*, [in:] U. Laffi, *Studi di storia romana e di diritto*Roma 2001, pp. 483–484; B. Santalucia, *Osservazioni...*, pp. 337–339.

187 T. Mommsen, *Römisches Strafrecht*, Leipzig 1899, p. 227, n. 2, who held that the decurions did not judge, but merely expressed an opinion. Cf. W. Simshäuser, *'Iuridici' und Munizipalgerichtsbarkeit in Italien*, München 1973, pp. 175–180.

188 Dion. Hal., *Ant. Rom.* 1,74,5: This is proved in many other ways, but particularly by the records of the censors, which the son receives in succession from the father and takes great care to transmit to posterity, like family rites; and there are many illustrious men of censorian families who preserve these records (transl. E. Cary).

189 These types of documents were kept in a *tablinum*. Cf. Cic., *Pro Sull.* 42; Plin. Mai. 35,6; E. Gabba, *Un documento censorio in Dionigi d'Alicarnasso 1.74.5*, [in:] *Synteleia Arangio-Ruiz*, I, eds. A. Guarino, L. Labruna, Napoli 1974, pp. 490–491; E.A. Meyer, *op. cit.*, pp. 27–29.

190 Cf. Cic., *Ad fam.* 3,10.

191 Cf. K. Tuori, J. Heikonen, *Spaces of Citizenship. The Census in Roman Republican Topography and Ideology*, "MEFRA" 134.2/2022, pp. 335–360.

192 Cf. C. De Boor, *op. cit.*, p. 3; T.R.S. Broughton, *op. cit.*, I, p. 61; J. Suolahti, *The Roman Censors...*, pp. 171–174; E. Reigadas Lavandero, *op. cit.*, pp. 57–62.
193 Liv. 4,22,7: In that year Gaius Furius Paculus and Marcus Geganius Macerinus the censors approved a public building erected in the Campus Martius, and the census of the people was taken there for the first time (transl. B.O. Foster). Cf. C. Nicolet, *The World of the Citizen in Republican Rome*, transl. P.S. Falla, Berkeley–Los Angeles, CA 1980, pp. 62–63.
194 Cf. Varr., *De re rust.* 3,1,2.
195 Cf. C. Nicolet, *The World of the Citizen...*, pp. 63–64.
196 N. Purcell, *'Atrium Libertatis'*, "PBSR" 61/1993, pp. 125–155.
197 Cf. K. Tuori, J. Heikonen, *op. cit.*, p. 335 ff.
198 On the process cf. below.
199 Liv. 43,16,12–13: The censors immediately mounted to the Hall of Liberty and, having there sealed the public accounts and closed the account-room and sent away the public slaves, declared that they would transact no public business until the judgment of the people upon them had been passed (transl. A.C. Schlesinger).
200 Gran. Licin. 28,10.
201 Liv. 45,15,5: This was argued between the two censors; finally they resorted to the following solution: they drew lots publicly in the Hall of Liberty for one of the four city tribes, to which they would consign all those who had been slaves. The lot of the Esquiline tribe was cast; Tiberius Gracchus announced that they had decided to enrol all freedmen in this tribe (transl. A.C. Schlesinger).
202 This was, of course, one of the urban tribes, as the draw of lots obviously included only these districts.
203 Cic., *Pro Mil.* 73: a man who set fire to the temple of the Nymphs, that he might erase the national records of the censor's registration that were printed in the national rolls (transl. N.H. Watts). The term *recensio* used by Cicero was a census by district, based on the declarations of the owners of tenements, which was used to control the population growth of the city, as well as those entitled to benefits such as frumentationes. Cf. Suet., *Div. Iul.*, 41,3; E. Lo Cascio, *Le procedure di recensus dalla tarda repubblica al. Tardo antico e il calcolo della popolazione di Roma*, [in:] *La Rome impériale: démographie et logistique*, ed. C. Virlouvet, Roma 1997, 3–76.
204 Cf. C. Nicolet, *The World of the Citizen...*, p. 199.
205 Liv. 29,37,12–15: When Gaius Claudius swore that he had acted according to law and went up to the treasury, he, among the names of those he demoted to the status of aerarii, left that of his colleague. Marcus Livius then came into the treasury; and there, with the exception of the Maecia tribe, which had not participated in his conviction but had also not elected him either consul or censor after the conviction, he left all the Roman people with the status of aerarii, all thirty-four tribes (transl. J.C. Yardley).
206 Cf. below.
207 Cf. Val. Max. 2,9,1; F. Millar, *The 'Aerarium' and Its Officials under the Empire*, "JRS" 54/1964, pp. 35–36.
208 Cf. G. Camodeca, *Il 'censorium' di Beneventum: un nuovo vocabolo del lessico latino*, [in:] *'Voce concordi'. Scritti per Claudio Zaccaria*, ed. F. Mainardis, Trieste 2016, pp. 119–126.
209 G. Polo Toribio, *La 'prorogatio' en la magistratura censoria*, "RGDR" 13/2009, passim.
210 Cf. Frontin., *De aquaed.* 94–95; Cf. M. Peachin, *Frontinus and the 'curae' of the 'curator aquarum'*, Stuttgart 2004, pp. 97–99; G. de Kleijn, *The Water Supply of Ancient Rome. City Area, Water and Population*, Amsterdam 2001, p. 94; O.F. Robinson, *Ancient Rome. City Planning and Administration*, London–New York 1992, pp. 96–97; C. Bruun, *Il funzionamento degli acquedotti romani*, [in:] *Roma imperiale. Una metropoli antica*, ed. E. Lo Cascio, Roma 2010, pp. 146–147; A. Tarwacka, *The Roman Censors as Protectors of Public Places*, "Diritto@Storia" 12/2014, http://

www.dirittoestoria.it/12/tradizione-romana/Tarwacka-Roman-Censors-Protectors-Public-Places.htm.

211 On the *lex Cornelia de XX quaestoribus* cf. E. Gabba, M.H. Crawford, *'Lex Cornelia de XX quaestoribus'*, [in:] *The Roman Statutes*, ed. M.H. Crawford, I, London 1996, pp. 293–300 with cited literature. Cf. A.E. Astin, *Censorships in the Late Republic*, "Historia" 34.2/1985, p. 176; A. Keaveney, *The Last Republican Sulla*², London–New York 2005, pp. 144–145. X. Ryan, *The 'lectio senatus'...*, p. 190, pointed out that the selection of members of the Senate was to some extent already determined from the *plebiscitum Atinium*, which introduced the principle of admitting former plebeian tribunes to the Senate. Both this plebiscite and *lex Cornelia de XX quaestoribus* thus caused a shift in the centre of gravity of the *lectio senatus*: from now on, the censors did not so much select new members, but rather took care to remove unworthy persons.

212 Cf. H. Hill, *Sulla's New Senators in 81 B.C.*, "CQ" 26.3–4/1932, pp. 170–177; T. Hantos, *'Res publica constituta'. Die Verfassung des Dictators Sulla*, Stuttgart 1988, pp. 45–61.

213 In contrast, it does not seem correct to say that Sulla's dictatorship also included the powers of the censors *in extenso*; so A. Keaveney, *op. cit.*, p. 145. Sulla achieved effects through other routes, most often through the legislative route, e.g. by reforming the composition of the Senate or introducing *lex sumptuaria*.

214 Cic., *Div. in Caec.* 8: The people of this country meanwhile have been visited with many hardships and many disabilities: yet in all the national life there is nothing whose loss they feel so much as the energy and sense of responsibility that our law-courts showed in times gone by. It is because they feel the lack of such courts that the agitation arose for restoring the tribunes' powers. It is the untrustworthiness of our courts that has excited the further demand for another class of citizens to serve on them. It is through the disgraceful conduct of our judges that the censorship, which in former times was seldom popular, is now being clamoured for, and has already come to be held an excellent and democratic institution (transl. L.H.G. Greenwood).

215 Vell. 2,30,4; cf. L. Polverini, *'Alius et idem'. Il tribunato della plebe nel corso della storia romana*, "Diritto@Storia" 7/2008, http://www.dirittoestoria.it/7/Memorie/Polverini-Tribunato-plebe-storia-romana.htm#_ftn23.

216 This interpretation is also supported by Cic., *In Pis.* 5,10, where Cicero speaks of the uninterrupted functioning of the *iudicium censorium* for almost 400 years. Cf. T. Mommsen, *Römisches Staatsrecht...*, II, p. 336, n. 3; E. Gabba, *Il ceto equestre e il senato di Silla*, "Athenaeum" 34.3–4/1956, p. 135; F.X. Ryan, *The `lectio senatus' after Sulla*, "RhM" 139/1996, p. 190.

217 Ps.-Ascon., *In Cic. Div. in Caec.* p. 103 ed. Orelli: This sad and rigid name was so hated by the Roman people that it was neglected for many years (transl. AT).

218 Schol. Gronov. p. 326 St.: Sulla, acting in the interests of the nobility, removed the tribunes and censors (transl. AT).

219 Cf. F. De Martino, *Storia...*, III, pp. 98–99.

220 Cf. T. Hantos, *op. cit.*, pp. 63–64.

221 Secretly, however, the *nobilitas* may have feared a census that would have resulted in a large number of new citizens being registered, which may have been the reason for the abandonment of the censorial election in 75 BC. Cf. E. Gabba, *Il ceto equestre...*, pp. 124–138. The holding of the census, on the other hand, may have already benefited Pompey, a man from Picenum, for whom the new citizens represented a potential electorate.

222 We know quite a lot about Sulla's legislation, which makes it all the more unlikely that the sources available to us could have overlooked such an important regulation.

223 The possibility of enacting such *a lex de censura* was questioned by L. Lange, *Römische Alterthümer*², I, Berlin 1863, p. 689; II, p. 319; III, p. 161. Its existence was also ruled out by G. Rotondi, *op. cit.*, p. 362.

224 Cf. A. Keaveney, *op. cit.*, p. 8.

225 Cf. G. Clemente, *I censori e il senato. I mores e la legge*, "Athenaeum" 104.2/2016, pp. 446–500.
226 More on this below.
227 Cf. Suet., *Div. Iul.* 76; cf. F. De Martino, *Storia…*, III, pp. 241–245.
228 Dio Cass. 43,14,4.
229 Cf. Suet., *Div. Iul.* 76,1.
230 Dio Cass. 44,5,3.
231 On the basis of this passage also Zon. 10,12.
232 Dio Cass. 44,7,1.
233 Dio Cass. 44,7,2: he accepted all but a very few of their decrees (transl. E. Cary).
234 Cf. T. Mommsen, *Römisches Staatsrecht…*, II, p. 706, fn. 1.
235 The exception was Buteo (cf. Liv. 23,23), who was designated *dictator senatui legendo*. This, however, probably had to do with the fact that he had already held the census before and his re-election to this office would have been a violation of the prohibition of *iteratio*. However, even he did not conduct the census, but only the *lectio senatus*. Cf. A. Tarwacka, *'Dictator senatui legendo'. The Unusual Dictatorship of M. Fabius Buteo*, "Zeszyty Prawnicze" 13.1/2013, pp. 185–196; P. Buongiorno, *Sui fondamenti della dittatura di Marco Fabio Buteone (216 a.C.)*, [in:] *La dittatura romana*, red. L. Garofalo, III, Napoli 2022, pp. 255–277.
236 P. De Francisci, *Arcana imperii…*, III.1, p. 190.
237 Cf. H. Siber, *Cäsars Diktatur und das Prinzipat des Augustus*, "ZSS" 55/1935, pp. 125–127.
238 Cf. G. Rotondi, *op. cit.*, p. 421.
239 Cf. F. De Martino, *Storia…*, III, p. 243.
240 Caesar verified the lists of those entitled to *frumentationes* (cf. Suet., *Div. Iul.* 41; Dio Cass. 43,25,2) and carried out a census (cf. App., *Bell. civ.* 2.425; Plut., *Caes.* 55,5).
241 This was the formulation used by Cicero, *Ad fam.* 9,15,5: Despite the foregoing, as long as our new Prefect of Morals remains in Rome, I shall defer to your advice (transl. D.R. Shackleton Bailey). However, it seems that he too was not writing about an office, but about someone who was placed in charge of customs.
242 Cf. Dio Cass., *Epit.* 67,4,3 cited below.
243 Cf. A.H.M. Jones, *The 'Imperium' of Augustus*, "JRS" 41.1–2/1951, p. 114.
244 *Res gestae* 8,2–3; cf. A.E. Cooley, *'Res gestae Divi Augusti'. Text, Translation, and Commentary*, Cambridge 2009, pp. 66–67.
245 On the *lex Iulia de maritandis ordinibus* see G. Rotondi, *op. cit.*, pp. 443–445; E.C. Green, A.D.E. Lewis, M.H. Crawford, '*Lex Iulia de maritandis ordinibus. Lex Papia Poppaea*', [in:] *The Roman Statutes*, ed. M.H. Crawford, II, London 1996, pp. 801–809.
246 Liv., *Per.* 59: Censor Quintus Metellus proposed that everyone should be compelled to marry in order to produce children. His speech is preserved, and was read by Augustus Caesar before the senate as though written for the present day, when the emperor was discussing the problem of marriage among the upper classes (transl. A.C. Schlesinger). Cf. C. De Boor, *op. cit.*, p. 21; T.R.S. Broughton, *op. cit.*, I, p. 500; J. Suolahti, *The Roman Censors…*, pp. 403–406.
247 This may have been the same speech, fragments of which were transmitted by Aulus Gellius in *Noctes Atticae*. Gellius, however, was referring to Metellus Numidicus, not Macedonicus. Scholars disagree as to whether the antiquarian made a mistake or whether two speeches by censors of the same lineage on the same subject were delivered. On this subject, see below, Chapter IV.
248 Cf. R. Syme, *The Roman Revolution*, Oxford 1939 (reprint 2002), pp. 444–445; T. Spagnuolo Vigorita, '*Casta domus*'. *Un seminario sulla legislazione matrimoniale augustea*^{2}, Napoli 2002, pp. 7–8.
249 Suet., *Aug.* 89,2: He even read entire volumes to the Senate and called the attention of the people to them by proclamations; for example, the speeches of Quintus Metellus

"On Increasing the Family," and of Rutilius "On the Height of Buildings"; to convince them that he was not the first to give attention to such matters, but that they had aroused the interest even of their forefathers (transl. J.C. Rolfe).

250 Consul in 105 BC; cf. T.R.S. Broughton, *op. cit.*, I, p. 555.

251 Cf. ORF 44 II, pp. 169–170; M. Schanz, C. Hosius, *op. cit.*, I, p. 208.

252 Cf. G. Rotondi, *op. cit.*, pp. 447–448.

253 Cf. Vitruv. 2,8,17; Plin. Mai. 35,173.

254 Macrob., *Sat.* 2,4,25.

255 See below. Cf. also C. De Boor, *op. cit.*, pp. 30–31; J. Suolahti, *The Roman Censors…*, pp. 501–506; R. Syme, *Paullus the Censor*, "Athenaeum" 65.1–2/1987, pp. 7–24; A. Wright, *Velleius Paterculus and L. Munatius Plancus*, "CP" 97.2/2002, pp. 178–184.

256 Suet., *Claud.* 16,1: He also assumed the censorship,48 which had long been discontinued, ever since the term of Plancus and Paulus, but in this office too he was variable, and both his theory and his practice were inconsistent (transl. J.C. Rolfe).

257 *Res gestae* 8,2–3: In my sixth consulship, with Marcus Agrippa as colleague, I made a census of the people. I performed the lustration after forty-one years. In this lustration the number of Roman citizens was four million and sixty-three thousand. Again assuming the consular power in the consulship of Gaius Censorinus and Gaius Asinius, I alone performed the lustration. At this census the number of Roman citizens was four million, two hundred and thirty thousand. A third time, assuming the consular power in the consulship of Sextus Pompeius and Sextus Appuleius, with Tiberius Cæsar as colleague, I performed the lustration. At this lustration the number of Roman citizens was four million, nine hundred and thirty-seven thousand (transl. W. Fairley). Cf. commentary by A.E. Cooley, *op. cit.*, pp. 138–143.

258 Cf. H. Markowski, *On Censuses during the Reign of Emperor Augustus*, "CQ" 5.1/1931, pp. 13–20; P.A. Brunt, *Italian Manpower 225 B.C.-A.D. 14*, Oxford 1971, pp. 113–120; E. Lo Cascio, *The Size of the Roman Population: Beloch and the Meaning of the Augustan Census Figures*, "JRS" 84/1994, pp. 23–40; Idem, *La popolazione*, [in:] E. Lo Cascio, *Roma imperiale. Una metropoli antica*, Roma 2010, p. 43; G. Kron, *The Augustan Census Figures and the Population of Italy*, "Athenaeum" 93.2/2005, pp. 441–495.

259 Suet., *Tib.* 21: Since the consuls caused a law to be passed soon after this that he should govern the provinces jointly with Augustus and hold the census with him, he set out for Illyricum on the conclusion of the lustral ceremonies (transl. J.C. Rolfe).

260 Suet., *Aug.* 38–39; cf. Ovid., *Trist.* 2,1,89–93; 541–542; L.R. Taylor, *Republican and Augustan Writers Enrolled in the Equestrian Centuries*, "TAPA" 99/1968, pp. 480–482.

261 *Res gestae* 6,1: During the consulship of Marcus Vinucius and Quintus Lucretius, and afterwards in that of Publius and Cnaeus Lentulus, and a third time in that of Paullus Fabius Maximus and Quintus Tubero, by the consent of the senate and the Roman people I was voted the sole charge of the laws and of morals, with the fullest power; but I accepted the proffer of no office which was contrary to the customs of the country. The measures of which the senate at that time wished me to take charge, I accomplished in virtue of my possession of the tribunitian power (transl. W. Fairley). Cf. commentary by A.E. Cooley, *op. cit.*, pp. 130–132.

262 Suet., *Aug.* 27,5: He received the tribunician power for life, and once or twice chose a colleague in the office for periods of five years each. He was also given the supervision of morals and of the laws for all time, and by the virtue of this position, although without the title of censor, he nevertheless took the census thrice, the first and last time with a colleague, the second time alone (transl. J.C. Rolfe).

263 This happened in 23 BC. Cf. M.H. Dettenhofer, *Herrschaft und Widerstand im augusteischen Prinzipat*, Stuttgart 2000, pp. 103–109.

264 In 45 BC, by virtue of the *lex Cassia de plebeis in patricios adlegendis*, the plebeian family of Octavius was admitted as a patrician family. Cf. Suet., *Aug.* 2; Dio Cass., 45,1,7; G. Rotondi, *op. cit.*, p. 426.

265 Dio Cass. 54,10,5.
266 On the chronology, cf. T. Mommsen, *Römisches Staatsrecht*..., II.1, p. 337; J.C. Stobart, *The Senate under Augustus*, "CQ" 2.4/1908, pp. 296–303; F. Blumenthal, *Zur zensorischen Tätigkeit des Augustus*, "Klio" 9/1909, pp. 493–500; A.H.M. Jones, *The Censorial Powers of Augustus*, [in] A.H.M. Jones, *Studies in Roman Government and Law*, Oxford 1960 (reprint 1968), pp. 19–26; A.E. Astin, *Augustus*..., pp. 226–235.
267 Cf. F. De Martino, *Storia*..., IV.1, pp. 196–197. See also G. Tibiletti, *The 'Comitia' during the Decline of the Roman Republic*, "SDHI" 25/1959, p. 126, who, however, believed that Agrippa was also a consul.
268 Cf. J. Rüpke, *Kalender und Öffentlichkeit. Die Geschichte der Repräsentation und religiösen Qualifikation von Zeit in Rom*, Berlin 1995, pp. 109–113.
269 Dio Cass. 52,42,1: *Καὶ μετὰ ταῦτα τιμητεύσας σὺν τῷ Ἀγρίππᾳ ἄλλα τέ τινα διώρθωσε καὶ τὴν βουλὴν ἐξήτασε.* [After this he became censor with Agrippa as his colleague, and in addition to other reforms which he instituted, he purged the Senate – transl. E. Cary, H.B. Foster].
270 A.H.M. Jones, *The Censorial Powers*..., pp. 23–24 wrote: Dio opens his account of the 'lectio' of 29 BC with the statement that Augustus held the censorship with Agrippa. Similarly, A.E. Astin, *Augustus and 'Censoria Potestas'*, "Latomus" 22.2/1963, p. 232.
271 Exerçant des pouvoirs censoriaux: G. Pieri, *L'histoire du cens jusqu'à la fin de la République romaine*, Paris 1968, p. 196.
272 Cf. Suet., *Aug.* 35; see also below.
273 M.A. Levi, *Augusto e il suo tempo*, Milano 1994, pp. 252–253 and 298, fn. 7.
274 Cf. G. Rotondi, *op. cit.*, p. 440.
275 Tac., *Ann.* 11,25; Dio Cass. 52,42,5; *Res gestae* 2,1.
276 Cf. A.H.M. Jones, *The Censorial Powers*..., pp. 23–24; A.E. Astin, *Augustus*..., p. 232; F. De Martino, *Storia*..., IV.1, pp. 196–201. Differently E.G. Hardy, *'Lectio Senatus' and 'Census' under Augustus*, "CQ" 13.1/1919, pp. 45–46.
277 Cf. R. Syme, *The Roman Revolution*..., p. 339.
278 Vell. 2,95,3: Before this had occurred the censorship of Plancus and Paulus, which, exercised as it was with mutual discord, was little credit to themselves or little benefit to the state, for the one lacked the force, the other the character, in keeping with the office; Paulus was scarcely capable of filling the censor's office, while Plancus had only too much reason to fear it, nor was there any charge which he could make against young men, or hear others make, of which he, old though he was, could not recognize himself as guilty (transl. F.W. Shipley).
279 Cf. Dio Cass. 54,2,1.
280 Cf. Dio Cass. 54,2,3–5.
281 Cf. A.E. Astin, *Augustus*..., pp. 230–231.
282 Cf. Suet., *Aug.* 37,1.
283 Cf. A.H.M. Jones, *The Censorial Powers*..., passim; T. Spagnuolo Vigorita, *op. cit.*, pp. 5–7. See also A.E. Astin, *Augustus*..., pp. 231–235, who, however, did not present a clear-cut view. Cf. also P. De Francisci, *'Arcana imperii'*..., III.1, pp. 284–289, who considered that Augustus did not accept the office of *curator legum et morum* as incompatible with ancestral customs, but accepted the *cura legum et morum*, the function itself.
284 A. Von Premerstein, *Vom Werden und Wesen des Prinzipats*, München 1937, p. 150 ff.
285 Hor., *Epist.* 1,2–3; cf. D. Little, *Politics in Augustan Poetry*, "ANRW" II.30.1/1983, p. 285.
286 For example, the census in 14 AD Augustus conducted with Tiberius on the basis of a law; cf. Suet., *Tib.* 21.
287 Cf. F. De Martino, *Storia*..., IV.1, pp. 201–207; P. Grenade, *Essai sur les origines du principat. Investiturenet renouvellement des pouvoirs impériaux*, Paris 1961, p. 334,

expresses the view that Augustus adopted *cura morum* as a duty rather than a legally defined competence, but is convinced that the emperor twice adopted *potestas censoria* for five years.

288 Suet., *Aug.* 35; cf. Dio Cass. 52,42,2; R.J. Evans, *The Augustan Purge of the Senate and the Census of 86 BC*, "Acta Classica" 40/1997, pp. 77–86.

289 Dio Cass. 52,42,1; cf. E.G. Hardy, *op. cit.*, p. 45.

290 Cf. L.F. Raditsa, *Augustus' Legislation Concerning Marriage, Procreation, Love Affairs and Adultery*, "ANRW" II.13/1980, pp. 305–307.

291 Cf. A.H.M. Jones, *The 'Imperium'...*, pp. 112–119.

292 *Res gestae* 34,3: After this time I excelled all in influence [auctoritas], although I possessed no more official power [potestas] than others who were my colleagues in the several magistracies (transl. P.A. Brunt, J.M. Moore). Cf. P. Zanker, *The Power of Images in the Age of Augustus*, transl. A. Shapiro, Ann Arbor, MI 1990, pp. 89 ff.

293 Cic., *De leg.* 3,7; cf. C.W. Keyes, *Original Elements in Cicero's Ideal Constitution*, "AJP" 42.4/1921, p. 316; A.E. Astin, *Cicero and the Censorship...*, pp. 233–239.

294 According to Stobart (*op. cit.*, p. 302), Augustus just tried to hold as few offices as possible at the same time.

295 In addition to the marriage legislation, the *lex Iulia sumptuaria*, already mentioned, should be mentioned.

296 Ovid, describing the case of the stigmatised Vedius Pollio, wrote explicitly (*Fast.* 6,647–648): That is the way to exercise the censorship; that is the way to set an example, when an upholder of law does himself what he warns others to do (transl. J.G. Frazer). For him, therefore, Augustus was simply a censor. Cf. P. Zanker, *op. cit.*, pp. 137–138. For more extensively on the case of Vedius, who punished slaves by throwing them to the morays and Augustus' reaction, cf. Sen., *De ir.* 3,40; Dio Cass. 54,23,2–4; J.-C. Dumont, *'Servus'. Rome et l'esclavage sous la république*, Rome 1987, pp. 144–146.

297 Cf. P. Zanker, *op. cit.*, pp. 101 ff.

298 Cf. A.H.J. Greenidge, *Infamia. Its Place in Roman Public and Private Law*, Oxford 1894, pp. 58–59.

299 Cf. J. Suolahti, *The Roman Censors...*, pp. 507–513. B. Levick, *Claudius*, London 1990 (reprint 2001), pp. 98–99, also emphasises that by assuming this office Claudius was trying to raise his prestige.

300 Suet., *Claud.* 16,1: He also assumed the censorship, which had long been discontinued, ever since the term of Plancus and Paulus (transl. J.C. Rolfe).

301 Cf. Suet., *Vit.* 2,3; Tac., *Hist.* 3,66; cf. C. De Boor, *op. cit.*, p. 32.

302 Cf. J. Osgood, *Claudius Caesar. Image and Power in the Early Roman Empire*, Cambridge 2011, pp. 147–167.

303 Since from the time of Tiberius the electoral functions of the popular assemblies were taken over by the Senate (Tac., *Ann.* 1,15; Vell. 2,126; cf., however, Suet., *Calig.* 16,2), it can be assumed that the election of the censors was made by the senators themselves. The assembly could only confirm this choice (cf. Dio Cass. 58,20). The relevant resolution of the Senate is recorded by P. Buongiorno, *'Senatus consulta Claudianis temporibus facta'. Una palingenesi delle deliberazioni senatorie dell'età di Claudio (41-54 D.C.)*, Napoli 2010, pp. 232–234, as *sc. de censura*, dating it to the first quarter of 47 AD.

304 Cf. Plin. Mai. 7,159. At the time of the census, T. Fullonius was recorded as 150 years old. The emperor took the trouble to check the documents confirming this unusual age. On this census more extensively J. Osgood, *op. cit.*, pp. 158–159.

305 The equestrian Flavius Proculus brought before the emperor during the censure four hundred freedmen usurping the status of equestrians (Plin. Mai. 33,33). Cf. G. Poma, *Provvedimenti legislativi e attività censoria di Claudio verso gli schiavi e i liberti*, "Rivista storica dell' antichità" 12/1982, pp. 153–156.

306 Cf. CIL VI,919.

307 Cf. Suet., *Claud.* 16; Tac., *Ann.* 12,4.

308 Claudius was aware of the financial difficulties of some senators and therefore sometimes supported them to retain the necessary censure. Cf. B. Levick, *Claudius*..., p. 99. On Claudius' control of the Senate, cf. D. McAlindon, *Claudius and the Senators*, "AJP" 78.3/1957, pp. 279–286. Protests were caused by the admission to the Senate of a freedman who had previously been adrogated by an equestrian (Suet, *Claud.* 24,1), which Claudius justified by referring to the actions of his ancestor censor Appius Claudius the Blind, who had admitted freedmen to the Senate (cf. above). The emperor was accused of misunderstanding the term *libertinus*, which formerly meant the son of a freedman and not, as in those days, the freedman himself. Claudius, who was an avid antiquarian, was attempted to be ridiculed in this way. Cf. G. Poma, *Provvedimenti*..., pp. 151–152. The attainment of *ingenui* status by arrogated freedmen was condemned by the jurist Sabinus; cf. Gell. 5,19,11–12.

309 Cf. Tac., *Ann.* 11,23–25; FIRA I; B. Levick, *Claudius*..., p. 101; O.F. Robinson, *The Sources of Roman Law. Problems and Methods for Ancient Historians*, London–New York 1997, pp. 125–126.

310 However, the emperor followed a policy of defending Roman citizenship, forbidding foreigners to bear Roman names (Suet., *Claud.* 25,3) and declaring knowledge of Latin essential for citizens (Suet., *Claud.* 16,2; Dio Cass. 60,17,4). Cf. G. Poma, *Provvedimenti*..., p. 150.

311 Suet., *Vesp.* 11: He reformed the two great orders, reduced by a series of murders and sullied by long standing neglect, and added to their numbers, holding a review of the senate and the knights, expelling those who least deserved the honour and enrolling the most distinguished of the Italians and provincials. Furthermore, to let it be known that the two orders differed from each other not so much in their privileges as in their rank, in the case of an altercation between a senator and a Roman knight, he rendered this decision: "Unseemly language should not be used towards senators, but to return their insults in kind is proper and lawful" (transl. J.C. Rolfe). Cf. B. Levick, *Vespasian*, London 1999 (reprint 2005), pp. 170–171.

312 Cf. Suet., *Tit.* 6; C. De Boor, *op. cit.*, p. 33; J. Suolahti, *The Roman Censors*..., pp. 513–515; A.B. Bosworth, *Vespasian and the Provinces: Some Problems of the Early 70's A.D.*, "Athenaeum" 51.1–2/1973, pp. 49–50. Numerous numismatic testimonies exist for their censorship.

313 The controversial thesis that Vespasian was censor until 79 AD, i.e. until his death, and thus embraced *censura perpetua*, is presented by A. Torrent, *Para una interpretacion de la 'potestas censoria' en los emperadores flavios*, "Emerita" 36/1968, pp. 213–229; cf. B.W. Jones, *A Note on the Flavians' Attitude to the Censorship*, "Historia" 21.1/1972, p. 128. However, this thesis is convincingly falsified by G.W. Houston, *The Duration of the Censorship of Vespasian and Titus*, "Emerita" 44/1976, pp. 397–402.

314 Palfurius Sura, who under Nero fought in the arena with a Spartan virgin, was removed from the Senate. Cf. *Schol. ad Iuv. Sat.* 4,53. The censorship of Vespasian and Titus is also associated with their acceptance of new families into the patrician ranks, which, however, was not characteristic for the office until the Principate. Cf. H. Dessau, *A Roman Senator under Domitian and Trajan*, "JRS" 3.2/1913, p. 304.

315 Cf. Censorin, *De die nat.* 14.

316 Cf. B.W. Jones, *Some Thoughts on Domitian's Perpetual Censorship*, "CJ" 68/1973, pp. 276–277; T.V. Buttrey, *Domitian's Perpetual Censorship and the Numismatic Evidence*, "CJ" 71/1975, s. 26–34.

317 Dio Cass., *Epit.* 67,4,3: However, being still more puffed up by his folly, he was elected consul for ten years in succession and censor for life, being the first and only man, whether private citizen or emperor, to be given this latter honour... (transl. E. Cary). Cf. Dio Cass. 53,18,5.

318 Cf. Stat., *Silv.* 4,3.
319 Cf. E.S. Ramage, *Juvenal and the Establishment: Denigration of Predecessor in the 'Satires'*, "ANRW" II.33.1/1989, p. 690; R. Stewart, *Domitian and Roman Religion: Juvenal, Satires Two and Four*, "TAPA" 124/1994, pp. 309–332.
320 This refers to his relationship with his niece Iulia Flavia. Cf. Dio Cass., *Epit.* 67,3,2; cf. C.S. Razzini, *op. cit.*, p. 67; R. Stewart, *Domitian...*, p. 310.
321 Cf. C.S. Razzini, *op. cit.*, pp. 67–68; R. Stewart, *Domitian...*, pp. 310–313; cf. also Mart. 6,7,1: Iulia lex populis ex quo, Faustine, renata est... [It is less than thirty days or certainly not more since the Julian law was reborn for the peoples... - transl. D.R. Shacleton Bailey].
322 Iuv., *Sat.* 2,44. However, it does not appear from the text that Domitian reinstated this law. Laronia, speaking in the passage, advises him to reinstate norms sanctioning sexual misconduct by men rather than women. On the *lex Scantinia* cf. above.
323 Cf. F. Grelle, *La 'correctio morum' nella legislazione flavia*, "ANRW" II.13/1980, pp. 345–346. It can be assumed that these were censor edicts, since the emperor implemented the *regimen morum* on their basis. Cf. Suet., *Dom.* 8: Having undertaken the correction of public morals, he put an end to the licence at the theatres, where the general public occupied the seats reserved for the knights; did away with the prevailing publication of scurrilous lampoons, in which distinguished men and women were attacked, and imposed ignominious penalties on their authors; expelled an exquaestor from the senate, because he was given to acting and dancing (transl. J.C. Rolfe).
324 The black colour of the raven's feathers was a punishment for denunciation. The once white bird informed Apollo of the betrayal of his beloved Coronis. The god killed the girl but punished the raven in such a way that the raven could no longer compare with the undefiled pigeons. Cf. Ovid, *Met.* 2,534–550 and 596–632, especially 534–536: thy plumage, talking raven, though white before, had been suddenly changed to black. For he had once been a bird of silvery-white plumage, so that he rivalled the spotless doves (transl. G.P. Goold).
325 Cf. Plin. Mai. 10,104: Next to partridges the habits of pigeons are most noticeable for a similar reason. These possess the greatest modesty, and adultery is unknown to either sex; they do not violate the faith of wedlock, and they keep house in company—unless unmated or widowed a pigeon does not leave its nest (transl. H. Rackham).
326 E.S. Ramage, *op. cit.*, p. 690, rightly pointed out that Juvenal's criticism of Domitian's censorship was a praise of Trajan's decision.
327 Plin. Min., *Paneg.* 45,6: and if you have not yet assumed the censorship and superintendence of our morals, it is because you would rather test our character by benefits than correctives. Besides, I fancy that a ruler may do more for the morals of his country by permitting good conduct than by compelling it (transl. B. Radice).
328 For Hadrian in Apul., *Apol.* 11.4: *imperator et censor divus Hadrianus*; for Septimius Severus and Caracalla on a Greek inscription found in Antalya: *AE* 1986.689.
329 The authenticity of the story, including the senate meeting, is questioned because Decius was already dead at the time described. Cf. H.A. Pohlsander, *The Religious Policy of Decius*, "ANRW" II.16.3/1986, p. 1830; A. Chastagnol, *La "censure" de Valérien*, [in:] *Historiae Augustae Colloquium Maceratense. Atti dei Convegni sulla 'Historia Augusta'*, ed. G. Bonamente, G. Paci, III, Bari 1995, pp. 139–150; S. Roncati, *'Censor legibus scribundis'?*, [in:] *Studi in onore di Franca De Marini Avonzo*, eds. M. Bianchini, G. Viarengo, Torino 1999, pp. 325–326.
330 SHA, *Valer.* 5,4: the senate convened in the Temple of Castor and Pollux, and each senator was asked his opinion as to the man to whom the office of censor should be offered (for the Decii had left this in the power of the most illustrious senate). When the praetor had first announced the question, "What do you think, conscript fathers, about choosing a censor?" and then asked the opinion of the one who was then the head of the senate in the absence of Valerian (for at that time he was in military service

with Decius), then everyone, interrupting the usual procedure for voting, spoke with one voice: "Valerian's life is a censorship. Let him judge all, who is better than all. Let him judge the senate, who is free from guilt. Let him judge our lives, against whom no complaint can be brought. From early childhood, Valerian has been a censor. All his life, Valerian has been a censor. A wise senator, a modest senator, a respected senator. The friend of good men, the enemy of tyrants, the enemy of crimes, the enemy of vices. We all accept him as censor, we all desire to imitate him" (transl. D. Magie).

331 SHA, *Valer.* 6,8: The office of censor has settled upon you, for a common man is not able to fill it. (transl. D. Magie).

332 E. Gibbon, *The History of The Decline and Fall of the Roman Empire*, I, Oxford 1827 (reprint), p. 295.

333 SHA, *Valer*. 6,2–6.

334 Cf. S. Roncati, *'Censor legibus scribundis'?*, [in:] *Studi in onore di Franca De Marini Avonzo*, eds. M. Bianchini, G. Viarengo, Torino 1999, pp. 321–327.

335 SHA, *Car., Carin., Numer.* 20,3: In fact, when Diocletian himself presented spectacles, after inviting people from every nation, he was most sparing in his generosity, declaring that there should be more restraint in the games when a censor was watching – transl. D. Magie).

336 Cf. Athan., *Apol. contra Arianos* 65–67 and Socr. Schol., *Hist. eccl.* 1,27,19–21, which uses the term *κήνσωρ*, which may suggest that it is precisely the epithet rather than the function that is meant.

337 M. Schanz, C. Hosius, *op. cit.*, IV.1, München 1970, p. 123.

338 Symmach., *Ep.* 5,9.

339 Symmach., *Ep.* 4,45; 4,29.

340 Cf. T. Mommsen, *Römisches Staatsrecht…*, II.1, p. 468.

341 Dio Cass. 52,1–40.

342 Dio Cass. 52,21,5.

343 Dio Cass. 52,19.

344 Dio Cass. 52,21,3–7; cf. G. Urso, *op. cit.*, p. 147, n. 60.

II Census-related powers of the censors

1. Preliminary remarks

Census tasks were of colossal importance for the state. They made it possible to estimate the number of citizens, prepared the ground for enhanced army conscription, and contained the information necessary for the collection of taxes. However, the appointment of specialised officials to carry out the census was only the beginning of the process of evaluating the population. Over time, when the censors were given the power to review the equestrian *centuriae* and to determine the composition of the Senate, it fell to them to control society and uphold the Republican system. It was on them that political careers largely depended; they provided the impetus for desirable behaviour. The sacral aspect of this magistracy, that is, the

Figure 1 The census scene from the Altar of Domitius Ahenobarbus, second century BC, Musée du Louvre, phot. Jastrow.

DOI: 10.4324/9781003486664-3

Figure 2 The lustration scene from the Altar of Domitius Ahenobarbus, second century BC, Musée du Louvre, phot. Jastrow.

lustration ceremony crowning the term of office of the censors, also played a considerable role.

An iconographic representation of these censorial activities can be seen in the already mentioned so-called Altar of Domitius Ahenobarbus, a relief from the Temple of Neptune in the Field of Mars, dated to the end of the second century BC.[1] It depicts both a census scene and a *lustrum*. In the central part of the former, a censor is seated, placing his hand on the shoulder of a citizen assigned to a particular property class in a sovereign manner. The second seated figure accepts and inscribes into the *tabulae censoriae* a declaration from another citizen who holds a *codex accepti et expensi* documenting his expenses and income. This figure is probably an *iurator*, although it cannot be ruled out whether it is the second censor or not. The scene of the lustration sacrifice, on the other hand, shows the censor with a wreath on his head at the altar, to which the sacrificial animals – a boar, a ram, and a bull – are being led. Another figure carries a banner (*vexillum*); this is also presumably an auxiliary official, although some identify this figure as the second censor. The scene also includes soldiers: infantrymen and horsemen participating in the purification ceremony.

2. Census

The institution of the census was, according to sources, introduced by the penultimate king, Servius Tullius. Plutarch even called him the first censor – *τιμητὴς πρῶτος*.[2]

> Liv. 1,42,5[3]: *Censum enim instituit, rem saluberrimam tanto futuro imperio, ex quo belli pacisque munia non viritim, ut ante, sed pro habitu pecuniarum fierent; tum classes centuriasque et hunc ordinem ex censu discripsit, vel paci decorum vel bello.*
>
> *For he instituted the census, a most useful thing for a government destined to such wide dominion, since it would enable the burdens of war and peace to be borne not indiscriminately, as heretofore, but in proportion to men's wealth. He then distributed the people into classes and centuries according to the following scale, which was based upon the census and was suitable either for peace or war.*
>
> (Transl. B.O. Foster)

According to Livy,[4] the king introduced a census so that henceforth the burdens, both in peace and war, would not be distributed among the citizens equally, but according to their wealth. In accordance with this principle, he divided the people into classes based on property and into centuries. Although the source accounts of these events seem to idealise to a certain extent,[5] they are generally considered reliable, at least regarding the timing of the introduction of the institution itself is concerned.[6] The institution of a census was known in the ancient world and also existed among the Etruscans,[7] which makes its introduction by a king originating from there plausible. In the early days of the Republic, the censuses were carried out by the consuls, and later censors were appointed specifically for this task.

The start date of the census and any information on the rules for it were announced in an edict. The censors also issued a *lex censui censendo* containing detailed regulations for the census. Some scholars identify it with the edict,[8] but it seems that the edict merely announced the publication of the *lex*.[9]

We know the formalities involved in the commencement of the census from the excerpts of the *tabulae censoriae* preserved in Varro's account.[10] After the nightly auspices[11] were held, the censor directed the usher to convene the people. At dawn, the censors drew lots among themselves as to which of them would conduct the *lustrum*, and that censor presided over the *contio*. It should be added that Varro separately mentioned the superintendents of all the *tribus*, whom the usher also summoned and who presumably assisted the censors during the census, as well as the officials – praetors and plebeian tribunes, who probably constituted the council (*consilium*) of the censors.

The census was held in the *Villa Publica* complex in the Field of Mars. Crowds of citizens flocked to Rome on this occasion.[12] It was not until the end of the Republican period that regular censuses were also carried out in the municipalities and colonies,[13] and later also in the provinces. The documentation compiled by local officials was then sent to Rome.[14]

On behalf of the whole family, registration was made by the *pater familias*,[15] widows and orphans were declared by the tutor.[16] The declaration included a range of personal and property data,[17] and was made in the form of a *iusiurandum*.

> *Tab. Her.* 144–148: *eorumque nomina praenomina patres aut patronos tribus cognomina et quot annos/ quisque eorum habe<bi>t et rationem pecuniae ex formula census, quae Romae ab eo, qui tum censum/ populi acturus erit, proposita erit, a ieis iurateis accipito.*
>
> *He shall accept from them under oath their names, praenomens, parents or patrons, tribes, cognomens, the age of each citizen, and the statement of his property in accordance with the pattern of the census, which shall be posted at Rome by the official who is about to take the census of the people at that time.*
>
> (Transl. A.C. Johnson, P.R. Coleman-Norton, F.C. Bourne)

The *Tabula Heracleensis* shows[18] that the declarant should provide the family name, first name, father's name or patronymic, the name of the *tribus*, age, and estate according to the *forma censualis*[19] issued in Rome by the census official. Sources also indicate that the citizens provided details of their offspring and wife.[20] The term *forma censualis* refers to the detailed guidelines for conducting a census. During the Republican period, these issues were addressed in the edicts of the censors and the *lex censui censendo*, issued shortly after they took office, which announced how the census would proceed.[21]

Land suitable for declaration was called *praedia censui censendo*.[22] These were properties subject to Quiritarian ownership, belonging to the category of *res mancipi*, which could also be collateral at *locationes censoriae*.[23]

As the censors were not able to personally receive all the declarations, they were assisted by *iuratores*.[24] The final compilation of the lists, however, was done by the *scribae*.

Incensus

The census had political as well as sacral significance for the Romans, due to the lustration sacrifice that ended it. Therefore, attendance and submission to the census were basic duties of citizenship, the non-fulfilment of which resulted in serious sanctions for the *incensus*.[25]

Information on the penalties for not submitting to the census can be found in sources on the reforms of King Servius Tullius.[26] According to Dionysius of Halicarnassus,[27] those who did not submit to the census were subject to the penalty of property confiscation and were sold after being flogged. This norm remained in force among the Romans for a long time. Flogging served as an aggravation of the punishment. Writing a little further on the dictatorship of Larcius,[28] Dionysius mentioned as punishments for *incensi* the loss of property and citizenship.[29] This information refers to the regulations introduced by Servius Tullius, which were applied by the first Roman dictator to conduct a census. It seems that the historian has mentioned a fact here with which the reader should already be aware. The loss of citizenship should therefore not be interpreted narrowly but rather taken to refer to the sanction mentioned earlier, involving the sale of *incensus*.

The norms introduced by Servius Tullius were presented in a slightly different way by Livy,[30] who provided information about the *lex de incensis* – a law establishing penalties for not submitting to the census. The sanctions he mentioned were imprisonment and death. There is, therefore, a major discrepancy regarding the regulations related to avoiding the census regarding whether *incensus* was punishable by death or by being sold into slavery.

In order to determine the sanction envisaged for *incensi*, it is therefore necessary to examine more sources concerning this institution. In his *Pro Caecina* speech, Cicero dealt with the loss of liberty and citizenship.[31] His client, Aulus Caecina, was a citizen of the city of Volaterra and was in dispute before the *recuperatores* over a landed estate with Aebutius. Since the opposing party's argument was based on the claim that the citizens of Volaterra had been deprived of their Roman citizenship by the *comitia centuriata* at Sulla's request, Cicero sought to prove that citizenship, once acquired, could not be revoked by law (*lege aut rogatione*). He first cited the case of a person who evaded military service and was sold.[32] In his opinion, it was not the people who took away freedom in this case, but the person himself, who did not want to endanger himself, renounced it. The speaker went on to deal with *incensus* by contrasting his situation with the *manumissio censu*,[33] whereby those who were in legal bondage were manumitted. He who refused to submit to the census was himself giving up his freedom, and being sold was merely a consequence of his own decision. Cicero thus seems to suggest that a person's status is determined by his enrolment: its existence means that the person is a free citizen, and deliberate evasion of it results in loss of freedom.

Gaius gave the case of *incensus* as an example of *capitis deminutio maxima*, a situation in which a Roman lost both his citizenship and his freedom:[34]

> G. 1,160: *Maxima est capitis deminutio, cum aliquis simul et civitatem et libertatem amittit; quae accidit incensis, qui ex forma censuali venire iubentur; quod ius p………………… ex leg(e)………… qui contra eam legem in urbe Roma domicilium habuerint; item feminae, quae ex senatus consulto Claudiano ancillae fiunt eorum dominorum, quibus invitis et denuntiantibus cum servis eorum coierint.*
>
> *The greatest 'capitis deminutio' is the simultaneous loss of citizenship and freedom, which happens to those who having evaded inscription on the censorial register are sold into slavery according to the regulations of the census, also under the — law when persons in violation of it make Rome their place of residence, and also under the Sc. Claudianum in case of persistent intercourse on the part of a free woman with another person's slave in spite of the dissent and denunciation of the owner.*
>
> (Transl. E. Poste)

According to him, those who had not submitted to the census were ordered to be sold under the *forma censualis*. The text of the *Institutes* is corrupt at this point. Attempts at reconstruction included adding the information that the sanction for not submitting to the census was no longer valid (*quod ius proprie in usu non est*). However, this cannot be accepted because even in later texts, it appears as an institution still in use.[35] In addition to *incensi*, Gaius seems to have mentioned the *peregrini dediticii ex lege Aelia Sentia*, who had settled in Rome in contravention of the law, and further a woman who was subject to the sanction imposed by the *senatusconsultum Claudianum* for cohabiting with another's slave.[36]

As can be seen from G. 1,160, the *forma censualis* also regulated that the person who did not submit to the census should be sold. Initially, therefore, the penalties for not submitting to the census stemmed from Numa's *lex de incensis*. Then, they were probably regulated in the edict of the censors and the *lex censui censendo*. After the disappearance of the censors' office, they were still found in the *forma censualis*.

Also, Ulpian mentioned the sale[37] of a person who did not submit to the census as an example of *capitis deminutio maxima*:

> Ulp. 11,11: *Maxima capitis deminutio est, per quam et civitas et libertas amittitur, veluti cum incensus aliquis venierit, aut quod mulier alieno servo se iunxerit denuntiante domino et ancilla facta fuerit ex senatus consulto Claudiano.*

> *The greatest is that by which both citizenship and freedom are lost; for instance, where anyone is sold for not having returned his property to the censor; or where a woman has formed a union with the slave of another, in defiance of the warning of his master, and has become a slave under the Claudian Decree of the Senate.*
>
> (Transl. S.P. Scott)

Although the above excerpt was taken from the post-classical compilation *Tituli ex corpore Ulpiani*, it is rather to be supposed that such a unique example came from the jurist himself. In addition to *incensus*, the jurist gave, like Gaius, the example of a woman becoming a slave by virtue of *senatus consultum Claudianum*.

Confiscation of property, death or being sold into slavery after being flogged are mentioned in the sources as punishments for failing to turn up for the census. According to jurists, *incensus* suffered *capitis deminutio maxima*.

These differences raise several questions. Therefore, it should be attempted to establish what sanction was envisaged for *incensi*, whether it changed over time, and according to what rules it was applied: *ipso iure* or under some procedure.

The penalties mentioned in the sources – death and sale – occur together also in another case, namely that of an insolvent debtor. The enforcement procedure was regulated in the third table of the Twelve Tables,[38] but it is to be assumed that these regulations already existed earlier and that the decemvirs codified them. According to Gellius,[39] insolvent debtors who did not reach a settlement with their creditor were held in bonds for sixty days. During that time, they were brought three times on market days before the praetor[40] for a *comitium*, where the amount of the debt was announced. After three market days, they were sold beyond the Tiber or *capite poenas dabant*.[41] The latter phrase can be interpreted as a death penalty[42] but also as losing one's *caput*,[43] i.e. one's legal capacity, and therefore falling into dependence on the creditor. Although Sextus Caecilius, whose views were cited by Gellius, clearly had the death penalty in mind,[44] it cannot be ruled out that the loss of *caput* in the legal sense was envisaged in the law.

However, if it were assumed that an insolvent debtor could be punished by death or sold, this would provide an analogy with the situation of *incensus*. It is also possible to hypothesise that the Numa statute provided for *poena capitis*, which Livy understood as the death penalty, but which may have meant the loss of *caput* in the legal sense instead. It should further be noted that – according to Livy – *incensus* was also threatened with *vincula*, which parallels Gellius' account: the creditor held the adjudged in bonds for sixty days. Failure to submit to the census was most often to avoid military service or the payment of tax, and *incensus* could therefore be considered a debtor to the Roman people. It seems that this is why his situation resembled that of other debtors. However, the analogy certainly cannot be overstated. *Incensus* broke the rules of public law. Therefore, the *lex Poetelia Papiria*[45] did not exclude the possibility of selling him.

There has also been a hypothesis in the literature[46] that *incensus* was considered *sacer*,[47] i.e. deprived of the protection of divine and human law, during the royal period because the census was sacred in nature and failure to submit to it constituted an imbalance between the worlds of deities and humans (*pax deorum*). However, the sources quoted do not provide a basis for such a theory.[48] It should also be noted that *sacertas* as a sanction appears essentially only in the norms attributed to the first kings, Romulus and Numa. Perhaps the authority to impose such a sanction was linked to their sacerdotal powers. Indeed, during the Latin monarchy, the king was the high priest. The kings of the Etruscan monarchical period, on the other hand, were probably devoid of the sacral dimension of power, although, with the exception of Tarquin the Proud, they were inaugurated.[49] Therefore, it is difficult to suppose that Servius Tullius would have ordered the recognition of *incensus* as *sacer*.[50]

It can be hypothesised that the originally introduced sanction for not submitting to the census was death, loss of *caput*, or sale. However, since there was a profit from selling the *incensus*, this sanction prevailed. According to Theodor Mommsen, this may also have had something to do with the institution of *provocatio ad populum*,[51] introduced perhaps as early as the beginning of the Republic, since an official could not sentence a citizen to death without giving him the right of appeal to the assembly.

In legal texts, *incensus* was mentioned in the context of *capitis deminutio maxima*. However, there is no precise information as to when exactly it occurred.

> Fragmenta Parisina 1, *Responsa Papiniani* (Paris. ZRG XVIII, 170.176):[52] *Servos ab eo, qui non condit[o] cens[u] ante crimen inlatum manumis[it], ad libertatem pervenire placuit. manumissi quoque similiter ut patronus incensorum crimine tenebuntur.*
>
> *Ulpianus. Quame (?) census tempore non fuerint libertatem……*
>
> *Paulus. Si cluso censu manumissi sunt nec postea census [condit]us est, incensorum poenis n[on tenentur].*
>
> *Paulus. Quare ipsi si cluso cen[su manu]missi sunt… libertatem……*
>
> *Apud [ve]teres autem antequam [in]census do[min]us iudicare[tur, liberta]tes obtine[r]e constitit……*
>
> *It is approved that slaves of the one who was accused of a crime and earlier he manumitted them before the completion of the census, should come to liberty. The manumitted will be charged with a crime of the ones who failed to submit to the census just like their patron.*
>
> *Ulpian: At the time of the census their freedom was not…*
>
> *Paulus: If they were manumitted after the closure of the census and afterwards no census was held, they will not be subject to the punishment for those who failed to submit to the census.*
>
> *Paulus: Because of that if they were manumitted after the closure of the census… freedom…*
>
> *By the ancestors however before the master was convicted as incensus, it was certain that freedom was acquired.*
>
> (Transl. AT)

The above excerpt from Papinian's *Responsa* was found in Egypt at the end of the nineteenth century.[53] It contains Papinian's statements interspersed with comments by Ulpian and Paulus. It deals with issues relating to the freedmen of a master who did not submit to the census. Papinian stated that slaves manumitted before an accusation[54] was brought against their owner for a crime committed were granted freedom, but – on a par with the patron – were held responsible for not submitting to the census. What follows is a statement by Ulpian, not preserved in its entirety, concerning those slaves who had not yet been freed at the time of the census. Paulus explained that – if the manumission occurred after the census had closed – the freedmen would not be subject to the penalty for *incensi*. A further section of the text contains part of Papinian's antiquarian commentary, in which the jurist conveyed that in the times of the forefathers – before an owner was convicted of not submitting to the census – he could effectively manumit a slave. It seems, therefore, that only a convicted *incensus* lost the right to perform a valid *manumissio*.

This passage provides especially important information about the *incensi*. Firstly, it testifies to the fact that punishments for them were still applied during the classical law period, in the third century BC.[55] Although the office of the censor no longer existed during this period, censuses were still carried out. Secondly, failure to submit to the census was treated as a *crimen*, which was subject to standard criminal procedure by private prosecution. This information seems to indicate that *capitis deminutio maxima* did not – at least in this period – occur *ipso iure* but was conditional on a conviction in a criminal trial, and only then did the convicted person lose his rights and property and the ability to dispose of it. The question arises as to when a prosecution could be brought. The term *cluso censu* appears in the text. Initially, the census ended with a lustration ceremony, which, however, was discontinued in the first century AD.[56] It may therefore be that at first the prosecution for *infrequentia*, i.e. failure to appear, followed the *lutratio*, and then, when it was abandoned, the census itself.

The mode of dealing with *incensus* must have been changing. The mention of the *lex de incensis* by Servius Tullius does not provide information on how the case was handled. It can be inferred that flogging was administered as part of the *coërcitio*.[57] Further, the *incensus* case was dealt with in a criminal trial. The convicted person (*iudicatus*) – already deprived of his *caput* – was probably held in bonds until the punishment in the form of a sale was carried out. During the classical law period, with the development of the *cognitio extra ordinem*, a procedure involving formal prosecution and sentencing by a judge had certainly already developed.

However, who carried out the *incensus* sale and how did it take place? The insolvent debtor was sold in enforcement proceedings by the creditor by whom he was *in mancipio*. In the case of a failure to submit to the census, the creditor was the state, on whose behalf an official, one presumes, acted. According to Theodor Mommsen, the consul dealt with the sale of the person, and the censor with the *incensus* estate.[58] The German scholar based this thesis on an excerpt from the work of Zonaras,[59] who stated that those whose property or themselves were not listed at the time of the census were dealt with as follows: the property was sold by the censors and the individuals themselves by the consuls.

Emanuel Hoffmann[60] argued that this division of responsibilities was due to a difference in competences: the censor was to ensure that the treasury obtained the best price for the property by auction, while the consul, as commander-in-chief, had the power to punish evaders from military service. The sale of *incensus* was supposed, according to Hoffmann,[61] to take place beyond the Tiber (*trans Tiberim*) and result in the convict only becoming a slave in the community that bought him. This view cannot be reconciled with the Papinian passage quoted above, from which *capitis deminutio maxima* occurred upon conviction for not submitting to the census. Edoardo Volterra[62] argued that there was no reason to believe that the *incensus* was sold beyond the Tiber and not into Roman territory. In his argument, however, he failed to consider that the absence of such information in the texts of jurists of the classical period does not prove that such a rule was not originally applied.

An excerpt from *De Oratore*[63] may provide some clues. Cicero, analysing the case of C. Mancinus who was handed over to the enemies and not accepted by them,[64] stated the principle, still remembered in his times, that one who had been sold by his *pater familias* or by the people, or had been handed over to the enemies (*deditio*) by a priest of the college of fetiales (*pater patratus*), was not entitled to the right of return (*ius postliminii*). Although Cicero did not mention *incensus*, it is a case of being sold by the people.[65] And since Cicero mentioned *postliminium*, the sale had to be made outside the borders of Rome, i.e. precisely *trans Tiberim*.[66] It seems that as long as Rome was a small state, it tended to avoid selling former citizens within its own territory.[67] Later, on the other hand, it became impossible to adhere to this rule for practical reasons related to expansion.

Volterra was also convinced that the *capitis deminutio maxima* of a person who did not submit to the census occurred even before the sale, but he gives other, not entirely convincing, arguments. Namely, he is of the opinion that mere non-enrolment resulted in loss of citizenship, and since it was not possible for an individual to exist without *status civitatis*,[68] this also entailed slavery. It is difficult to agree with this view given, for example, the existence of such an institution as deprivation of access to water and fire (*interdictio aquae et ignis*).[69] A citizen who went into exile voluntarily ceased to be a Roman citizen only when he was accepted by the community to which he went. However, the situation was different in the case of a sentence in a trial. Gema Polo Toribio[70] is of the opinion that, resulting from a deliberate act, failure to register resulted in loss of citizenship, but only being sold resulted in falling into slavery.

Papinian's *Responsa* shows that mere non-enrolment did not yet cause any negative consequences. The reason for this is probably that only deliberate avoidance of the census was punishable, while non-enrolment due to excused absence did not entail any sanction.[71] Therefore, in a trial, it had to be proven that there had been a wilful failure to appear (*dolo malo infrequentia*), and the sentence resulted in *capitis deminutio maxima*.

According to Zonaras, the property of *incensus* was also sold. This constituted the duty of the censors. Dionysius of Halicarnassus, on the other hand, conveyed that the property was subject to confiscation. Additional information related to this problem is provided by the *lex Osca tabulae Bantinae*,[72] preserved in epigraphic form, which regulated the city of Bantia in Lucania. The tabulae were found at the end of the eighteenth century. It is uncertain to which period the document inscribed on it should be dated. It is possible that it dates back to the time of Sulla's dictatorship. The text was written in the Oscan language. The content of the document probably reflects Roman solutions, with the principles of *cursus honorum* being respected.

In the light of the relevant passage,[73] the censors, or local officials, took a census of the inhabitants of Bantia. If someone deliberately failed to report, he was to be condemned, sold at a *comitium* presided over by an official in the presence of the people. His *familia* was sold and the *pecunia* he did not report at the time of the census became public.[74]

According to Volterra, the term *familia* refers to persons under the authority of the *pater familias* who did not submit to the census. This interpretation, however, contradicts the source texts. Firstly, one should recall the passage by Festus[75] concerning the word *famulus*, which the antiquarian derived from the Oscan *famelo* meaning slave. This is precisely the term found in the Oscan version of the text. In addition, the phrase *familia pecuniaque* was often used in connection with the census, as indicated by the reference in Cicero's *De Legibus*,[76] in which he assigned censors the task of conducting census declarations of citizens. The information provided was to include age, *suboles* – offspring, *familias*[77] – slaves, and *pecunias*[78] – property. Since Cicero listed offspring and *familia* separately, it must be thought that the latter term did not include free persons remaining under *patria potestas* or *manus*.

It is, therefore, impossible to share the view that not only the *incensus* but also the persons under his authority were subject to sale into slavery. On the other hand, his property: both movables, including slaves and real estate, became the property of the state and was sold at auction. The *capitis deminutio maxima* of the family superior meant that persons hitherto subject to him became *sui iuris*. Although they did not receive property, as this was forfeited, they seemingly maintained the *sacra familiaria*. Thus, the family could be preserved.

It can also be inferred from the provision of the *lex Osca tabulae Bantinae* that recognition of *incensus* was not made *ipso iure* but was established by proceeding. The procedure described indicates that it was a *iudicium populi*. Considering the provision of the Twelve Tables ordering the highest assembly to decide on capital cases (*de capite civis in maximo comitiatu*),[79] it can be assumed that in Rome, such a trial would have taken place at the *comitia centuriata*. It should be noted that Mommsen's opinion, mentioned above, concerning the abolition of the death penalty for *incensi* in connection with the introduction of the *provocatio*, is untenable because this penalty during the Republican period was not imposed by an official taking advantage of his *coërcitio*, but by the people.

The sources cited allow conclusions to be drawn about the sanctions for *incensi*. The obligation to submit to the census probably appeared as early as the time of Servius Tullius, who was also the author of the *lex de incensis* imposing penalties: this was probably the *poena capitis*, interpreted as the death penalty or the loss of *caput*, or the penalty of being sold. These were combined with additional flogging. During the Republican period, the punishment of being sold into slavery persisted, initially *trans Tiberim*, with the sold person not having the *ius postliminii*; later, however, the sale may have been carried out on Roman territory. The sale was supervised by the consul. The property of the *incensus* was subject to confiscation. It appears that the auction may have been overseen by the censor if he was still in office.

The *incensus* was not *ipso iure* subject to these penalties. He had to be sentenced because only intentional (*dolo malo*) failure to submit to the census was sanctioned, and therefore, those who were absent for excusable reasons at the time of the census were not punished. The trial took place during the Republican period at the *comitia centuriata*, and in the Principate at the *cognitio extra ordinem*. For an indictment to be brought, the census must have already been completed, initially probably also culminating in the form of lustration until this rite was abandoned in the time of Vespasian. Therefore, the censors may have already finished their term of office. Still, it appears that they were the ones who could, in most cases, bring charges against those who did not appear for the census.

The convicted *incensus* suffered *capitis deminutio maxima*. By contrast, it does not appear that persons found under the power of the condemned were subject to the penalty. They became *sui iuris*, but could not receive property, while *sacra* passed to them.

Such harsh sanctions for not submitting to the census were due to the culprit acting to the detriment of the state – on the one hand financially, as he evaded paying the tax, on the other militarily, as he avoided military service.

Incensus appears in the sources essentially theoretically. It is possible to research what sanctions were threatened for not submitting to the census, but there are no actual cases of their application. The only text in which a more practical mention of this institution can be found is an excerpt from the never-delivered first part of the *actio secunda* in the trial of Verres, which Cicero published after the former governor had already gone into voluntary exile in Massilia.

> Cic., *In Verr.* 2,1,104: *P. Annius Asellus mortuus est C. Sacerdote praetore. Is cum haberet unicam filiam neque census esset, quod eum natura hortabatur, lex nulla prohibebat, fecit ut filiam bonis suis heredem institueret. Heres erat filia. Faciebant omnia cum pupilla, leges, aequitas, voluntas patris, edicta praetorum, consuetudo iuris eius quod erat tum cum Asellus est mortuus.*
>
> *During the praetorship of Gaius Sacerdos, there died one Publius Annius Asellus. He, being the father of an only child, a daughter, and not having been registered, had taken the step, which his natural feelings prompted and there was no law to forbid, of making his daughter his heir: and she was so accordingly. All the arguments were in the child's favour—equity, the father's wishes, the edicts of past praetors, and the legal usage existing at the date of Asellus's death.*
>
> (Transl. L.H.G. Greenwood)

In this speech, Cicero addressed the praetorship of Verres, who held the dignity of *praetor urbanus* in 74 BC.[80] He subjected to crushing criticism above all his edict containing retroactive clauses[81] related to the interpretation of the *lex Voconia*,[82] the victim of which was Annia, daughter of P. Annius Asellus, who had established her as his heir in his will.[83]

In the first chapter of the Voconian plebiscite, there was a prohibition on the establishment of female heirs to persons who had been entered in the first class of property from the census of A. Postumius and Q. Fulvius. According to Cicero, if someone was not listed in the *census*, the restriction did not apply to them.[84] Meanwhile, Verres is likely to have extended the application of this norm to those who, although not listed in the first class, nevertheless had assets worth at least 100,000 asses. In doing so, he also extended these provisions to wills made before the edict was promulgated, using the clause *qui testamentum fecit fecerit*, i.e. 'whoever has made or will make a will.'

A scholarly debate exists on the case of Annius. Salvatore Cassisi[85] argued that Verres' edict struck *incensi*, interpreting the phrase *neque census esset* as referring to those who did not submit to the census. Claude Nicolet[86] expressed that Annius had escaped the rules laid down in the *lex Voconia* because no census had taken place since at least 86 BC. He added that – as a senator – Annius could not have avoided making a declaration of assets. However, this last argument is not plausible, since the *lectio* usually took place before the census itself began and without the participation of the senators concerned and those who might have become senators (unless the censors summoned someone or allowed proceedings in case of a threat of *nota*). As for the interval between censuses, the census was not conducted, but it seems that Cicero was speaking in general terms about the fact that if someone were not inscribed, they could avoid the restrictions of the law. Such a general formulation suggests that he was not just referring to this exceptional situation.

Suzanne Dixon,[87] on the other hand, saw in the case of Annius an expression of the practice of breaking the law to achieve socially approved outcomes. She acknowledged that a blind eye was turned to the fact that the richest citizens did not submit to the census to retain their freedom of instituting heirs.

The treatment of Annius as *incensus* seems to contradict the sources entirely. If one were to consider that he deliberately did not submit to the census, one would have to conclude – following this line of thought – that penalties for *incensi* were not applied during this period. Yet Cicero himself[88] explicitly referred to them as being in force. It is difficult to suppose that in the interval of only a few years, during which both speeches were written, the legal *status quo* had changed so much.

In my view, it is unacceptable to interpret the phrase *neque census esset* as referring to *incensus*. Nicolet's argument seems more plausible. Indeed, after 86 BC no further censors were elected until 70.[89] This does not mean, however, that lists were not drawn up. It is known that Sulla completed the composition of the Senate, presumably taking into account the wealth of its members. On the other hand, it cannot be ruled out that a census was not taken during this period. Perhaps Annius benefited from this. However, it seems that a more general interpretation can be applied here. From Cicero's words,[90] it appears that excused failure to appear for the census was not punished. A citizen eligible for the first class who wished to establish his daughter as heir could therefore find a suitable reason allowing him not to attend the census. This would perhaps be an action to circumvent the law (*in fraudem legis*), but not an offence punishable by *capitis deminutio maxima*.

It is a fact, on the other hand, that Verres' edict sought, in theory, to close a loophole, something that Cicero deliberately seemed to overlook. The speaker was merely highlighting how the former praetor had unfairly exploited the amendment. The argument about retroactivity was certainly exceptionally good. It must also have appealed to the audience that excused non-appearance at the census was considered an acceptable way of avoiding the restrictions introduced by *lex Voconia*. From a rhetorical point of view, it was therefore an excellent tactic.

Manumissio censu

Manumissio censu, one of the formal modes of manumission,[91] is intricately linked to the institution of the census. Formal manumission could basically take place in three ways in Roman law: in a will (*manumissio testamentaria*), in a proceeding *in iure* before an official endowed with jurisdiction (*manumissio vindicta*), or during a census (*manumissio censu*). Cicero, in his work *Topica*, written already after Caesar's death in 44 BC, explained what the enumeration of parts consisted of, using the example of manumission. He wrote that if a slave had not been manumitted either at the time of the census, *in iure* proceedings, or in a will, he was not free.[92] Thus, the list provided is *numerus clausus*. Only the accomplishment of one of the three *manumissiones* resulted in freedom.

> G. 1,17: *Nam in cuius personam tria haec concurrunt, ut maior sit annorum triginta et ex iure Quiritum domini et iusta ac legitima manumissione liberetur, id est vindicta aut censu aut testamento, is civis Romanus fit, sin vero aliquid eorum deerit, Latinus erit.*
>
> *A slave in whose person these three conditions are united, thirty years of age, quiritary ownership of the manumitter, liberation by a civil and statutory mode of manumission, i. e. by the form of vindicta, by entry on the censor's register, by testamentary disposition, becomes a citizen of Rome: a slave who fails to satisfy any one of these conditions becomes only a Latin.*
>
> (Transl. E. Poste)

In the first book of the *Institutes*, Gaius considered not only the problem of obtaining freedom but also the acquisition of Roman citizenship. In his view, the group of legitimate and lawful forms of manumission (*iustae ac legitimae manumissiones*) included *manumissio censu*, *vindicta* and *testamento*.[93] The jurist added that, in order to obtain citizenship, in addition to being manumitted in one of these ways, the freedman also had to be at least thirty years of age, as required by the *lex Aelia Sentia*[94] and had to be under Quiritarian ownership.[95]

It is therefore clear from the source texts that *manumissio censu* resulted in the acquisition of freedom and Roman citizenship. However, it remains to be examined how it took place and what prerequisites had to be fulfilled for it to occur. Furthermore, it is necessary to consider when a freed person obtained freedom and citizenship: at the time of entry by the censor or only after the *lustratio*, as well as the nature of the slave's entry on the list of citizens – declarative or constitutive.

The *manumissio censu* was carried out during a census. As mentioned above, the institution of the census was introduced according to sources by the penultimate king, Servius Tullius. Dionysius of Halicarnassus relayed that the king allowed freedmen to obtain citizenship and ordered them to be enrolled along with the other citizens.[96] They were also to be enrolled in the *tribus*. The king therefore did not introduce a new mode of manumission but allowed those who had previously been manumitted to be granted citizenship.[97] It must therefore be inferred that by this time, the Romans were manumitting slaves by merely granting them freedom without citizenship.[98] Such a practice was characteristic of ancient states whose inhabitants guarded their political rights quite jealously.

Whether the reform of Servius Tullius immediately resulted in the formation of the *manumissio censu* cannot be clearly determined from the sources. It should be added that this type of manumission provided for an element of state control, since the person making the entry in the list of citizens was first the king and then the *magistratus*, and it was on their decision that the entry depended.[99] The censor could refuse to put someone's name on the list if he had doubts about their identity. This was, for example, the case of the censor Quintus Metellus, who refused to list Lucius Equitius claiming to be the son of Tiberius Gracchus.[100]

An important issue is the conduct and requirements of the *manumissio censu*. In particular, the question of the role of the owner, the censor (or another person carrying out the *census*), and the slave himself must be considered.

An excerpt from *Tituli ex corpore Ulpiani*[101] states that those who were manumitted *censu* were slaves who, at the time of the Roman census, at the behest of their owners, came forward to be enrolled among the Roman citizens.[102] It was therefore the slave who reported to the censor after receiving the relevant order (*iussum*) from the owner[103] and made the census declaration (*professio*). David Daube[104] rightly points out the important semantic difference between the *iussum* at *manumissio censu* and the use of the verb form *iubere* in the phrase *Stichum serum meum liberum esse iubeo* at the making of a will when the owner frees the slave in imperative form. While in the first case, the owner ordered the slave to appear before the censor, indicating that he had not yet relinquished his property right, in the second case, he himself granted the slave freedom, limited only by a date (*dies a quo*). It also seems worth noting a possible analogy with the *actio quod iussu* developed later in praetorian law, which presupposed the owner's liability for the slave's contractual debts incurred by virtue of the *iussum*. Such a command by the owner, however, had to be known to the slave's counterparty. Also, in the case of *manumissio censu*, the owner did not issue a command to the slave – for how then could it be verified? – but addressed the censor directly. This could have happened, for example, already during the census, when the *pater familias* reported himself and his *familia*; the censor, informed by him, would then accept the declaration of his slave.

In such a case, the presence of the owner at the enrolment of his slave as a citizen was quite natural.[105] This seems to be confirmed by the reference to the law and edict of the consul C. Claudius of 177 BC[106] concerning the problem of the Original Latins (*Latini prisci*) acquiring citizenship through the *ius migrandi*, i.e. by settling in Rome.[107] A Latin wishing to exercise this entitlement had to leave a son in his hometown. This requirement was circumvented by surrendering oneself to a Roman citizen, who then performed a *manumissio* with the effect of conferring citizenship. The law and the edict of the consul Claudius forbade such circumvention practices and ordered Latins on the citizens' lists of their communities to return to those *civitates* and set up an appropriate tribunal chaired by the praetor.[108] The Senate, however, additionally enacted the *senatusconsultum*, under which an owner wishing to manumit a slave had to submit a *iusiurandum* that he was not manumitting to allow a change of citizenship; otherwise the official was obliged to refuse manumission. This injunction seems to have applied to both *manumissio censu* and *vindicta*, since it was addressed not only to present and future censors but also to dictators, consuls, interrexes, and praetors.[109] Since the owner was required to take an oath, it was standard for him to be present during the enrolment of the slave as a citizen.

It remains to be established whose decision formed the basis of the *manumissio censu*. The slave reported at the behest of the owner, but it seems that – since it was the censor who made the entry – he had the final say in the matter.[110]

> G. 1,140: *Quin etiam invito quoque eo, cuius in mancipio sunt, censu libertatem consequi possunt, excepto eo, quem pater ea lege mancipio dedit, ut sibi remancipetur; nam quodam modo tunc pater potestatem propriam reservare sibi videtur eo ipso, quod mancipio recipit. Ac ne is quidem dicitur invito eo cuius in mancipio est censu libertatem consequi, quem pater ex noxali causa mancipio dedit, veluti quod furti eius nomine damnatus est, et eum mancipio actori dedit; nam hunc actor pro pecunia habet.*
>
> *But even though the assent of the holder in mancipation is withheld, freedom may be acquired by entry on the register of the censor, except when a son has been mancipated by a father with a condition of remancipation, then the father is deemed to have reserved in a way his own power in consequence of the condition that he is to have him back in mancipation; nor can liberty be acquired without the assent of the holder in mancipation by entry on the censor's register when a delinquent son has been surrendered by his father in consequence of a noxal suit; when, for instance, the father has been condemned in an action for a theft committed by the son, and has by mancipation surrendered his son to the plaintiff, for in this case the plaintiff holds him in lieu of pecuniary damages.*
>
> (Transl. E. Poste)

Gaius dealt with the status of persons who were *in mancipio*, i.e. sold by their family superiors, and who could obtain their freedom through *manumissio censu*, *vindicta*, or *testamento*, thus becoming persons *sui iuris*.[111] In the passage quoted above, on the other hand, he argued that the *manumissio censu* of such a person could also take place without the consent of the one in whose power he was. This was excluded when the *pater familias* reserved the obligation to return (*remancipatio*) the person surrendered *in mancipium*, and also in the case of surrender to the injured party in case of a delict (*noxae datio*) – in that case, depriving the injured party of the right to decide the fate of the *persona in mancipio* would be detrimental to him, since he had received the perpetrator as compensation for the damage. It can be concluded from this text that – since *manumissio censu* could take place here without the consent of the holder of the power – the decision rested in the hands of the censor.

Researchers have also posed the question of the nature of the entry made by the censor: whether it was declarative or constitutive. Theodor Mommsen[112] put forward the thesis that by inscribing a slave on the list of citizens, the censor assumed the fiction that the slave was already a Roman citizen. Proponents of this view primarily cite a passage from Cicero's speech in defence of the poet Archias delivered in 62 BC:[113]

> Cic., *Pro Arch.* 11: *...quoniam census non ius civitatis confirmat, ac tantum modo indicat eum qui sit census [ita] se iam tum gessisse pro cive.*
>
> *But, since the census-roll is no proof of a man's civil status, and since the appearance of his name there does but indicate that when the census was taken he lived as a citizen...*
>
> (Transl. N.H. Watts)

The orator argued that an entry in the list did not confirm the right to citizenship but only indicated that the person entered was already acting as a citizen. Later in the speech, Cicero pointed out that Archias had, on several occasions, made wills that complied with the requirements of Roman law and was himself an heir. This passage would indicate that – in order to be enrolled – one already had to be a citizen. A slave would therefore have to be treated by the censor as if he were already a citizen.

In my opinion, however, Cicero's words have a slightly different implication: that a citizen who, for excusable reasons[114] (such as Archias, who was with Lucullus in his provinces at the time of the last census), was not enrolled in the list retained his *status civitatis*, which was merely noted at the time of the census. By contrast, there is no basis for concluding from Cicero's words that listing always merely confirmed an already existing *status civitatis*. In the case of a slave, it was the censor who decided whether to enrol him and thus to grant citizenship. This power of the official was the result of a kind of mandate[115] given to him by the *comitia centuriata*, which enacted the *lex centuriata* for him, since the ability to confer citizenship during the Republican period was available only to the *comitia*. Other entities acquired this possibility by delegation. It therefore does not seem necessary, or even useful, to apply the assumption of citizenship to the *manumissio censu*.[116] On the other hand, there is no reason to assume that the census entry was absolute: in the event of an error, it was not valid and did not result in the acquisition of citizenship.

The question can be raised as to whether every slave could be manumitted *censu*. Jane Gardner[117] stated that the *manumissio censu* applied only to men. Such a view probably stems from the belief that it was men *sui iuris* who came forward at the time of the census to state the status of their family and property. However, since the censors also kept a register of widows and orphans, perhaps female slaves were not automatically excluded from the possibility of the *manumissio censu* being applied to them. It seems that this type of manumission could theoretically have been applied regardless of gender, although in practice, it tended to apply to men.

There was a fierce dispute in antiquity as to when the effect of *manumissio censu* occurred.

> Cic., *De or.* 1,183: *Quid? De libertate, quo iudicium gravius esse nullum potest, nonne ex iure civili potest esse contentio, cum quaeritur, is, qui domini voluntate census sit, continuone, an, ubi lustrum sit conditum, liber sit?*
>
> *Then as to freedom, the most serious issue there can be, may not controversy arise out of the common law, on the question whether a slave, enrolled with his master's consent on the censor's list, is to date his enfranchisement from that moment, or from completion of the lustrum?*
>
> (Transl. E.W. Sutton, H. Rackham)

Cicero, discussing the intricacies of *ius civile* in his treatise *De Oratore*, found the problem of whether a slave who was enrolled as a citizen at the will of the owner became free immediately or only after *lustrum*[118] extremely difficult.

Such a doubt was also expressed by a jurist of the classical period, whose views are preserved in the *Fragmentum Dositheanum.*[119] This forms part of a textbook for the study of Latin by Pseudo-Dositheus.[120] This work, written at the beginning of the third century AD, probably consisted of twelve books, with the fifth book, on the manumission of slaves, composed in 207 AD or slightly earlier. The whole work is preserved in two manuscripts housed in Leiden and Paris, containing the Latin text written in parallel columns alongside its translation into Greek.

The question of the authorship of the work used by Pseudo-Dositheus, and, by extension, the time of its creation, is uncertain. Anthony Maurice Honoré[121] has convincingly argued that the author in question is the same as the author of a work called *Regulae*, created in the second half of the second century, and has hypothesised that this jurist may have been Gaius.[122]

> *FD* 17: *Et qui censu manumittitur, si triginta annos habeat, civitatem Romanam nanciscitur. Census autem Romae agi solet et peracto censu lustrum conditur: est autem lustrum quiquennale tempus quo Roma lustratur. Sed debet hic servus ex iure Quiritium manumissoris esse, ut civis Romanus fiat. Magna autem dissensio est inter peritos, utrum eo tempore vires accipiant omnia, in quo census, an eo tempore, quo lustrum conditur. Sunt enim qui existimant non alias vires accipere quae in censu aguntur, nisi haec dies sequatur, qua lustrum conditur; existimant enim censum descendere ad diem lustri, non lustrum recurrere ad diem census. Quod ideo quaesitum est, quoniam omnia quae in censu aguntur lustro confirmantur. Sed in urbe Roma*

tantum censum agi notum est; in provinciis autem magis professionibus utuntur.

The one who was manumitted at the census was given Roman citizenship provided he was thirty years of age. The census is usually performed in Rome and after its completion lustrum is carried out: lustrum is a time when Rome is purified every five years. But the slave has to be in the manumissor's Quiritarian ownership so that he can become a Roman citizen. There was a great disagreement between the experts if everything [that has been done during the census] gains force when the census or the lustrum is completed. There are those who are of the opinion that the census lasts until the day of the lustrum, but the lustrum does not turn back to the day of the census. And this has been investigated, because everything that is done in the census is confirmed by the lustrum. The census however is only performed in Rome; in the provinces on the other hand declarations are rather used.

(Transl. AT)

According to the text, a manumitted *censu* acquired Roman citizenship as long as he was at least thirty years old and was under Quiritarian ownership. There was, however, a dispute concerning the moment of the acquisition of rights: whether it happened as soon as the census itself was completed or only after the ceremony of *lustrum condere*. The elegant wording that *the census lasts until the day of the lustrum, but the lustrum does not revert to the day of the census* means that lustration makes the manumission and other census acts valid but only *ex nunc* and not *ex tunc*.

Censorin., *De die nat.* 13–14: *Idem tempus anni magni Romanis fuit, quod lustrum appellabant, ita quidem a Servio Tullio institutum, ut quinto quoque anno censu civium habito lustrum conderetur; sed non ita a posteris servatum. Nam cum inter primum a Servio rege conditum lustrum et id, quod ab imperatore Vespasiano V et T. Caesare III cons. factum est, anni interfuerunt paulo minus DCL, lustra tamen per ea tempora non plura quam LXXV sunt facta et postea plane fieri desierunt.*

The Great Year of the Romans is the same thing as the interval of time which they have called lustrum. This institution dates back to Servius Tullius, who ordered that at the end of every fifth year, we should solemnly proceed, after having made the census of citizens, to the closure of the lustrum. But this was also changed, because from the first lustrum closed by King Servius, to that which was made by the Emperor Vespasian, consul for the fifth time, and by Titus Caesar, under his third consulate, nearly 650 years had passed while only 75 lustra were closed in the interval. Since this epoch the ceremony has been altogether neglected.

(Transl. W. Maude)

Censorinus, a grammarian and antiquarian who lived in the first half of the third century AD, relates in his work *De die natali* that King Servius Tullius decided that a *lustrum* should be held in Rome every five years after the end of the census.[123] However, this custom was not followed consistently. In the approximately 650 years between the time of Servius (around 566 BC) and the reign of Vespasian (the last *lustrum* took place in 74 AD), *lustra* were conducted no more than seventy-five times before being abandoned altogether.

It seems that doubts about linking the effects of the census to the *lustrum* may have arisen due to their relatively low frequency. Not every census ended with sacrifices,[124] which may have caused a lot of confusion and uncertainty.

It is clear from the source texts that a definitive solution to this problem could not be reached. The voices of those who were convinced that only the *lustrum* confirms the decisions made at the time of the census were likely contested by those who considered the impracticality of such a solution. That the opinion of the latter may have been used in practice is indirectly evidenced by a passage from Festus' *De verborum significatu*:

> Fest. 454 L., s.v. *senatores*: *et nunc cum senatores adesse iubentur "quibuscumque in senatu[m] sententiam dicere licet"; quia hi, qui post lustrum conditum ex iunioribus magistratum ceperunt, et in senatu sententiam dicunt, et non vocantur senatores ante quam in senioribus sunt censi.*
>
> *and now, whenever the senators are summoned into session, [the expression is added] and those who are permitted to give their opinion in the senate; this is because these men were enrolled in junior centuries when the last census was completed, but subsequently obtained a magistracy and give their opinions in the senate and are not called senators until they are enrolled in senior centuries.*
>
> (Transl. W.J. Tatum)

In the Senate, opinions could also be expressed by those who had taken up offices entitling them to do so after the *lustrum*. However, they were not then called senators[125] until they had been enrolled in the senior centuria (*seniores*) at the time of the next census. The attainment of the title of senator therefore occurred at the time of entry and did not need to be confirmed at the time of the *lustrum*. While this is only circumstantial evidence, it seems likely to show that, in practice, it was the entry and not the *lustrum* that produced legal effects.

It is also impossible to exclude the possibility that at the time the entry was made, the manumitted person was already treated as a free person, but only began to enjoy the privileges of citizenship after the *lustrum*. One can attempt to divide the effects of *manumissio censu* into private and public law. In private law, the freedman would come immediately under the patronage, but in public law, he would receive his entitlements later. This arrangement would give the patron the possibility to recall him to a state of bondage (*revocatio in servitutem*) if the freedman proved ungrateful. Additionally, the censor could, in principle, change the entry until the purificatory offerings were made. It is also important to note the sacral aspect of the *lustrum*: until it was carried out, the freedman was not treated as a citizen in the realm of *fas* and did not have the approval of the gods[126] for being *civis Romanus*, which could be expressed, for example, in not being able to perform private auspices.

The additional requirement for manumission at the time of the census was pointed out by Cicero:

> Cic., *Por Caec.* 99: *Iam populus cum eum vendit qui miles factus non est, non adimit ei libertatem, sed iudicat non esse eum liberum qui, ut liber sit, adire periculum noluit; cum autem incensum vendit, hoc iudicat, cum ei qui in servitute iusta fuerunt censu liberentur, eum qui, cum liber esset, censeri noluerit, ipsum sibi libertatem abiudicavisse.*
>
> *So too the state, by selling a man who has evaded military service, does not take away his freedom but decrees that one who has refused to face danger for his freedom's sake is not a free man. By selling a man who has evaded the census, the state decrees that, whereas those who have been slaves in the normal way gain their freedom by being included in the census, one who has refused to be included in it although free, has of his own accord repudiated his freedom.*
>
> (Transl. H. Grose Hodge)

The orator emphasised that those who were in legal bondage (*in servitute iusta*) were granted freedom by being enrolled as citizens. This passage is taken from the speech *Pro Caecina.* Cicero addressed the possibility of a person losing their liberty by evading military service and by *incensus*, claiming that they themselves had, as it were, given up their *libertas*. He contrasted these situations with the case of those who obtained liberty at the time of the census, highlighting that it was a case of those who were in *iusta servitus*.

Furthermore, according to Gaius, only those who were freed from legal bondage (*iusta servitus*) were considered *libertini.*[127] *A contrario*, one who was not a *iustus servus*, could not become a freedman according to *ius civile*, even if a *manumissio* had been performed for him.[128] Such a situation could happen when someone who was not aware that he was free *(liber homo bona fide serviens)* was manumitted, or when it was a person captured by pirates who retained their freedom. In such cases, the manumitted person retained the same status as before.

Finally, it remains to answer the question of until when the *manumissio censu* was applied. Since this form of manumission was intricately linked to the institution of the census, its existence was possible as long as censuses were performed. In 22 BC, censors were appointed by the decision of Augustus, but later the censorial powers were assumed by the emperors. Sometimes a *princeps* assumed the office of censor by selecting a colleague. For the Principate period, there is no mention of the exercise of *manumissio censu*, but Gaius and the jurist whom Pseudo-Dositheus quotes wrote about this institution as still existing. It was only in the *Regulae Ulpiani* that the phrase *olim* was used referring to an institution that had already fallen out of use. Therefore, it must be assumed that the *manumissio censu* may still have been in use in the first to second centuries AD, and perhaps even in the third, but rather exceptionally, before disappearing altogether.[129]

3. Recognitio equitum

King Servius Tullius was to appoint eighteen equestrian centuries from among the wealthiest citizens.[130] These were *equites equo publico*, who received horses from the state.[131] For the purchase of horses, they were given ten thousand asses,[132] while the upkeep of the horses was charged to widows, who paid two thousand asses a year.

Gaius reported that the *equites* were entitled to *pignoris capio* on account of money for the purchase of a horse (*aes equestre*) and also for fodder (*aes hordiarium*).[133] This referred to the possibility of seizing items as security for these dues.[134]

Celebrations of the equestrian order took place quite frequently in Rome and are sometimes confused with the census of the *equites*, i.e. the *recognitio* or *recensio equitum* conducted by the censors. However, all of them, it should be stressed, concerned a narrow group of 1,800 *equites equo publico*.[135] According to Valerius Maximus,[136] the feast of the equestrian youth was the *Lupercalia*, a celebration commemorating the joy of Romulus and Remus when their grandfather Numitor allowed them to found a city at the foot of the Palatine, the place where they grew up. After making sacrifices and killing goats, they were so carried away by their merriment that, having divided the shepherds, girded with the skins of the sacrificial animals, they playfully attacked those on the opposing side. This merriment was recalled every year during the feast which fell on 15 February.

On the Ides of July,[137] the *transvectio equitum* took place. It was established by the censor Q. Fabius. The equites were dressed in *trabeae*, togas with purple stripes. The ceremonial procession set off from under the temple of Mars and proceeded to the temple of Castor and Pollux.

The two censors together[138] carried out the *recognitio*[139] *equitum* in the *forum Romanum*. The knights were called by the usher, *praeco*, by name according to *tribus*.[140]A decision was then taken: if the rider gained approval, he heard *transduc equum*[141] and could leave with his horse; a negative decision by the censors, on the other hand, is referred to in the sources as *equum adimere*[142] or *equum vendere iubere*,[143] and thus involved taking away the horse or ordering its sale.

An equestrian was subject to a censorial mark for acts commonly punished by censors, or for acts that were specific only to horsemen, i.e. closely related to their status and duties. It is worth taking a closer look at examples of the latter.

> Gell. 4,12,2–3: *Item, quis eques Romanus equum habere gracilentum aut parum nitidum visus erat, "inpolitiae" notabatur; id verbum significat, quasi tu dicas "incuriae". Cuius rei utriusque auctoritates sunt, et M. Cato id saepenumero adtestatus est.*
>
> *So too, any Roman knight, if his horse seemed to be skinny or not well groomed, was charged with 'inpolitiae', a word which means the same thing as negligence.*
>
> (Transl. J.C. Rolfe)

Among the memorable instances of the use of the censorial mark, Gellius noted situations where the horse was too thin or not well-groomed, a neglect of the horse referred to by the censors as *inpolitia*. Such a reason for the *nota* was given in writing in the *subscriptio*.

The term *inpolitia* was also explained by Festus, whose account is, however, only preserved in an abridged version by Paulus Diaconus.

> Fest. (Paul.) 95 L., s.v. *inpolitias*: *Inpolitias censores facere dicebantur, cum equiti aes abnegabant ob equum male curatum.*
>
> *The censors were said to do 'inpolitias' when they refused to pay the money to an equestrian because of a horse that had been badly cared for.*
>
> (Transl. AT)

Neglect of the horse consequently resulted in a refusal to pay the money – *aes*. This phrasing suggests that the knight did not receive *aes hordearium*. A comparison of the two texts allows additional conclusions to be drawn. It appears that the *inpolitia* resulted in a censorial mark, which only had the effect of removing the right of the horseman to collect the money intended to feed the horse. However, it was unlikely to lead to the equestrian's removal from his century.

> Gell. 4,20,11: *Item aliud refert Sabinus Masurius in septimo memoriali severe factum: "Censores" inquit "Publius Scipio Nasica et Marcus Popilius cum equitum censum agerent, equum nimis strigosum et male habitum, sed equitem eius uberrimum et habitissimum viderunt et "cur" inquiunt "ita est, ut tu sis quam equus curatior?" "Quoniam" inquit "ego me curo, equum Statius nihili servos." Visum est parum esse reverens responsum, relatusque in aerarios, ut mos est."*
>
> *Sabinus Masurius too in the seventh book of his Memoirs relates a third instance of severity. He says: "When the censors Publius Scipio Nasica and Marcus Popilius were holding a review of the knights, they saw a horse that was very thin and ill-kept, while its rider was plump and in the best of condition. 'Why is it,' said they, 'that you are better cared for than your mount?' 'Because,' he replied, 'I take care of myself, but Statius, a worthless slave, takes care of the horse.' This answer did not seem sufficiently respectful, and the man was reduced to a commoner, according to custom."*
>
> (Transl. J.C. Rolfe)

A little further on, Gellius wrote about censorial severity, quoting a passage from Massurius Sabinus' work entitled *Libri memoralium*. The jurist recorded an incident concerning the censorship of Scipio Nasica and Popillius in 159 BC.[144] Observing a well-groomed knight leading an emaciated horse, the censors asked why the master appeared better than the animal. They received the answer that the rider was looking after himself while the horse was attended by the useless slave Statius. The knight was punished by being transferred to the ranks of the *aerarii*, as custom dictated. Such a severe sanction, however, was not only due to the neglect of the horse, but also to the disrespectful words directed at the censors.

> Gell. 6,22: *Nimis pingui homini et corpulento censores equum adimere solitos scilicet minus idoneum ratos esse cum tanti corporis pondere ad faciendum equitis munus. Non enim poena id fuit, ut quidam existimant, sed munus sine ignominia remittebatur. Tamen Cato in oratione, quam de sacrificio commisso scripsit, obicit hanc rem criminosius, uti magis videri possit cum ignominia fuisse. Quod si ita accipias, id profecto existimandum est non omnino inculpatum neque indesidem visum esse, cuius corpus in tam inmodicum modum luxuriasset exuberassetque.*
>
> *The censors used to take his horse from a man who was too fat and corpulent, evidently because they thought that so heavy a person was unfit to perform the duties of a knight. For this was not a punishment, as some think, but the knight was relieved of duty without loss of rank. Yet Cato, in the speech which he wrote On Neglecting Sacrifice, makes such an occurrence a somewhat serious charge, thus apparently indicating that it was attended with disgrace. If you understand that to have been the case, you must certainly assume that it was because a man was not looked upon as wholly free from the reproach of slothfulness, if his body had bulked and swollen to such unwieldy dimensions.*
>
> (Transl. J.C. Rolfe)

Gellius further noted that the censors also used to deprive excessively fat and obese equestrians of their horses, considering them unfit to bear the hardships of horsemanship at such a weight. However, this was not a punishment, as they were dismissed without the stigma of *ignominia*, i.e. without insult to their good name. Further on, Gellius quoted Cato's opinion as expressed in his speech *de sacrificio commisso*. Cato regarded obesity as a serious charge, suggesting that it should be associated with *ignominia*. According to Gellius, the reason for this interpretation was that bringing one's body to such a state was a manifestation of excess. The speech of Cato mentioned above was probably directed against L. Veturius,[145] accused of neglecting his worship and also of bringing himself to a state that made it impossible to serve as a centurion of horsemen.[146] The speech was evidently cutting, as some attributed passages can attest. Plutarch records that Cato, rebuking the fat knight, said: "How can such a body serve the state when everything from the throat to the groin occupies the belly?"[147] A quote preserved in Servius' commentary on the *Aeneid* concerns the fact that the rider could not sit on a horse that was shaking under his weight.[148]

It appears, therefore, that obese horsemen were removed from the equestrian centuries, while whether this involved the stigma of *ignominia* depended on the censors currently in office and also involved other charges. In the case of Veturius, obesity was an additional charge, alongside neglect of the *sacra*.[149]

> Fest. (Paul.) 47 L., s.v. *censionem facere*: *Censionem facere dicebatur censor, cum multam equiti inrogabat.*

The censor was said to make a 'censio' when he punished an equestrian with a fine.

(Transl. AT)

A text by Paulus preserved information about fines imposed by the censors on the knights, referred to by the phrase *censionem facere*. The question arises, however, under what circumstances this might have happened.

In Plautus' comedy *Rudens*, Plesidippus says: *Adsum equidem, ne censionem semper facias.*[150] He thus informs that he is present so that Trachalio ceases *censionem facere*. In this scene, the young man is talking to the slave, and the wordplay revolves around the verb *censere* in its various meanings.[151] It can be inferred that the imposition of the fine was linked to a failure to appear. Such a situation was possible at the time of *recognitio* when the usher summoned horsemen by name according to *tribus*. A similar conclusion can be drawn from Placidus' glossa. *Censio*, wrote the grammarian, was a fine that the censor imposed on those who failed to appear when summoned.[152]

The termination of service in a horsemen's centuria also involved dismissal, but with honour. Such a situation was described by Plutarch,[153] according to whom the knight (in this case Pompey himself) would then lead the horse before the censors in the forum, giving the names of the chiefs under whom he served and reporting on his service. The censors would then decide his fame or infamy.

Since the late Republic, it was not possible for a knight to be a senator. Entering the Senate required surrendering the horse. This rule was introduced in 129 BC by the *plebiscitum reddendorum equorum*.[154] The censors had to consider this norm when appointing new senators. In the situation described by Plutarch, Pompey, who was entering the Senate and about to assume the consulship, ended his career as an equestrian by announcing before the censors that he had served as much as was required, and under his own command.

4. Lectio senatus

The composition of the Senate was initially determined by the king, and then by the consuls. This authority passed to the censors through an act usually titled *lex Ovinia*, known primarily from a single source text, namely a passage by Festus.

> Fest. 290 L., s.v. *praeteriti senatores*: *Praeteriti senatores quondam in opprobrio non erant, quod, ut reges sibi legebant, sublegebantque, quos in consilio publico haberent, ita post exactos eos consules quoque et tribuni militum consulari potestate coniunctissimos sibi quosque patriciorum, et deinde plebeiorum legebant; donec Ovinia tribunicia intervenit, qua sanctum est, ut censores ex omni ordine optimum quemque curiatim in senatum legerent. Quo factum est, ut qui praeteriti essent et loco moti, haberentur ignominiosi.*
>
> *Passed-over senators: in the past there was no opprobrium associated with this expression, because just as it was the custom for the kings to choose for themselves their public counsellors – and to choose their*

> *replacements – so, after the expulsion of the kings, the consuls and the military tribunes with consular power used to choose as their public counsellors those men of the patrician order with whom they had the closest ties. Later they included those members of the plebeian order with whom they had the closest ties. This practice continued until the Ovinian plebiscite supervened, by means of which it was made the law that censors enrol in the senate the best men from each order. Consequently, whenever men were passed over and removed from their position, they were disgraced.*
>
> (Transl. W.J. Tatum)

The antiquarian relayed that the omitted senators were not subject to disgrace because just as kings chose and replaced the members of the public council, so after their expulsion, the consuls and military tribunes with consular power also chose the senators first from among the patricians, then also the plebeians. This continued until the tribunician *Ovinia* intervened and stipulated that the censors should elect the best from each state to the Senate. Therefore, those who were overlooked and removed from their seats were treated as disgraced.

A huge debate arises over the dating of the *lex Ovinia*. Since the *lectio* carried out in 312 BC by Appius Claudius and Plautius Venox is widely described in the sources, it is most often dated between 318 and 312 BC.[155] Thomas R.S. Broughton even places Ovinius as a plebeian tribune in 313 BC.[156] However, Diodorus of Sicily relayed,[157] that – when the consuls refused to convene the Senate as elected by Appius Claudius and his colleague,[158] mainly due to the admission of the sons of the freedmen[159] – the Senate was convened according to the list drawn up by the previous censors, i.e. in 318 BC, which moves the *terminus ante quem* by four years.[160]

Another issue closely related to dating is the nature of the *lex Ovinia*. The wording of Festus *Ovinia tribunicia* suggests that it refers to a plebiscite. Meanwhile, the practice of giving of the plebiscite resolutions the force of laws began roughly half a century after its enactment. Therefore, some scholars[161] have pushed the date of the enactment of the *lex Ovinia* to the period after 287 BC, considering the information about earlier *lectiones* as an annalistic invention.

There is, of course, the possibility that the *rogatio* was brought not by a plebeian tribune but by a military tribune with consular powers. In that case, however, the date of enactment would have to be placed to the period before the *leges Liciniae Sextiae* of 367 BC, since the election of tribunes ceased at that time.

There is, however, no obstacle to considering the act in question as a plebiscite even if its enactment date is retained prior to 318 BC. The equating of plebiscites with *leges* by virtue of the *lex Hortensia* is mentioned in many sources,[162] while Livy also cited two earlier regulations concerning the universally binding force of plebiscites: *lex Valeria Horatia*[163] and *lex Publilia Philonis*.[164] The former stipulated that resolutions passed by the plebs after their return from *Mons Sacer* were binding on the whole people, while the latter recognised as binding on all citizens those plebiscites that obtained *auctoritas patrum*,[165] which seems very likely, especially in light of the reading of Gaius' text *quae sine auctoritate*.[166]

Therefore, it is possible that the *plebiscitum Ovinium* was enacted after 339 BC and received *auctoritas patrum*, making it binding on the whole people. Such an interpretation, however, provokes consideration of its impact about the senators. For it must be proven that it was a regulation favourable to the Senate to be certain that the granting of *auctoritas* was in its interest.

Although it is generally accepted[167] that membership of the Senate was for life in regal period and in the early days of the Republic, and that it was rare for senators to be removed, the text of Festus shows the exact opposite.[168] Both the kings and the highest Republican officials selected persons closely related to them to the Senate and could also replace them with others.[169] *Plebiscitum Ovinium* would therefore have been a step towards strengthening the sense of security of the senators, elected no longer on the subjective criterion of *coniunctissimi regis* (*consulis*), but on the fairly objective one of *optimus quisque*.

This last criterion, however, requires deeper analysis. According to Festus, the censors were to elect to the Senate *ex omni ordine optimum quemque curiatim*, i.e. 'the best of each state according to the curia.' The last word is a conjecture of the unintelligible *curiati* from *codex Farnesinus*. Another possible reading is *iurati* – 'sworn,' very plausible from a palaeographical point of view, but regarded as a *lectio facilior*. The excerpt raises numerous questions.

The phrase *ex omni ordine* may be understood in different ways. It can be interpreted as a choice between plebeians and patricians, where *ordo* means social order.[170] However, it is rightly argued that then the text should rather be *ex utroque ordine*.[171] Some[172] supplement *ordo magistratuum* by recognising that it refers to election from among former curule magistrates. However, it seems that the term *ordo* originally meant a certain social group, not necessarily in the political sense.[173] A somewhat similar interpretation was proposed by Tim Cornell,[174] arguing that the phrase *ex omni ordine* should be understood not so much distributively, but rather as 'from the whole state,' i.e. from among all citizens. However, Francesco De Martino[175] rightly argued that on the basis of this formulation, a practice was established: a customary order of appointment of senators, which was scrupulously adhered to by the dictator Buteo, who was appointed to compile the list of the Senate.[176] Some indication may also be provided by the information given by Gellius that the performance of certain functions, above all the holding of the curule office, predestined one to be a senator to the extent that such persons were admitted to the deliberations. It seems, therefore, that the censors were even expected to take these candidates into account when making the *lectio senatus*. This may indicate that the *plebiscitum Ovinium* introduced strict criteria for selecting the composition of the Senate, to which the censors had to adhere.[177] This state of affairs is confirmed by the anecdote quoted by Valerius Maximus about how Q. Fabius Maximus divulged the contents of a secret meeting to Crassus, thinking that he – since he had held the quaestorship three years ago – had already been listed by the censors.[178]

Another interpretative difficulty arises with the formulation *optimum quemque*. Who were these 'best'? It seems that this is not a very objective criterion, but rather a kind of general clause. However, the source texts indicate that *vir bonus* is someone who is morally blameless,[179] as well as financially well-off,[180] from the higher social strata.[181] It can therefore be assumed that the censors were to select from among citizens with a high wealth status those who were characterised by appropriate moral qualities. The point of reference must have been that of the *mores maiorum*.[182]

Each of the aforementioned conjectures regarding the corrupted term *curiati* has its supporters. Adopting the reading *curiatim* implies that censors were to select senators according to curia.[183] The reading *iurati* would suggest that censors would have to take an oath.[184]

The election of senators according to the curia is not supported by the sources. Besides, the censors had little in common with the curial organisation. They were elected at the *comitia centuriata*, the same assembly confirmed their election, and during the census, on the other hand, no fixed lists of curiae were created, as they depended on family affiliation.

In contrast, selecting under oath was a standard procedure used, for example, when appointing judges. The *iurati* lesson therefore seems more likely.[185] Additionally, senators would certainly be calmer knowing that their appointment depends on officials bound by *iusiurandum*.

The granting of the Senate's approval for the *plebiscitum Ovinium – auctoritas patrum* – seems to be beyond doubt in the light of the analysis of differences in the way the composition of the Senate was determined before and after its enactment. The arbitrary and completely unrestricted decisions of the consuls were replaced by decisions of the censors based on specific criteria. They had a great deal of freedom, but not as wide-ranging. This interpretation is also supported by the introduction of *ignominia* for *senatores praeteriti*, as it affected those who objectively failed to observe basic social norms dictated above all by *mores maiorum*, which at the time were unquestionable models of behaviour.

There were, however, some situations in which *ignominia* seems not to have been applied to *praeteriti*. The case of P. Popilius, described by Cicero in his *Pro Cluentio*,[186] suggests that the loss of good name could be spared for those whose *praeteritio* was based on objective grounds without any fault on their part. Popilius was accused of bribery by one of the censors during the *lectio senatus* and was thus threatened with a censorial mark, but the other censor blocked his colleague's decision. Nevertheless, Popilius was not admitted to the Senate due to being the son of a freedman. However, he was not subjected to ignominy and retained a senatorial seat at the games (this was probably a privilege of those expecting to be admitted to the Senate and having the *ius sententiae dicendae*). Such a decision by the censors must have been based on their earlier announcement in the edict that they would not admit the sons of freedmen.

Perhaps some light could be shed on the problem of dating the first censorial *lectio senatus* by an inscription discovered in 1950 in Brindisi containing the text of the elogium, unfortunately largely incomplete.

AE 1954.216: *PRIMUS SENATUM LEGIT ET COMITI…………*
BARBULA COS. CIRCUM SEDIT VI……………

> *DIUMQUE HANNIBALIS ET PRAE...............*
> *MILITARIBUS PRAECIPUAM GLOR...............*
>
> *He first reviewed the senate and (reorganized?) the popular assembly ... during the consulship of ... and ... Barbula, and he surrounded and ... (took?) the camp of Hannibal and ..., for his military exploits (he earned?) particular glory.*
>
> (Transl. S. Bernard)

Researchers have attempted to establish the identity of the person to whom the elogium was dedicated. The consular date contained in the inscription is the primary interpretative clue. Consuls with the nickname Barbula held office in the following years: 317, 311, 281, and 230 BC.[187]

Initially, the prevailing view was that it referred to Fabius Cunctator,[188] which would explain the mention of Hannibal but makes absolutely no sense in relation to the *lectio senatus*. There is also a view that refers to some unknown municipal official.[189] More recently, the hypothesis has been put forward that the elogium refers to Appius Claudius,[190] and the decisive argument is the phrase *primus senatum legit*, which, according to scholars, must refer to him because he was the first to elect senators under the *lex Ovinia*. Such reasoning is fundamentally flawed, as dating the Ovinian plebiscite to the years 318–312 BC is highly questionable and cannot be the basis for further conclusions.

However, another thesis can be proposed: that the consular year mentioned in the inscription is 317 BC and that the person to whom the elogium refers is the censor elected to office the year before, Gaius Maenius.[191]

As consul in 338 BC[192] Maenius, together with Camillus, subjugated Latium to Rome, which Livy describes as 'conquered by force' (*vi capta*).[193] Maenius held a triumph because of this, and the prows of the ships he seized at Antium adorned the Rostra.

Under the censorship of Maenius, two new *tribus* were added: the Oufentina and the Falerna, the latter created in the previously conquered territories of Latium.[194] The authority to create *tribus* lay with the censors. Therefore, the beginning of the word *comiti* might refer to the addition of new territorial units to the assembly.

The reference to Hannibal is the most difficult to interpret. Of course, the famous leader and conqueror of the Romans is not the only Carthaginian known to us by that name. During the period in question, battles were being fought near Sicily, as the Carthaginians vied for domination.

Thomas Lenschau[195] has listed twelve people named Hannibal. The third of these fits chronologically, as he was the commander of the Carthaginian army at the beginning of the First Punic War and died shortly afterwards. It is also possible that the inscription refers to some otherwise unknown Hannibal who commanded an army or conducted some military operation for a time.

The strongest arguments, therefore, suggest that the *plebiscitum Ovinium* was enacted shortly before or in 318 BC. This *plebiscitum* brought the *lectio senatus* into the hands of the censors, allowing them to select the best candidates and – *a contrario* – remove those who did not meet this criterion. From this point onwards, the powers of the censors to assess their fellow citizens from a moral point of view were institutionalised,[196] particularly concerning the observance of *mores maiorum*. The *regimen morum* thus finally formed covered not only the senators but all citizens. While previously the censors had exercised this oversight based on a custom, trying to develop instruments for such oversight, after the plebiscite was passed, it began to take on a more concrete framework.

5. Lustrum condere

The crowning task of the censors' tenure was to perform a purification ritual, referred to by the phrase *lustrum condere.*[197] Ceremonies of this kind were also performed to purify the field[198] or army.[199] In this case, however, the verb *condere* was not used, but the more general *facere*.[200]

The regulations for carrying out this rite were found in the *tabulae censoriae*, excerpts of which were provided by Varro.[201] It is clear from the text that which of the censors was to carry out the lustration was determined by drawing lots. However, it is difficult to imagine the actual application of this rule between 351 and 280 BC. Despite the admission of plebeians to exercise censorship, the lustration always fell to the patrician censor. Only later were plebeian censors allowed to perform the ceremony. However, it must be stressed that despite the draw, both censors were needed to carry out the lustration. This was referred to by the term *ambilustrium*, which Servius used when commenting on Virgil's *Aeneid*, meaning that it was not legal to purify the state without both censors.[202]

We do not know the exact course of the ceremony. At the head of the procession was a *scriba* reading out the formula for the prayer (*precatio*).[203] The text of the *precatio* is similar to the one used when convoking the citizens for the *census*.[204] It remained unchanged for a long time, and the circumstances of its amendment were presented by Valerius Maximus:

> Val. Max. 4,1,10: *qui censor, cum lustrum conderet inque solitaurilium sacrificio scriba ex publicis tabulis sollemne ei precationis carmen praeiret, quo di immortales ut populi Romani res meliores amplioresque facerent rogabantur, 'satis' inquit 'bonae et magnae sunt: itaque precor ut eas perpetuo incolumes servent', ac protinus in publicis tabulis ad hunc modum carmen emendari iussit. qua votorum verecundia deinceps censores in condendis lustris usi sunt.*
>
> *When as Censor he was winding up the census and in the sacrifice of solitaurilia the scribe was reciting before him from the public tables the formula of prayer in which the immortal gods were asked to make the state of the Roman people better and greater, "It is good and great enough," said Scipio. "So I pray the gods to keep it safe in perpetuity." And on the words he gave order that the formula in the public tables be emended accordingly. From that time on Censors have used this modest form of prayer in winding up censuses.*
>
> (Transl. D.R. Shackleton Bailey)

At the time of his censorship, Scipio ordered a change in the formula of the *precatio*,[205] in which the immortal deities had hitherto been asked to improve the situation of the Roman people. The victor of Hannibal felt that it was already good enough and asked that this should never change. He also ordered this change to be made to the *tabulae publicae*.[206]

The lustration sacrifice consisted of a boar, a ram, and a bull.[207] These were *suovetaurilia*[208] for Mars.[209] This very deity can be seen at the central point of the so-called altar of Domitius Ahenobarbus in the lustration section.[210] The sacrifice was offered on the Field of Mars.

Animals could only be led, as Cicero pointed out,[211] by people with good names (*bonis nominibus*). It can be inferred from Festus' account[212] that names such as Valerius, Salvius, and Statorius were considered auspicious.

An additional limitation was reported by Cassius Dio when writing about Agrippa's funeral. Augustus delivered an elogium on this occasion, but first fenced off the body of the deceased with a screen, which was incomprehensible to the historian.[213] According to the opinions cited by Cassius, Augustus' behaviour was caused either by his function as *pontifex maximus* or by his censorial tasks. However, both of these suppositions were considered by the historian to be incorrect, as the *pontifex maximus* was allowed to view the dead,[214] while the censor was only forbidden to do so for the duration of the lustration ceremony. If he had seen the body before it was finished, he had to start from the beginning.[215]

As reported by Athenaios[216] the censor was dressed in a purple toga and had a wreath on his head when killing sacrificial animals with an axe. This is confirmed by an iconographic source, as on the Ahenobarbus' altar mentioned above, the censor actually has a wreath. Varro reported,[217] that later the censor led the army[218] to the city[219] *ad vexillum* (to the banner). Firstly, it is important to consider the meaning of the term *exercitus*. Botsford[220] argues that this could not have been about a regular army, but about citizens who volunteered to be enrolled in the census. However, it appears that it was rather those who were destined to serve in the army who participated in the lustration ceremony. It is difficult to believe that such an important ritual would not have been attended by the *alieni iuris* sons, who were, after all, registered by their *patres familiarum*, and that widows, for example, would have been admitted to it. It is clear from Varro's account that this involved the so-called *exercitus urbanus*.

The phrasing *ad vexillum* raises doubts, particularly whether the banner was carried by the censor followed by the army, or if it was located in the city with the censor at the head of the *exercitus* proceeding towards it. The fact that the *vexillum* was carried in a lustration procession is evidenced by the altar of Domitius Ahenobarbus, where a figure with a covered head is depicted carrying a banner next to the sacrificial ram. However, its identification is questionable. Mario Torelli[221] expressed the belief that it was an auxiliary official, an *accensus* called *velatus*, who, despite his military affiliation, was distinguished by his robe called *velum* rather than by his military coat.[222] Erich Gruen,[223] on the other hand, argued that it was the censor himself. He drew this conclusion based on Varro's text, which, however, does not unequivocally indicate that it was the censor who carried the *vexillum*. It seems unlikely that the magistrate himself carried the sizable burden; rather, it was likely carried by *an apparitor*, whose attire in this case identifies him as an *accensus velatus* with a high degree of probability.

Certainly, a particularly important detail of this ceremony should be noted. As a rule, the army could not enter the city, which is why the *comitia centuriata*, having a military nature, occurred outside the *pomerium* on the Field of Mars.[224] An exception to this rule was the triumph, during which the victorious leader entered Rome through the triumphal gate at the head of his army to perform a solemn sacrifice on the Capitoline Hill. The lustration was apparently the second exception.[225]

It is not known where this procession ended; one can only speculate. Perhaps – since the ceremony was dedicated to Mars – it proceeded to the *sacrarium Martis* in the *Regia*. It was only after the construction of the temple of Mars Ultor in the *Forum Augusti* that the first *princeps* ordered the censors finishing their term of office to drive a nail there.[226] It can therefore be assumed that the purifying ceremony henceforth ended in this temple.

The proper conduct of lustration guaranteed the state's prosperity until the next ceremony. The phraseological compound *lustrum felix* was used to describe this situation.

There is, for example, a surviving reference to Cato's speech *De lustri sui felicitate*.[227]

> Eumen., *Paneg.* 13: *Praeclara fertur Catonis oratio de lustri sui felicitate. Iam tunc enim in illa vetere republica, ad censorum laudem pertinebat si lustrum felix condidissent, si horrea messis implesset, si vindemia redundasset, si oliveta larga fluxissent.*
>
> *Cato's speech on the good fortune of his lustrum [term as censor] is celebrated as famous. For then already, in that ancient res publica, it was relevant to the esteem of censors whether they had concluded a fortunate lustrum, whether the harvest had filled the barns, whether the vintage had been in copious supply, whether the olive yards had given a great yield.*
>
> (Transl. G. Manuwald)

The author of the panegyric, in explaining the title of Cato's speech, mentioned that during the Republic, the censor was praised to have conducted an auspicious *lustrum* if the granaries were full and if there was an abundant vintage and harvest in the olive groves. It seems, therefore, that purely practical circumstances such as a rich harvest were associated with the concept of *felicitas lustri*. A crop failure was associated with an improperly offered sacrifice.

Perhaps initially, the augural doctrine allowed only a patrician censor to perform the purification sacrifice, since otherwise it would not have ensured prosperity.[228] This principle was probably only abandoned in 280 BC when lustration was first carried out by a plebeian.[229]

It is worth mentioning at this point Asellus' accusations against Scipio regarding the unsuccessful *lustrum*.[230] The lustration was performed by Scipio's colleague in office,[231] L. Mummius, who revoked the *nota* imposed by Scipio on Asellus. Scipio regarded Mummius' *intercessio* as detrimental to the state (*religiosa*).[232] The disruption of the balance with the world of the deities was believed to have caused the failure of the purification sacrifice.

The fact that the censor's action considered *religiosum* resulted in the lack of success of the *lustrum* is also evidenced by the information preserved in Festus.

> Fest. 366 L, s.v. *referri diem prodictam*: *Referri diem prodictam, id est anteferri, religiosum est, ut ait Veranius in eo, qui est auspiciorum de comitiis: idque exemplo conprobat L. Iuli et P. Licini censorum, qui id fecerint sine ullo decreto augurum, et ob id lustrum parum felix fuerit.*
>
> *It is sacrally forbidden to anticipate a fixed day, as Veranius says in his book on the auspices concerning the assemblies: and his proves it with an example of the censors Lucius Iulius and Paublius Licinius who did this without any decree of the augurs and because of that the lustrum was not fortunate.*
>
> (Transl. AT)

Festus quoted Veranius' opinion from his work *Liber auspiciorum de comitiis*, according to which it was considered *religiosum* to move a predetermined date without the decree of the augurs. This was done by the censors L. Iulius Caesar and P. Licinius Crassus in 89 BC, resulting in an unfortunate *lustrum* (*parum felix*).[233] A very interesting interpretation of this excerpt was presented by Jerzy Linderski.[234] According to the researcher, the censors performed the *lustrum* earlier than the announcement placed in the edict and therefore – according to augural law – on a *dies religiosus*, which resulted in the ceremony being *infelix*. Linderski went on to argue that this meant it was considered invalid because it was conducted in a defective manner (*vitio*). Due to the correlation between the occurrence of the legal effects of the census and the performance of the *lustrum*,[235] new censors had to be elected.

It seems that the *lustrum* recognised as *infelix* formally by the augurs was treated as invalid. On the other hand, private allegations related to the lack of success of the purification ceremony were not considered relevant.

6. Summary

Performing the census was the primary task of the censors. They began their activities by issuing an edict and a *lex censui censendo*. Then, on the appointed day after the auspices were taken, they would convene the citizens for a *contio* and begin the census. At the time of the census, slaves could report to the censors, usually at the behest of their owners, whom the censors included on the list of citizens, granting them their freedom. Unexcused absence from the census could result in conviction in a criminal trial, leading to loss of liberty and citizenship and being sold into slavery.

In addition to this, the censors also compiled a list of senators. They were granted this authority by the *plebiscitum Ovinium*, enacted around 318 BC.

When reviewing the equestrian centuries, the censors decided whether the knights were allowed to retain their horses. Taking back the mount could occur due to termination of service or as a punishment, which was additionally associated with loss of reputation.

The effect of the census depended on the lustration ceremony, which culminated the censors' activities and was performed by one of them, chosen by lot. This censor would convene the *comitia centuriata* and lead the armed citizens into the city. He would make a ceremonial sacrifice to Mars of a boar, a ram, and a bull, ensuring the prosperity of the state.

Notes

1 M. Torelli, *Typology & Structure of Roman Historical Reliefs*, Ann Arbor, MI 1982, pp. 8–20; C. Bur, *Le spectacle du cens. Relecture du déroulement de la professio sous la République romaine*, "Athenaeum" 2/2017, pp. 520–550. Cf. a different interpretation by D. Maschek, *Not Census But Deductio: Reconsidering the 'Ara of Domitius Ahenobarbus'*, "JRS" 108/2018, pp. 27–52, who identifies the relief as illustrating a *deductio coloniae*. See Figure 1 and 2.

2 Plut., *Mor.* 322 c; cf. G. Dumézil, *Essai sur la fonction sociale de Louange et de Blâme et sur les éléments indo-européens du cens romain*, Paris 1943, pp. 174–175.

3 This passage is included in the reconstruction of the *leges regiae* (Serv. Tull. 5, FIRA I). Cf. G. Franciosi (ed.), *'Leges regiae'*, Napoli 2003, pp. 160–161.

4 Cf. *Pap. Oxy.* XVII, 2088; Cic., *De rep.* 2,39; Dion. Hal., *Ant. Rom.* 4,19–22; Eutrop., *Brev.* 1,7.

5 Cf. M. Humm, *Servius Tullius et la censure: élaboration d'un modèle institutionnel*, [in:] *Invention des grands hommes de la Rome antique*, eds. M. Coudry, T. Späth, Paris 2001, pp. 221–247.

6 Cf. P. De Francisci, *Primordia civitatis*, Roma 1959, pp. 668 ff; H. Last, *The Servian Reforms*, "JRS" 35/1945, pp. 30–48; C. Nicolet, *The World of the Citizen in Republican Rome*, transl. P.S. Falla, Berkeley–Los Angeles, CA 1980, pp. 52–53; E. Lo Cascio, *Il census a Roma e la sua evoluzione dall'età "serviana" alla prima età imperiale*, "MEFRA" 113.2/2001, pp. 565–603.

7 Cf. Fest. 358 L, s.v. *rituales*.

8 Cf. G. Pieri, *L'histoire du cens jusqu'à la fin de la République romaine*, Paris 1968, p. 130.

9 The censors announced in the edict that they would issue a *lex censui censendo* (Liv. 43,14,5: *legem censui censendo dicturos esse*). Therefore, it should rather be inferred that the edict was an announcement that the censors would issue the lex *dicta*. Cf. A. Magdelain, *La loi à Rome. Histoire d'un concept*, Paris 1978, pp. 72–74.

10 Varr., *L.L.* 6,87 cited above. However, cf. A. Magdelain, *Recherches sur l''imperium'. La loi curiate et les auspices d'investiture*, Paris 1968, pp. 49–51 and J. Linderski, *The Augural Law*, "ANRW" II.16.3/1986, p. 2189, n. 157, who believe that these excerpts refer to the commencement of the *lustrum* ceremony. However, since the reference is made to an order to appear for those who wish to make declarations (*si quis pro se sive pro altero rationem dari volet*), it seems to refer to the beginning of the census. Cf. T. Mommsen, *Römisches Staatsrecht*[3], I, Graz 1952, p. 81, fn. 2.

11 The censors were entitled to perform *auspicia maxima*. Cf. Gell. 13,15,4; P. Catalano, *Contributi allo studio del diritto augurale*, Torino 1960, pp. 444–450.

12 Cic., *In Verr.* 1,18,54: I will not permit the settlement of this case to be delayed until after the departure from Rome of these multitudes that have simultaneously assembled, from all parts of Italy, to attend the elections, the games, and the census (transl. L.H.G. Greenwood).

13 Cf. *Tab. Her.* 142–156. On the *Tabula Heracleensis* cf. C. Nicolet, M.H. Crawford, *'Tabula Heracleensis'*, [in:] *The Roman Statutes*, ed. M.H. Crawford, I, London 1996, pp. 355–391 with cited literature. Cf. also C. Nicolet, *Censeurs et publicains. Économie et fiscalité dans la Rome antique*, Paris 2000, pp. 202–208; J.F. Rodríguez Neila, *Cuestiones en torno a la censura municipal romana*, "Gerion" 4/1986, pp. 61–99; D. Kremer, *Il censo nelle colonie latine prima della guerra sociale*, [in:] *Gli statuti municipali*, eds. L. Capogrossi Colognesi, E. Gabba, Pavia 2006, pp. 627–645; G. Greco, *Census. Profili storico-giuridici delle attività di censimento a Roma*, Torino 2022, pp. 153 ff.

14 *Tab. Her.* 148–156: He shall enter all this on the public records of his municipality. He shall dispatch these registers to the censors at Rome by means of the envoys chosen for this purpose by the majority vote of the Senate when this matter is voted. He shall provide that the census shall be completed and that the envoys shall appear before the censors at Rome and shall deliver the registers of the respective municipalities, colonies, or prefectures more than sixty days before the census at Rome is completed. This censor, or whatever other magistrate conducts the census of the people in the next five days after the arrival of the envoys, shall accept without fraudulent intent the registers of the census from them. From these registers of the communities, he shall provide that the entries shall be copied in the public records and that such records shall be filed in the same place where are filed the other public records containing the census of the people (transl. A.C. Johnson, P.R. Coleman-Norton, F.C. Bourne).

15 For the *pater familias* who registered a son, the term *duicensus* was introduced. Cf. Fest. (Paul.) 58 L., s.v. *duicensus*.

16 *Tabula Her.* 4–6. For the discussion on the transformation of the meaning of citizenship, see C. Ando, *Census, Censor, Citizenship. Republican Subjectivity in Advance of Monarchy*, [in:] *Citizenship in Antiquity*, eds. J. Filonik, C. Plastow, R. Zelnick-Abramovitz, London 2023, pp. 616–626.

17 Cic., *De leg.* 3,7: Censors shall make a list of the citizens, recording their ages, families, slaves, and other property (transl. C.W Keyes). Cf. E. De Ruggiero, *Dizionario epigrafico di antichità romane*, Roma 1900, s.v. censor.

18 Although the regulations contained in the *Tabula Heracleensis* appear to concern local censuses, they refer to general rules related to censuses.

19 Ulpian, in his work *De censibus* (D. 50,15,4 pr.), explained that under the *forma censualis* it was established that land had to be declared in a certain way at the time of the census. It was necessary to state the name of the land and whose property it was and where it was located, the names of the two nearest neighbours, as well as to report what crops would be grown on the land in the next ten years, what the acreage of the land was, what kind of vegetation was on it (vines, olive trees, meadows, pastures, forests). All of this should be valued by the citizen coming forward for the census. In the same work, Ulpian also gave rules for reporting slaves (D. 50,15,4,5). It can probably be assumed that the norms contained in the *forma censualis* discussed by Ulpian were largely a repetition of the rules of the Republican period. Only where the rules changed, e.g. with regard to the collection of taxes, the rules for the compilation of censuses also had to be adjusted.

20 Cf. Gell. 4,20,2–6 discussed below.

21 Cf. A. Magdelain, *La loi à Rome...*, pp. 72–74.

22 Fest. 50 L., s.v. *Censui censendo*: We call lands "liable for inclusion in the census" which can be bought and sold according to civil law (transl. S.T. Roselaar); Cic., *Pro Flacc.* 79: I ask these questions: are those estates capable of being returned in the census, do they admit of a legal right, are they in your formal possession or not, can they be entered as surety at the treasury or with the censor? (transl. C. Macdonald).

23 *Schol. Bob.* 102 St.: Property that was not legally owned could not be pledged to the treasury or to the censors. And the reason for pledging was that those who leased the

collection of taxes, or who stood surety for the purchaser (manceps), obliged their estates as a pledge to the republic until the contractors (redemptores) paid all the money due because of the taxes leased (transl. AT).

24 Cf. C. Bur, *Le spectacle du cens...*, pp. 531 ff.

25 Cf. C. Gizewski, *Incensus*, [in:] *Brill's New Pauly. Encyclopedia of the Ancient World. Antiquity*, VI, eds. H. Schneider, M. Landfester, H. Cancik, Leiden–Boston, MA 2005, p. 753; A. Tarwacka, *The Consequences of Avoiding Census in Roman Law*, "Revista General de Derecho Romano" 21/2013, s. 1–16, http://www.iustel.com/v2/revistas/detalle_revista.asp?id_noticia=414019&d=1.

26 Cf. F. Desserteaux, *Études sur la formation historique de la 'capitis deminutio'*, I, Dijon 1919, pp. 339–340.

27 Dion. Hal., *Ant. Rom.* 4,15,6. This passage is included in the reconstruction of the *leges regiae* (Serv. Tull. 2, FIRA I). Cf. G. Franciosi (ed.), *op. cit.*, pp. 163–164.

28 Cf. T.R.S. Broughton, *The Magistrates of the Roman Republic*, I, Atlanta, GA 1951 (reprint 1986), p. 9.

29 Dion. Hal., *Ant. Rom.* 5,75,3.

30 Liv. 1,44,1: Upon the completion of the census, which had been expedited by fear of a law that threatened with death and imprisonment those who failed to register, Servius issued a proclamation calling on all Roman citizens, both horse and foot, to assemble at daybreak, each in his own century, in the Campus Martius (transl. B.O. Foster). Cf. G. Franciosi (ed.), *op. cit.*, p. 185.

31 Cic., *Pro Caec.* 99–100: So too the state, by selling a man who has evaded military service, does not take away his freedom but decrees that one who has refused to face danger for his freedom's sake is not a free man. By selling a man who has evaded the census, the state decrees that, whereas those who have been slaves in the normal way gain their freedom by being included in the census, one who has refused to be included in it although free, has of his own accord repudiated his freedom. Now if these are the special grounds on which citizenship and liberty can be lost, do those who quote them fail to understand that our forefathers, by intending that loss of liberty should be possible in these circumstances, intended that it should be impossible in any others? For as they have produced these instances from our law, I wish they would also produce instances in which people have been deprived of their citizenship or their liberty by any statute or proposal (transl. H. Grose Hodge). Cf. L. Fotheringham, *Repetition and Unity in a Civil Law Speech: The 'Pro Caecina'*, [in:] *Cicero the Advocate*, eds. J. Powell, J. Paterson, Oxford 2004, pp. 253–276.

32 The case of selling an *indelectus*, i.e. an evader of military service, and his property was also described by Valerius Maximus (6,3,4). Suetonius (*Aug.* 24), on the other hand, reported that Augustus ordered the sale of an equestrian and his property when the knight cut off his sons' thumbs to render them unfit for military service. The position of the *indelectus* was similar to that of the *incensus*, for he too was subject to *capitis deminutio maxima*.

33 Cf. A. Tarwacka, *Appunti su requisiti, percorso ed effetti della 'manumissio censu'*, "Diritto@Storia" 13/2015, http://www.dirittoestoria.it/13/tradizione-romana/Tarwacka-Requisiti-percorso-effetti-manumissio-censu.htm#_ftn1.

34 Cf. F. Desserteaux, *op. cit.*, I, pp. 113–116.

35 Cf. the *excerpts* from *Responsa* Papiniana analysed below, as well as *Tituli ex corpore Ulpiani*. Cf. F. Desserteaux, *op. cit.*, I, p. 116.

36 On the subject of sc. Claudianum cf. G. Poma, *Provvedimenti legislativi e attività censoria di Claudio verso gli schiavi e i liberti*, "Rivista storica dell' antichità" 12/1982, pp. 166–174; C. Masi Doria, *In Margine a PS. 2,21A,11*, [in:] *Au-delà des fontierès. Mélanges de droit romain offers à Witold Wołodkiewicz*, I, eds. M. Zabłocka, J. Krzynówek, J. Urbanik. Z. Służewska, Warsaw 2000, pp. 507–519; Eadem, *La denuntiatio nel senatusconsultum Claudianum: i legittimati e la struttura del procedimento,*

[in:] *Parti e giudici nel processo: dai diritti antichi all'attualità*, eds. C. Cascione. E. Germino, C. Masi Doria, Napoli 2006, pp. 125–156; A. Kacprzak, *The Senatusconsultum Claudianum and the Mysterious Lex Concerning the Status of Children Born to Free Women Cohabiting with Slaves (G. 1,86)*, "Zeszyty Prawnicze" 20.4/2020, pp. 53–89.

37 E. Volterra, *Sull' 'incensus' in diritto romano*, [in:] E. Volterra, *Scritti giuridici*, II, Napoli 1991, p. 308, noted the lack of mention of censors in the Ulpian text. However, he misinterpreted the word *aliquis*, which refers to *incensus* (this should be translated as 'someone who did not submit to the censor') and not to the person who sold.

38 Tab. 3,1–6 (FIRA I).

39 Gell. 20,1,46–47 (=Tab. 3,5): In the meantime the right of compromising the case was allowed, and if they did not compromise it, debtors were confined for sixty days. During that time on three successive market-days they were brought before the praetor and the amount of the judgment against them was announced. But on the third-day they were capitally condemned or sent across the Tiber to be sold abroad (transl. J.C. Rolfe).

40 The office of praetor did not come into existence until 367 BC by virtue of a compromise reached within the *leges Liciniae Sextiae*. In the earlier period, the jurisdictional functions were performed by the consuls, who, however, were still then also called *praetores* (cf. Cic., *De leg.* 3,8). Gellius may therefore have had this former name of consuls in mind, or he may have been writing about officials who were commonly associated with the exercise of jurisdiction.

41 Cf. J. Zabłocki, *Procedura esecutiva nella legge delle XII Tavole*, [in:] *Studi in onore di Antonino Metro*, ed. C. Russo Ruggeri, VI, Milano 2010, pp. 513–534.

42 In this sense, the phrase *capite poenas* in combination with the verb was used, for example, by Sallustius (*Iug.* 69), Tacitus (*Ann.* 12,19), Seneca (*Ag.* 1001). Cf. E. Levy, *Die römische Kapitalstrafe*, [in:] E. Levy, *Gesamelte Schriften*, II, Köln-Graz 1963, pp. 327–332.

43 The phrase *poena capitis* was used in this sense by Cicero (*De dom.* 45). Cf. G. Mac Cormack, '*Partes secanto*', "TR" 36/1968, pp. 511–515. The institution of *capitis deminutio* is linked with the phrase *capite census* by H. Kornhardt, '*Postliminium' in republikanischer Zeit*, "SDHI" 19/1953, pp. 21–23, considering that it refers to the loss of status resulting from a change of place in the census lists or deletion from them. Cf. F. Desserteaux, *op. cit*, I, pp. 355–359.

44 This follows from Gell. 20,1,48.

45 Cf. G. Rotondi, *'Leges publicae populi Romani'. Elenco cronologico con una introduzione sull'attività legislativa dei comizi romani*, Milano 1912, pp. 230–231.

46 Cf. I. Pfaff, '*Incensus*', "RE" IX.2/1916, pp. 1245–1246. This hypothesis was considered plausible by B. Santalucia, *Alle origini del processo penale romano*, "Iura" 35/1984, p. 50, fn. 8; Idem, *Processo penale*, [in:] B. Santalucia, *Studi di diritto penale romano*, Roma 1994, p. 147, fn. 8.

47 On the sacer extensively L. Garofalo, *Sulla condizione di 'homo sacer' in età arcaica*, [in:] L. Garofalo, *Studi sulla sacertà*, Padova 2005, pp. 11–50; R. Fiori, *'Homo sacer'. Dinamica politico-costituzionale di una sanzione giuridico-religiosa*, Napoli 1996, passim.

48 Cf. L. Garofalo, *op. cit.*, p. 22, fn. 38.

49 Cf. A. Burdese, *Manuale di diritto pubblico romano*[3], Torino 2005, pp. 18–20.

50 Servius Tullius is credited with the norm prescribing that a son, or more broadly a descendant, who would strike his father (ascendant) be considered *sacer*– Fest. 260 L. s.v. *plorare* (*leges regiae* Serv. Tull. 6; cf. G. Franciosi (ed.), *op. cit.*, p. 184. However, there is an assumption that Servius Tullius only extended this norm to the daughter-in-law, and that Festus would therefore have erroneously attributed the rules to the kings. Cf. R. Fiori, *op. cit.*, pp. 187–190.

51 Cf. T. Mommsen, *Römisches Staatsrecht…*, II.1, p. 367; see, however, below.
52 Cf. O. Lenel, *Palingenesia iuris civilis*, Graz 1960, I, col. 926, no. 624. The passage was placed in Book IX of the *Responsa* under the title *De manumissionibus et liberali causa*.
53 Cf. L. Wenger, *Die Quellen des römischen Rechts*, Wien 1953, pp. 513–514.
54 The phrase *crimen inferre* is a technical term used to describe the accusatory action of bringing a charge. Cf. *Rhet. Her.* 4,47: Accusatoris officium est inferre crimina [The duty of the prosecutor is to bring the charges – transl. H. Caplan].
55 L. Gagliardi, *I censimenti romani della tarda repubblica e il caso dei 'proletarii'*, "BIDR" 117/2023, pp. 81–89, rightly argues that in Republican times the *proletarii* had absolutely no reason to appear for the census since they had no property to declare and were not conscripted into the army. But I would still think that the only way they could be excused was by a decision of the censors themselves, expressed in the edict. This does not exclude the existence of a punishment for *incensi.*
56 The last *lustrum* took place in 74 AD during the reign of Vespasian. Cf. Censorin, *De die nat.* 14.
57 The *coërcitio* of the censors does not appear to have included the infliction of flogging. Therefore, it must be thought that, at the time of their appointment at the latest, this additional penal ailment had fallen out of use.
58 Cf. T. Mommsen, *Römisches Staatsrecht…*, II.1, p. 367. This was the so-called *sectio bonorum*; cf. G. Scherillo, *Appunti sulla 'sectio bonorum'*, "Iura" 4/1953, pp. 197–205; M. García Morcillo, *Staging Power and Authority at Roman Auctions*, "Ancient Society" 38/2008, p. 155; P. Buongiorno, *'Sectio', 'Sectores', 'Interdictum sectorium': origini e disciplina in epoca repubblicana*, [in:] *I beni di interesse pubblico nell'esperienza giuridica romana*, ed. L. Garofalo. Napoli 2016, pp. 635-671. The purchaser of the property obtained Quiritarian ownership, as well as protection in the form of *interdictum sectorium*. Cf. G. 4,146.
59 Zonar. 7,19: If any persons did not have their property and themselves registered in the census lists, the censors sold the property and the consuls the men (transl. E. Cary).
60 E. Hoffmann, *Das Gesetz der Zwölf-Tafeln von der Forcten und Sanaten*, "Zeitschrift für die österreichischen Gymnasien" 17/1866, pp. 600–601. cf. C.S. Tomulescu, *Quelques petites études de droit romain*, "BIDR" 82/1979, s. 95–102.
61 So also O. Robleda, *Il diritto degli schiavi nella Roma antica*, Roma 1976, p. 30.
62 E. Volterra, *Sull' 'incensus'…*, pp. 301 ff.
63 Cic., *De or.* 1,181: the traditional rule was that a man sold by his father or by the people, or delivered up by the pater patratus, had no right of return (ius postliminii) (transl. E.W Sutton, H. Rackham, adapted).
64 Cf. D. 50,7,18 (Pomp. 37 *ad Q. Muc.*); G. Crifò, *Sul caso di C. Ostilio Mancino*, [in:] *Studies in Roman Law in Memory of A. Arthur Schiller*, eds. R.S. Bagnall, W.V. Harris, New York 1986, pp. 19–32; A. Maffi, *Ricerche sul 'postliminium'*, Milano 1992, pp. 63–69; M.F. Cursi, *La struttura del 'postliminium' nella repubblica e nel principato,* Napoli 1996, pp. 57–73; J. Harries, *Cicero and the Jurists. From Citizen's Law to the Lawful State*, Bodmin 2006, pp. 144–148.
65 Cf. F. Desserteaux, *op. cit.*, I, p. 343; II, p. 403; M.F. Cursi, *op. cit.*, p. 70, fn. 105.
66 Cf. F. Desserteaux, *op. cit.*, II, pp. 67–69; O. Robleda, *Il diritto degli schiavi…*, p. 34.
67 Cf. K.W. Welwei, *Piraterie und Sklaverei in der frühen römischen Republik*, [in:] *Fünfzig Jahre Forschungen zur Antiken Sklaverei an der Mainzer Akademie 1950-2000. Miscellanea zum Iubiläum*, eds. H. Bellen, H. Heinen, Stuttgart 2001, p. 79. However, F. De Martino, *Intorno all' origine della schiavitù a Roma*, "Labeo" 20/1974, pp. 170–171 argues that *trans Tiberim* sales were only made when no buyer could be found among the Romans or Latins.
68 Cf. E. Volterra, *Manomissione e cittadinanza*, [in:] *Studi in onore di Ugo Enrico Paoli*, Firenze 1956, pp. 695–699. O. Robleda (*Il diritto degli schiavi…*, pp. 28–29) is of

the same opinion. He cites Cic., *Pro Caec.* 96: if once it is possible to take away citizenship it is impossible to preserve liberty (transl. H. Grose Hodge). However, this excerpt, completely out of context, does not constitute any evidence. Cicero argued that neither liberty nor citizenship could be taken away from a citizen by law. He went on to argue that allowing a statute to deprive a citizen of his citizenship would similarly allow liberty to be deprived by this means. There seems to be no convincing argument that the loss of citizenship while retaining liberty was not possible. Cf. E. Levy, *'Libertas' und 'civitas'*, [in:] E. Levy, *Gesamelte Schriften*, II, Köln-Graz 1963, pp. 3–24. On the other hand, one can agree that someone deprived of citizenship, and thus of the protection afforded by the community and its laws, could easily be taken as a slave. Cf. H. Kornhardt, *op. cit.*, pp. 21–23.

69 Cf. D. 50,7,18 (Pomp. 37 *ad Q. Muc.*).

70 G. Polo Toribio, *Algunas puntualizaciones entorno a la figura jurídica del incensus*, "RGDR" 12/2009, pp. 10–11; Eadem, *Manumissio. Libertas. Census. Civis. Incensus*, Madrid 2023, pp. 119 ff.

71 Cf. Cic., *Pro Arch.* 11. In addition, it should be noted that in the period of the decline of the Republic, it was not necessary to appear in person at the time of the census, as deplored by Scipio Aemilianus (Gell. 5,19,16). Previously, however, citizens from the provinces were summoned at the time of the census (cf. Vell. 2,7,7). Cf. R. Pfeilschifter, *Die Brüchigkeit der Rituale. Bemerkungen zum Niedergang der römischen Zensur*, "Klio" 84.2/2002, pp. 450–452.

72 Cf. FIRA I, pp. 163–165; M.H. Crawford, R.G. Coleman, (H. Galsterer), *'Lex Osca Tabulae Bantinae'*, [in:] *The Roman Statutes*, ed. M.H. Crawford, I, London 1996, pp. 271–292 with cited literature.

73 *Lex Osca tabulae Bantinae* 4,10: But if anyone shall with wrongful deceit not have come to the census and is convicted of that, he himself should be flogged in the comitium, by virtue of the magistracy in the presence of the people, without wrongful deceit (of the magistrate) and the whole of his estate is to be sold and the whole of his property, which shall have been his and which shall not have been listed, is to be (made) public (transl. M.H. Crawford).

74 Cf. D. Kremer, *op. cit.*, p. 644.

75 Fest. 77 L., s.v. *famuli*: The word 'famulus' comes from the Oscans, among whom a slave was called 'famel', hence 'familia' (transl. AT).

76 Cic., *De leg.* 3,7.

77 The term *familia* indeed had many meanings: it could refer to both persons and things. In the Law of the Twelve Tables, it was used both to refer to persons under the authority of a single familial superior and to property. This multiplicity of meanings was emphasised by Ulpian – an excerpt concerning this issue from the 46th book of his commentary on the edict is given in D. 50,16,195,1. In the excerpt in question, it certainly does not refer to free subjects of authority due to the presence of the term *suboles* meaning offspring in its vicinity. According to O. Karlowa, *Römische Rechtsgeschichte. I. Staatsrecht und Rechtsquellen*, Leipzig 1885, p. 237, the term *familia* here means *res mancipi*, i.e. slaves but also land.

78 Cf. D. 50,16,222 (Hermogen. 2 *iuris epit.*).

79 Tab. 9,2 based on Cic., *De leg.* 3,44.

80 Cf. T.R.S. Broughton, *op. cit.*, II, p. 101.

81 Cf. M. Bartošek, *Variazioni metodologiche su tema ciceroniano ('Lex Voconia', 'ius novum', retroattività)*, [in:] *Studi in onore di Gaetano Scherillo*, ed. G. Grosso, II, Milano 1972, pp. 648–679.

82 G. Rotondi, *op. cit.*, pp. 283–284.

83 Cf. Cic., *In Verr.* 2,1,104–113.

84 Cicero also argued that persons who were not registered were also not prohibited from establishing legates in excess of the heir's share of the estate. Cic., *In Verr.* 2,1,110:

What of his bequeathing away more than comes to the heir or heirs? That by the Voconian law is legal for a person not registered at a census: why do you not guard against this action, since it belongs to the same class? (transl. L.H.G. Greenwood).

85 S. Cassisi, *L'editto di Verre e la 'lex Voconia'*, "Annali del Seminario Guiridico Università di Catania" 3/1948–1949, pp. 490–505.

86 C. Nicolet, *The World of the Citizen...*, p. 72.

87 S. Dixon, *Breaking the Law to Do the Right Thing: The Gradual Erosion of the Voconian Law in Ancient Rome*, "Adelaide Law Review" 9/1985, pp. 519–534. However, this researcher, contrary to the source accounts, attributes Verres' decisions to the period of his governorship in Sicily and not to the praetorship. Cf. P. Cañas Navarro, *Aspectos jurídicos del censo romano (II)*, "Revista de Derecho UNED", 4/2009, p. 119.

88 Cf. Cic., *Pro Caec.* 99–100 cited above.

89 On Sulla's attitude to censorship, see below.

90 Cic., *Pro Arch.* 11.

91 Cf. E. Weiss, *'Manumissio'*, "RE" 14.2/1930, pp. 1366–1377; W.W. Buckland, *The Roman Law of Slavery. The Condition of the Slave in Private Law from Augustus to Justinian*, Cambridge 1908, p. 437 ff.; A.M. Duff, *Freedmen in the Early Roman Empire*, Cambridge 1958, p. 23 ff.; S. Treggiari, *Roman Freedmen during the Late Republic*, Oxford 1969 (reprint London 2000), p. 20 ss.; O. Robleda, *Il diritto degli schiavi...*, p. 105 ff.; A. Watson, *The Law of Persons in the Later Roman Republic*, Oxford 1967, p. 185 ff.; Idem, *Roman Slave Law*, Baltimore, MD–London 1987, p. 24 ff.; C. Masi Doria, *'Civitas, operae, obsequium'. Tre studi sulla codizione giuridica dei liberti*, Napoli 1999, p. 1 ff.; P. López Barja de Quiroga, *Historia de la manumisión en Roma. De los orígenes a los Severos*, Madrid 2007, pp. 16–37. Formal manumission resulted in the granting of Roman citizenship. This caused surprise among foreigners. Cf. F. Reduzzi Merola, *'Servo parere'. Studi sulla condizione degli schiavi vicari e dei sottoposti a schiavi nelle esperienze greca e romana*, Napoli 1990, pp. 37–38; C. Masi Doria, *'Civitas, operae, obsequium'...*, pp. 1–4.

92 Cic., *Top.* 10: Sometimes there is an enumeration of parts, and this is handled in the following manner: So-and-So is not a free man unless he has been set free by entry in the census roll, or by touching with the rod, or by will. None of these conditions has been fulfilled, therefore he is not free (transl. H.M. Hubbell).

93 Cf. FD 5: In the past, there was only one freedom, and manumission was done by rod (vindicta) or by will or by census, and the manumitted had the right to Roman citizenship: this was called just manumission (transl. AT).

94 Cf. G. Rotondi, *op. cit.*, pp. 455–456; see also W.W. Buckland, *op. cit.*, p. 542. It is worth adding that the *manumissio censu* did not apply to the limitation of the number of freed slaves under the *lex Fufia Caninia*– G. 1,44: Nor does the statute apply to any but testamentary manumission, so that by the form of vindicta or inscription on the censor's register, or by attestation of friends, a proprietor of slaves may manumit his whole household, provided that there is no other let or hindrance to impede their manumission (transl. E. Poste).

95 Cf. FD 17, analysed below.

96 Dion. Hal., *Ant. Rom.* 4,22 = *Leg. reg.* Serv. Tull. 3; G. Franciosi (ed.), *op. cit.*, pp. 159–160; cf. G. Poma, *Dionigi d'Alicarnasso e la cittadinanza romana*, "MEFRA" 101.1/1989, pp. 192–197.

97 Cf A. Watson, *Roman Slave Law*, Baltimore–London 1987, p. 24.

98 E. Volterra, *Manomissione e cittadinanza...*, pp. 695–699 argues that it was unthinkable in the ancient world for a free person to have no citizenship, and thus argues that it was impossible to confer freedom itself. See, however, H. Chantraine, *Zur Entstehung der Freilassung mit Bürgerrechtserwerb in Rom*, "ANRW" I.2/1972, pp. 59–63, who points out that the Roman custom of granting citizenship to freedmen was seen as peculiar. This author also rightly points out that the Romans did not know of such

categories of population as, for example, the metics, who did not have citizenship but were nevertheless a part, however impaired, of society. Cf. also T. Mommsen, *Römisches Staatsrecht*..., III, pp. 58–64, who believes that initially only patricians had citizenship, which neither clients nor plebeians had. M. Kaser, *Die Anfänge der 'manumissio' und das fiduziarisch gebundene Eigentum*, "ZSS" 61/1941, pp. 153–186, considers that only the *manumissio testamento* conferred client status, the others citizenship. Cf. C. Masi Doria, *'Civitas, operae, obsequium'*..., pp. 9–15.

99 Cf. C. Cosentini, *Studi sui liberti*, I, Catania 1948, p. 15.

100 CIL VI,40942 = CIL VI,31604 = AE 1891.00124: Q(uintus) Caec[ilius L(uci) f(ilius) Metellus] / [Numidicus] / [// complures civitates in] / [pote]state[m accepit de rege Iugurtha triumphavit] / [ce]nsor L(ucium) Eq[uitium qui se Ti(beri) Gracchi filium mentiebatur] / [in cen]s[um non recepit. [Quintus Caecilius, son of Lucius Metellus Numidicus, took power over many societies, he triumphed over King Jughurta; as censor, he refused to enrol Lucius Equitius during the census, who lied that he was the son of Tiberius Gracchus - transl. AT].

101 Ulp. 1,8: Those manumitted by the census are such as formerly, at the Lustral Census of Rome, by the order of their masters, offered themselves to be enrolled among Roman citizens (transl. S.P. Scott).

102 Cf. Boëth, *Ad Cic. Top.* 1,2,10: If someone gave his name in the census with the knowledge or on the orders of his owner, he became a Roman citizen and was freed from the bonds of slavery (transl. AT). P. López Barja de Quiroga, *Historia*..., p. 32, interprets the phrase *olim* as a post-classical change. According to him, back in Ulpian times the *manumissio censu* was still an institution in use.

103 Cicero wrote about *voluntas domini* (*De or.* 1,40,183) and Theophilus about *κέλευσις* (1,5,4).

104 D. Daube, *Two Early Patterns of Manumission*, "JRS" 36/1946, pp. 63–66.

105 Differently D. Daube, *Two Early Patterns*..., pp. 66–68. Cf. also S. Treggiari, *Roman Freedmen*..., p. 27, who argues that an owner living outside Rome could send a slave himself to the census. However, this reasoning seems to be flawed, since the owner, after all, also had to appear before the censors at the time of the census.

106 Liv. 41,9,9–12: Then Gaius Claudius, with the authorization of the senate, proposed a law concerning the allies, and issued a proclamation to the effect that all allies of the Latin confederacy, in the event that they themselves or their ancestors had been registered among the allies of the Latin confederacy in the censorship of Marcus Claudius and Titus Quinctius or thereafter, should all return, each to his own state, before the Kalends of November. The investigation of those who should not have returned in this fashion was decreed to Lucius Mummius the praetor. To this law and proclamation of the consul a decree of the senate was added, that a dictator, consul, interrex, censor, or praetor, who was at the time in office or should henceforth be in office, before any one of whom a slave was brought for manumission and for the assertion of his claim to freedom, should require that an oath be given that the person who was manumitting the slave was not manumitting him for the purpose of changing his citizenship; in any case in which this oath was not taken, they decreed that the manumission should not take place (transl. E.T. Sage, E.C. Schlesinger).

107 Cf. L. Gagliardi, *'Romam commigrare'. I Romani, I Latini e l'immigrazione*, Milano 2023, pp. 83–176.

108 Cf. P. Frezza, *Note esegetiche di diritto pubblico romano*, [in:] *Studi in onore di Pietro De Francisci*, I, Milano 1956, pp. 204–206.

109 F. Cancelli, *Studi sui censores e sull' arbitratus della lex contractus*, Milano 1960, pp. 44–46 considered that this passage proves that the censors could perform *vindicatio in libertatem*, since he is of the opinion that Livy meant only *manumissio vindicta.* It seems to me that such a view is unwarranted, since Livy's text did not necessarily refer to only one type of manumission.

110 Cf. W.W. Buckland, *op. cit.*, p. 440; H. Last, *op. cit.*, pp. 37–38. A remarkably interesting case is highlighted by P. López Barja de Quiroga, *La fundación de Carteya y la 'manumissio cens'*, "Latomus" 56.1/1997, pp. 83–93, who, interpreting the passage in Liv. 43,3,1–4, concluded that the sons of Roman soldiers and Spaniards, with whom there was no *conubium*, having performed the act of *deditio*, were given the opportunity to found a Latin colony, and the governor of the province was entrusted with the task of taking a census, during which he could accept as colonists those whom he manumitted *censu* after they had performed a *professio*. The role of *iussum domini* was fulfilled in this case by a resolution of the Senate. Although the freedmen were not slaves but *dediticii*, the case seems to confirm the overriding role of the decision of the official, who probably had the right to refuse manumission.

111 G. 1,138. cf. S. Solazzi, *'Manumissio ex mancipatione'*, [in:] S. Solazzi, *Scritti di diritto romano*, III, Napoli 1960, pp. 199–218. Such manumission may also have been aimed at achieving an emancipation effect.

112 T. Mommsen, *Römisches Staatsrecht*..., III, pp. 58–59; Cf. C. Cosentini, *Studi sui liberti*..., I, pp. 15–16; P. Frezza, *op. cit.*, p. 206; G. Greco, *op. cit.*, p. 130.

113 Cf. G. Polo Toribio, *La pretendida prueba material en la defensa del poeta Arquías*, "Diritto@Storia" 8/2009, http://www.dirittoestoria.it/8/Tradizione-Romana/PoloToribio-Defensa-poeta-Arquias.htm.

114 Cf. *Schol. Bob.* 177 St.

115 Cf. F. De Visscher, *De l'acquisition du droit de cité romaine par l'affranchissement*, "SDHI" 12/1946, p. 72.

116 Cf. G. Pieri, *op. cit.*, pp. 41–42.

117 J.F. Gardner, *Women in Roman Society and Law*, London 1986 (reprint 1995), p. 222.

118 Cf. S. Treggiari, *Roman Freedmen*..., p. 25.

119 FIRA II.

120 Cf. P. Jörs, *'Dositheanum fragmentum'*, "RE" 10/ 1905, pp. 1603–1605; cf. L. Wenger, *op. cit.*, pp. 528–529; A.M. Honoré, *The 'Fragmentum Dositheanum'*, "RIDA" 12/1965, s. 301–323.

121 A.M. Honoré, *op. cit.*, pp. 301–323.

122 Gaius' *regulae* are reconstructed by O. Lenel, *Palingenesia*..., col. 251.

123 Cf. Varr., *L.L.* 6,11.

124 *Lustrum* did not take place in 459 and 214 BC. Cf. Liv. 3,22; 24,43; J.V. Melničuk, *'Lustrum' en su aspecto marcial*, "Diritto@Storia" 4/2005, http://www.dirittoestoria.it/4/Tradizione-Romana/Melniciuk-Lustrum.htm.

125 On the meaning of the phrase *quibus in senatu sententiam dicere licet* cf. F.X. Ryan, *Rank and Participation in the Republican Senate*, Stuttgart 1998, pp. 72–87.

126 This aspect is emphasised by M. Lemosse, *L'affranchisement par le* cens, "RHD" 27/1949, pp. 178–179, cf. R. Danieli, *Contributi alla storia delle manomissioni romane*, Milano 1953, p. 52.

127 G. 1,11: The freeborn are free by birth; freedmen by manumission from legal slavery (transl. E. Poste). The *iusta servitus* happened where a slave was made by someone who had fallen into slavery to enemies, was born of a slave mother (these ways derived from the *ius gentium*) or, if he was over 20 years old, allowed himself to be sold in order to deceive the buyer and profit from it (slavery *iure civili*). Cf. D. 1,5,5,1 (Marc. 1 *inst.*). See also A. Watson, *The Law of Persons*..., p. 162; M.F. Cursi, *'Captivitas' e 'capitis deminutio'. La posizione del 'servus hostium' tra 'ius civile' e 'ius gentium'*, [in:] *'Iuris vincula'. Studi in onore di Mario Talamanca*, II, Napoli 2001, pp. 300–301. Differently E. Volterra, *Manomissione e cittadinanza*..., pp. 708–709.

128 Cf. A. Tarwacka, *Romans and Pirates. Legal Perspective*, Warszawa 2009, pp. 91–92.

129 A.M. Duff, *op. cit.*, pp. 24–25 expresses the belief that by the period of the Principate *manumissio censu* was no longer in use and that mentions of it in the works of jurists had no reference to reality.

130 Cf. Liv. 1,43. Cicero (*De rep.* 2,20), however, attributed the organisation of the horsemen's centuries to Tarquin the Elder. On the subject of the *equites*, cf. F. De Martino, *Sulla storia dell'equitatus romano*, [in:] F. De Martino, *Diritto, economia e società nel mondo romano. II. Diritto pubblico*, Napoli 1996, pp. 281–298.

131 There were also *equites equo privato*, who bought the horses themselves; cf. H. Hill, *Livy's Account of the 'Equites'*, "CP" 25.3/1930, pp. 244–249. On the formation of the *equester ordo* cf. M.I. Henderson, *The Establishment of the 'Equester Ordo'*, "JRS" 53/1963, s. 51–62.

132 Liv. 1,43,9: For the purchase of horses, they were allowed 10,000 asses each from the state treasury, and for the maintenance of these horses unmarried women were designated, who had to pay 2,000 asses each, every year (transl. B.O. Foster). Varro (*L.L.* 8,71), on the other hand, gave the following price: *et non equum publicum mille assarium esse, sed mille assariorum* [a cavalryman's horse is worth not a thousand assariumc 'of assarii,' but a thousand assariorum – transl. R.G. Kent]. Presumably, therefore, it is a thousand asses. An increase of this amount was requested in the Senate by Cato (Prisc. GL 2,318–319): Cato [says] in the speech by which he advised in the Senate that there should be more allowances for purchasing horses: "Now I believe that there should be arranged the provision of no fewer than two thousand and two hundred allowances for purchasing horses." In the same [text]: "as for the allowances for purchasing horses arrangements having been made concerning two thousand" (transl. G. Manuwald). Cf. P. Fraccaro, *Ricerche storiche e letterarie sulla censura del 184/183 (M. Porcio Catone L. Valerio Flacco)*, [in:] P. Fraccaro, *Opuscula*, I, Pavia 1956, pp. 449–450.

133 G. 4,27: Pignoris capio was employed (…) by custom, in obligations connected with military service; for the soldier could distrain upon his paymaster for his pay, called aes militare; for money to buy a horse, called aes equestre; and for money to buy barley for his horse, called aes hordiarium (transl. E. Poste).

134 Cf. A. Carcaterra, *La 'pignoris capio' nel diritto pubblico romano*, " Ann. Bari" 5/1942, pp. 59–79; W. Kunkel, R. Wittmann, *Staatsordnung und Staatspraxis der römischen Republik. Zweiter Abschnitt. Die Magistratur*, München 1995, pp. 392–393.

135 The separation of the proper equestrian state probably occurred at the end of the third century BC. The equestrian census was 400,000 sesterces.

136 Val. Max. 2,2,9.

137 Cf. Liv. 9,46,15: It was Fabius too, so it is said, who instituted the parade of the knights on the fifteenth of July (transl. B.O. Foster). The date was the anniversary of the victory at Lake Regillus. Cf. Dion. Hal., *Ant. Rom.* 13,13.

138 Cf. Plut., *Pomp.* 22,5.

139 Cf. A. Giovannini, *Cheval public et ordre équestre à la fin de la République*, "Athenaeum" 98.2/2010, pp. 356–357.

140 Liv. 29,37,8: Census of equestrians began next; and both censors happened to have a public horse. When they came to the Pollia tribe, in which Livius was enrolled, and the herald hesitated in calling out the name of the censor himself... (transl. J.C. Yardley)

141 Cf. Val. Max. 4,1,10; cf. also Ovid., *Trist.* 2,1,541–542: I had published verse when thou wert censuring our sins and I passed thee so many times, a knight uncriticized (transl. A.L. Wheeler).

142 Cf. Gell. 6,22.

143 Cf. Liv. 29,37.

144 Cf. C. De Boor, *Fasti censorii*, Berolini 1873, p. 19; T.R.S. Broughton, *op. cit.*, I, pp. 445–446; J. Suolahti, *The Roman Censors…*, pp. 382–387.

145 Cf. ORF 8 XII, pp. 34–36; P. Fraccaro, *Ricerche…*, pp. 444–448; F. della Corte, *Catone Censore. La vita e la fortuna*, Torino 1949, p. 26; A.E. Astin, *Cato the Censor*, Oxford 1978, pp. 81–82; F. Zevi, *Catone e i cavalieri grassi. Il culto di Vulcano ad Ostia: una proposta di lettura storica*, "MEFRA" 121.2/2009, pp. 505–513.

146 Cato also took the horse from L. Scipio. Cf. Liv. 39,44,1; Plut., *Cat. Mai.* 18,1.
147 Plut., *Cat. Mai.* 9,6.
148 Serv., *In Verg. Aen.* 4,121: Cato [says]: "he cannot sit on a trembling horse" (transl. G. Manuwald).
149 Cf. below, Chapter V.
150 Plaut., *Rud.* 1273.
151 Cf. more extensively A. Tarwacka, *The Censors and Their Duties in the Comedies of Plautus*, "RGDR" 23/2014, http://www.iustel.com/v2/revistas/detalle_revista.asp?id_noticia=415488.
152 Placidus, p. 27 (ed. Deuerling): 'Censio' is a fine that the censor used to punish those who failed to appear when summoned (transl. AT).
153 Plut., *Pomp.* 22,4–6. cf. M.H. Crawford, *The Roman Republic*², Cambridge, MA 1992, pp. 200–202.
154 Cf. Cic., *De rep.* 4,2; C. Nicolet, *L'ordre équestre à l'époque républicaine*, I, Paris 1966, pp. 103–111.
155 Cf. P. Willems, *Le sénat de la république romaine*, I, 1878 (reprint Aalen 1968), pp. 155–157; T. Mommsen, *Römisches Staatsrecht*..., II.1, pp. 318–319; G. Rotondi, *op. cit.*, pp. 233–234; J. Suolahti, *The Roman Censors*..., p. 53; M.V. Giangrieco Pessi, *Dalla 'lex Aemilia' al plebiscito Ovinio: Problemi e riflessioni*, [in:] *Leggi e società nella repubblica romana*, ed. F. Serrao, II, Napoli 2000, pp. 332–338; C. Busacca, *Sulla datazione del 'plebiscitum Ovinium'*, [in:] Scritti per Alessandro Corbino, ed. I. Piro, I, Tricase 2016, pp. 429–452. Supporters of this thesis cite the text of Lydus (*De mag.* 1,43), who identified Appius Claudius as the first censor.
156 T.R.S. Broughton, *op. cit.*, I, pp. 158–159.
157 Diod. Sic. 20,36,5.
158 A very controversial thesis related to this information was presented by E. Ferenczy, *The Censorship of Appius Claudius Caecus*, "AAH" 15/1967, pp. 38–50. This researcher, namely, considered the *lectio* made by Appius Claudius as the first and only one carried out under the *plebiscitum Ovinium*. He based his thesis primarily on the absence of any mention of this plebiscite in sources other than Festus. In his view, the *lex Ovinia* allowed people from all social orders, including descendants of slaves, to be elected as senators, for which there was no social consensus. Consequently, the *nobilitas* refused to recognise *lex Ovinia* as binding. This reasoning seems doubtful. Firstly, it assumes *a priori* that the *lectio* of Appius Claudius was the first one. Ferenczy also made a comparison between the election of senators and the Athenian election of the *βουλή*. This led him into a trap, since Athenian law presupposed for these elections the principle of indirect democracy, blandly incompatible with the *lectio senatus*.
159 Appius Claudius' reform of the *tribus* was also controversial, with the censor distributing the freedmen to all *tribus* and admitting those citizens who had no land. Cf. Liv. 9,46; Diod. Sic. 20,36; P. De Francisci, *'Arcana imperii'*..., III.1, p. 89; E. Gintowt, *Le changement du caractère de la 'tribus' romaine, attribué à Appius Claudius Caecus*, "Eos" 43.1/1949, pp. 198–210; M. Humm, *Le Comitium du forum romain et la réforme des tribus d'Appius Claudius Caecus*, "MEFRA" 111.2/1999, pp. 625–694.
160 Cf. especially the comprehensive article by T.J. Cornell, *The 'Lex Ovinia' and the Emancipation of the Senate*, [in:] *The Roman Middle Republic. Politics, Religion and Historiography*, ed. C. Bruun, Rome 2000, pp. 69–89, who expressed the belief that *the lex Ovinia* was enacted between 342 and 318. In the older literature, this view was represented by L. Lange, *Römische Alterthümer*², Berlin 1863, II, pp. 313–314; Idem, *De plebiscitis Ovinio et Atinio Disputatio*, Lipsiae 1879 (reprint), pp. 3–5, who postpones the *terminus post quem* to 367 BC. Cf. also H. Beck, *Karriere und Hierarchie. Die römische Aristokratie und die Anfänge des 'cursus honorum' in der mittleren Republik*, Berlin 2005, p. 78.

161 Cf. H. Siber, *Die plebeischen Magistraturen bis zur 'lex Hortensia'*, Leipzig 1936, pp. 48–49; A. Momigliano, *An Interim Report on the Origins of Rome*, "JRS" 53/1963, p. 111.
162 Plin. Mai. 16,37; G. 1,3; Gell. 15,27,4; D. 1,2,2,8; I. 1,2,4; G. Rotondi, *op. cit.*, pp. 238–240.
163 Cf. Liv. 3,55,1–7; G. Rotondi, *op. cit.*, pp. 203–204.
164 Cf. Liv. 8,12,14–16; G. Rotondi, *op. cit.*, pp. 226–227.
165 Cf. App., *Bell. civ.* 1,59; A. Biscardi, *'Auctoritas patrum'. Problemi di storia del diritto pubblico romano*, Napoli 1987, pp. 75–90; J. Bleicken, *Das Volkstribunat der klassischen Republik*, München 1955, pp. 22–26; J. Zabłocki, *'Leges votatae' nelle assemblee popolari*, "Diritto@Storia 10/2011-2012 ; cf. also dissenting views: P. Willems, *Le sénat...*, I, p. 81 and, following him, F. Stella Maranca, *Il tribunato della plebe dalla 'lex Hortensia' alla 'lex Cornelia'*, Lanciano 1901 (reprint Napoli 1982), pp. 3–7 considered that *lex Publilia Philonis* required for plebiscites the prior consent of the Senate, as for laws. A. Guarino, *L' 'exaequatio legibus' dei 'plebisscita'*, [in:] *Festschrift Fritz Schulz*, eds. H. Niedermeyer, W. Flume, I, Weimar 1951, pp. 458–465 argues, on the other hand, that the *lex Publilia Philonis* recognised as valid only those plebiscites which were subsequently voted by the whole people at the *comitia centuriata*.
166 G.1,3: unde olim patricii dicebant plebiscitis se non teneri, [quia] <quae> sine auctoritate eorum facta essent; sed postea lex Hortensia lata est, qua cautum est, ut plebiscita universum populum tenerent: Itaque eo modo legibus exaequata sunt. [Whence in former times the patricians maintained that they were not bound by the plebiscites, as passed without their authority; but afterwards a statute called the lex Hortensia was enacted, which provided that the plebiscites should bind the people, and thus plebiscites were made co-ordinate with statutes (transl. E. Poste)].
167 Cf. T. Mommsen, *Römisches Staatsrecht...*, II.1, p. 418; K.-J. Hölkeskamp, *Die Entstehung der Nobilität*, Stuttgart 1987, pp. 142–143.
168 Cf. T.J. Cornell, *op. cit.*, pp. 70 ff.
169 Cf. C. Busacca, *Qualche riflessione sull'attribuzione della 'lectio senatus' ai censori*, [in:] *Scritti in onore di G. Silvestri*, ed. A. Ruggeri, I, Torino 2016, pp. 333–346.
170 Cf. J. Bleicken, *'Lex publica'. Gesetz und Recht in der römischen Republik*, Berlin 1975, p. 379.
171 Cf. W. Kunkel, R. Wittmann, *op. cit.*, p. 438.
172 P. Willems, *Le sénat...*, I, pp. 158 ff.
173 Cf. W. Kunkel, R. Wittmann, *op. cit.*, pp. 438–439.
174 T.J. Cornell, *op. cit.*, pp. 380–385.
175 F. De Martino, *Storia della costituzione romana*[2], II, Napoli 1973, pp. 185–189.
176 Liv. 23,23,3–6: After reading out the list of the old senate, Fabius first replaced deceased members with men who had held curule offices after the censorship of Lucius Aemilius and Gaius Flaminius but who had not yet been selected for the senate; and he prioritized them according to who had been elected first. He then chose those who had been aediles, plebeian tribunes, or quaestors and, after them, men who, while they had not gained magistracies, had spoils from the enemy affixed to their houses or had received the civic crown (transl. J.C. Yardley). Cf. A. Tarwacka, *Dictator senatui legendo. The Unusual Dictatorship of M. Fabius Buteo*, "Zeszyty Prawnicze" 13.1/2013, pp. 185–196; P. Buongiorno, *Sui fondamenti della dittatura di Marco Fabio Buteone (216 a.C.)*, [in:] *La dittatura romana*, ed. L. Garofalo, Napoli 2022, pp. 255–277.
177 Gellius also wrote about the plebiscitum Atinium, by virtue of which former plebeian tribunes were to be included in the Senate. Gell. 14,8,2: "For the tribunes of the commons also," says Capito, "had the right of convening the senate although before the bill of Atinius6 they were not senators" (transl. J.C. Rolfe). Cf. G. Rotondi, *op. cit.*, p. 330; W.J. Tatum, *The Plebiscitum Atinium Once More*, "Res Historica" 29/2010, pp. 189–208.

178 Cf. Val. Max. 2,2,1; J. Zabłocki, *Il segreto nel diritto romano,* [in:] *Scritti per Alessandro Corbino,* ed. I. Piro, VII, Tricase 2016, pp. 589–599.
179 Cf. e.g. Cic., *Tusc.* 5,10,28.
180 Cf. e.g. Cat., *De agr.* 143; D. 17,1,35 (Nerv. 5 *membr.*).
181 Cf. e.g. Plaut., *Curc.* 475.
182 G. Clemente, *When the Senators Became 'The Best',* [in:] *Institutions and Ideology in Republican Rome. Speech, Audience and Decision,* eds. H. van der Blom, C. Gray, C. Steel, Cambridge 2018, pp. 206–221.
183 Cf. F.X. Ryan, *Rank and Participation...,* pp. 151–156.
184 Cf. T.J. Cornell, *op. cit.,* pp. 80 ff.
185 Cf. G. Clemente, *When the Senators Became 'The Best'...,* p. 206.
186 Cic., *Pro Cluent.* 132.
187 In 317 and 311 it was Q. Aemilius Barbula; cf. T.R.S. Broughton, op. *cit.,* I, pp. 155 and 161. In 281 it was L. Aemilius Barbula; cf. T.R.S. Broughton, *op. cit.,* I, p. 190, and in 230 it was M. Aemilius Barbula; cf. T.R.S. Broughton, *op. cit.,* I, p. 226.
188 Cf. G. Vitucci, *Intorno a un nuovo frammento di 'elogium',* "Rivista di Filologia e di Istruzione Classica" 81/1953, pp. 43–61; F. Cássola, *Ancora sull' elogio di Brindisi,* "Labeo" 8.3/1962, pp. 307–316.
189 Cf. E. Gabba, *L'elogio di Brindisi,* "Athenaeum" 36.1–2/1958, pp. 90–105.
190 Cf. R. Develin, *Appius Claudius Caecus and the Brindisi 'elogium',* "Historia" 25/1976, pp. 484–487; J.D. *Muccigrosso, The Brindisi 'Elogium' and the Rejected 'lectio senatus' of Appius Claudius Caecus,* "Historia" 52.4/2003, pp. 496–501.
191 Cf. C. De Boor, *op. cit.,* p. 8; F. Münzer, *C. Maenius (9),* "RE" XIV.1/1928, pp. 152–155; T.R.S. Broughton, *op. cit.,* I, p. 155; J. Suolahti, *The Roman Censors...,* pp. 218–220; E. Reigadas Lavandero, *Censura y res publica: aportación constitucional y protagonismo político,* Madrid 2000, pp. 129–133.
192 Cf. T.R.S. Broughton, *op. cit.,* I, p. 138.
193 Cf. Liv. 8,13.
194 Cf. E. Lo Cascio, *Il census a Roma...,* p. 579.
195 T. Lenschau, *Hannibal,* "RE" VII,2/1912, pp. 2318–2351.
196 Cf. C.E. Jarcke, *Versuch einer Darstellung des censorischen Strafrechts der Römer: ein Beytrag zur Geschichte des Criminalrechts,* Bonn 1824, pp. 3–9, who concluded that even before the appointment of censors, the *regimen morum* was at the discretion of the consuls conducting the census. See also J.F. Keseberg, *De censoribus Romanorum commentatio,* Quedlinburg 1829, pp. 7–8, who argued that the *regimen morum* was at the discretion of the censors from the time of their appointment in 443 BC.
197 Cf. R.M. Ogilvie, *'Lustrum Condere',* "JRS" 51.1–2/1961, pp. 31–39; G. Pieri, *op. cit.,* pp. 77–82.
198 Cf. Cat., *De agr.* 141; Ovid., *Fast.* 1,669; on the *lustratio* of sheep cf. Ovid., *Fast.* 4,735–778.
199 Cf. Cic., *Ad Att.* 5,20,2; App., *Bell. civ.* 5,96.
200 Cf. O. Leuze, *Zur Geschichte der römischen Censur,* Halle 1912, pp. 71–79; R.M. Ogilvie, *op. cit.,* p. 31.
201 Varr., *L.L.* 6,87–88 cited above.
202 Serv., *In Verg. Aen.* 1,283.
203 Cf. Mag. et sac. p. R. exp. 41b, s.v. *censores.*
204 Varr., *L.L.* 6,87. See Chapter II.
205 Cf. J.V. Melničuk, *Некоторые аспекты римского сакрального ритуала 'lustrum',* "Ius Antiquum" 1(11)/2003, pp. 54–55. Cf. however Cic., *De or.* 2,268, who notes that the *lustrum* was carried out not by Scipio, but by his colleague L. Mummius.
206 Scipio was later accused of a *lustrum infelix* and this is probably why Varro quotes the original *precatio* formula. See below, Chapter III.

207 The animals were guided around the congregation three times. Cf. Varr. *De re rust.* 2,1,10: when the Roman people is purified by the suovetaurilia, a boar, a ram, and a bull are driven around (transl. W.D. Hooper, H.B. Ash . Cf. Dion. Hal., *Ant. Rom.* 4,22,1; W.F. Otto, *Lustrum*, "RhM" 71/1916, pp. 17–40.
208 On the etymology see Charis., *Ars* 139 (ed. Barwick); cf. Fest. 372 L., s.v. *solitaurilia*; J.F. Keseberg, *op. cit.*, p. 5. Cf. Serv., *In Verg. Aen.* 8,183: Lustral or fat: because it was customary for the censors to offer fat sacrifices at the end of the lustrum (...) or because the city was purified by these sacrifices for five years. Others say 'lustral' of those animals that were taken with both hands and put on the altar by the pontifex or the censor (transl. AT). It can be inferred from Servius' commentary on the Aeneid that the sacrificial animals had to be fat. The censor took them from the handlers with both hands and placed them on the altar in their entirety, without dividing them into parts as was the case with most blood sacrifices. Cf. D. Baudy, *Römische Umgangsriten. Eine ethologische Untersuchung der Funktion von Wiederholung für religiöses Verhalten*, Berlin–New York 1998, pp. 223–261.
209 Cf. Dion. Hal., *Ant. Rom.* 4,22,1.
210 See Figure 2.
211 Cic., *De div.*, 1,102: So too, when the sacred ceremony of purification was held by one starting on an expedition to found a colony, or when the commander-in-chief was reviewing his army, or the censor was taking his census, it was the rule to choose men with names of good omen to lead the victims (transl. W.A. Falconer).
212 Festus noted that persons with these names were called first at army enlistment and censuses; Fest. 108 L., s.v. *Lacus Lucrinus*.
213 Dio Cass. 54,28,4; cf. M. Lemosse, *Mort e 'lustratio'. Á propos de Dio Cass. 54,28,4*, "TR" 36/1968, pp. 519–524; A. Manzo, *'Lustratio' e divieto del 'suffectus': due aspetti sacerdotali del censore?*, "Teoria e storia del diritto privato" 12/2019, pp. 1–22.
214 The priest who could not touch the dead, however, was the *flamen Dialis*. Cf. Gell. 10,15,24.
215 W. Kunkel, R. Wittmann, *op. cit.*, p. 469, considered such a *lustrum* to be invalid, which, however, contradicts the source text.
216 Athen. 14,660 c. Cf. above.
217 Varr., *L.L.* 6,93: because the censor arranges in centuries the citizen-army for a period of five years, when he must ceremonially purify it and lead it to the city under its standards (transl. D.R. Shackleton Bailey).
218 Cf. Dion. Hal., *Ant. Rom.* 4,22,1, where it is mentioned that citizens were armed. Although this transmission relates to the *lustrum* of Servius Tullius, it seems that also during the republican period armed men participated in the ceremony, as the relief from the altar of Domitius Ahenobarbus also indicates. Differently W. Kunkel, R. Wittmann, *op. cit.*, p. 466, n. 252. Cf. also G. Greco, *op. cit.*, pp. 170 ff., who discusses the problem of who was actually present at the lustration and the ethymological difference between *lŭstrum* and *lūstrum*.
219 W. Kunkel, R. Wittmann, *op. cit.*, p. 467, wrote that the censor only led the people to the city gate. This view is not justified in the light of Varro's formulation *in urbem*.
220 Cf. G.W. Botsford, *op. cit.*, pp. 203–205.
221 M. Torelli, *op. cit.*, pp. 11–12.
222 Cf. P. Fraccaro, *'Accensi'*, [in:] P. Fraccaro, *Opuscula*, II, Pavia 1957, p. 319.
223 E.S. Gruen, *Culture and National Identity in Republican Rome*, New York 1992, p. 148.
224 Cf. Gell. 15,27,5.
225 The similarities between *lustrum* and triumph ceremonies were pointed out by J. Gagé, *Les rites anciens de lustration du Populus et les attributs «triomphaux» des censeurs*, "MEFRA" 82.1/1970, pp. 43–71. cf. Ja. V. Melničuk, *'Lustrum' en su aspecto marcial....*

226 Dio Cass. 55,10,4.
227 Cf. ORF 8 XXXII, pp. 51–53; F. della Corte, *op. cit.* pp. 29–30; R. Stark, *Catos Rede 'de lustri sui felicitate'*, "RhM" 96/1953, pp. 184–187.
228 Cf. H. Beck, *op. cit.*, p. 77.
229 Liv., *Per.* 13.
230 More on this below.
231 About the conflict between them Val. Max. 6,4,2; *De vir. ill.* 58,9.
232 Cf. Fest. 360 L, s.v. *religionis*. Lindsay has not reconstructed this badly corrupt passage, but a proposal for completing the lacuna is cited by A. Cenderelli, *Varroniana. Istituti e terminologia giuridica nelle opere di M. Terenzio Varrone*, Milano 1973, p. 78.
233 T.P. Wiseman, *The Census in the First Century B.C.*, "JRS" 59.1–2/1969, pp. 63–64 even considers that this *lustrum* was not taken into account and therefore subsequent censors were elected as early as 86 BC.
234 J. Linderski, *The Augural Law*..., pp. 2186–2189.
235 Cf. FD 17; see also below.

III The principles of the *regimen morum*

1. Preliminary remarks

The censors, as guardians of morality exercising the *regimen morum* (supervision of customs), of course had a huge influence on social life. This power is often mentioned in the sources but usually only in an anecdotal context. As a result, this area of censorial activity tends to be treated as a series of ad hoc solutions, lacking internal logic and offering little insight into the course of legal development.

There are, however, indications that this view needs to be revised. Firstly, although the censors' decisions within the framework of the *regimen morum* were discretionary, there was a certain procedure that was followed in the proceedings before the censors. It is also worth noting that the catalogue of actions the censors considered punishable, even if it varied widely, was used to develop legal protection in various situations, both public and private. It can be assumed that the censorial *ignominia* or blemish on the name was the origin of the institution of infamy and that the censorial mark was the source of Augustus' solutions in his marriage laws. It was the censors who paved the way for punishing forgery, perjury, dishonesty, and extravagance.

2. Rules for the application of the censorial mark

As a guarantee of stability and balance, censorship was an extremely important element of the Republican system. In its various aspects, the *regimen morum* influenced the development of the law. In private law, censorial sanctions often preceded and sometimes reinforced the protection introduced by the praetor's edict. In public law, censorship and the censorial mark were major factors in its development. The guardianship of the observance of the *mores maiorum* was much more than anecdotal stories about the kissing of wives or the beheading of convicts at parties. Censorship was as much about systemic balance as ensuring that basic moral principles were not violated. This also had an impact on the development of criminal law. The abuse of official authority, bribery, and perjury were punishable by a censorial mark. It can therefore be assumed that censorship completes the picture of both law and procedure in the Republican period.

It is noteworthy that the censorial mark was only applied to men, while women's morals were watched over by their fathers and husbands.[1] The view that it was the

DOI: 10.4324/9781003486664-4

husband who was supposed to be the guardian of his wife's morals[2] and therefore acted as a censor towards her was widespread among the Romans.

> Cic., *De rep.* 4,6 apud Non. 499 M. (ed. Müller): *Nec vero mulieribus praefectus praeponatur, qui apud Graecos creari solet, sed sit censor, qui viros doceat moderari uxoribus.*
>
> *Nor indeed should there be a governor placed over women, as is usually done among the Greeks, but there should be a censor to teach men to rule their wives.*
>
> (Transl. C.W. Keyes)

From the passage of *De re publica* preserved by Nonius, it appears that Cicero believed that officials controlling women's morals (*praefectus mulierum, γυναικονόμος*) should not be appointed, as was the case with the Greeks,[3] but that it was the censor who should teach men how to restrain women. *Regimen morum mulieris* was therefore the responsibility of the man who exercised authority over a woman, and it seems, of her closest relatives.[4] This issue is addressed in a fragment of Cato's speech *De dote*,[5] preserved in the *Noctes Atticae* by Aulus Gellius, which is of great interest to scholars but also very controversial.[6]

> Gell. 10,23,4: *Verba Marci Catonis adscripsi ex oratione, quae inscribitur De dote, in qua id quoque scriptum est in adulterio uxores deprehensas ius fuisse maritis necare: "Vir" inquit "cum divortium fecit, mulieri iudex pro censore est, imperium quod videtur habet, si quid perverse taetreque factum est a muliere; multitatur, si vinum bibit; si cum alieno viro probri quid fecit, condemnatur."*
>
> *I have copied Marcus Cato's words from the oration entitled 'On the Dowry', in which it is also stated that husbands had the right to kill wives taken in adultery: "When a husband put away his wife," says he, "he judges the woman as a censor would, and has full powers if she has been guilty of any wrong or shameful act; she is punished if she has drunk wine; if she has done wrong with another man, she is condemned."*
>
> (Transl. J.C. Rolfe, adapted)

Gellius first reported that the speech Cato had referred to stated that husbands had the right to kill wives caught in adultery. This is followed by a quotation, the interpretation of which is complicated. Cato stated that someone exercised the function of censor for a woman: the husband or the judge. In view of the difficulties posed by the analysis of this excerpt, it is necessary to refer again to its grammatical content: *Vir cum divortium fecit mulieri iudex pro censore est.* A significant detail might be to consider the principles of *consecutio temporum.* Cato's reasoning would then have to be interpreted as follows: the husband, having carried out a divorce, lost the right to control the customs of his ex-wife, so that the functions of 'censor' towards her were taken over by the judge. Such an understanding of the text is confirmed by verb forms: *fecit* is *indicativus perfecti activi*, and *est – indicativus praesentis activi*, which clearly indicates that the divorce has already taken place, and the one acting as censor is now performing his duties. Cato's sentence, therefore, does not at all contradict the fact that it was the husband who controlled his wife's customs, but supplements this information with an additional detail. Since the dissolution of the marriage interrupted the husband's control,[7] the judge could still assess the woman's behaviour during the marriage and – if necessary – deprive her of part of her dowry. The quoted excerpt would therefore have to be translated as follows: "after the husband divorced, the judge acts as a censor towards the woman."

In his speech, therefore, Cato stated that, during the course of the marriage, the husband had the right to react, even violently, to his wife's transgressions. If he caught her in adultery, he could even kill her in extreme cases. By contrast, after divorce, the right to judge a woman's morals passed to the judge. The verbs *multitare* and *condemnare* refer to the judgement concerning the dowry.[8]

It should be remembered, however, that the divorce mentioned by Cato could lead to proceedings before the censors insofar as the latter considered the *repudium* to be unfounded. Then the customs of the woman became indirectly the object of interest of the officials.

The term 'censorial mark' itself (*nota censoria, notatio censoria, animadversio censoria*) is the general name for the sanction applied by the censors. Its effects could, however, vary depending on the status of the punished and the will of the officials themselves. There is a description of the punishments used by the censors as part of the *regimen morum* in a commentary on one of Cicero's speeches (*Divinatio in Caecilium*).

> Ps.-Ascon., *In. Cic. div. in Caec.* p. 103 ed. Orelli: *Regendis moribus civitatis censores quinto quoque anno creari solebant. Hi prorsus cives sic notabant: ut, qui senator esset, eiiceretve senatu; qui eques Romanus, equum publicum perderet; qui plebeius, in Caeritum tabulas referretur et aerarius fieret, ac per hoc [non] esset in albo centuriae suae, sed ad hoc non esset civis, tantummodo ut pro capite suo tributi nomine aera praeberet.*
>
> *It was also customary to appoint censors every five years to control the morals of the community. They were the ones who punished citizens in this way: if someone was a senator, he was removed from the senate; if he was a Roman horseman, he lost his public horse; if he was a plebeian, he was entered on the tables of the Caerites and became a commoner and because of that he was [not] on the list of his century but he was not a citizen in a sense that he had to pay taxes for his head.*
>
> (Transl. AT)

Pseudo-Asconius noted that senators were removed from the Senate, knights were removed from the equestrian centuries, and plebeians were transferred to the *tabulae Caeritum* and to the ranks of the *aerarii*, so that they were not listed in their original century. In addition, it was clarified that the sanctioned were not[9] only citizens in the sense that they paid the poll tax (*tributum*) for themselves. Although the text does not provide a complete overview of the sanctions used by the censors, it can nevertheless be considered as a starting point.

The interest of the censors was certainly, though not exclusively, focused on the upper strata of society. As far as senators were concerned, the basic, and very severe, punishment was the deletion of their names from the senate list. However, in the source texts, in addition to the phrase *senatu eicere* or *senatu movere*, i.e. 'to expel from the senate,' there is also the phrase *praeterire*, i.e. 'to omit.'

As mentioned above, after the enactment of *lex Ovinia*, citizens who held offices giving them the right to enter the Senate had to wait for another *lectio* to actually sit in the curia. However, it did happen that the censors, who were after all not absolutely obliged to include someone on the list, deemed the person unworthy and simply omitted him. The verb *movere* or *eicere* therefore denotes the removal from the Senate of an existing member, while *praeterire* denotes the omission of one who, according to the *lex Ovinia*, could count on being included in the list of senators.[10]

Another category of people mentioned by Pseudo-Asconius who could be subject to a censorial mark were the equestrians, who were entitled to a public horse, fed, and maintained at state expense. The horse was taken away (*equum adimere*) from the punished rider, thus excluding him from the elite *centuria*. It is worth recalling that the catalogue of acts for which the censors punished the equestrians with a mark was extended to include specific behaviour peculiar to this group: the basic charge was neglect of the horse. Excessive obesity, on the other hand, did lead to exclusion from the equestrian century but was not associated with loss of reputation.

Finally, the commentator mentioned plebeians, a term that should be understood as referring to poor citizens, not those who came from plebeian families. Although the division between patricians and plebeians had political significance for quite a long time (if only in the context of being able to be elected to the office of plebeian tribune), the colloquial language of the late Republican period developed a connotation of the word 'plebs' with a group of citizens of low social status. In any case, anyone who was neither a senator nor a knight was, according to this source, subject to two parallel sanctions: entry on the *tabulae Caeritum* and transfer to the ranks of the *aerarii*.

> Gell. 16,13,7: *Primos autem municipes sine suffragii iure Caerites esse factos accepimus concessumque illis, ut civitatis Romanae honorem quidem caperent, sed negotiis tamen atque oneribus vacarent pro sacris bello Gallico receptis custoditisque. Hinc "tabulae Caerites" appellatae versa vice, in quas censores referri iubebant, quos notae causa suffragiis privabant.*
>
> *We learn besides that the people of Caere were the first municipes without the right of suffrage, and that it was allowed them to assume the honour of Roman citizenship, but yet to be free from service and burdens, in return for receiving and guarding sacred objects during the war with the Gauls. Hence by contraries those tablets were called Caerites on which the censors ordered those to be enrolled whom they deprived of their votes by way of disgrace.*
>
> (Transl. J.C. Rolfe)

The name *tabulae Caeritum*[11] derives from the city of Caere, whose inhabitants were the first to be granted *civitas sine suffragio*,[12] as noted by Gellius. The antiquarian added that on these tabulae, the censors inscribed those whom they punished with a mark, thus depriving them of the right to vote. Inscription on the *tabulae Caeritum* therefore meant, in practice, depriving the citizen of the *ius suffragii*.

As for the phrase of the *aerarium facere*, it was linked to the removal of a citizen from the list of his *centuria*[13] and the necessity to pay a *tributum*,[14] an obligation from which citizens enjoying full rights were exempted from 167 BC. Prior to that year, those punished probably had to pay a larger amount than the rest.[15] This is possibly why, after the census had been completed, the censors carried the list of *aerarii* to the temple of Saturn, where the treasury (*aerarium*) was located,[16] and handed it to the quaestors.

It is interesting to note that the term *aerarium facere* appears in other source texts. However, it is never accompanied by information about entry in the *tabulae Caeritum*. Instead, many authors mention another sanction: *tribu movere*, i.e. change of tribe. Is there a difference between these two punishments? Let us start by noting that Caere, which was located in Etruria, was later incorporated into the *tribus Arniensis*. It is therefore possible that this was a case of transfer to another tribe. Initially, those punished by the *nota* were listed as residents of Caere in order to deprive them of the *ius suffragii*, but later the sanction was generalised to include transfer to an 'inferior' *tribus* and not just the *tabulae Caeritum*. It should be noted that the category of citizens without the right to vote (*cives sine suffragio*) seems to have disappeared at the end of the second century BC. For this reason, the term *tabulae Caeritum* is only rarely found in the sources. The change of *tribus*, on the other hand, began to involve the citizen moving from a rural *tribus* to an urban one, where the number of citizens was much greater and therefore their votes in the assembly were of negligible value.

The listed sanctions could also be applied cumulatively: a citizen removed from the Senate or from the equestrian century could additionally be enrolled as an *aerarius* or transferred to another *tribus*, leading in practice to a significant reduction in their political participation.

In addition, the imposition of a censorial mark was also associated with the loss of reputation already mentioned – *ignominia*. According to Cicero, the censorial mark brought the punished person into disrepute[17] – 'blush,' as he put it.[18] The subject of *ignominia* was not deprived of political rights: he could still run for office,[19] although, if removed from the Senate, he had to attain a position that entitled him to sit in it.[20] Punishment could even provide the impetus for a brilliant career, as exemplified by the two cases described by Valerius Maximus[21] of senators removed from the Senate who later became censors themselves. Geta and Valerius Messala were so embarrassed by their marks that they did their best to show their fellow citizens that they were worthy to hold censorial duties.[22] Cicero's view was that censorship should be a source of fear, not a lifelong effect.[23] A mark could not only be removed by a second censor, it could also be ignored by a popular assembly, a judge, or an official without drawing consequences from its imposition.[24]

It is necessary to clarify the terminology used in the sources. To denote dishonour, both the terms *ignominia* and *infamia* are used. The former usually denotes a loss of reputaion due to a censorial mark, while the latter denotes a loss of honour, although it should be noted that ancient authors did not always use them accurately.

Romanist studies often emphasise the distinctiveness of these two legal institutions and the lack of correlation between them. In a recent work on infamy, a different perspective was taken by Clément Bur,[25] who argued that the institution was homogeneous and developed gradually: from the punishments applied as part of military discipline, through the censorial *regimen morum*, the *actiones famosae*, the infamy applied in trials before *quaestiones perpetuae*, in the *iudicia publica*, and finally the praetorian infamy. This linear conception is remarkably interesting as it highlights the relationship between the different stages of the evolution of infamy.

Nevertheless, I believe that the thesis that the terms *ignominia* and *infamia* are technically distinct should be maintained. This does not mean, however, that there is no connection between the two. The *regimen morum* had a significant influence on the development of the concept of infamy. It should also be emphasised that for a long time the word *infamia* itself was often used in a non-technical sense (apart from the strictly technical meaning referring to defamatory complaints): it was intended to describe the status of persons who had been disgraced for various reasons. It was only in the legal language of late antiquity that the term began to be used more broadly in a strict sense concerning every case of loss of honour. This seems to be confirmed, for example, by the fact that the praetor's edict did not originally contain a section on infamy, but only a prohibition to appear in court – the *postulatio*.

The influence of the *regimen morum* on praetorian regulations seems indisputable. The censorial mark may have been applied in various circumstances, depending on the views of the current pair of censors. The sources describe many cases of punishment for one-off acts. Often, the stigmatised person could also count on the fact that the next pair of censors would no longer apply sanctions against him. However, there was a large group of acts associated with a mark of a permanent nature, repeated on the occasion of each census. Such were the sanctions against those bearing false witness, committing perjury, theft, and other offences sanctioned by defamatory complaints, as well as practising disgraceful professions such as acting, gladiatorial, or animal fighting. The patterns established in censorial practice thus influenced the creation of written regulations, particularly the development of the praetor's edict.

3. Procedure applied by the censors

Sources on the procedure followed in proceedings before the censors often refer to it as a court – *censorium iudicium*[26] or *iudicium de moribus*.[27] A fragment of the Altar of Domitius Ahenobarbus mentioned above seems to be an iconographic representation of the censorial actions. The seated censor places his hand on the citizen standing beside him in the section depicting the census. This gesture can be interpreted as denoting authority and power[28] – *manus* – of the official over the Romans. It seems to refer precisely to the *regimen morum*, which allowed for a degradation of a citizen by removing him from the social group to which he belonged.

The censorial mark could be applied both during the census itself and when the lists of senators and equestrians were drawn up. The reason for the punishment had to be recorded next to the citizen's name in the form of *subscriptio censoria*.[29] It must be stressed that not every citizen stood directly before the censors every five years. The census was such a huge undertaking that the officials were assisted in it by a staff of helpers, primarily the *iuratores* receiving the census declarations. Consequently, citizens from the higher social strata (senators and knights) and those who were subject to the mark for a reason that was permanent, such as having a disgraceful profession, had to reckon with punishment in the first place. It could, however, happen that the censors took an interest in a person after receiving information about him indicating the existence of grounds for punishment. Such a situation occurred both when officials received a denunciation or an informal message, as well as when someone made a formal accusation.

Valerius Maximus, describing the censorship of Scipio Aemilianus, admired his moderation[30] during the *recognitio equitum*.[31] Deciding on the case of Gaius Licinius Sacerdos, the censor stated that he knew the man was guilty of perjury at *verba concepta*[32] and encouraged those assembled to lead the charge. However, as no one came forward, he allowed the knight to leave with his horse, sparing him a mark. He justified this by saying that he did not want to assume the roles of accuser, witness, and judge in one case.[33]

There is a well-known excerpt of Cato's accusatory speech *apud censores in Lentulum*.[34] In this speech, Cato seems to have accused Lentulus of having abused his guardianship or patronage. Gaius Gracchus was also accused before the censors and asked to be given the opportunity to defend himself.[35] Therefore, it appears that conducting adversarial proceedings was not the rule, but only optional.

The defence of a person threatened with a mark could be undertaken by friends as well as advocates, although their admission was subject to the decision of the censors. Cicero, speaking in defence of Cluentius,[36] cited the case of the judge Publius Popillius, who had been punished with a mark by the censor Lucius Gellius with the following *subscriptio*: *quod is pecuniam accepisset, quo innocentem condemnaret* ('because he accepted money to condemn an innocent man'). Cicero stressed that no one was allowed to speak up in defence of Popillius and others punished equally recklessly.[37] In similar circumstances during his censorship, Lepidus deprived a rider of his horse. The friends of the punished man inquired how he should explain the punishment to his father. They argued to the censor that the equestrian who had been subjected to the mark was an exemplary farmer, suggesting that the punishment was unjustified. Lepidus replied that he did not believe this[38] and therefore did not allow any evidence to be presented.

There is an interesting passage preserved in *Rhetorica ad Herennium*, which appears to have come from an accusatory speech delivered before the censors, but which was considered imperfect due to faulty argumentation.[39] The textbook's author stated that it was flawed to cite one tentative argument in support of another. In this situation, the case concerned a failure to appear by a person who had taken the relevant oath. It is difficult to reconstruct the case based on such scanty information. However, it can be assumed that the proceedings concerned the imposition of a censorial mark for breach of oath. The prosecutor argued that it was not enough to say that one could not appear if one had taken the oath and added that such an explanation would certainly not have been accepted if it had been made to a military tribunal by someone who had failed to appear in the army. As far as conscription to the army was concerned, those who had been called up took a *iusiurandum*, swearing to appear at the appointed time, with excuses for absence only possible under certain circumstances.[40] Failure to be excused resulted in being considered *infrequens*.[41] With regard to the case discussed in the source text, a doubt arises as to what the oath in dispute may have been about. The term *iuratus* seems to indicate the performing of a *iusiurandum*. It is not possible to resolve this question definitively, but it can be assumed that it refers to *iusiurandum iudicio sisti*, i.e. an oath to appear before the court. Jurists of the classical period held that the absence had to be explained by giving a reason (e.g. matters of state, sea storm, illness, trickery of the other party in the trial).[42] In the absence of an adequate explanation, a party was not excused. One may think that during the Republican period, censors were particularly sensitive to such situations. In the case in question, apparently the citizen threatened with a mark said that he could not appear, which, according to the prosecution, was not enough.

It seems, therefore, that the censors could have conducted the proceedings by admitting both the accuser and the defence counsel, as well as the witnesses. However, they were not obliged to do so.

It is worth noting that this issue has been questioned by scholars. Clément Bur stated[43] that the *lectio senatus* took place behind closed doors, and that therefore the censors' decisions on the matter were made arbitrarily and without any proceedings. This view is convincing because indeed the *lectio* was carried out quickly, and therefore there may not have been time for possible trials. However, it cannot be ruled out that here too, in case of doubt, the censors could have allowed proceedings, particularly the presentation of evidence, avoiding publicity.

An interesting relationship is observed between the trial before a private judge and the trial before the censors concerning morals (*apud censores de moribus*). Varro emphasised that praetorian regulations acted *ad legem*, or 'according to the law,' while the censorial court acted *ad aequum*, or 'according to equity.'[44] The decisions of the censors should therefore observe the principles of equity. An interesting aspect of this relationship was also described by Gellius.[45] The writer himself, appointed as a judge, was to decide a case concerning a money loan.[46] The lender was unable to produce evidence: neither an *expensilatio* (a record from the accounting book), nor a bank account, nor a debenture, nor certified *tabulae*, nor witnesses; but he was a good and trustworthy man. The defendant – a person leading a dishonest life – claimed the release and conviction of the plaintiff on account of *calumnia* (bringing a false accusation). He also argued that the assessment of character should have no relevance in this trial, as it was a private dispute over money and not a trial before the censors dealing with customs. Gellius' opinion on this was that, although no evidence of the payment of money was presented, he, as a judge, did not want to release the defendant and expose the plaintiff to a *calumnia* penalty, but he did not want to adjudicate either, because the character evidence seemed to him insufficient. However, it can be concluded that Gellius was inwardly convinced that the plaintiff was right. Why? The defendant did not deny the allegations of lack of fairness. The argument that customs can only be judged by censors was only used when the integrity of a party could not be proven, that is, as a last resort. Therefore, this meant that, in fact, the defendant was probably an untrustworthy liar, and Gellius was right not to pass judgement in his favour. However, just because someone is a fraudster in general does not mean that they are lying in a particular case. So, what is to be done? Gellius managed to extricate himself from his predicament: he was dismissed from the case after swearing that he could not settle the dispute (*sibi non liquere*).

However, this case raises the question: where did the argument about dealing with censors come from in the first place, when that office was already a thing of the past? Gellius wrote that the defendant had many advocates (*patrones*).[47] It can be assumed that they were the ones who employed this strategy. Rhetorical textbooks advised it as a last resort.[48] It seems, therefore, that court speakers, especially those who were not highly creative, used certain patterns in their work, and that such tactics were precisely the typical, even schoolyard solution. Censorship was an office which, although it had disappeared, was known, and the reference to its powers had to be legible and understandable.

It can therefore be inferred that the procedure used in the *iudicium de moribus* provided for both formal prosecution and adversarial proceedings involving lawyers and witnesses. Its application, however, was subject to the decision of the censors, who had full discretion both in this respect and in the application of the mark itself. There were only two limitations to this discretion. Firstly, the censors were bound by an oath in which they pledged to be guided neither by gratitude nor hatred, but to have the common good in mind.[49] This promise should not be taken lightly, since one of the acts most severely condemned by the censors was perjury.[50] Secondly, the principle of collegiality was particularly strong in the case of the office of censor.[51] Both censors were elected simultaneously, care was taken to ensure that there were no conflicts between them, and the death of one censor resulted in his colleague having to resign his office. Collegiality was also expressed in the right to apply *intercessio* against the official decision of the other censor.[52] This concerned, above all, issues related to the displacement of citizens in the social hierarchy because of the application of the censorial mark. The most desirable state of affairs seems to have been the unanimity of the censors. *Intercessiones* were, of course, not uncommon, but a serious conflict dividing the censors could lead to a complete blocking of their ability to perform their official functions.

All of the above restrictions on censorship power did not limit the arbitrary nature of decisions related to the imposition of the mark. In 58 BC, however, a plebiscite was enacted to contribute to changing this situation. This is the *lex*

Clodia de censoria notione,[53] one of the four[54] plebiscites P. Clodius promulgated on the first day of his term as plebeian tribune.

Among the sources on *lex Clodia*, there are passages from Cicero's speeches and commentaries on them, as well as excerpts from Cassius Dio's work. As far as Cicero's speeches are concerned, it must be remembered that the orator was hostile to Clodius (with reciprocation, by the way). This makes it necessary to interpret his words with care, considering possible exaggerations of key points. In his speech *Pro Sestio*, for example, Cicero[55] tried to prove that Clodius's tribunate was illegitimate, based on force, rather than law. He also insisted that the plebiscites enacted were detrimental to the state and contrary to constitutional principles. In his view, Clodius removed the censorial mark and the harshest court of the most sacred office from the state. On the other hand, in his *De haruspicum responsis* speech, he stated that Clodius had completely abolished censorship.[56] Such a radical formulation was intended to discredit the former tribune and facilitate Cicero's efforts to regain the house he had lost after Clodius ordered its consecration.

Speaking after the death of Clodius in his speech *De provinciis consularibus*, Cicero had to explain his change of attitude towards Caesar. He argued that if one considered Caesar's laws to be invalid, one would also have to assume that the censorial court, the *nota*, and the strictest control of customs had not been removed from society by virtue of the wicked *leges*.[57] The orator had in mind here the problem of the legality of laws passed during Caesar's consulship, when Bibulus blocked legislation by conducting an observation of the sky in search of signs (*spectio de caelo*). He stressed that the *acta Caesaris* cannot be considered ineffective (*inrita*) if it is assumed that Clodius, who was not even entitled to become a tribune, could legitimately push through all his plebiscites.[58]

Speaking against Piso, the man who contributed to his exile, Cicero necessarily wanted to remind his audience of the controversial legislation of Clodius by which censorship, the former guardian of manners and modesty, was abolished.[59] He argued that the censorial mark had existed for almost 400 years[60] and no one had ever dared to block the holding of a court over customs every five years.

Based on these sources, one would have to assume that the censors were completely stripped of their authority to guard customs. However, all the texts quoted are strongly rhetorical, which makes it necessary to treat them with detachment. There is also a curious circumstance that may affect the perception of Cicero's statements: regardless of the limitations cited, the orator himself decided to run for the office of censor.

In a letter to Atticus dated the first half of October 57 BC, Cicero informed his friend that he had accepted the function of legate from Pompey, on the condition, however, that he should not be restricted in his political plans. If subsequent consuls announced elections for censors, he intended to submit his candidacy.[61] He also wished to remain in Rome, in full view of his fellow citizens, which was necessary for a possible election campaign. This declaration is evidence that censorship seemed to Cicero still worth fighting for and therefore could not be completely abolished. The powers were certainly curtailed, but the office itself remained the pinnacle of a political career.

Among the source texts on *lex Clodia*, there are also commentaries on Cicero's speeches. One of the commentators is Asconius, a writer almost contemporary with Cicero, and the other is a medieval scholiast. Commenting on the *In Pisonem*, Asconius wrote that, by virtue of the fourth of Clodius' plebiscites, censors could only omit someone during the *lectio senatus* or punish a senator with a mark if he had been accused and convicted before them by the sentences of both colleagues.[62] The scholiast, on the other hand, mentioned the *lex Clodia* which forbade the censors to omit someone during the *lectio senatus* unless the person had been convicted.[63]

Cassius Dio,[64] an author free of Ciceronian influence, stated that the plebiscite of Clodius forbade censors from removing and punishing someone with a mark unless the individual had been tried and convicted by both censors.

These texts appear to contradict with each other, making it difficult to establish the actual content of the plebiscite, which evidently sparked controversy even among contemporaries. This is evidenced by its repeal just six years after its enactment, when Consul Metellus Scipio proposed the *lex Caecilia de censoribus.*[65] Metellus aimed to restore the censors to their former powers. By adopting his proposal, the popular assembly revoked *lex Clodia*, thus allowing the censors to decide independently whether to remove someone from the Senate or the equestrian state. However, it turned out that Clodius' regulations had actually facilitated officials' decisions. Suddenly, it became challenging to punish citizens openly and pit them against each other. On the other hand, the censors' failure to act when someone deserved a mark also drew criticism. Therefore, according to Dio, censorship lost its popularity and hardly anyone sought the office.

The abolition of *lex Clodia* was probably the reason we know so little about it. It only influenced the censorship of M. Valerius Messala Niger and P. Servilius Vatia Isauricus in 55 BC.[66] From Cicero's letter to Atticus dated 1 October 54 BC, it can be inferred[67] that trials under *lex Clodia*[68] prevented the censors from completing their tasks and carrying out the *lustrum*.

According to Theodor Mommsen's opinion[69] on the Clodian plebiscite, it was evident that the mark had to be imposed by both censors in unison and in the form of a trial, which prevented them from punishing without evidence, and at the same time deprived them of initiative in the proceedings.

The most in-depth analysis to date on this subject has been carried out by W. Jeffrey Tatum.[70] This researcher has argued that Clodius was trying to gain the support of the Senate, particularly the *senatores pedarii*. Since the time of Sulla, former quaestors had to be admitted to the Senate,[71] which was already overcrowded. A severe purge of the current members was inevitable. Clodius was convinced that the senators threatened with removal would thank him for the new regulations[72] because from now on the *lectio* would no longer take place behind closed doors, and everyone would be able to defend themselves.

Tatum also argued that the censors were not deprived of their right to prosecute. In his view, the only novelty of the regulation in question was the change to the *lectio senatus* procedure, during which hitherto the censors had been completely unrestricted and independent of any external factors. A similar view was presented by Clément Bur,[73] according to whom the *lex Clodia* mandated formal proceedings during the *lectio senatus*.

The tribune's reasons for introducing the draft of the plebiscite in question were probably personal. Clodius was an extremely controversial politician and may have feared for his place in the Senate. The thesis of his desire to secure support among the senators seems correct.

The *lex Clodia* probably introduced uniform procedures for dealing with all censorial actions related to the *regimen morum*: *lectio senatus*, *recognitio equitum*, and census.[74] The reason some sources only mention the determination of the composition of the Senate is probably because they were written from the perspective of those in the senatorial state. It may also be that during the census of 55 BC no action beyond *lectio* could be taken because the processes took so long, and only this was remembered later.

However, I disagree with the statement that the plebiscite of Clodius only changed the way *lectio* was carried out. In my opinion, it strongly influenced all activities related to the *regimen morum*. Until its enactment, the rules were different. Firstly, the decision of one censor was sufficient as long as the other did not oppose it, whether he knew about it or not. Now both censors had to act unanimously. Besides, it does not seem that previously the censors were obliged to allow a defence when threatening a mark, and certainly did not have to give time to prepare for it. Now, on the other hand, a regular trial was conducted, ending in a conviction – *damnatio*.

It remains questionable whether the accusation must have come from outside, or whether it could have been brought by the censors themselves. We have only one probable testimony, which is the case of L. Libo accused by Helvius Mancia Formianus[75] before the said censors of 55 BC. The trial was public; even Pompey arrived. However, this does not prove that the initiative was taken away from the censors.

One may venture the thesis that the real novelty introduced in *lex Clodia* was the necessity for the censors to accept all accusations made. This explains why they were unable to complete their work and carry out the *lustrum*, which probably weakened the venerable office the most.

The very construction of the *regimen morum* makes it a difficult institution to interpret. It penetrated deeply into the lives of Romans,[76] addressing their dignity. The censors were given control over the most vital areas of political and social life, demonstrating the level of trust placed in them. Their authority meant that citizens naturally submitted to them.[77]

All decisions related to the custody of morality were to be based on *mores maiorum*,[78] to which the censors often referred when introducing new rules in their edicts.[79] The power of these officials was subject to restrictions designed to ensure the validity of their decisions. However, none of these restrictions were able to prevent a censor who wanted to punish someone with a mark. Such cases were not common. The sources mention severe rather than unjust censors.

The final period of the Roman Republic witnessed a crisis in most of its political institutions, including censorship. After the dictatorship of Sulla,[80] establishing new rules for conducting the *lectio* of the overcrowded Senate became challenging. The plebiscite of Clodius aimed to resolve this issue in favour of the incumbent senators by hindering their removal. However, it seems too far-fetched to consider it a step towards increasing the impartiality of the *regimen.*

Mores maiorum ceased to be seen as a fundamental determinant of the rules[81] and became quite oppressive. Clodius wanted to create a situation where penalties would not be imposed for deviating from old customs. However, he probably did not anticipate the consequences of this reform, such as an endless series of trials that made lustration impossible. This is why the plebiscite was repealed after only one term of censors.

Cicero's reaction to the *lex Clodia* was certainly political – he wanted to discredit his opponent as much as possible. However, this was not the only reason. For the orator, censorship was one of the most crucial legal institutions of the Republic,[82] upholding tradition and preventing degeneration. He probably feared that without this respectable office, the Republic would go astray. Simultaneously, it should not be forgotten that Cicero himself aspired to the censorship and was probably extremely disappointed that he failed to attain it in time and had to be content with what was left of it after the reform.

It therefore seems that – since the censors took over the supervision of the observance of *mores maiorum* – the censorial mark was imposed in a discretionary manner. This does not change the fact that the officials could carry out the procedure by giving the person threatened with punishment an opportunity to defend themselves, as well as allowing prosecution. However, there were only two censors, which meant that the procedure was only used in exceptional cases. The *lex Clodia* provides evidence of how destructive it would have been to carry out the full procedure in every case.

However, this state of affairs had its consequences: the decision of the censors had no prejudicial value and was not permanent. In the aforementioned speech delivered in defence of Cluentius, Cicero stressed that a censor could not only criticise but also annul his colleague's decision.[83] He was therefore trying to prove that the censors' verdict did not constitute a settled case (*res iudicata*). This view implied further consequences because, according to the speaker, *res iudicatae* were a source of law[84] and as such were binding. If the adjudicated case could constitute evidence in a subsequent trial, it was treated as a prejudicial circumstance in the subsequent proceedings (*praeiudicium*). Likewise, if the judgment entailed further consequences, as in the case of an adjudication from a defamatory complaint (*iudicium famosum*),[85] officials and judges had to take this into account when denying the adjudicator the right to act as judge, witness, or guardian and the possibility of *postulatio.* The censorial mark, on the other hand, had no such effect.

Bearing in mind that the mark was imposed by a given censor or a pair of censors and that its permanence covered only the following five years or *lustrum*, it is nevertheless important to note a certain regularity. There were situations where the mark was indeed a one-off, but there were also cases where its validity extended for the life of the punished person. What was the difference? A mark could result from both single behaviours and long-lasting actions, sometimes even constituting a way of life. It was one thing to break an engagement, for example, and another to practise a disgraceful profession, such as acting. The cessation of behaviour contrary to *mores maiorum* usually resulted in successive censors not putting a mark next to a citizen's name. If one deserved social advancement, they could reward one by including him in the list of senators.[86] On the other hand, when disgraceful behaviour persisted, each successive pair of censors renewed the mark.[87] It can be assumed that this subsequently developed into other sanctions referring to the loss of honour.

4. Accountability of the censors

The question arises whether and to what extent the censors were responsible[88] for their actions in relation to the *regimen morum*. Could they have been prosecuted during or after the termination of their office?

From the words that Dionysius of Halicarnassus attributed to Fabricius speaking to King Pyrrhus of Epirus in 280 BC,[89] it follows that the power of the censors was free from any responsibility.[90] However, this is too general a statement to draw further conclusions from. It is necessary to examine the sources that refer to accusations made against the censors in connection with their decisions related to the *regimen morum*.

The first case concerns the censors Publius Furius Philus and Marcus Atilius Regulus.[91] During the *recognitio equitum*, they dealt very harshly with equestrians who had formed a conspiracy to leave Italy after the defeat at Cannae. The quaestor Marcus Metellus was the ringleader of this action. He and the others were removed by the censors from the horsemen's centuries and transferred to the ranks of the *aerarii*.[92] The justification for such a sanction was cowardice – *turpis metus*. It is noteworthy that Valerius Maximus, who described the censors as guardians of peace, considered that this decision was a manifestation of their shift from the forum to the military camp.[93]

Livy's account shows[94] that shortly after this harsh review of the equestrian centuries, Metellus took office as plebeian tribune and immediately set the censors on trial before the popular assembly. The other nine tribunes granted *auxilium* to the censors, forbidding their trial during their term of office and setting them free.

Firstly, it should be stressed that the above text clearly points out that there is no objection whatsoever to censors being held accountable for official acts, even during their tenure.[95] However, what exactly was the allegation made by the tribune? It is difficult to imagine him speaking directly about the wrongfully imposed *nota*. Italian scholar Orazio Licandro believes that Metellus sought to exclude military matters from the scope of acts covered by the *regimen morum*.[96] However, this does not appear to be an exclusion. As mentioned, Valerius Maximus regarded the decisions of the censors as pioneering, since they were entering the camp from the forum. So Metellus most likely accused them of abusing their powers, arguing that the *regimen morum* should be limited to matters of a civil nature. One may hazard a guess that he accused them of treason – *perduellio*. The support of the other tribunes seems to have sealed the fact that the censors were able to stigmatise cowardice and disloyalty, a *de facto* extension of their powers.

Another case concerns the censorship of Marcus Livius Salinator and Gaius Claudius Nero in 204/203 BC.[97] Livy reported[98] that – because the censors were unpopular – the plebeian tribune Cn. Baebius[99] saw this as an opportunity to improve his position and set a trial date for them before the assembly. However, these proceedings were halted by a unanimous decision of the senators, preventing the censors from being subjected to the whims of the people.

Valerius Maximus's[100] account adds important details to the story. Primarily, it shows that the tribune accused the censors of excessive severity while in office. The Senate relieved them of the need to defend themselves by passing a decree exonerating the censors. The term *ratio* used in the text refers to the declarations received by the censors at the time of the census: the censors should *exigere rationem* – 'demand declarations, accounts' – and not *reddere rationem* – 'make declarations, give accounts.'

The interpretation of this situation must be preceded by a short account of the tenure of Livius Salinator and Claudius Nero.[101] These politicians had previously held the consulship unanimously in 207 BC. There were also no disputes regarding the *lectio senatus* and the leasing of public contracts. Only during the review of the equestrian centuries did a dispute arise: the two censors tried to take horses from each other. Furthermore, Nero included his colleague in the list of *aerarii* Salinator's response was to degrade thirty-four *tribus* to this category. None of these actions could produce effects due to the disagreement between the censors. Each censor was certainly applying *intecessio* against the other. Nevertheless, the whole situation was quite scandalous and – above all – embarrassing. Therefore, it should not be surprising that the plebeian tribune saw this as an opportunity to gain political capital.

Baebius' accusation was allegedly about the excessive severity of the bickering officials. The question of when it was brought is of considerable importance: before the end of the censors' term of office or after it had already ended. Livy's account first mentions the holding of a lustration ceremony, and only then the *recognitio equitum*, after which the censors made an *iusiurandum in leges* and handed over the lists of *aerarii* to the quaestors. Baebius then brought an accusation. He therefore appears to have initiated a process against the now former censors.[102]

The Senate prohibited the trial. From the account of Valerius Maximus, it appears that a *decretum* was passed, which in this context should be understood as a decision of a personal rather than a general nature. Allowing the proceedings before the assembly would have amounted to acquiescence in putting censors on trial for official decisions. By halting the trial, the Senate hoped that censorship would not be subject to judgement in the future as well. It can be assumed that there had previously been no prohibition against prosecuting former censors for their actions related to the *regimen morum*. Baebius therefore attempted to prosecute unpopular politicians and gain notoriety. However, the Senate recognised the danger in setting such a precedent. The decree was therefore an attempt to curb the ambitions of Baebius and subsequent plebeian tribunes, and to strengthen the position of the censors. If censors could be punished for imposing a censorial mark, their office would lose its independence, despite there being no avenue for appealing against such a mark.

There may be doubts whether such a decision of the Senate had the force of universally binding law. However, it is likely that for the Romans, such a manifestation of the Senate's opinion was a sufficient sign that censors would not be criminally liable for official decisions (i.e. those related to the *regimen morum*, as well as the leasing of public contracts).

So, what could a person do who felt they had been unfairly punished with a censorial mark? Get over it and get on with life, trying to regain their lost good name and position? Some tried to prove that they were even worthy of becoming censors and they succeeded.[103] But the others? Basically, they could only hope that the next pair of censors would be more sympathetic to them.

Some clues may be provided by the history of the conflict involving the censors of 169 BC: Tiberius Sempronius Gracchus and Gaius Claudius Pulcher,[104] and the plebeian tribune Publius Rutilius.[105] The censors upset the equestrians with a very harsh review of the horsemen's centuries and issued an edict removing the right to apply for public contracts from those who had leased them by decision of previous censors.[106] The publicans obtained the support of the tribune Rutilius.[107] Importantly, they had previously tried to persuade the Senate[108] to set limits on the censors' power. The equestrians alleged that the *potestas censoria* was unlimited and they probably had both aspects in mind: the *regimen morum* and the *locationes censoriae*. However, since the Senate, it seems, only had influence over the censorial public contracts,[109] the request of the publicans must have been to annul the *locationes* and to conclude new ones under different conditions.

Rutilius had a private quarrel with the censors[110] because they ordered his client to demolish a building erected on public land, sent agents to seize security, and imposed a fine, even though he had appealed[111] to the tribunes. This is why Rutilius filed an *intercessio*.[112] To help the publicans, the exasperated official decided to bring a plebiscite motion to annul the *locationes* concluded by the censors and to lead to a re-run of the auctions in which all those willing could participate.[113] The subsequent stages of this dispute are quite convoluted.

During the *contio* convened by Rutilius, the censors tried to dissuade the plebs from voting on the resolution proposed by the tribune.[114] Gracchus' speech was listened to in silence, while his colleague had to ask an usher to silence the assembled people, which the tribune interpreted as taking away his *contio* and treating him as a private person.

The following day, Rutilius began to act as if his sacrosanctity had been violated.[115] He first addressed the issue of his intercession being disregarded regarding the censors' decision to impose a fine on his client, for which he carried out the consecration of the estates[116] of the censor Tiberius Gracchus. He then set a trial date for Claudius in connection with the *contio* being taken away from him. Finally, he announced his intention to accuse them both of *perduellio* and asked the urban praetor[117] Sulpicius to set a date for the assembly, which, as the censors did not shy away from standing trial, he scheduled for the eighteenth day before the calends of October.

The ongoing trial before the *comitia centuriata* took a dramatic course.[118] Firstly, the assembly was to decide the fate of Claudius. When the vote took an unfavourable turn, Gracchus – despite being convinced that he was in no danger – tipped the scales in favour of his colleague, vowing to go into exile with him in the event of a conviction, without waiting for a decision on his own case.[119] The conviction was avoided by a vote of only eight centuries. The acquittal of Claudius caused Rutilius to withdraw[120] the charges against Gracchus.

Several points should be noted throughout this case. First of all, Rutilius initially did indeed try to act against the censors as officials by bringing in a plebiscite motion. However, this plebiscite probably constituted an encroachment into the area of competence of the Senate. The tribune therefore abandoned it rather easily, which may indicate that he had only been trying to provoke the censors. What was he aiming at, then? Apparently, he was looking for a pretext that would allow him to accuse them of violating his sacrosanctity. He already had one reason, as his *intercessio* had previously been ignored, but he was looking for something more spectacular, and the *contio*, during which the commotion arose, was perfect for this, as there were crowds of people there. The accusation of *perduellio* was going in a similar direction. Rutilius made no accusations against the censorial activities of Gracchus and Claudius but claimed that his integrity had been violated and that he had not been treated as the dignity of the tribune's office dictated.

It must therefore be emphasised that Rutilius did not wish to challenge the official decisions of the censors. This may indicate that the Senate resolution discussed above introduced a binding norm in this respect.

It is worth tracing how censors were dealt with in the later period. The conflict between Scipio Africanus,[121] Hannibal's conqueror, and the plebeian tribune Tiberius Claudius Asellus[122] is quite unusual. Asellus was punished by Scipio with a mark, resulting in his removal from the equestrian century. However, this ultimately did not happen due to the *intercessio* of the second censor, Mummius.[123] Asellus then brought an accusation against Scipio, the basis of which was given by Gellius who quoted a relevant passage from Lucilius' *Satires*.

> Gell. 4,17: *Lucilii ex XI. versus sunt:*
> *Scipiadae magno improbus obiciebat Asellus*
> *lustrum illo censore malum infelixque fuisse.*
> *In the eleventh book of Lucilius are these lines: Thus base Asellus did great Scipio taunt: Unlucky was his censorship and bad.*
> (Transl. J.C. Rolfe)

The accusation[124] concerned irregularities in the performance of lustration, which had the effect of failing to ensure the prosperity of the state.[125] It should, therefore, be emphasised that he did not attempt to challenge the censor's decision. On the other hand, it should be noted that the removal of Asellus from the equestrian century did not eventually take place because Mummius did not agree to it. Still, the knight's fury was so deep that he decided to attack Scipio after he had already completed his term of office.

This episode allows some conclusions to be drawn about the possibility of making accusations against the censors. Firstly, Asellus only acted when Scipio was already a private person, not in office. It is also interesting to note that the accusation concerned a sacral issue. The Romans regarded the *lustrum* as an extremely important ceremony. After all, the office of censor was established and initially reserved only for patricians precisely so that plebeians aspiring to the consulship would not be given the opportunity to perform this sacrifice. Even when one of the censors could already be a plebeian, the purification ceremony was for a long time[126] carried out by a patrician anyway. This is why Asellus hoped that citizens would want to punish a censor who failed in this crucial duty.

A major problem with this case is that it is uncertain whether it was actually Scipio who carried out the lustration. The source texts seem to contradict each other. Cicero quoted an anecdote about how Scipio, in response to Asellus's accusation of the *lustrum*'s unsuccessfulness, countered that there was nothing to be surprised about since the sacrifice was made by the censor who reversed the decision to place him among the *aerarii*,[127] that is, Mummius. Valerius Maximus, on the other hand, wrote that during the lustration, Scipio changed the content of the prayer addressed to the deities.[128] It seems that Mummius was offering the sacrifice, but Scipio, present after all, interfered in the ceremony. It may therefore be – but this is only a hypothesis – that the basis of the accusation was precisely that the conqueror of Carthage dared to change the *precatio*, the text of which was strictly fixed and inscribed in the *tabulae censoriae*, which was supposed to have prejudiced the success of the whole ceremony.

The case of Quintus Metellus, nicknamed Macedonicus, the officiating censor in 131 BC,[129] who became famous for a speech aimed at persuading fellow citizens to marry and seek offspring,[130] is also interesting. The story of Metellus was most fully described by Pliny the Elder.[131] During an extremely strict *lectio senatus*, Metellus punished Gaius Atinius Labeo, nicknamed Macerio. This man, while holding the office of plebeian tribune,[132] committed an almost unbelievable deed: in the middle of the day, when the forum and the Capitol were deserted, he dragged[133] the censor to the Tarpeian Rock, intending to throw him down. Metellus' four sons rallied but could do nothing due to the fact that the tribunitian sacrosanctity prevented Atinius' attack from being repelled. Metellus was saved from death by the *intercessio* of another tribune, but even so, a *consecratio bonorum* was carried out against his property, and in addition the tribune tied a rope around his neck so tightly that blood came out of his ears. It should be added here that Pliny regarded the act of Atinius as felonious audacity – *scelerata audacia* – and was surprised that it was not avenged.[134]

The story was also described by Livy, but his account is preserved only in an abridged version of the epitome.[135] It appears from the text that the tribune Atinius ordered the censor Metellus, who had overlooked him in drawing up the list of senators, to be thrown off a cliff, which was prevented by other plebeian tribunes giving *auxilium*.

There is a major difference between the texts referred to: Pliny claimed that Atinius was removed from the Senate, whereas Livy's *epitome* mentions the omission[136] of his name during the *lectio senatus*. Both authors, on the other hand, cited Metellus as the author of the decision. This may either indicate that his colleague, Quintus Pompeius, did not object or, on the contrary, Pompeius did protest, and the tribune remained in the Senate, but he harboured such hatred towards Metellus that he decided to take revenge for the attempt to deprive him of his senatorial dignity.

The episode in question was also referred to by Cicero in his *De domo sua* speech.[137] Chronologically, it is of course the first testimony, but the speaker used the story as an example without giving details. It is therefore a good complement to the other sources.

Cicero, having suffered *consecratio bonorum* through Clodius,[138] tried to prove at all costs that this measure had not been applied legally. He claimed that, although Atinius had sacrificed Metellus' goods by placing a sacrificial vessel on the rostra and summoning a flute player,[139] his actions had no negative effect on Metellus. The speaker also added that a similar fate had befallen the censor Gnaeus Lentulus,[140] which, however, did not lead to the property being charged with any sacerdotal obligation. Cicero therefore suggested that the *consecratio bonorum* carried out by the plebeian tribune did not have any legal effect,[141] which analogously also applied to his estate consecrated by Clodius.

The stories cited allow some conclusions to be drawn. It seems that initially there was no prohibition against censors being indicted either during or after their term of office. By a decree of the Senate in 203 BC, the censors were exempted from having to appear for criminal trial. The Senate also expressed the general opinion that censors should not be held accountable for official decisions. The authority of the Senate was, it seems, so strong that from that time onwards no attempt was made to institute trials relating to the censors' decisions concerning the *regimen morum* or *locationes censoriae*.

Censorship was a peculiar office, and the decisions of officials often caused grief and anger, especially among citizens punished with a censorial mark. The lack of recourse sometimes caused frustration. Most of those punished simply sought to regain their good name. There was, on the other hand, one path that made it possible not to hold the censors accountable but rather to take revenge on them. Namely, one had to become a plebeian tribune[142] (which, of course, closed the path for patricians to seek revenge…). The tribunate, as an office primarily with blocking powers, offered the possibility of resorting to unusual means, such as *consecratio bonorum* or accusation of *perduellio*, and in extreme cases, even throwing the censors off the Tarpeian Rock. It was enough to accuse the censors of violating the tribunician sacrosanctity.

However, it should be noted that such actions by tribunes were political games and were considered as such. The censors usually enjoyed widespread respect. Therefore, the inclinations of tribunes usually met with opposition from their colleagues in office. The stories of these conflicts are extremely colourful. However, they should be regarded as attempts (usually not remarkably successful) to overcome powerlessness in the face of the censors, who held an office of colossal systemic importance during the Republic. The fact that the censors could not formally be held accountable was, of course, deeply justified: their powers were of a controlling nature and served as a guarantee for the stability of the state. However, this peculiar immunity was so irritating that attempts were made to circumvent it by various methods.

5. Summary

Regimen morum as an authority of the censors developed gradually. Although it is usually linked to its emergence with the enactment of the *lex Ovinia*, it can be argued that censors had previously attempted measures to sanction behaviour contrary to ancestral customs.

A censorial mark could result in exclusion from the Senate or the equestrian centuries, transfer to the ranks of *aerarii*, transfer to another ('inferior') *tribus* or the imposition of *ignominia* or loss of reputation. While this institution was separate from infamy, it may have preceded it in some cases: particularly when a citizen was punished regularly for repeated misbehaviour or behaviour that permanently stigmatised them among fellow citizens as unworthy of respect and trust.

In applying the mark, censors took discretionary decisions. Their discretion was limited by the need to take an oath of impartiality, as well as by the principle of collegiality within the office and the possibility of dissent from a colleague.

It was possible to hold a trial in which the person threatened with a mark could defend themselves (alone or through a lawyer), witnesses, and the accuser could appear. Initially it was up to the censors to decide whether to allow the proceedings to take place, but under the *lex Clodia*, they were obliged to do so, which paralysed the operation of the office for some time.

It can therefore be assumed that the censorial mark was largely an instrument of control for the upper classes, but not exclusively so. Ordinary citizens could also have feared it, particularly when their activities contrary to *mores maiorum* were of a permanent nature. These included, above all, engaging in disgraceful activities such as acting or fighting in the arena.

The effects of a censorial mark lasted in principle for the entire *lustrum*, while the next pair of censors could re-impose the *nota* at their discretion. This is what distinguishes a censorial *ignominia* or blemish on a name, from infamy, which was a loss of honour for a lifetime.

As a rule, censors were not held responsible for decisions made during their term of office (from 203 BC onwards), but there were times when they fell victim to retribution from plebeian tribunes.

Notes

1 Cf. A. Tarwacka, *Vir cum divortium fecit mulieri iudex pro censore est. Were the woman's morals examined and assessed during or out of a lawsuit?*, [in:] *Alternative Dispute Resolution: From Roman Law to Contemporary Regulations*, eds. B. Sitek, J. Szczerbowski, K. Ciućkowska-Leszczewicz, C. Lázaro Guillamón, S. Kursa, A. Bauknecht, Warsaw 2016, pp. 181–188.

2 Cf. A.H.J. Greenidge, *Infamia. Its Place in Roman Public and Private Law*, Oxford 1894, p. 63.

3 The term *praefectus* seems to have been used by Cicero to describe an office of *γυναικονόμος* existing in various Greek *poleis*. Cf. Arist., *Pol.* 1299a22; 1322b39; Plaut., *Aulul.* 503–504; E. Schmähling, *Die Sittenaufsicht der Censoren. Ein Beitrag zur Sittengeschichte der römischen Republik*, Stuttgart 1938, p. 10; A. Banfi, *Gynaikonomein. Intorno ad una magistratura ateniese del IV secolo ed alla sua presenza*

nelle fonti teatrali greche e romane, [in:] *Diritto e teatro in Grecia e Roma*, eds. E. Cantarella, L. Gagliardi, Milano 2007, pp. 17–29.

4 Cf. Dion. Hal., *Ant. Rom.* 2,25,6 = *leg. reg.* Rom. 7 (FIRA I). A form of control of women's customs was also certainly the *ius osculi*, i.e. checking whether she drunk wine by kissing her on the lips. Cf. Plin. Mai. 14,90; Plut., *Mor.* 265 b–e; Athen. 10,440e–441b; Tert., *Apol.* 6; J. Zabłocki, *Illeciti delle donne romane*, "Ius Antiquum" 1.8/2001, pp. 75 ff.; Idem, *The Prohibition on Women Drinking Wine in Ancient Rome*, [in:] J. Zabłocki, *Scripta Gelliana*, Warszawa 2020, pp. 93 ff.

5 Cf. ORF 8 LXIX, pp. 89–90; D. Kienast, *Cato der Zensor. Seine Persönlichkeit und seine Zeit*, Darmstadt 1979, p. 166; A.E. Astin, *Cato the Censor*, Oxford 1978, p. 116, fn. 41; R.A. Bauman, *Lawyers in Roman Transitional Politics. A Study of the Roman Jurists in Their Political Setting in the Late Republic and Triumvirate*, München 1985, pp. 157 ff.

6 More extensively on this subject A. Tarwacka, *Vir cum divortium fecit...*, pp. 181–188.

7 This is not a matter of *manus mariti*, but of control of customs. In the case of divorce, there was no *ipso iure* rupture of *manus*, as this required a separate legal action.

8 For a more extensive discussion see A. Tarwacka, *Vir cum divortium fecit...*, pp. 186–188.

9 There are doubts as to whether there should be a *non* after the words *ad hoc* in the text. However, it seems that the author did not have in mind here the loss of citizenship in general, but only the inclusion in the category of the *tributum* payers, from which citizens residing in Italy were exempted. Cf. E. Lo Cascio, *Il census a Roma e la sua evoluzione dall'età "serviana" alla prima età imperiale*, "MEFRA" 113.2/2001, p. 583.

10 Cf. C. Bur, *La citoyenneté dégradée. Une histoire de l'infamie à Rome (312 av. J.-C.-96 apr. J.-C.)*, Rome 2018, pp. 124 ff., on the link between *praeteritio* and *ius sententiae dicendae*.

11 Cf. Strab. 5,2,3; Hor., *Epist.* 1,6,62–63.

12 In 353 or as late as 270 BC. Cf. P.A. Brunt, *Italian Manpower 225 B.C.-A.D. 14*, Oxford 1971, pp. 515 ff.

13 They may have been enrolled in a special *centuria*, which C. Nicolet, *Les listes des centuries: La prétendue centurie 'Niquis scivit'*, "MEFRA" 113.2/2001, pp. 723–734, identifies it with the *centuria niquis scivit* mentioned by Festus (184 L.).

14 Cf. M. Humm, *Il 'regimen morum' dei censori e le identità dei cittadini*, [in:] *'Homo, caput, persona'. La costruzione giuridica dell' identità nel'esperienza romana*, eds. A. Corbino, M. Humbert, G. Negri, Pavia 2010, pp. 301–302. See, however, C. Bur, *Les censeurs privaient-ils du droit de vote ? Retour sur l'aerarium facere et le tribu mouere*, "MEFRA" 128.2/2016, pp. 419–437, who argues that both sanctions *aerarium facere* and *tribu movere* only served for the social degradation of the citizen and had no financial consequences.

15 Cf. P. Fraccaro, *'Tribules' ed 'aerarii'. Una ricerca di diritto pubblico romano*, [in:] P. Fraccaro, *Opuscula*, II, Pavia 1957, passim, especially pp. 168–170.

16 Liv. 29,37: ... Gaius Claudius (...) went up to the treasury, he, among the names of those he demoted to the status of aerarii, left that of his colleague. Marcus Livius then came into the treasury; and there, with the exception of the Maecia tribe, which had not participated in his conviction but had also not elected him either consul or censor after the conviction, he left all the Roman people with the status of aerarii, all thirty-four tribes... (transl. J.C. Yardley). The decisions of the censors, however, must have been consensual. In the case described by Livy, the actions of the censors were carried out, as it were, for show, since none of them could expect the approval of a colleague. Cf. Val. Max. 2,9,1; F. Millar, *The 'Aerarium' and Its Officials under the Empire*, "JRS" 54/1964, pp. 35–36; M.D. Thomas, *Censure of the Censors: Livy in a 'Comic' Mode*, "Ancient History Bulletin", 8.1/1994, pp. 18–27.

17 Cf. M. Ducos, *Les Romains et la loi. Recherches sur les rapports de la philosophie grecque et de la tradition romaine à la fin de la République*, Paris 1984, p. 385.
18 Cic., *De rep.* 4,6: The censor's judgment imposes almost no penalty except a blush upon the man he condemns. Therefore, as his decision affects nothing but the reputation, his condemnation is called "ignominy" (transl. C.W. Keyes). Cf. A. Wlosok, *'Nihil nisi ruborem' – über die Rolle der Scham in der römischen Rechtskultur*, "Grazer Beiträge" 9/1980, pp. 158 ff.; H.I. Flower, *Disgrace and Oblivion in Roman Political Culture*, Chapel Hill, NC 2006, p. 52. See also G. Greco, *Census. Profili storico-giuridici delle attività di censimento a Roma*, Torino 2022, pp. 134–135 on the concept of a culture where sanctions are based on shame.
19 Cic., *Pro Cluent.* 120: That is why in all statutes which contain clauses specifying the reasons which disqualify a man from holding public office, serving as a juror, or initiating a prosecution, the reason we are discussing, namely, ignominy, is never mentioned (transl. H. Grose Hodge). It should be added, however, that the punishment of placing a citizen on *tabulae Caeritum* resulted, as mentioned above, in the loss of *ius suffragii*.
20 P. Cornelius Lentulus Sura, consul in 71 BC, was removed from the Senate by the censors in 70 BC. He managed to win election as praetor in 63 BC and thus regain his seat in the Senate.
21 Val. Max. 2,9,9: Two examples of the same sort follow and it will suffice to add them. C. Geta was elected Censor after he had been expelled from the senate by Censors L. Metellus and Cn. Domitius. Likewise M. Valerius Messalla, after having been scraped by the censorial stigma, was later given the censorial power. Their humiliation whetted their energies. Urged by the shame of it, they strove with might and main to make their countrymen think them deserving to have the Censorship bestowed upon them rather than brought up against them (transl. D.R. Shackleton Bailey).
22 Cf. Cic., *Pro Cluent.* 119.
23 It was therefore preventive in nature. Cic., *Pro Cluent.* 120: because our forefathers intended to invest the censor's office with the power of inspiring fear, not of punishing for life (transl. H. Grose Hodge). Cf. E. Schmähling, *op. cit.*, p. 1.
24 Cic., *Pro Cluent.* 122: How then can it occur to you to give the name of verdict to decisions which you see annulled by the people, rejected by sworn jurors, passed over by magistrates, altered by successive wielders of the censor's power, a subject of variance between those who wield it jointly? (transl. H. Grose Hodge). However, it has been rightly pointed out by A.H.J. Greenidge, *Infamia…*, p. 54, that the disregard of the *nota* by officials or assemblies could not have been the rule, as this would have undermined the legitimacy of the *regimen morum*. Instead, it seems that after a certain period of time – when a citizen proved by his behaviour that his morals had improved – the people could decide to elect him to office.
25 C. Bur, *La citoyenneté dégradée…*, pp. 3 ff.
26 Cf. Varr., *L.L.* 6,71; Cic., *Pro Sest.* 135; Cic., *In Pis.* 4,10.
27 Cf. Cic., *De rep.* 4,6; Liv. 23,23,4.
28 See Figure 1. Cf. M. Torelli, *Typology & Structure of Roman Historical Reliefs*, Ann Arbor, MI 1982, p. 10; C. Bur, *Le spectacle du cens. Relecture du déroulement de la professio sous la République romaine*, "Athenaeum" 105.2/2017, pp. 520 ff.
29 Cf. Ascon. 84 C. The *intercessio* of the colleague resulted in the withdrawal of the note, but the censors did not have to agree on the *subscriptio*, as long as both wanted to punish the citizen. Cf. A. Fernández de Buján, *Derecho público romano*[26], Madrid 2023, pp. 174.
30 Val. Max. 4,1,10: Nor did his censorial moderation show itself less clearly on his tribunal. In reviewing the centuries of knights, he observed C. Licinius Sacerdos come forward as his name was called and said that he knew him to have committed perjury in set terms; therefore if anyone wished to charge him, his, Scipio's, testimony would

be at his disposal. But when nobody took the matter up, "Lead your horse across, Sacerdos," he said, "and go free of the censorial stigma. For I must not seem to have played the role of prosecutor cum witness cum jury in your particular" (transl. D.R. Shackleton Bailey). Cf. Cic., *De off.* 1,40; 3,111; 3,113; *Pro Cluent.* 134; Quint., *Inst. or.* 5,11,13; Plut., *Mor.* 200 e; C. Masi Doria, *'Exemplum pessimum': Quinto Mucio e il 'testimonium' in Val. Max. 4.1.11*, "Index" 38/2010, pp. 73–75; Eadem, *Status and Contract in Ancient Rome: With Some Thoughts on the 'Future of Obligations'*, [in:] *Obligations in Roman Law. Past, Present, and Future*, ed. by T.A.J. McGinn, Ann Arbor, MI 2012, pp. 109–112.

31 Cf. Cic., *Pro Cluent.* 134; Plut., *Mor.* 200 e; Quint., *Inst. or.* 5,11,13. P. Fraccaro, *Ricerche storiche e letterarie sulla censura del 184/183 (M. Porcio Catone L. Valerio Flacco)*, [in:] P. Fraccaro, *Opuscula*, I, Pavia 1956, p. 431.

32 The term *verba concepta* can mean a procedural formula (G. 4,30) or a formula of stipulation or oath. It seems, therefore, that the equestrian lied in a private trial.

33 Cf. Plut., *Mor.* 200 e. See C. Bur, *La citoyenneté dégradée…*, pp. 84–89.

34 Gell. 5,13,4 Cf. below.

35 This is according to Plutarch's account (*G. Gracch.* 2,4–5). In contrast, Gellius (15,12) cited the same speech as *an oratio ad populum in contione*. It must be remembered, however, that the censors convened the *contiones*, so the two do not contradict each other. Cf. also Cic., *Orat.* 233.

36 Cic., *Pro Cluent.* 131.

37 It must be added, however, that the second censor, Lentulus, disagreed with his colleague's decisions, which may have resulted in the mark ultimately not being applied. Cf. Cic., *Pro Cluent.* 132.

38 Cic., *De or.* 2,287: for example when the censor Lepidus had taken a horse from Marcus Antistius of Pyrgi and Antistius's friends made an outcry and kept asking him what answer he should give his father to explain why his horse had been taken away from him, a first-class farmer, and an extremely economical and moderate and thrifty person, he said his answer would be 'I don't accept any of that!' (transl. E.W. Sutton, H. Rackham).

39 *Rhet. Her.* 2,26,41: Again, it is a fault to refute one disputed point by another disputed point, as follows: "You should not be satisfied, Censors, when this defendant says that he was unable to be present as he had sworn he would be. I ask, would he have given this same excuse to the tribune of the soldiers if he had failed to appear for military duty?" This is faulty because a matter not clearly settled or adjudged, but entangled with difficulties and based on a like point of dispute is cited as an example (transl. H. Caplan).

40 Gell. 16,4,4: then an oath was taken, binding them to appear, with the addition of the following exceptions: 'Unless there be any of the following excuses: a funeral in his family or purification from a dead body (provided these were not appointed for that day in order that he might not appear on that day), a dangerous disease, or an omen which could not be passed by without expiatory rites, or an anniversary sacrifice which could not be properly celebrated unless he himself were present on that day, violence or the attack of enemies, a stated and appointed day with a foreigner; if anyone shall have any of these excuses, then on the day following that on which he is excused for these reasons he shall come and render service to the one who held the levy in that district, village or town' (transl. J.C. Rolfe).

41 Gell. 16,4,5: Also in the same book are these words: "When a soldier was absent on the appointed day and had not been excused, he was branded as a deserter" (transl. J.C. Rolfe).

42 D. 22,3,19,1 (Ulp. 7 *disp.*): Where anyone who promised to appear in court alleges as a reason for not doing so that he has been absent on public business, or that some malicious act of his adversary prevented him from appearing, or his health, or a storm hindered him, he must prove it (transl. S.P. Scott).

43 C. Bur, *La citoyenneté dégradée...*, pp. 99 ff.

44 Varr., *L.L.* 6,71. *Aequum* was a concept deeply rooted in Roman law. I do not think that the activities of censors can be considered to be *"ausserhalb des 'ius'-Bereiches"*, i.e. "outside the zone of ius", as argued by E. Pólay, *Das 'regimen morum' des Zensors und die sogenannte Hausgerichtsbarkeit*, [in:] *Studi in onore di Edoardo Volterra*, III, Milano 1971, passim (e.g. p. 277); cf. A. Wlosok, *op. cit.*, pp. 157–158. Customary law counted as *ius* just as other sources of law.

45 Gell. 14,2,8: He maintained that the testimony relating to the life and conduct of the two parties was irrelevant; for this was a case of claiming money before a private judge, not a question of morals inquired into by the censors (transl. J.C. Rolfe).

46 For a detailed discussion of this process, see J. Zabłocki, *Appunti sull''officium iudicis' nella 'Noctes Atticae'*, [in:] *Au-delà des fontierès. Mélanges de droit romain offers à Witold Wołodkiewicz*, II, eds. M. Zabłocka, J. Krzynówek, J. Urbanik, Z. Służewska, Varsovie 2000, pp. 1115–1126; Idem, *'Iudex qui iuravit rem sibi non liquere'*, [in:] J. Zabłocki, *Scripta Gelliana*, Warsaw 2020, pp. 241–255. Cf. L. Holford-Strevens, *Aulus Gellius. An Antonine Scholar and His Achievement*, Oxford 2003, pp. 295 ff.

47 Gell. 14,2,7.

48 Cf. Cic., *De inv.* 2,37; *Rhet. Her.* 2,3,5.

49 Cf. Zon. 7,19; D.F. Epstein, *Personal Enmity in Roman Politics 218-43 B.C.*, London–New York 1987 (reprint 1989), pp. 72–73.

50 Cic., *De off.* 3,113: That is clearly proved (...) by the investigations made by the censors and the penalties imposed by them; for there were no cases in which they used to render more rigorous decisions than in cases of violation of an oath (transl. W. Miller); Cic., *De off.* 1,40; Gell. 6,18,10: This dishonourable cleverness of theirs was considered so shameful, that they were generally despised and reprobated; and later the censors punished them with all possible fines and marks of disgrace, on the ground that they had not done what they had sworn to do (transl. J.C. Rolfe). Cf. Liv. 24,18; T. Mommsen, *Römisches Staatsrecht*[3], II.1, Graz 1952 (reprint), p. 380.

51 Cic. *De leg.* 3,7: They shall be two in number... (transl. C.W. Keyes). Cf. H. Siber, *Zur Kollegialität der römischen Zensoren,* [in:] *Festschrift Fritz Schulz*, I, ed. W. Flume, Weimar 1951, pp. 466–474; W. Kunkel, R. Wittmann, *Staatsordnung und Staatspraxis der römischen Republik. Zweiter Abschnitt. Die Magistratur*, München 1995, s. 199–201; R. Bunse, *Die frühe Zensur und die Entstehung der Kollegialität*, "Historia" 50.2/2001, pp. 145–162; N. El Beheiri, *Das regimen morum der Zensoren. Die Konstruktion des römischen Gemeinwesens*, Berlin 2012, pp. 127–131; C. Bur, *La citoyenneté dégradée...*, pp. 65–70.

52 Cic., *Pro Cluent.* 122. Cf. H. Siber, *Zur Kollegialität...*, pp. 466–474; F. De Martino, *Storia della costituzione romana*[2], II, Napoli 1973, pp. 266–267; R. Bunse, *op. cit.*, pp. 145–162.

53 Cf. G. Rotondi, *'Leges publicae populi Romani'. Elenco cronologico con una introduzione sull'attività legislativa dei comizi romani*, Milano 1912, p. 398.

54 The others are: *lex annonaria, lex de iure et tempore legum rogandarum, lex de collegiis*. Cf. Ascon. 8 C.; G. Rotondi, *op. cit.*, pp. 393–398; W.J. Tatum, *The Patrician Tribune Publius Clodius Pulcher*, Chapel Hill, NC 1999, pp. 114 ff.

55 Cic., *Pro Sest.* 55: ... to the effect that the censors' investigation of character, that is to say, the verdict, so authoritative, of a most hallowed magistracy, should be removed from the constitution (transl. R. Gardner).

56 Cic., *Har. resp.* 58: ... (scil. Clodius) swept away the censorship (transl. N.H. Watts).

57 Cic., *De prov. cons.* 46: You must, therefore, either decide that (...) that the censors' verdict and power of investigation and their most strict supervision of morals have not been removed from the State by pernicious laws (transl. R. Gardner).

58 Cf. Cic., *De prov. cons.* 45–46.

59 Cic., *In Pis.* 4,9: He too it was who, wallowing in unparalleled and abominable debaucheries, abolished the censorship, that ancient guardian of honour and chastity;

Cic., *In Pis.* 5,10: For nigh a century we had maintained the law of Aelius and Fufius, and for 400 the censor's prerogative of criticism and stigmatization—institutions which now and then a scoundrel has had the audacity, but none the power, to uproot; powers which none has with such wanton profligacy endeavoured to curtail, in order to prevent judgement being passed upon our morals once in every five years (transl. N.H. Watts).

60 This gives the year 455 BC, before the office of censor was even introduced. *Regimen morum* became the competence of censors gradually. It seems, therefore, that Cicero was greatly exaggerating here.

61 Cic., *Ad Att.* 4,2,6: I have let Pompey nominate me one of his Lieutenant Commissioners, but on the understanding that my hands are left quite free. If I did not want to leave it open to myself to stand for the Censorship if next year's Consuls hold an election to that office (transl. D.R. Shackleton Bailey).

62 Ascon. 8 C.: We have said that in the consulship of L. Piso and A. Gabinius P. Clodius, tribune of the plebs, passed four laws which endangered the Roman people: (...) the fourth to prevent the censors in selecting the Senate from passing over or branding with any mark of ill-repute any man who had not been charged before them and condemned by the declared verdict of both censors (transl. R.G. Lewis).

63 Schol. Bob. 132 St.: He enumerated the laws of Clodius, one of which was that the censor, when drawing up the list of the Senate, should not omit any person except those known to have been condemned (transl. AT).

64 Dio Cass. 38,13: He also forbade the censors to remove anybody from any order or to censure any one, except as he should be tried and convicted before them both (transl. E. Cary). Cf. Zon. 7,19: later it was determined that a man once enrolled in the senate should be a senator for life, and that his name should not be erased, unless he had been convicted of some crime and been deprived of his citizenship, or had been shown to be leading an evil life (transl. E. Cary). Perhaps in this passage Zonaras, relying on the work of Cassius Dio, referred to the *lex Clodia*, but he only wrote about *lectio senatus*.

65 Dio Cass. 40,57,1; cf. G. Rotondi, *op. cit.*, p. 412.

66 Cf. T.R.S. Broughton, *The Magistrates of the Roman Republic*, II, New York 1952, p. 215; J. Suolahti, *The Roman Censors. A Study on Social Structure*, Helsinki 1963, pp. 477–483; E. Reigadas Lavandero, *Censura y res publica: aportación constitucional y protagonismo político*, Madrid 2000, pp. 471–477.

67 Cic., *Ad Att.* 4,17,7: Well, there you have the news of Rome – I don't suppose you are interested in the census, which has now been given up as a bad job, or the trials under the lex Clodia (transl. D.R. Shackleton Bailey).

68 Ludwig Lange's conjecture in proposing to change the incomprehensible *lege Coctia* to *Clodia* seems most commendable here.

69 T. Mommsen, *Römisches Staatsrecht...*, II.1, pp. 386–387.

70 W.J. Tatum, *The 'lex Clodia de censoria notione'*, "CQ" 85.1/1990, pp. 34–43.

71 By virtue of the *lex Cornelia de quaestoribus XX creandis*. Cf. G. Rotondi, *op. cit.*, pp. 353–354.

72 Cf. H. Benner, *Die Politik des P. Clodius Pulcher. Untersuchungen zur Denaturierung des Clientelwesens in der ausgehenden römischen Republik*, Stuttgart 1987, pp. 51–52.

73 C. Bur, *La citoyenneté dégradée...*, pp. 107 ff.

74 Cf. C. Nicolet, *The World of the Citizen in Republican Rome*, transl. P.S. Falla, Berkeley–Los Angeles, CA 1980, p. 56.

75 Val. Max. 6,2,8.

76 Even to the bedroom – Dion. Hal., *Ant. Rom.* 20,13,3.

77 What is certified, however, are the cases of revenge, about which more below.

78 Cf. Dion. Hal., *Ant. Rom.* 19,19.

79 See my forthcoming paper on the censorial edicts.

80 Sulla does not seem to have abolished censorship, but in fact deprived it of certain powers. Cf. E. Gabba, *Il ceto equestre e il senato di Silla*, "Athenaeum" 34.3–4/1956, pp. 124–138; F.X. Ryan, *The 'lectio senatus' after Sulla*, "RhM" 139/1996, pp. 189–191; cf. above.

81 Cf. G. Clemente, *Cicerone, Clodio e la censura: la politica e l'ideale*, [in:] *'Munuscula'. Scritti in ricordo di Luigi Amirante*, ed. E. Dovere, Napoli 2010, pp. 72–73.

82 Cf. A.E. Astin, *Cicero and the Censorship*, "CP" 80.3/1985, pp. 233–239.

83 Cic., *Pro Cluent.* 122: And lastly, the censors themselves have time after time thrown over the verdicts—if you wish to call them such—of their predecessors. So little importance indeed do the censors themselves attach to each other's verdicts that one will not only arraign but even annul his colleague's verdict: one will propose to degrade a man from the Senate, while the other keeps him there, and holds him worthy of the most honourable rank. One orders him to be degraded or expelled from his tribe, the other forbids it (transl. H. Grose Hodge).

84 Cic., *Top.* 28: Secondly, definitions are made partly by enumeration and partly by analysis; by enumeration, when the thing which has been set up for definition is divided into its members as it were: for instance, if one should define the civil law as made up of statutes, decrees of the Senate, judicial decisions, opinions of those learned in the law, edicts of magistrates, custom, and equity (transl. H.M. Hubbell).

85 Cf. Cic., *Pro Rosc. Amer.* 111–115, where Cicero stated that someone who neglected a mandate should be condemned with an infamatory action, and equated *crimen mandati* with *furtum*. Other *famosa iudicia* in Cic., *Pro Caec.* 7–8; *Top.* 42 and D. 3,2,1 (Iulian. 1 *ad ed.*).

86 Cf. Val. Max. 2,9,9.

87 Cf. Cic., *De off.* 1,40; Liv. 24,18; Gell. 6,18.

88 Cf. in more detail A. Tarwacka, *Come vendicarsi dei censori? Scontri politici e responsabilità penale dei guardiani della morale*, "Diritto@Storia" 14/2016, http://www.dirittoestoria.it/14/tradizione/Tarwacka-Come-vendicarsi-dei-censori.htm.

89 Cf. T.R.S. Broughton, *op. cit.*, I, p. 192.

90 Dion. Hal., *Ant. Rom.* 19,16,5: those magistrates who are subject to no accounting for their administration, the officials we call censors (transl. E. Cary).

91 Cf. C. De Boor, *Fasti censorii*, Berolini 1873, p. 13; T.R.S. Broughton, *op. cit.*, I, p. 259; J. Suolahti, *The Roman Censors…*, pp. 309–315; E. Reigadas Lavandero, *op. cit.*, pp. 251–256.

92 Liv. 24,18; Val. Max. 2,9,8. The same censors also punished with a mark those who did not keep their oath to Hannibal that they would return to his camp if Rome rejected the proposal for an exchange of prisoners they were to submit to the Senate. Cf. Gell. 6,18.

93 Val. Max. 2,9,8: Now this Censorship has passed from the Forum to the camp, unwilling that the enemy should be either feared or deceived (transl. D.R. Shackleton Bailey).

94 Liv. 24,43,2–3: At Rome, as soon as the new tribunes of the plebs entered office, an indictment to appear before the people was immediately issued to the censors Publius Furius and Marcus Atilius by one of these tribunes, Marcus Metellus. The previous year, when Metellus was quaestor, they had deprived him of his horse, expelled him from his tribe, and degraded him to the status of aerarius over the conspiracy to abandon Italy that had been hatched at Cannae. However, aided by nine tribunes, who ruled against their being tried while in office, they were released (transl. J.C. Yardley).

95 There is no doubt about this, since the *lustrum* did not take place due to the death of Furius, after which Atilius resigned the office. Cf. Liv. 24,43,4.

96 O. Licandro, *'In magistratu damnari'. Ricerche sulla responsabilità dei magistrati romani durante l'esercizio delle funzioni*, Torino 1999, pp. 201–205.

97 Cf. C. De Boor, *op. cit.*, pp. 15–16; T.R.S. Broughton, *op. cit.*, I, p. 306; J. Suolahti, *The Roman Censors…*, pp. 325–331; E. Reigadas Lavandero, *op. cit.*, pp. 269–278.

98 Liv. 29,37,17: As the censors were now in disrepute, the plebeian tribune Gnaeus Baebius, thinking he had a chance to make political capital at their expense, served a summons on both. The procedure was blocked by a unanimous decision of the senators for fear that the office of censor might later be subject to the whim of the people (transl. J.C. Yardley).
99 Cf. T.R.S. Broughton, *op. cit.*, I, pp. 307 and 312.
100 Val. Max. 7,2,6: When the same two were accused from the rostra by Tribune of the Plebs Cn. Baebius because of their unduly harsh exercise of the Censorship, the senate by its decree exempted them from answering the charge. They made that office clear of any apprehension of judicial action; it should demand justification, not provide it (transl. D.R. Shackleton Bailey).
101 Cf. Liv. 29,37; D.F. Epstein, *op. cit.*, p. 17; M.D. Thomas, *op. cit.*, pp. 18–27.
102 Differently, O. Licandro, *op. cit.*, p. 208, who considered that the trial was initiated against the censors in office.
103 Cf. Val. Max. 2,9,9.
104 Cf. C. De Boor, *op. cit.*, p. 18; T.R.S. Broughton, *op. cit.*, I, pp. 423–424; J. Suolahti, *The Roman Censors…*, pp. 371–376; E. Reigadas Lavandero, *op. cit.*, pp. 331–342.
105 Cf. T.R.S. Broughton, *op. cit.*, I, p. 425.
106 Liv. 43,16,1–2: In reviewing the knights, the censorship of these officials was rather stern and harsh; they deprived many of their horses. When in this matter they had offended the order of knights, they added fire to the grudge by a proclamation, in which they proclaimed that none of those who in the censorship of Quintus Fulvius and Aulus Postumius had farmed the public revenues or the public works should appear at the auction of Claudius and Sempronius, or should be a partner or sharer in the contracting (transl. A.C. Schlesinger).
107 Liv. 43,16,3: When, after many complaints about this decree, the veteran tax-gatherers were unable to induce the Senate to set a limit to the censors' power, at last in a tribune of the people, Publius Rutilius, who was angry with the censors over a dispute concerning a private matter, they found an advocate for their cause (transl. A.C. Schlesinger).
108 The existence of a conflict between publicans and equestrians on the one hand and senators on the other was highlighted by F. Salerno, *Dalla consecratio alla publicatio bonorum*, Napoli 1990, pp. 116–118.
109 Cf. Polyb. 6,17,5; Cic., *Ad. Att.* 1,17,9.
110 E. Reigadas Lavandero, *op. cit.*, p. 336, fn. 39, concluded that Rutilius was not included in the list of the Senate (*praeteritus*) by the censors and hence his anger. However, this opinion is not supported by the sources.
111 The verb *appellare* here refers to the use of the *ius auxilii*.
112 Cf. Liv. 43,16,4–5; Val. Max. 6,5,3.
113 Liv. 43,16,6–7: A dispute having arisen from this cause, when the veteran tax-gatherers had resorted to the tribune, a proposed law was suddenly published under the name of the one tribune, stating that whereas Gaius Claudius and Tiberius Sempronius had let certain public revenues and public works, the letting of these should be void; they should be let anew, and everyone without restriction should have the right of farming and contracting (transl. A.C. Schlesinger). Cf. G. Rotondi, *op. cit.*, pp. 284–285; J. Bleicken, *Das Volkstribunat der klassischen Republik*, München 1955, p. 62.
114 Liv. 43,16,8–13: The tribune of the people announced for the assembly a day for voting on this proposal. When this day came, as the censors came forward to advise against the law, while Gracchus was speaking there was silence; when heckling greeted Claudius, he ordered the herald to bring the meeting to order. When this was done, the tribune, complaining that the meeting had been taken out of his hands and that he had been deprived of his authority, left the Capitol, where the assembly was. Next day he raised a great uproar. He first dedicated to the gods the property of Tiberius Gracchus because in the matter of the fine and the bonds imposed on one who had appealed to a

tribune, Gracchus had, by not obeying the tribune's interposition, deprived him of his authority; he set a day for the trial of Gaius Claudius on the charge of taking the meeting away from him; and he announced that he judged each censor guilty of treason, and asked of Gaius Sulpicius the city praetor a day for an assembly. Since the censors did not object to having the people pass judgment on them at the first possible moment, the day for the assembly-trial for treason was set for the twenty-third and twenty-fourth of September (transl. A.C. Schlesinger).

115 The tribune therefore *exercised* his *summa coërcendi potestas*; cf. B. Santalucia, *Processo penale*, [in:] B. Santalucia, *Studi di diritto penale romano*, Roma 1994, pp. 165–166.

116 *Consecratio bonorum* in favour of the temple of Ceres. Cf. T. Mommsen, *Römisches Staatsrecht…*, I, p. 137; W. Kunkel, R. Wittmann, *op. cit.*, p. 173.

117 The tribune could not convene the *comitia centuriata* himself. Cf. Liv. 26,3,9; Gell. 6,9,9; B. Santalucia, *I tribuni e le centurie*, [in:] B. Santalucia, *Studi di diritto penale romano*, Roma 1994, p. 56 ff.

118 Liv. 43,16,14–16: Claudius pleaded his cause first; and when of the twelve centuries of knights eight had condemned the censor, along with many other centuries of the first class, at once the leading men of the state, in the sight of the people, laid aside their gold rings and put on mourning, in order to go about entreating the commons. Chiefly, however, Tiberius Gracchus is said to have changed men's minds, because, although there was everywhere shouting from the commons that Gracchus was in no danger, he swore in formal terms that if his colleague were condemned he would not await the outcome of his own trial, but would accompany Claudius into exile. None the less, so near did the defendant come to the last ray of hope that only eight centuries were lacking for condemnation. When Claudius had been acquitted, the tribune of the people said that he did not care about the case of Gracchus (transl. A.C. Schlesinger).

119 Cf. Gell. 6,9,9: Cicero, in the sixth book of his Republic, wrote: "Which indeed was so much the more remarkable, because, while the colleagues were in the same case, they not only did not incur the same hatred, but the affection felt for Gracchus even averted (deprecabatur) the unpopularity of Claudius" (transl. J.C. Rolfe).

120 T. Mommsen, *Römisches Staatsrecht…*, I, p. 146, was convinced that the tribune presided over the assembly. However, it seems more likely that it was a higher official, in this case the city praetor, who presided. Cf. B. Santalucia, *I tribuni…*, pp. 56 ff.

121 Cf. C. De Boor, *op. cit.*, p. 20; T.R.S. Broughton, *op. cit.*, I, pp. 474–475; J. Suolahti, *The Roman Censors…*, pp. 393–394.

122 Cf. T.R.S. Broughton, *op. cit.*, I, p. 480.

123 Cf. Gell. 16,8. The censors were at odds with each other; cf. Val. Max. 6,4,2; *De vir. ill.* 58,9.

124 Cf. M.C. Alexander, *Trials in the Late Roman Republic, 149 BC to 50 BC*, Toronto–Buffalo–London 1990, p. 5.

125 On *lustrum infelix* cf. Fest 366 L, s.v. *referri diem prodictam*; J. Linderski, *The Augural Law*, "ANRW" II.16.3/1986, pp. 2186–2189.

126 By 280 BC.

127 Cic., *De or.* 2,268: Compare with this the retort of Africanus, when Asellus taxed him with that unfortunate purification of his.a 'Do not be surprised,' said Africanus, 'for he who delivered you from disfranchisement completed the purification by sacrificing the bull' (transl. E.W. Sutton, H. Rackham).

128 Val. Max. 4,1,10: When as Censor he was winding up the census and in the sacrifice of solitaurilia the scribe was reciting before him from the public tables the formula of prayer in which the immortal gods were asked to make the state of the Roman people better and greater, "It is good and great enough," said Scipio. "So I pray the gods to keep it safe in perpetuity." And on the words he gave order that the formula in the public tables be emended accordingly. From that time on Censors have used this modest form of prayer in winding up censuses (transl. D.R. Shackleton Bailey).

129 Cf. C. De Boor, *op. cit.*, p. 21; T.R.S. Broughton, *op. cit.*, I, p. 500; J. Suolahti, *The Roman Censors*..., pp. 403–406; E. Reigadas Lavandero, *op. cit.*, pp. 377–386.

130 Liv., *Per.* 59; cf. below.

131 Plin. Mai. 7,143–144: Nevertheless at the very height of his distinguished career, when coming back from the Field at midday, the market place and Capitol being empty, he was carried off to the Tarpeian Rock by Gaius Atinius Labeo, surnamed Macerio, tribune of the plebs, whom when censor he had ejected from the Senate, with the intention of hurling him down the cliff; the numerous company of persons who called him their father did it is true hasten to his aid, but as was inevitable in this sudden emergency, too late and as if coming for his funeral, and as he had not the right to resist and to repel the hallowed person of a tribune his virtue and his strictness would have resulted in his destruction, but with difficulty another tribune was found to intercede, and he was recalled from the very threshold of death; and subsequently he lived on the charity of another, as his own property had immediately been confiscated on the proposal of the very man whom he had himself caused to be condemned, just as though the penalty exacted from him of having his throat tied in a rope and the blood forced out through his ears were not sufficient! (transl. H. Rackham).

132 Cf. T.R.S. Broughton, *op. cit.*, I, pp. 500–501.

133 Further on, Pliny (7,145) wrote about dragging the censor through the middle of the city: ...*per mediam urbem censore tracto*...

134 Plin. Mai. 7,146: For the rest I know not whether it counts to the credit of our morals or increases the anguish of our indignation that among all the many Metelli that criminal audacity of Gaius Atinius for ever went unpunished (transl. H. Rackham).

135 Liv., *Per.* 59: Gaius Atinius Labeo, tribune of the commons, ordered Censor Quintus Metellus, who had passed him by in revising the roll of the Senate, to be thrown from the Tarpeian Rock; the other tribunes of the commons came to the aid of Metellus to prevent this from taking place (transl. A.C. Schlesinger).

136 Perhaps the *plebiscitum Atinium*, by virtue of which holding the tribunate entitled one to a seat in the Senate, was already in force at that time. If this Atinius was the proposer, he may indeed have felt offended by such a blatant violation of the rules introduced by the plebiscite. Cf. G. Rotondi, *op. cit.*, p. 330; W. Kunkel, R. Wittmann, *op. cit.*, p. 172, fn. 272.

137 Cic., *De dom.* 123–124: And yet our fathers could remember how Gaius Atinius, with brazier duly placed upon the rostra and with flute-player in attendance, so devoted the property of Quintus Metellus, who, in his capacity of censor, had ejected him from the senate, your grandfather, Quintus Metellus, and yours, Publius Servilius, and your great-grandfather, Publius Scipio. And what was the result? Were these mad proceedings, inspired by several examples afforded by our earliest history, detrimental to that great and renowned gentleman Metellus? Assuredly not. We have seen the censor Gnaeus Lentulus treated in the same manner by a tribune of the plebs; and was that tribune able by so doing to put any religious embarrassment upon the property of Lentulus? (transl. N.H. Watts).

138 Cf. D. Stockton, *Cicero: a Political Biography*, Oxford 1971, pp. 196 ff.; M. Fuhrmann, *Cicero und die römische Republik*, Düsseldorf 2006, pp. 128 ff.

139 On the rituals accompanying the *consecratio*, F. Salerno, *op. cit.*, pp. 14 ff.

140 Cf. C. De Boor, *op. cit.*, p. 26; T.R.S. Broughton, *op. cit.*, II, p. 126; E. Reigadas Lavandero, *op. cit.*, pp. 447–454.

141 Cf. T. Mommsen, *Römisches Staatsrecht*..., I, p. 138.

142 Cf. App., *Bell. civ.*, 1,28.

IV Censorial mark concerning morality in family life

1. Preliminary remarks

Dionysius of Halicarnassus handed down to posterity an extraordinarily vivid picture of a Roman censor looking into the bedrooms of his fellow citizens and controlling every manifestation of domestic life.[1] Plutarch, too, emphasised that among the Romans, neither marriage, child-rearing, daily life, nor feasting could be outside the control and evaluation exercised by the censors.[2] These opinions indicate that it seemed strange to foreigners for magistrates to interfere in the affairs of the family, which they felt should be a private sphere of life. However, such an arrangement had specific reasons.

The family had not only social or economic importance in Republican Rome but also political importance.[3] It was headed by the *pater familias*, who exercised domestic worship (*sacra familiaria*), owned property, and wielded unlimited power over the free members of the family: the descendants (*patria potestas*) and the wife (*manus*), as well as the slaves (*dominica potestas*), and those in a position similar to slaves. His actions could have a serious impact on the functioning of the state: the presence of sons in the political and military structures, the payment of taxes, and even the balance between the world of men and the world of deities (*pax deorum*). Therefore, the family was not completely outside the control of the state. An instrument of this oversight was the supervision of customs – *regimen morum*. Officials could impose a censorial mark on a citizen whom they considered guilty of negligence.

From the Greek authors' texts cited, it was considered reprehensible to punish slaves excessively cruelly, to be too harsh or, on the contrary, lenient in the upbringing of children, to deal unjustly with one's wife, and when children were disobedient to aged parents, as well as when brothers wanted to obtain more than their due share of property. It was also forbidden to organise all-night feasts, deprave the youth, neglect ancestor worship and funerals.[4] Cases of the application of the censorial mark in family matters should therefore be analysed in more detail based on further source texts.

However, it should be noted that due to their high narrative potential, some of the situations discussed took on an anecdotal character. Therefore, they cannot be seen as evidence of systematic reprehension for certain behaviour, but rather as

DOI: 10.4324/9781003486664-5

one-off cases. An example of such a situation is the decision of Cato the Elder. Plutarch noted[5] that Cato had removed Manilius, who had been likely to attain the dignity of consul, from the Senate for having kissed his wife in the daytime in the presence of his daughter.[6] Cato himself claimed that he only embraced his wife when thunder was heard and joked that, when Jupiter thundered, he was a happy man.

It seems that Ammianus Marcellinus had the same story in mind[7] when he condemned the behaviour of citizens, pointing out that in the time of their ancestors, a senator was punished with a censorial mark for kissing his wife in the presence of his daughter. This example cannot prove the existence of a rigid rule followed by all censors, but only the severity of Cato, which was even proverbial. The whole affair grew over time into an anecdote detached from specific personal details and became a general example of censorial severity.

2. Marriage

Firstly, it is necessary to discuss situations in which the censors interfered in matters related to marriage. However, since the nuptial ceremony was usually preceded by the engagement, it should be examined whether this preliminary step was subject to magisterial control.

The object of the censors' interest was the various cases of reneging on concluded contracts, and the Roman *sponsalia*, or betrothal,[8] were initially contractual in nature.

> Varr., *L.L.* 6,71: *Qui spoponderat filiam, despondisse dicebant, quod de sponte eius, id est de voluntate, exierat: non enim si volebat, dabat, quod sponsu erat alligatus: nam ut in comoediis vides dici: "Sponden tuam gnatam filio uxorem meo?". Quod tum et praetorium ius ad legem et censorium iudicium ad aequum existimabatur.*
>
> *He who spoponderat 'had promised' his daughter, they said, despondisse 'had promised her away,' because she had gone out of the power of his sponte 'inclination,' that is, from the control of his voluntas 'desire': for even if he wished not to give her, still he gave her, because he was bound by his sponsus 'formal promise': for you see it said, as in comedies: Do you now promise your daughter to my son as wife? This was at that time considered a principle established by the praetors to supplement the statutes, and a decision of the censors for the sake of fairness.*
>
> (Transl. R.G. Kent)

Varro relayed that when a father pledged his daughter to someone for marriage, it was called *despondere*, indicating that the decision was no longer dependent on his will. This refers to giving up the possibility of making a different decision in the future and being bound by an oath. The giving of a daughter in marriage no longer depended solely on the father's will but on the pledge he had made. The antiquarian also cited the question asked by the father of the future bride: "Do you promise your daughter to be my son's wife?" pointing out that this appeared in comedies.[9] Failure to fulfil such a betrothal *sponsio* was then sanctioned both in praetorian law *ad legem*, i.e. according to statute law, and in the court of censor *ad aequum*, i.e. according to equity and ancestral customs. The fiancé's father could therefore avail himself of the complaint for breaking the promise – *actio ex stipulatu*, while the woman's *pater familias* had to additionally face a censorial mark. However, a doubt arises concerning the breaking of the betrothal by the fiancé or his father.

In his *Attic Nights*, Aulus Gellius quotes an excerpt from *De dotibus* by the jurist Servius Sulpicius Rufus, which describes how betrothals were celebrated in the Latium area until the *lex Iulia de civitate Latinis danda* of 90 BC.[10] This involved a verbal *sponsio* contract between the father of the bride-to-be and the fiancé, with the unilateral breaking of the contract entitling the other party to bring an action (*actio ex stipulatu*). The judge appointed in the suit assessed the validity of the claim and, if he considered the rupture of the betrothal to be unjustified, awarded an amount based on his assessment of the dispute's value. The described procedure seems to coincide with that described by Varro. It can be assumed that in both Rome and Latium, breaking an engagement could lead to a legal complaint, but over time, the possibility of a clause guaranteeing the payment of a fine was abolished. In Latium, therefore, this custom ceased to exist after the *Lex Iulia*.

In the case of betrothal, the censorial mark was complementary to the protection provided by the praetor. However, it can be assumed that the censorial regulations were earlier, as indicated by the archaic nature of the institution of engagement.[11] It should be noted that Varro wrote about these sanctions as an ancient institution, using the past tense, which means that they were no longer in use at the end of the Republic. In the case of the censorial mark, this may have been related to the crisis of the censor's office. However, it was certainly also because the very conclusion of *sponsio* at an engagement had fallen out of use.[12]

Finding a suitable wife was a key issue in Republican Rome.[13] In the upper classes, for example, it could have meant a political alliance to facilitate a career. An unsuitable marriage was associated with many social problems. Whether a disapproved relationship could be sanctioned, and possibly how, is debatable.

The crux of further consideration will be the question of the applicability of a censorial mark to a man who married an unsuitable woman. This problem was, of course, the subject of later regulations, above all the marriage laws of Augustus,[14] while the Republican era represents a less documented period in this respect.

Marriage was within the orbit of interest of the censors. These officials carried out various activities to curb the problem of celibacy and encouraged the pursuit of offspring. They promoted procreation as a factor for the survival of the state.[15] However, they may have been mindful of the fact that not every marriage was suitable to serve the public benefit. Any restrictions, therefore, stemmed from the realm of customs, which the censors upheld, and which were not reflected in statutory law. Therefore, it is not possible to speak of a lack of *conubium* regarding women considered unsuitable.[16]

Some introductory remarks still need to be made. Firstly, the censorial sanctions, as mentioned, could only cover men, and therefore it was they who could be punished for marrying an unsuitable woman. Secondly, the issue concerns which relationships were at stake. Doubts could potentially be raised about freedwomen and *feminae famosae*, as indicated by later legislation from the time of Augustus. However, it should be noted that, from a legal point of view, the unions of a former owner, i.e. the patron, with his freedwoman had a special status, and *manumissio matrimonii causa* was not at all uncommon.[17]

Inappropriate marriage figures in the lists of reasons for the application of the censorial mark were formulated by scholars[18] with a passage from Livy's work on Bacchanalia cited as the source.

> Liv. 39,19,3–5: *Sp. Postumius aliquanto post Romam venit: eo referente de P. Aebutii et Hispalae Faeceniae praemio, quod eorum opera indicata Bacchanalia essent, senatus consultum factum est, [...] utique ei [scil. Faeceniae Hispalae] ingenuo nubere liceret, neu quid ei qui eam duxisset ob id fraudi ignominiaeve esset.*
>
> *Some time later Spurius Postumius came to Rome. He proposed to the senate a reward for Publius Aebutius and Hispala Faecenia since it was thanks to them that the Bacchanalia had been brought to light, and the following senatorial decree was passed: (...) that she [scil. Hispala Faecenia] be permitted to marry a freeborn man, and that whosoever married her suffer thereby no prejudice or loss of status.*
>
> (Transl. E.T. Sage)

Describing the affair of 186 BC,[19] Livy emphasised the role of Hispala Faecenia in uncovering the whole scandal. Hispala, a freedwoman and prostitute,[20] warned her lover Publius Aebutius about the initiation into the Bacchic cult, who then reported everything to the consul. They were both rewarded for their testimony by a plebiscite passed under the *senatus consultum*, the contents of which the historian quoted in full. One of the privileges[21] given to Hispala was the possibility of marrying a freeborn citizen and that marriage with her would not be regarded as a *fraus*[22] (deceit, crime) or cause him to lose his good name. The term *ignominia*[23] is a clear reference to the *regimen morum*, and so it must be inferred that – if the privilege had not been granted – anyone who married Hispala would be subject to the mark.[24] This does not mean, however, that every pair of censors scrupulously punished such unions. Rather, it seems that a mark could be expected by citizens from the upper classes, primarily senators and equestrians.

It can be inferred from the case of Hispala that a freeborn Roman citizen who married a prostitute, or perhaps a freedwoman (although not likely his own), would commit *fraus* and lose his reputation, i.e. break the customary law, and expose himself to a censorial mark.[25]

A passage from Cicero's speech in defence of Sestius in 56 BC is cited as evidence that marriages with freedwomen were permitted in the late Republic.[26]

> Cic., *Pro Sest.* 110: *...qui [scil. Gellius], ut credo, non libidinis causa, sed ut plebicola videretur, libertinam duxit uxorem.*

...and has married a freedwoman, not, I suppose, to gratify his lust, but that he might appear to be "a friend of the commons."

(Transl. R. Gardner)

Cicero mentioned the knight Lucius Gellius, who – not even for lust, but to demonstrate his proplebeian inclinations – married a freedwoman. It is worth noting that Cicero was mocking his opponent by referring to his nickname: the full *tria nomina* of the knight were Lucius Gellius Publicola. His *cognomen* Publicola meant 'one who cares for the plebs,' so the speaker ironically suggested that the marriage was to make amends for his name. Above all, Cicero tried to prove that Gellius was a man unworthy of equestrian status, a wastrel, and a subversive. The list of acts imputed to him included this marriage, which then must have been considered improper. Why, then, did it go unpunished? The office of the censor, and above all the *regimen morum*, was undergoing a serious crisis at this time, since, by virtue of the *lex Clodia de censoria notione*, enacted in 58 BC, censors had to conduct a trial upon the application of the mark and accept all accusations made, which significantly prolonged the procedure and led to a de facto blockage of official functions.[27] Therefore, there is nothing unusual in the fact that no one bothered with the *nota censoria* just then.

However, the implication of the episode is that a knight should not be in a marriage with a freedwoman. It is worth noting that things were apparently different for the plebs: in this social stratum, such a marriage would hardly have been regarded as bad. The question is only how the term 'plebs' should be interpreted? In the first century BC, the division between patricians and plebeians still existed, but it was mainly of historical significance. Members of wealthy plebeian families sometimes courted *adlectio inter patricios*, which could be ennobling. On the other hand, to become a plebeian tribune, one had to be a plebeian. Over time, the colloquial meaning of the term 'plebs' gradually developed, and it began to be used to describe the poor as early as in the second century BC. Thus, while a poor citizen could take a freedwoman as his wife, a knight or senator should not have done so.

The problem of the incompatibility of the relationship between a nobleman and women of low status with the customs of the ancestors can be illuminated by the source texts on the relationships of Mark Antony.[28]

Antony's first wife was Fadia, daughter of the freedman Q. Fadius. This union was the cause of much ridicule from Cicero.

Cic., *Phil.* 2,3: *Sed hoc idcirco commemoratum a te puto, ut te infimo ordini commendares, cum omnes te recordarentur libertini generum et liberos tuos nepotes Q. Fadi, libertini hominis fuisse.*

But I imagine you brought up this incident to recommend yourself to the lowest tier of citizens, since they will all bear in mind that you were a freedman's son-in-law and that your children were the grandchildren of a freedman, Quintus Fadius.

(Transl. D.R. Shackleton Bailey)

In the Second Philippic, the speaker scoffed that his opponent could win the favour of the low strata of society if everyone remembered that he was the son-in-law of a freedman and that his children were grandchildren of Fadius.[29] In the Thirteenth Philippic, he reproached Antony for daring to despise someone else's lowly position when he himself had raised[30] the children Fadia bore him.[31]

This case is certainly not direct evidence, but only an indirect indication of the attitude of the Romans towards marriages with former slaves. Fadia herself was not a freedwoman; she was born free, whereas her father was manumitted. The fact is that the rights of the sons of freedmen in public law were limited, as they could not run for office. On the other hand, even if marriages between freeborn (*ingenui*) and former slaves were looked down upon, Fadia was not one of them; she was a free-born Roman citizen. However, Cicero must have been sure that his words would fall on fertile ground. Descent from a former slave was seen as an inconvenience, as a quality standing in the way of marriage to someone of good birth, a member of the *nobilitas*.

According to Plutarch,[32] Antony was said to spend a lot of time in the company of actors, often being a guest at their weddings, which did not make him popular. He was accompanied on his travels by a mime actress named Cytheris, who was also a freedwoman. This relationship became the subject of Cicero's derision. In a letter to Atticus, the Arpinate scoffed[33] that Antony had ordered Cytheris to be carried behind him in a litter as if she were his second wife. The phrase *alteram uxorem* suggests that Antony was married, and the actress was his mistress. He made no secret of his affair and treated Cytheris as his spouse. The sources actually indicate that he was then married to Antonia, his cousin.

Cicero's intention was to discredit Antony by pointing out that he, being a married man, treated another woman, who was in addition a mime actress, as his wife. The affair itself was not unusual, but it had to be within a certain framework. By flaunting it, Antony overstepped the boundaries of good taste. Cicero, of course, used this theme in his Philippics.

In his second speech against Antony, Cicero highlighted the dissonance of the solemnity of the official's retinue, a plebeian tribune[34] escorted by lictors, with the litter in which the mime actress was carried.[35] He added that the inhabitants of the municipalities visited by Antony, aware of how serious he was about his affair, addressed Cytheris by her family name (derived from the patron who had manumitted her): Volumnia. The entire retinue was completed by a carriage with pimps, and in addition, Cytheris was followed by Antony's rejected mother, as if she were her daughter-in-law. Cicero noted that Antony thus travelled around all the municipalities, prefectures, and colonies, encompassing the whole of Italy. Interestingly, Pliny's *Natural History*[36] shows that Antony was the first man to harness lions to a chariot and rode like this, not only alone but with Cytheris.

In the same Philippic, Cicero extended the theme of quasi-marriage with an actress even further.

> Cic., *Phil.* 2,69: *Huius in sedibus pro cubiculis stabula, pro conclavibus popinae sunt. Etsi iam negat. Nolite quaerere; frugi factus est; mimulam suam suas res sibi habere iussit, ex duodecim tabulis clavis ademit, exegit. Quam*

> *porro spectatus civis, quam probatus! Cuius ex omni vita nihil est honestius, quam quod cum mima fecit divortium.*
>
> *Now in this man's dwelling there are brothels in place of bedrooms, cheap eateries in place of dining rooms. Oh, but he now denies it! Don't ask questions; he has become frugal. He has told that mistress of his to get her own things together, he has taken away her keys according to the provisions of the Twelve Tables, he has put her out of doors. What a respectable citizen he is, what an upright one, out of whose whole life the most creditable action is to have divorced a mime actress!*
>
> (Transl. D.R. Shackleton Bailey)

Since Cytheris was treated by Antony as his wife, the interruption of their relationship could be equated to a divorce. Cicero made use of a provision of the Law of the Twelve Tables. The treatment is rhetorical in nature, contrasting an elevated and respected legal provision with behaviour unworthy of a Roman citizen.

According to the speaker, Antony ordered Cytheris to take her belongings, took the keys from her, and then drove her out. It is this passage that forms the basis for the reconstruction of the provision of the Twelve Tables.[37] Cicero's aim was to discredit his opponent. It seems, therefore, that his reference to the law must have been precise for this to give him the best rhetorical effect: the contrast of the solemnity of the decemviral law with the scandalous affair of the controversial politician. The provision in question thus contained, as one might assume, a divorce formula: *Res tuas tibi habeto*, as well as a norm for taking away the keys from the wife. The latter was an exact reversal of the gesture made during the marriage ceremony, when the wife received the keys to the house where she was to live with her husband.[38] Moreover, it seems that we are dealing here with a provision that regulated the form for evidentiary purposes. Since divorce, like marriage, was an informal legal act, it was nevertheless important to determine the moment of its beginning (due to the problem of gifts between spouses or the time of conception). The decemvirs described the usual formulas and gestures.[39]

Finally, Cicero further stressed that the most honest thing Antony had done in his life was to divorce a mime actress.

None of the Ciceronian texts mention a censorial mark, but it is quite clear from them that the public perception of marriages between men from the *nobilitas* and women who were themselves freedwomen or had manumitted fathers was rather poor. A formalised relationship with an actress was not an option at all.

Because of the plebiscite passed in 58 BC, the aforementioned *lex Clodia de censoria notione*, neither Gellius Publicola nor Antony had to fear the censors. Moreover, in the case of Antony, none of the relationships described by Cicero constituted a marriage that could be subject to censorial sanctions: Fadia was not a freedwoman but the daughter of a freedman, and Cytheris certainly never became Antony's wife. Of course, a scrupulous censor would surely have found another reason to apply the sanction...

It is worth recalling in passing that Cicero himself dreamt of censorship.[40] It was the only dignity he lacked for his political career to be completed and crowned with the office even called *sanctissimus magistratus*.[41] Had he attained this honour, it is not difficult to guess that he would have applied the mark wherever, in his opinion, *mores maiorum* were violated, such as in the case of improper marriages.

The imposition of the mark by the censors was, as mentioned before, almost entirely discretionary. The only limitation was, in principle, the collegiality of the office, which provided a guarantee for citizens subjected to the census, the procedure for composing the list of senators (*lectio senatus*) or the review of the equestrian centuries. Any censor could block the decision of a colleague, thus saving the threatened from punishment.

The catalogue of acts that could result in a sanction was not fixed. Each pair of censors announced in an edict what they would be looking out for. However, there is no doubt that some actions were always (or almost always) punished with a mark. *Mores maiorum* may not have been a very precise term, but certain behaviours were widely regarded as contrary to ancestral customs. The *senatus consultum* enacted in the case of Hispala Faecenia seems to indicate that an improper marriage could be included in this category. The Senate considered that Hispala's future husband should be protected from loss of his good name, and from this it can be inferred that *ignominia* for taking a freedwoman or prostitute as a wife was a serious risk.

Of course, the reality of censorship must also be taken into account: officials closely scrutinised members of the upper classes, mainly senators and equestrians. The census declarations of other citizens were accepted by the *iuratores*, which significantly reduced the likelihood of a mark being applied to them. Therefore, sources indicate that among the poorer citizens, marriage to a freedwoman escaped unpunished.

An additional clue to the issue at hand may be found in an excerpt from Cassius Dio's work on the marriage regulations of Augustus.[42]

> Dio Cass. 54,16,2: *ἐπειδή τε πολὺ πλεῖον τὸ ἄρρεν τοῦ θήλεος τοῦ εὐγενοῦς ἦν, ἐπέτρεψε καὶ ἐξελευθέρας τοῖς ἐθέλουσι, πλὴν τῶν βουλευόντων, ἄγεσθαι, ἔννομον τὴν τεκνοποιίαν αὐτῶν εἶναι κελεύσας.*
>
> *And since among the nobility there were far more males than females, he allowed all who wished, except the senators, to marry freed women, and ordered that their offspring should be held legitimate.*
>
> (Transl. E. Cary, H.B. Foster)

The historian reported that the emperor allowed those among the well-born, with the exception of senators, to take freedwomen as wives and recognised the children of such unions as legitimate. It follows that a knight or a noble who was not a senator could conclude a legally recognised marriage (*iustum matrimonium*) with a freedwoman. From this formulation, however, it can be inferred *a contrario* that such unions had not previously been possible, and that Augustus granted new rights rather than restricted existing ones.

> D. 23,2,23 (Cels. 30 *dig.*): *Lege Papia cavetur omnibus ingenuis praeter senatores eorumque liberos libertinam uxorem habere licere.*

> *It is provided by the Lex Papia that all freeborn men, except Senators and their children, can marry freedwomen.*
>
> (Transl. S.P. Scott)

A passage in the *Digesta* by Celsus also addresses this issue. This text seems to indicate that Augustus allowed marriages that had not previously been permitted.

Most scholars usually assume that, on the contrary, the *princeps*' prohibition was a *novum*.[43] In light of the sources from the Republican period, however, this point can be clarified. Marriages with freedwomen were not forbidden by statutory law, but were, at least among the upper classes, considered behaviour contrary to good customs (*contra bonos mores*).[44] A man who entered such a union could expect a censorial mark.

The activity of censors focused on the sphere of *mores maiorum* was correlated with the sphere of *ius* in several ways. They could apply sanctions under the *regimen morum* when the law already provided for other means of protection. Often, however, the powers of the censors gave them wider scope for action. This was the case, for example, with spendthrifts: according to the *ius civile*, only a person who squandered property inherited by intestate succession from his ancestors to the detriment of his future heirs could be considered a *prodigus*,[45] while the censors could punish any manifestation of an excessively luxurious life. The same applied to sumptuary laws. In some cases, however, a censorial mark was the only possible sanction. This was precisely the case with inappropriate marriages.

Hence, why did Cassius Dio and Celsus write that Augustus allowed marriages previously not permitted? Although the first *princeps* never formally embraced censorship, he assumed its powers. Besides, he clearly assumed the role of a censor and imposed demands for the rectification of customs and a return to *mores maiorum*. Therefore, he announced that relationships with freedwomen would be permissible for all except senators and their sons.

Among the powers of the censors enumerated by Cicero in his treatise *De legibus*, there was mention of the prohibition on remaining unmarried (*caelibes*), which was to be enforced by these very officials.[46]

The census was conducted once every five years and was a task that, from the beginning, was the primary function of the censors. Each male citizen *sui iuris*,[47] or *pater familias*, made a declaration covering a range of personal and property data: name, origin, age, offspring, assets (particularly real estate and slaves).[48] These declarations were made in the form of an *iusiurandum* – an oath of a sacred nature dedicated to Jupiter, based on the Roman virtue of *fides*, or fidelity in private and public affairs.[49] When accepting the declarations, the censor or an auxiliary official, the *iurator*, would ask questions and the citizen would answer.

> Gell. 4,20,2–6: *Censor agebat de uxoribus sollemne iusiurandum; verba erant ita concepta: "Ut tu ex animi tui sententia uxorem habes?" Qui iurabat, cavillator quidam et canicula et nimis ridicularius fuit. Is locum esse sibi ioci dicundi ratus, cum ita, uti mos erat, censor dixisset "ut tu ex animi tui sententia uxorem habes?", "habeo equidem" inquit "uxorem, sed non hercle*

ex animi mei sententia." Tum censor eum, quod intempestive lascivisset, in aerarios rettulit causamque hanc ioci scurrilis apud se dicti subscripsit.

The censor was administering the usual oath regarding wives, which was worded as follows: "Have you, to the best of your knowledge and belief, a wife?" The man who was to take the oath was a jester, a sarcastic dog, and too much given to buffoonery. Thinking that he had a chance to crack a joke, when the censor asked him, as was customary, "Have you, to the best of your knowledge and belief, a wife?" he replied: "I indeed have a wife, but not, by Heaven! such a one as I could desire." Then the censor reduced him to a commoner for his untimely quip, and added that the reason for his action was a scurrilous joke made in his presence.

(Transl. J.C. Rolfe)

According to Gellius, one of the questions put to the citizen concerned marriage. Since the key factor for the existence of *iustum matrimonium* was *affectio maritalis*, i.e. a lasting will to remain in the relationship, perhaps the phrase *Ut tu ex animi tui sententia uxorem habes?* was intended to establish whether the husband expressed this will. The anecdote quoted is proof of the protagonist's dislike of his wife. Since he thought that the joke would be received positively, he must have been convinced that he was saying something genuinely funny. This is an indication that marriage could be the subject of jokes and that misogynistic attitudes were not perceived negatively. The censor's harsh reaction was due to the solemnity of the situation. The *iusiurandum* was sacred and therefore had to be submitted with solemnity. In addition, the official could perceive the joke as violating his dignity. Therefore, he imposed a mark on the joker and degraded him socially, transferring him to the ranks of the *aerarii.*

Cicero's treatise *De Oratore*[50] identifies both the censor and the joker. The former was none other than Cato, the epitome of austerity, while the latter was L. Nasica. However, the Arpinate made no mention of the censorial mark. This may indicate that Cato's decision was blocked by his colleague in office, Valerius Flaccus, especially as Gellius also mentions one censor. However, it cannot be excluded that Nasica was punished because Cato was definitely the censor who displayed a stronger personality, and his colleague rarely defied him.

From another passage in the *Attic Nights* by Aulus Gellius, it appears that yet another censorial question concerned marriage. The text is related to the famous divorce case of Spurius Carvilius Ruga.[51]

Gell. 4,3,2: ... *iurare a censoribus coactus erat uxorem se liberum quaerundum gratia habiturum.*

he set his regard for the oath which the censors had compelled him to take, that he would marry a wife for the purpose of begetting children.

(Transl. J.C. Rolfe)

Carvilius performed a unilateral divorce (*repudium*).[52] In justifying the dismissal of his wife on the grounds of her infertility, Ruga claimed that he had taken an oath before the censors to enter into such a marriage, which was intended to produce children.

The significance of the *iusiurandum* submitted at the census concerning marriage to seek offspring appears to have been part of a consistent policy by the censors aimed at increasing the birth rate of the population. However, the aim here was to draw the attention of citizens to the importance of the issue rather than to introduce an absolute rule.

Speeches delivered by censors urging fellow citizens to marry should be understood in a similar way. Such orations were delivered at informal gatherings of the people, i.e. *contiones*.[53]

> Gell. 1,6,1–2: *Multis et eruditis viris audientibus legebatur oratio Metelli Numidici, gravis ac diserti viri, quam in censura dixit ad populum de ducendis uxoribus, cum eum ad matrimonia capessenda hortaretur. in ea oratione ita scriptum fuit: "Si sine uxore possemus, Quirites, omnes ea molestia careremus; set quoniam ita natura tradidit, ut nec cum illis satis commode, nec sine illis uno modo vivi possit, saluti perpetuae potius quam brevi voluptati consulendum est."*
>
> *A number of learned men were listening to the reading of the speech which Metellus Numidicus, an earnest and eloquent man, delivered to the people when he was censor, On Marriage, urging them to be ready to undertake its obligations. In that speech these words were written: "If we could get on without a wife, Romans, we would all avoid that annoyance; but since nature has ordained that we can neither live very comfortably with them nor at all without them, we must take thought for our lasting well-being rather than for the pleasure of the moment."*
>
> (Transl. J.C. Rolfe)

Gellius quoted a passage from a speech by the censor Metellus Numidicus, in which the politician argued that, although the relationship with a wife could be burdensome, marriage was a necessity. It can be assumed that the phrase *salus perpetua* refers not so much to the well-being of the individual as to the benefit to the community as a whole, the state.[54] Gellius reported that the speech provoked a fierce discussion among readers. The censor was accused of discouraging marriage rather than encouraging it. Metellus was defended by Titus Castricius, who stated that an advocate and a censor speak differently: the former can resort to lies, as long as what he says has a semblance of probability, while the latter must above all be mindful of his own dignity and should, therefore, present the state of affairs honestly.

The censors also exhorted people to strive for offspring.

> Liv., *Per.* 59: *Q. Metellus censor censuit ut cogerentur omnes ducere uxores liberorum creandorum causa. Extat oratio eius, quam Augustus Caesar, cum de maritandis ordinibus ageret, velut in haec tempora scriptam in senatu recitavit.*

Censor Quintus Metellus proposed that everyone should be compelled to marry in order to produce children. His speech is preserved, and was read by Augustus Caesar before the senate as though written for the present day, when the emperor was discussing the problem of marriage among the upper classes.

(Transl. A.C. Schlesinger)

Livy's epitomator relayed that the censor Quintus Metellus, in 131 BC, called for marriages to foster offspring (*liberorum creandorum causa*). His speech must have been timeless, since more than a century later, Augustus made use of it when in 18 BC he presented the draft of the *lex Iulia de maritandis ordinibus*. The plebiscite, passed at the emperor's request, made it compulsory for citizens to remain married, and Augustus hoped that the censor's fiery speech would enable him to overcome the senators' reluctance to such a solution. Suetonius, too,[55] mentioned the reading of the speech, underlining the emperor's desire to prove that he was not the first to address the issue, that his ancestors had already considered similar problems.

It is not clear whether the speech quoted by Gellius and that used by Augustus are the same.[56] In the *Attic Nights*, Quintus Metellus Numidicus, a censor in 102 BC, is indicated as the author, while Livy's epitome mentions Quintus Metellus Macedonicus (131 BC), and Suetonius wrote only Quintus Metellus, without giving a *praenomen*. It should also be noted that Gellius quoted a speech on the necessity of marriage, while the other authors wrote of a speech encouraging people to seek offspring. There is no doubt that the argumentation given was very catchy and was probably used more than once. In fact, it sometimes happened that members of the same family consistently pushed the same political ideas. This was the case with the families of Valerii and Porcii, who proposed laws concerning *provocatio ad populum* (the right to appeal to the popular assembly),[57] or the famous brothers Gracchi and their agrarian legislation,[58] and we can also assume that this happened with the Metelli.

The censorial speeches had consequences. They foreshadowed the decisions made during the census. Therefore, it could be expected that those who did not live up to expectations would be punished.

Val. Max. 2,9,1: *Camillus et Postumius censores aera poenae nomine eos, qui ad senectutem caelibes pervenerant, in aerarium deferre iusserunt, iterum puniri dignos, si quo modo de tam iusta constitutione queri sunt ausi, cum in hunc modum increparentur: 'natura vobis quemadmodum nascendi, ita gignendi legem scribit, parentesque vos alendo nepotum nutriendorum debito, si quis est pudor, alligaverunt. accedit his quod etiam fortuna longam praestandi huiusce muneris advocationem estis adsecuti, cum interim consumpti sunt anni vestri et mariti et patris nomine vacui. ite igitur et non odiosam exsolvite stipem, utilem posteritati numerosae.'*

Censors Camillus and Postumius ordered persons who had reached old age as bachelors to pay copper coins to the treasury as a penalty. They deserved a second punishment for daring to protest against so just an ordinance in the face of a rebuke such as this: "Nature writes a law for us; as we are born, so must we beget. By raising you your parents bound you in decency with a debt to bring up grandchildren. Add that by the gift of Fortune you obtained a long adjournment of this obligation, during which time your years were squandered, void of the names of husband and father. Go then and loosen the knotty mite for the use of a numerous posterity."

(Transl. D.R. Shackleton Bailey)

The censors Camillus and Postumius[59] ordered citizens who remained unmarried to old age to pay a fine to the treasury[60] called *aes uxorium*.[61] This is the only instance described in the sources of the imposition of such a tax. Valerius Maximus quoted a passage from a speech in which the censors explained the reasons for their decision, arguing that by raising offspring one pays the debt incurred with one's parents, and therefore those who cannot boast of being called husbands and fathers must pay this debt in another way, in the form of money.

The details of this episode are further illuminated by Plutarch's account[62] in the *Life of Camillus*. The biographer wrote that the censor wanted to persuade unmarried men, using both methods of persuasion and the threat of financial penalties, to marry widows, of which there were many due to the numerous wars. Rome was at war with Veii at the time, conducting a siege of the city. It seems that the censors were trying to raise additional funds, as may be indicated by the fact that – in addition to the tax in question – they also made it compulsory for orphans to make census declarations.

One may wonder why, in this case, the censors used the rather peculiar instrument of imposing a financial penalty rather than the censorial mark typical for their office. This is probably because in the fifth century BC the authority to exercise guardianship over good customs had not yet developed. Originally, censors achieved their goals by interfering with citizens' property declarations. It was only with time that they began to apply the sanctions associated with the *regimen morum*. The evolution of the censors' powers in this respect presumably ended with the delegation to them of the power to draw up a list of senators by virtue of the *plebiscitum Ovinium* of around 318 BC.[63]

A detail from the biography of the Emperor Claudius by Suetonius is also worth considering in the context of the censors' activities concerning procreation. As mentioned above, already in the final period of the Republic, the office of the censor was experiencing a deep crisis, and from the time of Augustus, censors were not appointed at all. Claudius decided to reactivate the censorship in its traditional form. Clinging to tradition, the *princeps* retained the standard eighteen-month term as censor and selected a colleague, Lucius Vitellius.[64] They took office in 47 AD. Claudius heavily used the censorial mark, for which Suetonius severely criticised him. It is worth noting, however, that the emperor planned to apply the mark to the unmarried and childless.[65] Despite the validity of Augustus' laws[66] (*lex Iulia et Papia*), he sought to punish them in the traditional way by socially degrading them. This indicates that the promotion of procreation was seen as a typical task of the censors, who not only could, but even should, apply a *nota censoria* to those who were not married and had no children.[67]

When discussing the influence of the censors on the institution of marriage, the question of morality cannot be overlooked. It is conceivable that a man leading an overly casual lifestyle may have feared a censorial mark. A rhetorical exercise in which the principle *Bis adulterii notatus ignominiosus sit* ("One marked twice for aldultery shall bear the loss of good name")[68] is used as the legal basis may provide some clues. This text may represent a trace of censorship practice. It cannot be ruled out that the censorial mark could have been applied to a man who had been caught several times *in flagranti* with married women. Although the problem of adultery was treated as a private matter in the Republican period, settled between the interested parties themselves, nevertheless – since the censor was considered to look even into the bedroom – the imposition of penalties on adulterers is highly probable.

It should be added that Gellius mentioned the historian Sallustius as having been punished more than once with a mark.[69] Although it is not possible to deduce from the text what the reasons for this were, it seems that the accusations concerned immoral conduct, since there is a reference to Sallustius being caught in adultery by Milo, bruised and released after paying a ransom.

At this point, it is worth emphasising how greatly Augustus' legislative work was influenced by the Republican practice of censors exercising *regimen morum*. The emperor concluded that ad hoc measures and selectively applied penalties, speeches, and edicts were not enough. He therefore introduced regulation through statute law. In his speeches in the Senate, however, he referred to the policy of the censors to justify interference in the private lives of citizens. He tried to show that not much would actually change. In reality, however, the changes were revolutionary, mainly because of the sanctions being introduced. Financial penalties concerning inheritance were fixed for those not being married or without offspring, linked to the deprivation of the possibility of receiving all or part of testamentary benefits. Criminal sanctions were also introduced for extramarital relations.

Also deeply rooted in customary law were norms concerning the remarriage of a widow during a period of bereavement. One may ask whether these issues were within the orbit of the censors as well.[70] First of all, it should be emphasised again that the *regimen morum* did not include women. Therefore, only a man who took a widow as his wife could be subject to the mark, as well as a father who remarried his daughter during the period of mourning.

Unfortunately, there are no source texts that directly indicate a solution to this problem. However, some assumptions can be made. Firstly, regulations concerning *tempus lugendi* were already found in the laws of the kings, which became part of customary law – *mores maiorum* – during the Republican period. In many cases, the severe sanctions of the *leges regiae* were replaced by a censorial mark. Additionally, as noted above, there is an undoubted link between the censorial *regimen morum* and the regulations of the praetor's edict *de postulando*, which in turn formed the basis of the list of persons subject to infamy in the Digest.

> D. 3,2,1 (Iul. 1 *dig.*): *Praetoris verba dicunt: "infamia notatur (...) qui eam, quae in potestate eius esset, genero mortuo, cum eum mortuum esse sciret,*

intra id tempus, quo elugere virum moris est, antequam virum elugeret, in matrimonium collocaverit: eamve sciens quis uxorem duxerit non iussu eius, in cuius potestate est: et qui eum, quem in potestate haberet, eam, de qua supra comprehensum est, uxorem ducere passus fuerit..."

The words of the Praetor are as follows: "He (...) is branded with infamy (...) who gave his daughter, who was under his control in marriage after the death of his son-in-law, he knowing him to be dead before the time had elapsed which is customary for a widow to mourn for her husband; it also applies to one who married her, being also aware of this, without the order of the person under whose control he was; to him who permitted him to marry her while he was under his control, being aware of the above mentioned facts."

(Transl. S.P. Scott, adapted)

According to the text handed down in the Digest,[71] loss of honour was suffered by anyone who gave in marriage a woman under his authority while she was mourning her husband, by anyone who married her, and by anyone who allowed a man under his authority to marry her. Perhaps, therefore, the breach of the obligation to remain in mourning for the husband was first the basis for the application of the *nota censoria*,[72] then for the imposition of the *postulatio* ban, and finally for the punishment of infamy.

3. Divorce

Since one of the tasks of the censors was to induce fellow citizens to marry and seek offspring, it seems reasonable to assume that these officials also dealt with the issue of divorce.

The unilateral dissolution of marriage had probably been the subject of Roman law regulation since archaic times. According to Plutarch, Romulus himself was said to have been the first to address this legal institution.[73]

Plut., *Rom.* 22,3: *Ἔθηκε δὲ καὶ νόμους τινὰς (ὁ Ῥωμύλος) ὧν σφοδρὸς μὲν ἐστιν ὁ γυναικὶ μὴ διδοὺς ἀπολείπειν ἄνδρα, γυναῖκα δὲ διδοὺς ἐκβάλλειν ἐπὶ φαρμακείᾳ καὶ τέκνων ὑποβολῇ καὶ μοιχευθεῖσαν· εἰ δ' ἄλλως τις ἀποπέμψαιτο, τῆς οὐσίας αὐτοῦ τὸ μὲν τῆς γυναικὸς εἶναι, τὸ δὲ τῆς Δήμητρος ἱερὸν κελεύων. 4.*

He also enacted certain laws, and among them one of severity, which forbids a wife to leave her husband, but permits a husband to put away his wife for using poisons, for substituting children, and for adultery; but if a man for any other reason sends his wife away, the law prescribes that half his substance shall belong to his wife, and the other half be consecrate to Ceres.

(Transl. B. Perrin)

The king was to forbid women to leave their husbands, while men were allowed to divorce their wives on one of the listed grounds[74]: adultery, abortion, poisoning, or the substitution of the keys (these keyes were to the wine cellar so the offence meant here was drinking wine). A husband who divorced without stating any of these grounds was subject to the penalty of confiscation of his property, with part going to his wife and part being consecrated to the goddess Ceres (Demeter in Greek, as mentioned by Plutarch). The reliability of Plutarch's account can, of course, be questioned, but it is reasonable to assume that divorce was regulated in archaic law and that the unilateral dismissal of a wife was only possible for specific reasons.

During the Republican period, *the leges regiae* continued to be observed as custom. As far as family laws were concerned, the natural guardian was from the beginning the *pater familias*. Over time, however, the censors[75] equipped with the *regimen morum*, acquired a significant role. It can be assumed that performing a *repudium* without stating any of the reasons mentioned resulted in a censorial mark.

> Val. Max. 2,9,2: *Horum severitatem M. Valerius Maximus et C. Iunius Brutus Bubulcus censores consimili genere animadversionis imitati sunt: L. enim Annium senatu moverunt, quod quam virginem in matrimonium duxerat repudiasset nullo amicorum [in] consilio adhibito.*
>
> *Their severity was imitated by Censors M. Valerius Maximus and C. Junius Bubulcus Brutus with a dissimilar sort of visitation. They expelled L. Annius from the senate because he divorced the girl he had taken to wife without calling any council of friends.*
>
> (Transl. D.R. Shackleton Bailey)

The first case of interference by censors in divorce matters was described by Valerius Maximus. The antiquarian reported the decision of the censors in 307 BC – his namesake Marcus Valerius and Gaius Iunius[76] – who removed Lucius Annius from the Senate for having dismissed his wife, whom he had taken as a virgin, without consulting his friends.[77] The reason for the application of the mark was probably not that Annius had divorced without observing Romulus' reasons for *repudium*, but the lack of evidence in the form of witnesses, who should have been the friends summoned to the *consilium*.[78]

This case represents the first instance described in the sources of the application of a mark to a senator after the passing of the *plebiscitum Ovinium*, which gave censors the right to compile a list of senators (*lectio senatus*). The authenticity of this story is questioned[79] due to the scarcity of sources. It is also pointed out that the powers of the censors related to the *regimen morum* took shape gradually after the *plebiscitum Ovinium*, and that this case is too early to be considered genuine.

First of all, it should be noted that censorship was by no means initially a meaningless office. Livy's formulation of *res a parva origine orta* is a considerable understatement. Already in the early stages of the office's development, situations arose in which censors attempted to apply penalties as part of censorial operations, which later gradually developed into *regimen morum*. Such was the case with the dictator Marcus Aemilius Mamercus,[80] the initiator of the *lex Aemilia de censura minuenda*.[81] The censors, at the time, Gaius Furius and Marcus Geganius,[82] embittered by the diminution of their office, punished Mamercus[83] by transferring him to another *tribus* and by overestimating the value of his property eightfold, thus placing him among the *aerarii*.[84] Apparently, the censors wanted to increase the tax base, and therefore arbitrarily entered the higher value of this property.[85]

Regimen morum was not solely the result of giving censors the power to perform *lectio senatus*. It developed because senators were the social stratum in which the censors were most interested. However, the beginnings of this institution were already discernible before then. Therefore, it is difficult to consider definitively the case of Lucius Annius as a forgery.

Censors also formed a key part of what is perhaps the most famous Roman divorce story, dating to the consulship of Marcus Atilius and Publius Valerius in the 230 BC: the case of Spurius Carvilius Ruga,[86] the first Roman to divorce despite the non-existence of any of the causes permitted by the law of Romulus.

> Gell. 4,3,2: *Spurius Carvilius, cui Ruga cognomentum fuit, vir nobilis, divortium cum uxore fecit, quia liberi ex ea corporis vitio non gignerentur, anno urbis conditae quingentesimo vicesimo tertio M. Atilio P. Valerio consulibus. Atque is Carvilius traditur uxorem, quam dimisit, egregie dilexisse carissimamque morum eius gratia habuisse, set iurisiurandi religionem animo atque amori praevertisse, quod iurare a censoribus coactus erat uxorem se liberum quaerundum gratia habiturum.*
>
> *Spurius Carvilius, who was surnamed Ruga, a man of rank, put away his wife because, owing to some physical defect, no children were born from her; and that this happened in the five hundred and twenty-third year after the founding of the city, in the consulship of Marcus Atilius and Publius Valerius. And it is reported that this Carvilius dearly loved the wife whom he divorced, and held her in strong affection because of her character, but that above his devotion and his love he set his regard for the oath which the censors had compelled him to take, that he would marry a wife for the purpose of begetting children.*
>
> (Transl. J.C. Rolfe)

Ruga repudiated his wife on account of infertility, claiming that he had pledged[87] before the censors that he had married her to have children[88] (*liberorum procreandorum causa*).[89] The negative public reaction to this *repudium* indicates that despite the *iusiurandum*, there was no acquiescence in the repudiation of one's wife because of her infertility. However, for the censors, it was desirable behaviour for fellow citizens to marry and to pursue offspring.

The question then arises as to whether the censors had any involvement in the story other than, of course, administering the oath to Carvilius.

> Val. Max. 2,1,4: *Repudium inter uxorem et virum a condita urbe usque ad vicesimum et quingentesimum annum nullum intercessit. primus*

> *autem Sp. Carvilius uxorem sterilitatis causa dimisit. qui, quamquam tolerabili ratione motus videbatur, reprehensione tamen non caruit, quia ne cupiditatem quidem liberorum coniugali fidei praeponi debuisse arbitrabantur.*
>
> *From the founding of the city down to its five hundred and twentieth year there was no case of divorce between man and wife. Sp. Carvilius was the first to put his wife away for cause of barrenness. Although he was thought to have a tolerable reason for so doing, he did not escape criticism, because they considered that even desire for children ought not to have been placed ahead of conjugal loyalty.*
>
> (Transl. D.R. Shackleton Bailey)

The account of Valerius Maximus contains the information that Ruga, although driven by acceptable motives, did not escape reprimand because it was thought that he should not have prioritised procreative issues above marital fidelity. The antiquarian used the term *reprehensio*, which was sometimes used to describe the punishments inflicted by the censors,[90] and for this he used the verb *arbitror* in the third person *pluralis*. The passage seems incomplete, it is not clear who found the divorcee's motives insufficient and what this *reprehensio* consisted of. Since the office of the censor undoubtedly played a role in the whole affair, one may be tempted to venture a reconstruction of events.

It is certain that Carvilius repudiated his wife due to her infertility. It is also known that he called friends as witnesses to satisfy the legal requirements.[91] It can be assumed that Carvilius was threatened with a censorial mark and tried to defend himself by referring to the aforementioned oath taken before the censors. These officials were confronted with a very difficult choice: they could either punish the divorcee, thus concluding that marriage did not have to serve procreation at all, or they could pardon him, considering that, in the absence of offspring, it was safe to repudiate. Perhaps the censors were not in agreement and one of them wanted to impose a mark, to which the other objected. This would explain the use of the phrase *reprehensione non caruit*.

Carvilius Ruga's divorce initiated the introduction of safeguards designed to allow women who had been repudiated by their husbands to demand the return of their dowry (which had previously been only a moral obligation of the man): *cautio* and *actio rei uxoriae*.[92] It also undoubtedly contributed to an increase in the frequency of divorces.[93] However, this does not mean that the censors stopped taking an interest in the issue of *repudium*. It must be thought that they continued to punish with a mark in extreme cases where they considered that the divorce constituted an abuse of customary norms.

Traces of proceedings before the censors on these matters may perhaps be found in the declamations of the early Principate period.

> Quint., *Inst. or.* 7,4,36: *praeter haec finguntur in scholis et inscripti maleficii, in quibus aut hoc quaeritur, an inscriptum sit aut hoc, an maleficium sit, raro utrumque.*

> *In addition, we have in the schools fictitious cases of wrongdoing not specified by law, in which the Question is either whether the act is not so specified or whether it is wrongdoing; rarely both.*
>
> (Transl. D.A. Russel)

Quintilian mentioned the topics of rhetorical exercises given in schools concerning *inscripta maleficia*, or 'unwritten transgressions.' It seems that this term may refer to offences not regulated by state law, remaining within the realm of custom. And although Quintilian reported that the situations considered in the schools were fictional, it is not impossible that they were based on authentic cases.

One of the topics appearing in these declamations was the issue of wrongful divorce. The source texts mention the complaint for wrongful divorece – *actio iniusti repudii*,[94] the nature of which is disputed by scholars. It is considered to be fictitious,[95] although this view seems debatable.

> Quint., *Inst. or.* 7,4,38: *simpliciores illae iniusti repudii, sub qua lege controversiae illud proprium habent, quod a parte accusantis defensio est, a defendentis accusatio.*
>
> *Cases of Unjust Repudiation are simpler; the peculiarity of cases under this law is that the defence is made by the accuser, and the accusation by the defendant.*
>
> (Transl. D.A. Russel)

Quintilian pointed out a characteristic feature of proceedings based on *actio iniusti repudii*: it is the accuser who defends, while the defender accuses. This reversal of roles is due to the nature of the action itself, which concerns wrongful divorce, asserting that there were no valid grounds for the wife's dismissal. The woman[96] or someone on her behalf accuses, aiming to prove that there was no fault on her part, i.e. that the grounds for divorce did not exist. The husband, on the other hand, defends himself, (either personally or through an advocate), attempting to place the blame on the woman.

In the rhetorical exercises, the wife's adultery appears as a ground for divorce,[97] while another invoked ground is infertility, which may indicate they have a legal basis and are not entirely fictitious.

> Ps.-Quint., *Decl. min.* 327 pr.: *Introducta tribus privignis sterilitatis medicamentum bibit. Repudiata iniusti repudii agit.*
>
> *A woman who married the father of three sons drank a drug causing sterility. Divorced, she brings an action for wrongful divorce.*
>
> (Transl. D.R. Shacleton Bailey)

Declamation 327 attributed (probably erroneously) to Quintilian, concerns the remarriage of a father with three children. The stepmother deliberately took a remedy that made her infertile, in order not to harm her stepchildren.[98] It is clear from the text that the woman did not want to become a typical stepmother who would prioritise her own children over her husband's offspring from his first marriage. There must have been a topos of an evil stepmother in Rome, as evidenced by the phrase *fabulae novercarum* – "tales of bad stepmothers".[99] The woman also knew that her husband had already made a will[100] and did not want to compel him to change it or risk invalidation by the birth of another son.

Ultimately, however, the husband repudiated his wife, citing her infertility as the reason. The woman, on the other hand, brought an *actio iniusti repudii*. Her argument was based primarily on the fact that the husband already had children (three of them) and therefore did not need to marry in order to have offspring (*liberorum procreandorum gratia*), and the fact that he was already at an age when he should not desire progeny. Interestingly, the declamation completely omits the theme of Augustus' marriage laws; after all, the heroine should have had at least one child to avoid the consequences of the *lex Papia*. On the other hand, proving that the husband already had three children, thus enjoying the *ius trium liberorum*, could have led to the conclusion that he actually no longer needed more offspring. However, it should not be forgotten that as the father of three children, he did not have to remain in the marriage and was free to send his wife away. These glaring deficiencies in the argumentation may indicate that the casus was considered not so much based on state law as but rather on custom, which reinforces the suspicion that it fell more within the censor's jurisdiction.

Some conclusions can additionally be drawn from the declamation. Foremost, infertility was a legitimate ground for repudiation, although arguments could be sought to show that this was not a sufficient reason in a particular case.

However, there were other interesting formulations in the argument in favour of the wife.

> Ps.-Quint., *Decl. min.* 327,1,1: *Quod primum pertinet ad pudorem huius feminae, non adulterium obicitur, non aliqua adversus maritum licentia.*
>
> *What is first relevant to the honor of this woman, she is not taxed with adultery or any license against her husband.*
>
> (Transl. D.R. Shackleton Bailey)

Firstly, it was emphasised that the woman had not committed adultery or any other act against her husband. The term *licentia* is to be understood here as indecent behaviour.

> Ps.-Quint., *Decl. min.* 327,3,1: *Venenum paravit, insidiata est liberis tuis, vel, quod levissimum est, expugnare animum tuum voluit? Nihil horum.*
>
> *Did she prepare poison, did she plot against your children, or, what is the least of them, did she try to turn your mind against them? None of these.*
>
> (Transl. D.R. Shackleton Bailey)

Furthermore, it was made clear that the woman had not taken any action against her stepchildren.

Both passages illustrate a clear link[101] with the text referred to the source concerning the reasons for divorce established by Romulus. Both adultery and poisoning (also in the context of children, including abortion) were among the reasons that justified the dismissal of a wife. The declamation thus seems to indicate the existence of a link between the content of the rhetorical exercises and the *mores maiorum*.

> Ps.-Quint., *Decl. min.* 251 pr.: *Intra quinquennium non parientem repudiare liceat. Iniusti repudii sit actio. Quidam uxorem, quam ex raptu habere coeperat secundum optionem, intra quinquennium non parientem dimisit. Agit illa iniusti repudii.*
>
> *Let there be a license to divorce a wife who has not given birth within five years. Let an action lie for unjust divorce. A man divorced his wife whom he had taken after raping her in accordance with option, not having given birth within five years. She prosecutes for unjust divorce.*
>
> (Transl. D.R. Shackleton Bailey)

Another declamation of Pseudo-Quintilian contains a rule according to which a woman who had not given birth within five years (from the beginning of marriage, of course) could be divorced. In the cited source, however, this rule intersects with the rather fictitious *lex raptae*,[102] which allowed a raped woman to decide whether she preferred her rapist to suffer the death penalty or whether she wanted to marry him. The text invokes *boni mores*[103] – good customs – which dictate that in this case *iustitia* rather than *ius* should be invoked, that is, justice should be placed above statutory law. Since marriage here was an alternative to death, it can be argued that the spouse lost, as it were, the right to repudiate the wife he had married out of necessity.[104]

> Ps.-Quint., *Decl. min.* 262 pr.: *Iniusti repudii sit actio. Qui habebat uxorem rapuit virginem. Nuptias rapta optavit. Ille repudiavit uxorem. Agit illa iniusti repudii.*
>
> *Let there be an action for wrongful divorce. A man who had a wife raped a virgin. The victim opted for marriage. He divorced his wife. She brings action for wrongful divorce.*
>
> (Transl. D.R. Shackleton Bailey)

In another declamation, the combination of divorce and marriage to a raped woman appears again. This time, however, the man repudiated his wife to marry his victim. The divorce was thus carried out *ex necessitate*, with no fault on the part of the wife. In the text of the declamation, an interesting line of reasoning emerges, according to which the *repudium* was basically brought about by the man's decision to commit rape.[105]

In the context of wrongful divorce, the *actio ingrati* (complaint for ungratefulness),[106] the application of which was, however, broader, also appears in the declamations. As far as divorce is concerned, the declamation[107] in which a raped woman married her rapist against her father's will and was then repudiated by him for having supported that father in poverty without his consent seems interesting. However, the author himself pointed out that in the situation described, the woman could also use the *actio iniusti repudii.*[108]

The declamations clearly refer to *mores maiorum* when discussing divorce. Reasons are mentioned to justify a wife's dismissal, including those cited by Plutarch, as well as infertility, which first appeared in the case of Carvilius Ruga. It can therefore be assumed that the content of the exercises was drawn from censorial practice. It seems that the censors may have been punishing unjustified divorces that resulted in harm to the woman. It is worth noting that proceedings before censors may have been an important factor in convincing a man to return his ex-wife's dowry. These proceedings could continue even after the introduction of the *actio rei uxoriae*, constituting a complementary legal solution and remaining a tool of the censors' policy related to encouraging marriage and offspring. They lost their raison d'être with the decline of censorship and the enactment of Augustus' marriage laws, which *de facto* replaced the censorial solutions in this respect.

4. *Patria potestas*, guardianship, and patronage

Although the head of the household initially had far-reaching freedom in the exercise of *patria potestas*, he was gradually subjected to various restrictions. He could not freely use the *ius vitae ac necis*, he lost his authority over his son after the third sale, he had to secure the livelihood of those under his authority in a will (otherwise his last will was deemed a *testamentum inofficiosum*), and in cases of spendthrift behaviour, the praetor could limit his capacity for legal acts. However, there were also restrictions based on the powers of the censors. Bringing up children in an improper manner could prompt the censors to apply a mark. An example of this is Cato's decision, described above, to remove Manilius, who kissed his wife in the presence of his daughter, from the Senate. However, as mentioned, this story is anecdotal. It can only be generally inferred from it that the censors had the right to intervene in the case of a father scandalising his children.

According to Dionysius of Halicarnassus, a mark could result from excessively cruel punishment of slaves, excessive harshness or, conversely, leniency in the upbringing of children, and unfair treatment of a wife.[109] The text seems to indicate that a *pater familias* could be punished with a mark when he abused his authority over any of his subjects: slaves, children, or wife. However, it is also very general.

A notable example of censorial interference with *patria potestas*, on the other hand, is the edict of Gnaeus Domitius Ahenobarbus and Lucius Licinius Crassus of 92 BC concerning the schools of Latin rhetoricians, the text of which is preserved[110] in its entirety in the accounts of Suetonius and Gellius.[111]

> Gell. 15,11,2[112]: *Aliquot deinde annis post id senatusconsultum Cn. Domitius Ahenobarbus et L. Licinius Crassus censores de coërcendis rhetoribus Latinis ita edixerunt: "Renuntiatum est nobis esse homines, qui novum genus disciplinae instituerunt, ad quos iuventus in ludum conveniat; eos sibi nomen inposuisse Latinos rhetoras; ibi homines adulescentulos dies totos desidere.*

Maiores nostri, quae liberos suos discere et quos in ludos itare vellent, instituerunt. Haec nova, quae praeter consuetudinem ac morem maiorum fiunt, neque placent neque recta videntur. Quapropter et his, qui eos ludos habent, et his, qui eo venire consuerunt, visum est faciundum, ut ostenderemus nostram sententiam nobis non placere."

"It has been reported to us that there be men who have introduced a new kind of training, and that our young men frequent their schools; that these men have assumed the title of Latin rhetoricians, and that young men spend whole days with them in idleness. Our forefathers determined what they wished their children to learn and what schools they desired them to attend. These innovations in the customs and principles of our forefathers do not please us nor seem proper. Therefore it appears necessary to make our opinion known, both to those who have such schools and to those who are in the habit of attending them, that they are displeasing to us."

(Transl. J.C. Rolfe)

The censors described the whole situation in their edict: it had been reported to them that a new type of school had been introduced for young people to attend. They schools were run by people who called themselves *rhetores Latini* and they aimed to have young people spend their days there. Meanwhile, the ancestors had already decided how children should be educated and to which schools they should be sent. These new schools, which contradicted the customs and traditions of the ancestors, did not please the censors and did not seem right to them. Consequently, they decided that both those who ran these schools and those who attended them should be informed that the censors disapproved of them.

Both Suetonius and Gellius[113] quote, in addition to the edict, the provisions of a senate resolution from 161 BC concerning philosophers and rhetoricians. Praetor M. Pomponius was obliged to ensure that they did not remain in Rome. Therefore, the censorial edict was not the first regulation of its kind.

However, there is a major difference between the accounts of Suetonius and Gellius. Gellius gave the edict the title *de coërcendis rhetoribus Latinis*, suggesting that coercive measures were taken against the rhetors. This raised doubts among scholars.[114] After all, in the edict, the censors merely expressed their disapproval of the schools of *rhetores Latini* by directing it at the teachers themselves, as well as at those who had received education from them. Disregarding such a warning could certainly have resulted in a censorial mark. In the case at hand, the *nota* would often have been imposed on the *pater familias* who had improperly brought up his son by sending him to study with teachers who met with the disapproval of the censors. The edict of the censors could, however, have a double meaning: in addition to announcing the imposition of a censorial mark, it could provoke a reaction from other officials, particularly the aediles. In such a case, indeed, the *rhetores Latini* could have been removed from the city by the aediles using the *coërcitio*. A similar situation occurred when flutists (*tibicines*) were removed from Rome.[115] Therefore, one may conclude that the title *de coërcendis rhetoribus Latinis* given to the edict of Crassus and Domitius by Gellius was admittedly inaccurate, but nevertheless justifiable, which is further confirmed by the statement attributed to Crassus by Cicero concerning his removal of the teachers (*ego censor edicto meo sustuleram*).[116]

Researchers also have doubts about the reasons for issuing the edict. The censors themselves invoked *mores maiorum*, claiming that the ancestors decided how children should be educated and to which schools they should be sent. Crassus justified the decision on the grounds that the new schools provided no knowledge but only taught insolence.

The most commonly proposed explanation for the reasons behind the edict is political, specifically the struggle between the *optimates*, whose representatives both censors were,[117] and the *populares*. The schools of the *rhetores Latini* were seen as a political instrument in the hands of *populares*, especially Marius, whose close friendship with Plotius was mentioned by Cicero.[118] However, Manfredini[119] seems correct in suggesting that the *optimates* were more likely to try to make a deal with Marius during the period concerned. Furthermore, the connections between the great leader and the schools of rhetoric teachers are impossible to prove with certainty.[120]

It is also possible to see the edict as an attempt to prevent the egalitarisation of education, which had hitherto only been available to members of the *nobilitas* who knew Greek, and which was perhaps becoming more widespread through the *rhetores Latini.* In this light, the term *impudentia* takes on an additional meaning, namely that it could refer to the prosecution of *nobilitas* in criminal tribunals by people from the lower classes educated in the new schools.[121]

In my opinion, the closest to the truth seems to be the notion that the censors' actions stemmed from specific objections to the level presented by the new schools. The education of a politician, an orator, a statesman, could not consist merely in acquiring proficiency in the art of rhetoric. The political system of the Republic required a fluent knowledge of the realities of public life, as well as of the law. Sophistry alone could not suffice. This is why Crassus accused teachers of eloquence of not imparting any knowledge, but only teaching insolence.

Learning oratory skills was always a stage in a young person's education. Already the *grammaticus* taught it to children. Later, it was taken up again after the start of a political career. For example, the school of Molon on Rhodes[122] was popular in the last decades of the Republic. In Rome, on the other hand, young men were expected to learn state principles.[123]

In my opinion, the key to understanding the issue is a passage from the edict itself: *ibi homines adulescentulos dies totos desidere – "they want the young people to spend whole days there"*. Since teachers required young people to spend whole days in their schools, there was indeed no more time for other, more traditional, forms of learning. An eloquent speaker could only impress his audience if he knew how to defeat his opponent. Sophistry alone was no guarantee of victory in a court of law. It was a matter of knowledge of the realities of the forum, of witnessing political and legal speeches. At the very least, it was necessary to spend some time observing the activities of the magistrates and listening to the proceedings of the praetor (*tirocinium fori*).

Therefore, the edict of Crassus and Domitius in 92 BC should be seen as an attempt to provide the Republic with people capable of governing it and continuing the work of their ancestors, people able to co-determine the fate of the state, aware of themselves as citizens, and able to hold office in the interests of the Republic and to fight for it. The censors saw the *rhetores Latini* schools as a threat to these basic values.

The censor Publius Scipio Africanus had already encouraged his fellow citizens to observe the customs of their ancestors much earlier in a speech from 142 BC, giving examples of the harsh decisions of his predecessors.[124] It is likely that, in the same speech, he strongly condemned two behaviours contrary to *mores maiorum*[125]: treating adopted sons as if they were natural when counting offspring and granting adoptive fathers privileges, which he described as *praemia patrum*, and allowing a census declaration to be made *in absentia*.[126]

Scipio was appalled that an adopted son, who was not even enrolled in the *tribus* of his new *pater familias*, was treated as a native son and provided the benefits of having offspring. It does not appear that adoption as such could have caused the censors' objections. However, it may be that officials were sensitive to such adoptions, which were only intended to achieve the benefit of having offspring. It cannot be ruled out that such ties were simply later dissolved by emancipation. This would give the censors reason to apply the mark. The fact mentioned by Scipio, that father and son by adoption voted in different *tribus*, precisely indicates the fictitious nature of the legal action. While at the time of the adrogation itself, there was clearly strong control by both the pontiffs and the assembly, after the adrogation only the censors could react.[127]

What did these *praemia patrum* consist of? Livy,[128] for example, described the decision of the censors in 169 BC, who chose to enrol all freedmen in one of the four urban *tribus*, but made an exception for fathers with at least a five-year-old son, enrolling them where their names were in the previous census. Caesar's agrarian law, on the other hand, provided for the allocation of land to 20,000 citizens who had three or more children,[129] while a girl whose parents had three children could be exempted from appointment as a Vestal.[130] Presumably, having offspring could also be decisive when a choice had to be made between two candidates for an office (if only in the case of a tie).[131]

When discussing the hierarchy of duties, Gellius also quoted a very interesting excerpt from Cato's speech before the censors against Lentulus,[132] in which the order of loyalty to particular individuals was indicated.

> Gell. 5,13,4: *M. Cato in oratione, quam dixit apud censores in Lentulum, ita scripsit: "Quod maiores sanctius habuere defendi pupillos quam clientem non fallere. Adversus cognatos pro cliente testatur, testimonium adversus clientem nemo dicit. Patrem primum, postea patronum proximum nomen habuere."*
>
> *Marcus Cato in the speech which he delivered before the censors Against Lentulus wrote thus: "Our forefathers regarded it as a more sacred obligation to defend their wards than not to deceive a client. One testifies in a*

client's behalf against one's relatives; testimony against a client is given by no one. A father held the first position of honour; next after him a patron."
(Transl. J.C. Rolfe)

The ancestors placed duties under the guardianship first before those of the patron to the client. It was permissible to testify against relatives in the interests of the client. The father was held in the highest esteem, immediately followed by the patron. Cato made this speech cited in the *Attic Nights* before the censors, most likely being, as the title implies, the accuser.[133] Lentulus was probably threatened with a censorial mark, and Cato apparently accused him of neglecting his duties as a tutor or patron. If we consider the case of clients and patrons, the law of Romulus[134] was already intended to introduce a sanction for breach of the law of patronage, declaring the guilty party a *sacer* (a sacrally declared outlaw).[135] During the Republican era, these relationships naturally were, like the issue of divorce, within the sphere of interest of the censors. *Tutela* was a later institution than patronage, with the guardian initially only being liable for it in certain cases. Therefore, also in this situation, the intervention of the censors was necessary.

It is likely that Lentulus was a senator (possibly Cornelius Lentulus, consul in 275 BC), as it was this group that the censors addressed most meticulously during the *lectio senatus*. During the census, many tasks were performed by the auxiliary officials, the *iuratores*. The citizen threatened with a mark could defend himself by calling witnesses, but it could also happen that someone made an accusation, as in this case.

What Lentulus was accused of is difficult to ascertain. The excerpt from Cato's speech indicates that the accusation concerned some kind of breach of duty where the hierarchy of duties was violated. It can be assumed that Lentulus either acted against a ward in the interests of his client or testified against his client to help a relative. Both actions fell under the jurisdiction of the censors. For neglect of duty, the guardian was liable according to the *ius civile*. According to the Law of the Twelve Tables, anyone could bring an *accusatio suspecti tutoris* against a tutor to immediately remove him from his guardianship, while the ward himself could, upon reaching maturity, bring an *actio rationibus distrahendis*. Later, there was also an *actio tutelae*. However, the censors presumably had the authority to react not only in cases of financial harm but also in other cases of negligence by the guardian.

A final aspect worth mentioning in the context of superior authority within the family is the issue of censorial control in cases of abuse of the right to own slaves. Apart from the general information provided by Dionysius of Halicarnassus quoted above, it is difficult to find source texts that indicate the extent of such control. The only instance in the sources where the restriction of ownership rights is interfered in context of censorship is in a regulation from the time of Domitian, who, in the exercise of perpetual censorship, forbade castration. The poet Statius, in a poem dedicated to the construction of the Via Domitiana, mentions that the emperor, as censor, forbade the castration of adult males,[136] which is confirmed by the account of Suetonius.[137] It can be assumed that the prohibition applied to slaves who were castrated for profit, but it is also possible that it extended to free men. This regulation was supplemented by provisions aimed at reducing the price of eunuchs. It should be remembered that Cato, at the time of his censorship, also imposed a tax of three asses per thousand on slaves purchased after the last *lustrum* for 10,000 asses or more[138] (usually young boys bought for their beauty).[139] Therefore, it is possible that in some cases the censors interfered in the price level of goods considered luxurious in order to limit excess and regulate the market. In this case, however, the prohibition of castration can also be interpreted as a restriction on ownership.

It can therefore be concluded that the power of the *pater familias* was subject to censorial control both in the raising of children and in the performance of the duties of tutor or patron, as well as in his role as a slave owner.

5. Family inheritance

The pater familias was also responsible for his *patrimonium* – that which he had inherited from his ancestors, both in a sacral and material sense.

The exercise of family worship was subject to censorial control. Cato's words against Veturius probably addressed this problem.

> Fest. 466 L. s.v. *Stata sacrificia: Stata sacrificia sunt, quae certis diebus fieri debent. Cato in ea, quam scripsit de L. Veturio, de sacrificio commisso, cum ei equum ademit*: "*Quod tu, quod in te fuit, sacra stata, sollempnia, capite sancta deseruisti.*"
>
> *Fixed sacrifices are those that must take place on certain days. As Cato wrote of Lucius Veturius when he took his horse away from him: "Because you have abandoned the solemn worship [the performance of which] belonged to you, which is punishable by a capital penalty."*
>
> (Transl. AT)

Festus noted that the accused had abandoned the *sacra* (probably family *sacra*),[140] the celebration of which was cyclical and sanctioned *capite*. This may mean that Veturius may even have been threatened with death or *capitis deminutio*. The passage shows that Cato deprived Veturius of his horse, thus removing him from the equestrian century, a rather mild punishment in this case. The noted words of the censor appear to be the listed reason for the application of the mark or *subscriptio censoria*.

As mentioned above, the censors used to take away horses from overly bulky equestrians, deeming them unfit to bear the hardships of horsemanship at such a weight. However, this was not a punishment as they were usually dismissed without the stigma of *ignominia*, i.e. without losing their reputation. This depended on the censors currently in office. In the case of Veturius, the weight of the body was merely a supplementary ground for punishing with a mark, in addition to the abandonment of the *sacra*.

On the other hand, the censors' interest may have been piqued by the neglect of ancestral property.[141]

> Plin. Mai. 18,11: *agrum male colere censorium probrum iudicabatur, atque, ut refert Cato, cum virum bonum laudantes bonum agricolam bonumque colonum dixissent, amplissime laudasse existimabantur.*
>
> *Bad husbandry was judged an offence within the jurisdiction of the censors, and, as Cato tells us, to praise a man by saying he was a good farmer and a good husbandman was thought to be the highest form of commendation.*
>
> (Transl. H. Rackham)

Pliny the Elder reported that negligence in the cultivation of a field was regarded as *probrum censorium.*[142] He also added, citing Cato,[143] that it was considered a great praise to call someone a good farmer.[144]

> Gell. 4,12,1: *Si quis agrum suum passus fuerat sordescere eumque indiligenter curabat ac neque araverat neque purgaverat, sive quis arborem suam vineamque habuerat derelictui, non id sine poena fuit, sed erat opus censorium, censoresque aerarium faciebant.*
>
> *If anyone had allowed his land to run to waste and was not giving it sufficient attention, if he had neither ploughed nor weeded it, or if anyone had neglected his orchard or vineyard, such conduct did not go unpunished, but it was taken up by the censors, who reduced such a man to the lowest class of citizens.*
>
> (Transl. J.C. Rolfe)

Gellius, on the other hand, also citing Cato, pointed out that negligence in the cultivation of land caused the risk of being transferred to the ranks of the *aerarii*. To avoid exposing oneself to the mark, the field had to be cultivated and ritually cleansed by *lustratio*,[145] and the trees and vines had to be cared for.

> Plin. Mai. 18,32: *Modus hic probatur, ut neque fundus villam quaerat neque villa fundum, non, ut fecere iuxta diversis in eadem aetate exemplis L. Lucullus et Q. Scaevola, cum villa Scaevolae fructus non caperet, villam Luculli ager, quo in genere censoria castigatio erat minus arare quam verrere.*
>
> *The satisfactory plan is that the house shall not be inadequate to the farm nor the farm to the house, not as was done on adjacent estates by Lucius Lucullus and Quintus Scaevola, acting on opposite principles though at the same period, when Scaevola's farmhouse would not hold the produce of his farm and Lucullus's farm was not big enough for his house—a sort of extravagance that occasioned the censor's rebuke that there was less ground to plough than floor-space to sweep.*
>
> (Transl. H. Rackham)

It was also necessary to maintain the ratio between buildings and cultivated land to adequately store the harvest.[146] Pliny recorded that both the case of Scaevola, whose buildings could not accommodate all the harvested crops, and of Lucullus, whose estate had more land for sweeping than for ploughing, seemed reprehensible to the censors. Lucullus turned the farmland into marble-lined squares and alleys, the maintenance of which required a broom rather than a plough. The country estate could not produce a harvest in this case.

It can therefore be concluded that rural estates had to be run according to certain rules.[147] Adequate land had to be set aside for crops, and storage had to be provided in prepared buildings. An estate should not just provide entertainment; it was supposed to be profitable. This attitude of the censors was perhaps due to the belief that wage labour was disgraceful – income had to be derived from the land. This, in turn, indicates that the people subject to the control of the censors in this respect were citizens from the upper strata of society[148] who owned rural estates.

It should be stressed that the decisions of the censors concerning the care of the land constituted a serious infringement of the right to property. This right was restricted by obliging citizens to use rural estates in a certain way. It is worth noting that the censors had the power of care with regard to both public and private places (*ius publicorum privatorumque locorum*).[149] In the case of public places, the censors had extensive powers: they protected their status against usurpation by private individuals, granted concessions for use, for example, for the water supply from an aqueduct, could use coercive measures such as the imposition of a fine, the seizure of objects as security, and the order of demolition, had the right to demarcate the boundaries of public places, and could also acquire land for the state and change its status to public. This activity of the censors evolved later, leading to the development of various legal institutions, particularly the praetorian interdicts. The right to interfere in private property was the second element of their spatial power.

The issue of squandering wealth cannot be overlooked either. The primary problem considered by the censors was excessive luxury.[150] Here, however, it will be narrowed down to the problem of squandering.

An interesting contribution to these considerations may be the lawsuit brought against the former censor Scipio by Asellus, discussed above. The accusation concerned the failure of the *lustrum*, but Scipio apparently decided to allude in his speech to the problem of the legitimacy of punishing Asellus with a censorial mark. For it was common knowledge that the bringing of the accusation against him constituted revenge.

> Gell. 6,11,9: *P. Africanus pro se contra Tiberium Asellum de multa ad populum: "Omnia mala, probra, flagitia, quae homines faciunt, in duabus rebus sunt, malitia atque nequitia. Utrum defendis, malitiam an nequitiam an utrumque simul? Si nequitiam defendere vis, licet; si tu in uno scorto maiorem pecuniam absumpsisti, quam quanti omne instrumentum fundi Sabini in censum dedicavisti, si hoc ita est: qui spondet mille nummum? si tu plus tertia parte pecuniae paternae perdidisti atque absumpsisti in flagitiis, si hoc ita est: qui spondet mille nummum? Non vis nequitiam. Age malitiam saltem defende. Si tu verbis conceptis coniuravisti sciens sciente animo tuo, si hoc ita est: qui spondet mille nummum?"*

Publius Africanus, speaking In his own Defence against Tiberius Asellus in the matter of a fine, thus addressed the people: "All the evils, shameful deeds, and crimes that men commit come from two things, malice and profligacy (nequitia). Against which charge do you defend yourself, that of malice or profligacy, or both together? If you wish to defend yourself against the charge of profligacy, well and good; if you have squandered more money on one harlot than you reported for the census as the value of all the equipment of your Sabine estate; if this is so, who pledges a thousand sesterces? If you have wasted more than a third of your patrimony and spent it on your vices; if that is so, who pledges a thousand sesterces? You do not care to defend yourself against the charge of profligacy; at least refute the charge of malice. If you have sworn falsely in set terms knowingly and deliberately; if this is so, who pledges a thousand sesterces?"

(Transl. J.C. Rolfe)

Scipio asserted that all crimes committed by human beings have their origin in malice and profligacy. He employed a rhetorical tactic with an appeal to *sponsio*. Specifically, he called on the assembled people to take an oath affirming the unworthy behaviour of his trial opponent. It is difficult to interpret this passage, but it seems that he may be referring to some kind of preliminary *sponsio*.

With regard to profligacy (*nequitia*) – Scipio cited two behaviours of Asellus that deserved condemnation: firstly, that he had spent more money on one prostitute than the value of the farm equipment on Sabine land he had declared at the time of the census, and secondly, that he had lost and squandered more than a third of the property inherited from his father on shameful whims. On the other hand, he gave a false oath as proof of malice. Since the whole speech was related to the censorial mark previously imposed on Asellus, it can be assumed that these listed behaviours formed the basis of it. In the end, Asellus escaped punishment due to the *intercessio* applied by the second censor, but Scipio remained convinced of the righteousness of his decision.

From the wording of the speech, it can be inferred that both the squandering of paternal property, which was also subject to the praetorian *interdictio bonorum*, and profligacy in the broadest sense, i.e. spending large sums on amusements deemed undignified, were considered reprehensible. The definition of spendthrift was quite narrow, and therefore the mark could also serve as a sanction in cases where it was impossible to appoint a curator because of unmet prerequisites. In such cases, prodigality did not result in the loss of property or pose a threat to future heirs. It is worth noting, on the other hand, that the term *nequitia* used by Scipio refers to the content of the praetorian *interdictio bonorum*.[151]

Ascon. 84 C.: *Hunc Antonium Gellius et Lentulus censores sexennio quo haec dicerentur senatu moverunt titulosque subscripserunt, quod socios diripuerit, quod iudicium recusarit, quod propter aeris alieni magnitudinem praedia mancipari bonaque sua in potestate non habeat.*

> *Six years before this speech was delivered, the censors Gellius and Lentulus removed this Antonius from the senate and put their signatures to a public listing of their reasons—that he had plundered allies, rejected the judgment of a court, that on account of his vast debts he had made over estates and held no property in his own name.*
>
> (Transl. R.G. Lewis)

In a commentary on Cicero's speech in the Senate against the rival candidates in the consular election, Asconius wrote that the censors appointed in 70 BC, Gnaeus Cornelius Lentulus and Lucius Gellius Publicola, removed Antonius Hybrida (later Cicero's colleague during the consulship) from the Senate[152] for robbing allies in Greece, refusing to enter into litigation and for having, due to the enormity of his debts, divested himself of land ownership and not having his estates under his authority. These reasons were given in the *subscriptio*, which the commentator seems to quote verbatim. The last allegation is precisely about squandering. Antonius had forfeited his estates, so his behaviour clearly fell within the definition of *prodigus*. However, it seems that the only sanction he suffered was a censorial mark, while his capacity for legal acts was not restricted.

It may also be added that, among Augustus' actions as a censor, Macrobius mentioned the case of a knight accused of diminishing his wealth. However, the equestrian managed to prove that, on the contrary, he had multiplied it.[153] This mention seems to clearly confirm that squandering must have constituted a *probrum censorium*.

It is still worth recalling one of the reasons mentioned by Dionysius of Halicarnassus for the use of the *nota censoria*: when brothers wanted to obtain more than their due share of the inheritance estate.

> Dion. Hal., *Ant. Rom.* 20,13,3: *οὔτε ἀδελφοὺς γνησίους τὸ πλεῖον ἀντὶ τοῦ ἴσου διώκοντας...*
>
> *nor should own brothers strive for more than their equal share.*
>
> (Transl. E. Cary)

The historian's mention is very laconic, but it is worth trying to interpret it. The text mentions siblings, who – as one may assume – inherited the estate in fractional parts. This could have happened without a will or based on a will. In the first case, a *consortium ercto non cito*,[154] an archaic form of partnership, was created between the brothers. The dissolution of the community could be achieved using *actio familiae erciscundae*, but the source text refers to a situation in which the brothers did not divide the inheritance between themselves; instead, one of them seized the greater part, marginalising the role of the other in the management of the property.

It seems, therefore, that the censors kept a close eye on citizens' actions relating to their ancestral heritage, both in the sacral and property spheres, punishing negligence in this regard with a mark.

6. Summary

For the Romans, the family was an institution vital for the proper functioning of society, ensuring stability. The *pater familias* looked after the family *sacra*, raised offspring, cultivated the land, and participated in political life. Such important matters could not remain outside the control of the state. Gradually, they were placed under the jurisdiction of censors, who punished citizens for violating ancestral customs with a censorial mark.

The interference of state authorities in the private lives of citizens was quite a rarity in the ancient world. That is why Greek authors wrote about it with astonishment, unable to understand why censorial control of customs extended so far.

The censors progressively created mechanisms to sanction behaviours they believed posed a threat to society. It can be noted that the penalties they applied had a different relationship with private law norms. Sometimes, the censorial mark complemented the regulations contained in the *ius civile* because it had a broader application. For example, a restriction of the capacity for legal acts of a spendthrift could only take place in cases where ancestral property was squandered to the detriment of future heirs, while censors could punish any manifestation of profligacy contrary to ancestral customs. It could also happen that legal norms developed during the period of the kings were only sanctioned by the censors during the Republican era. An example is the penalties for wrongful divorce, which in the *leges regiae* included confiscation of the husband's property but were not retained. Only censors could thus react in cases of wrongful dismissal of a wife. In this case, the censorial mark was probably an important premise influencing the outcome of lawsuits for the return of the dowry. The evolution of norms related to marriage and procreation is also very interesting. The censors urged people to marry and have offspring in a variety of ways, while also reproving unions contrary to ancestral customs. Octavian Augustus, on the other hand, referring to censorial solutions, decided to regulate the issue in statutory law, leading to the enactment of *lex Iulia et Papia*.

Notes

1 Dion. Hal., *Ant. Rom.* 20,13,3: But the Romans, throwing open every house and extending the authority of the censors even to the bed-chamber, made that office the overseer and guardian of everything that took place in the homes (transl. E. Cary). Cf. Dion. Hal., *Ant. Rom.* 19,16,5; M. Coudry, *Denys d'Halicarnasse, Plutarque, Dion Cassius: trois visions grecques de la censure?*, [in:] *Visions grecques de Rome. Griechische Blicke auf Rom*, eds. M.L. Freyburger, D. Meyer, Paris 2007, pp. 36–46.

2 Plut., *Cat. Mai.* 16. Cf. M. Coudry, *op. cit.*, pp. 46–50.

3 Cf. J. Zabłocki, *The Image of a Roman Family in 'Noctes Atticae' by Aulus Gellius*, "Pomoerium" 2/1996, p. 36; Idem, *The Picture of a Roman Family in 'Noctes Atticae' by Aulus Gellius*, [in:] J. Zabłocki, *Scripta Gelliana*, Warszawa 2020, p. 47.

4 Dion. Hal., *Ant. Rom.* 20,13,3.

5 Plut., *Cat. Mai.* 17,7: Cato expelled another senator who was thought to have good prospects for the consulship, namely, Manilius, because he embraced his wife in open day before the eyes of his daughter. For his own part, he said, he never embraced his

wife unless it thundered loudly; and it was a pleasantry of his to remark that he was a happy man when it thundered (transl. B. Perrin). Cf. Plut., *Mor.* 139 e.

6 Cf. M. Nowak, *Die Strafverhängungen der Censoren*, Breslau 1909, pp. 24 and 59; O. Schönberger, *Der glückliche Cato*, "RhM" 112/1969, p. 190.

7 Amm. Marc. 28,4,9: And those who stoop to do such things are men in the time of whose forefathers a senator was punished with the censor's brand of infamy, if he had dared, while this was still considered unseemly, to kiss his wife in the presence of their own daughter (transl. J.C. Rolfe).

8 On the subject of betrothal cf. in particular E. Volterra, *Ricerche intorno agli sponsali in diritto romano*, [in:] E. Volterra, *Scritti giuridici*, I, Napoli 1991, pp. 339–420; H. Kupiszewski, *Das Verlöbnis im altrömischen Recht*, "ZSS" 77/1960, pp. 125–159; R. Astolfi, *Il fidanzamento nel diritto romano*, Padova 1987, pp. 9 ff.

9 Plaut., *Aul.* 204–205; *Curc.* 670–671; *Poen.* 1156–1157; *Trin.* 1156–1168; Ter., *Andr.* 73–75; *Phorm.* 924–925; cf. M.V. Bramante, *'Patres', 'filii' e 'filiae' nelle commedie di Plauto. Note sul diritto nel teatro*, [in:] *Diritto e teatro in Grecia e a Roma*, eds. E. Cantarella, L. Gagliardi, Milano 2007, pp. 108–113.

10 Gell. 4,4,2: "One who wished to take a wife," says he, "demanded of him from whom she was to be received a formal promise that she would be given in marriage. The man who was to take the woman to wife made a corresponding promise. That contract, based upon pledges given and received, was called sponsalia, or 'betrothal.' Thereafter, she who had been promised was called sponsa, and he who had asked her in marriage, sponsus. But if, after such an interchange of pledges, the bride to be was not given in marriage, or was not received, then he who had asked for her hand, or he who had promised her, brought suit on the ground of breach of contract. The court took cognizance of the case. The judge inquired why the woman was not given in marriage, or why she was not accepted. If no good and sufficient reason appeared, the judge then assigned a money value to the advantage to be derived from receiving or giving the woman in marriage, and condemned the one who had made the promise, or the one who had asked for it, to pay a fine of that amount" (transl. J.C. Rolfe). Cf. J. Zabłocki, *The Image…*, pp. 40–41; Idem, *The Picture…*, pp. 54–55.

11 Cf. D. 23,1,2 (Ulp. l. sing. *de sponsal.*): "Betrothal" is derived from the word "promise," for it was customary among the ancients to stipulate and promise wives to one another (transl. S.P. Scott).

12 Cf. C. Fayer, *La familia romana. Aspetti giuridici ed antiquari. Sponsalia. Matrimonio. Dote. Parte seconda*, Roma 2005, p. 52 ff.

13 Cf. S. Treggiari, *Roman Marriage. 'Iusti coniuges' from the Time of Cicero to the Time of Ulpian*, Oxford 1993, pp. 83 ff.; J.F. Gardner, *Women in Roman Society and Law*, London 1986 (reprint 1995), pp. 31 ff.

14 Cf. B. Biondi, *La legislazione di Augusto*, [in:] B. Biondi, *Scritti giuridici*, II, Milano 1965, pp. 77 ff.; L.F. Raditsa, *Augustus' Legislation Concerning Marriage, Procreation, Love Affairs and Adultery*, "ANRW" 2.13/1980, pp. 278 ff.

15 Cf. A. Tarwacka, *The Censors' Influence on Marriage in Republican Rome*, "Zeszyty Prawnicze" 18.1/2018, pp. 173–191. See also below.

16 Cf. R. Astolfi, *La 'lex Iulia et Papia'*, Padova 1986, pp. 104–105; J. Urbanik, *Husband and Wife*, [in:] *The Oxford Handbook of Roman Law and Society*, eds. P.J. du Plessis, C. Ando, K. Tuori, Oxford 2016, pp. 475 ff.

17 M.J. Perry, *Gender, Manumission, and the Roman Freedwoman*, Cambridge 2014, pp. 90 ff.

18 Cf. T. Mommsen, *Römisches Staatsrecht*^{3}, II.1, Graz 1952 (reprint), pp. 377–382; M. Nowak, *op. cit.*, p. 64; E. Schmähling, *Die Sittenaufsicht der Censoren. Ein Beitrag zur Sittengeschichte der römischen Republik*, Stuttgart 1938, p. 64. Cf. also O. Karlowa, *Römische Rechtsgeschichte. I. Staatsrecht und Rechtsquellen*, Leipzig 1885, p. 172.

19 On the Bacchanalia case cf. *inter alia* E.S. Gruen, *Studies in Greek Culture and Roman Policy*, Leiden 1990, pp. 34–78; R.A. Bauman, *Women and Politics in Ancient Rome*, London 1992 (reprint 2003), pp. 35 ff.

20 Livy (39,9,5) wrote: *scortum nobile libertina Hispala Faecenia*. Cf. T.A.J. McGinn, *Prostitution, Sexuality, and the Law in Ancient Rome*, Oxford 2003, pp. 86 ff.

21 On the tutela over Hispala, the question of her marriage and her inheritance, cf. A. Watson, *'Gentis enuptio'*, [in:] A. Watson, *Studies in Roman Private Law*, London–Rio Grande 1991, pp. 3–13.

22 On the term *fraus* cf. H. Krüger, M. Kaser, *'Fraus'*, "ZSS" 63/1943, pp. 117–174.

23 Cf. M. Kaser, *Infamia und ignominia in den römischen Rechtsquellen*, "ZSS" 73/1956, pp. 220–278; J.G. Wolf, *Das Stigma ignominia*, "ZSS" 126/2009, pp. 55–113; Idem, *Lo stigma dell'ignominia*, [in:] *Homo, caput, persona. La costruzione giuridica dell' identità nell'esperienza romana*, eds. A. Corbino, M. Humbert, G. Negri, Pavia 2010, pp. 491–550.

24 It is uncertain whether this was due to the fact that she was a freedwoman or a prostitute – perhaps both reasons were sufficient in themselves. On this subject cf. T. Mommsen, *Römisches Staatsrecht...*, III, pp. 429–431; M. Humbert, *Hispala Faecenia et l'endogamie des affranchis sous la Republique*, "Index" 15/1987, pp. 131–140; S. Treggiari, *Roman Marriage...*, p. 64; T.A.J. McGinn, *Prostitution...*, pp. 86–91.

25 Cf., however, O. Karlowa, *Römische Rechtsgeschichte*, II, Leipzig 1901, p. 172, who expressed the cautious view of the non-existence of *iustum matrimonium* between freeborn and manumitted persons.

26 Cf. L. Villers, *Le mariage envisagé comme institution d'État dans le droit classique de Rome*, "ANRW" II.14/1982, pp. 295–296; T.A.J. McGinn, *Prostitution...*, p. 85, fn. 159.

27 On this subject, see above.

28 Cf. E.G. Huzar, *Mark Antony. Marriages vs. Careers*, "CJ" 81.2/1986, pp. 97 ff.

29 Cf. Cic., *Ad Att.* 16,11,1.

30 On the meaning in this context of the verb *sustulerit*, cf. B.D. Shaw, *Raising and Killing Children. Two Roman Myths*, "Mnemosyne" 54.1/2001, p. 39.

31 Cic., *Phil.* 13,23: And does the father of Fadia's children dare to despise anybody's lowly social origins? (transl. D.R. Shackleton Bailey).

32 Plut., *Ant.* 9,4.

33 Cic., *Ad Att.* 10,10,5: But this worthy here is carrying Cytheris around with him in an open litter, a second wife (transl. D.R. Shackleton Bailey). Cf. Cic., *Ad Att.* 15,22.

34 It is worth noting that Antony himself was a plebeian, but his membership of the *nobilitas* meant that his relationships with women of ill repute and freedwomen were frowned upon.

35 Cic., *Phil.* 2,58: As tribune of the plebs, he used to ride about in a two-wheeled 58 carriage; lictors decked with laurel led the way, 63 and in their midst a mime actress 64 was carried in an open litter. Respectable folk from the country towns, who were obliged to come out and meet the cortege, greeted her not by her well-known stage name but as "Volumnia." Then followed a carriage full of pimps, Antonius' utterly worthless entourage. His mother, relegated to the rear, followed her worthless son's mistress as if a daughter-in-law. Poor unfortunate woman, to be mother of that brood! He left the traces of these infamies in every town, prefecture, and colony, in fact throughout Italy (transl. D.R. Shackleton Bailey).

36 Plin. Mai. 8,55.

37 Tab. 4,3 (FIRA I), with the word *illam* instead of *mimulam* appearing in the reconstruction. The exact wording of the provision is uncertain. In the edition of M.H. Crawford, *The Roman Statutes*, II, London 1996, pp. 580 and 632–633, the reconstruction reads *<<repudium mittito>>*. Cf. R. Yaron, *Minutiae on Roman Divorce*, "TR" 28/1960, pp. 1–12; A. Watson, *The Divorce of Carvilius Ruga*, "TR" 33/1965, p. 42.

38 Cf. Athen. 10, 440e–441b.

39 Cf. J. Urbanik, *'Tuas res tibi habeto': la funzione delle 'parole approvate' nel divorzio*, [in:] *Dire le droit: normes, juges, jurisconsultes*, ed. B. Anagnostou-Canas, Paris 2006, pp. 87–98.

40 Cic., *Ad Att.* 4,2,6 cited above.

41 Cic., *Pro Sest.* 55; Quint., *Inst. or.* 4, pr. 3; *Nov. Mar.* 4,2; cf. also Plut., *Aem. Paul.* 38,7; *Camill.* 14,1; *Flam.* 18,1.

42 Cf. Dio Cass. 56,7,2.

43 Cf. J. Urbanik, *Husband and Wife*..., pp. 475–476 with cited literature.

44 Cf. R. Astolfi, *La 'lex Iulia et Papia'*..., p. 104, who wrote of "matrimoni (...) riprovevoli per la società".

45 See also below.

46 Cic., *De leg.* 3,7: ...they shall prohibit celibacy... (transl. C.W. Keyes). Cf. N. El Beheiri, *Das regimen morum der Zensoren. Die Konstruktion des römischen Gemeinwesens*, Berlin 2012, pp. 140–143.

47 The declarations were also made by divorced women and widows as well as by orphans, but a tutor acted for them.

48 Cf. *Tabula Heracleensis* 144–148; D. 50,15,4 pr. (Ulp. 3 *de cens.*).

49 Cf. Cic., *De off.* 3,104.

50 Cic., *De or.* 2,260: Laughable again was the response of Lucius Nasica to the interrogatory of Cato the censor, 'On your conscience, are you satisfied that you are a married man?' 'Married for certain,' returned Nasica, 'but verily not to my entire satisfaction!' (transl. E.W. Sutton, H. Rackham).

51 On this divorce and the censorial mark in the case of the wife's repudiation, see below.

52 Gellius used the term *divortium*, which rather meant divorce with the consent of both parties (cf. Gai. D. 24,2,2, pr.-1). This discrepancy is due to the fact that the source texts referring to divorce lack terminological consistency. Cf. O. Robleda, *El matrimonio en el dercho romano. Esencia, requisitos de validez, efectos, disolubilidad*, Roma 1970, p. 258 ff.

53 Gell. 13,16,3. Cf. G.W. Botsford, *The Roman Assemblies from Their Origin to the End of the Republic*, New York 1909 (reprint New Jersey 2001), pp. 139–151; L.R. Taylor, *Roman Voting Assemblies. From the Hannibalic War to the Dictatorship of Caesar*, Ann Arbor, MI 1966 (reprint 2003), pp. 2–3; F. Pina Polo, *Las 'contiones' civiles y militares en Roma*, Zaragoza 1989, pp. 4–11 and 41–42; J. Zabłocki, *'Leges votatae' nelle assemblee popolari*, "Diritto@Storia" 10–11/2011/2012, https://www.dirittoestoria.it/10/Tradizione-Romana/Zablocki-Leges-voto-assemblee-popolari.htm; R. Frolov, *Public Meetings in Ancient Rome. Definitions of the 'Contiones' in the Sources*, "Graeco-Latina Brunensia" 18/2013, pp. 75–84. On the censorial *contiones* cf. Varr., *L.L.* 6,90; Val. Max. 4,1,3.

54 Metellus was explicit about the interest of the state (*salus rei publicae*) - Gell. 1,6,6: he then found it no difficult or uphill work to convince them of what was the soundest and truest of principles, that the State cannot survive without numerous marriages (transl. J.C. Rolfe).

55 Suet., *Aug.* 89,2.

56 A. Berger, *Note on Gellius, N.A., I,6*, AJP 67.4/1946, pp. 323–328 argues that Gellius was mistaken, similarly L. Holford-Strevens, *Aulus Gellius. An Antonine Scholar and His Achievement*, Oxford 2003, p. 318. M. McDonnell, *The Speech of Numidicus at Gellius, N.A.1.6*, "AJP" 108.1/1987, pp. 81–94 argues instead that Metellus Numidicus also made a speech about the necessity of marriage. Cf. ORF 18 III, pp. 107–108.

57 Cf. *inter alia* E. Tassi Scandone, *'Leges Valeriae de provocatione'. Repressione criminale e garanzie costituzionali nella Roma repubblicana*, Napoli 2008, *passim*.

58 Cf. D. Stockton, *The Gracchi*, Oxford 1979 (reprint 2002), pp. 40 ff.; 131 ff.

59 403 BC. Cf. C. De Boor, *Fasti censorii*, Berolini 1873, p. 4; T.R.S. Broughton, *The Magistrates of the Roman Republic*, I, Atlanta 1951 (reprint 1986), p. 82; J. Suolahti, *The Roman Censors. A Study on Social Structure*, Helsinki 1963, pp. 176–178; E. Reigadas Lavandero, *Censura y res publica: aportación constitucional y protagonismo político*, Madrid 2000. pp. 71–75.
60 Cf. M. Nowak, *op. cit.*, p. 10.
61 Fest. (Paul.) 519 L., s.v. *uxorium*: Uxorium pependisse dicitur, qui quod uxorem non habuerit res populo dedit. [It is said that he paid 'wife fee' who, because he had no wife, gave something to the people – transl. AT]. Mommsen's conjecture, which proposed to replace *res* by *aes*, is to be received with appreciation.
62 Plut., *Camill.* 2,2.
63 See Chapter II.
64 Cf. Suet., *Vit.* 2,3; Tac., *Hist.* 3,66 Cf. C. De Boor, *op. cit.*, p. 32.
65 Suet., *Claud.* 16,3: for owing to the great carelessness of his agents, but to his own greater shame, those whom he accused of celibacy, childlessness, or lack of means proved that they were married, or fathers, or well-to-do (transl. J.C. Rolfe).
66 In Augustus' own actions, we can also find links between the marriage laws and censorship. This is evidenced firstly by the censorial speech *de prole augenda* delivered in the Senate, and also by the fact that the charge of celibacy was linked in the sources to the *regimen morum*– cf. Macrob., *Sat.* 2,4,25: 'As censor Augustus displayed a striking and praiseworthy forbearance. (…) he reproached the same man for not obeying the laws prescribing marriage, but the man said he had a wife and three children, and added, "From now on, Caesar, give honorable men the job of investigating honorable men" (transl. R.A. Kaster).
67 Sanctions imposed on childless bachelors were not the only element of the policy to promote procreation. Fathers could count on various kinds of rewards and bonuses since Republican times. This is discussed in more detail below.
68 Ps.-Quint., *Decl. min.* 310 pr. Cf. Ps.-Quint., *Decl. min.* 310,2,1: Well, none of us denies that it is written in the law: "Let him who has twice been found guilty of adultery be under stigma" (transl. D.R. Shackleton Bailey).
69 Gell. 17,18: Marcus Varro, a man of great trustworthiness and authority in his writings and in his life, in the work which he entitled Pius, or On Peace, says that Gaius Sallustius, the author of those austere and dignified works, whom we see in his history writing and acting like a censor, was taken in adultery by Annius Milo, soundly beaten with thongs, and allowed to escape only after paying a sum of money (transl. J.C. Rolfe).
70 By contrast, it does not seem likely that there was a penalty in the form of a censorial mark for persisting in mourning beyond the statutory time, a view put forward by some scholars on the basis of the text of Sen. Rhet., *Contr.* 4,1: Who is this man who claims to be censor of grief over a weeping father? Flung among all the disgraceful actions provoked by greed and lust, worthy of branding by every censor, he makes up rules for the age; he claims to know how much a father should weep for three lost sons: his father would weep for him, if he were alive (transl. M. Winterbottom). Cf. J. Garcia Sanchez, *Algunas consideraciones sobre el 'tempus lugendi'*, "RIDA", 23/1976, p. 147, who, however, misunderstood Seneca's text, thinking that it referred to a deceased father who, had he lived, would have mourned his three dead children. It should be noted that Numa's law limited mourning for children ten years and older to one year, for younger children to as many months as they were old, but children under three years of age were not mourned at all. Cf. *Leg. reg.* Numa 10 = Plut., *Numa* 12 (FIRA I); cf. G. Franciosi (ed.), *'Leges regiae'*, Napoli 2003, p. 98–99; *Frag. Vat.* 321. From D. 3,2,23 (Ulp. 8 *ad ed.*), however, it appears that the time of mourning for children was determined by each individual himself *secundum pietatis rationem et animi sui patientiam, prout quisque voluerit* that is according to the criterion of virtue and patience of his mind so far as each would like. Perhaps, therefore, over time, the

norms of statutory law ceased to apply, and a time of mourning was not imposed for deceased children. However, this issue is complicated by the suspicion of interpolation. Cf. more extensively A. Tarwacka, *As Far as the Bedroom… The Censor's Mark in Family Matters in Republican Rome*, "Zeszyty Prawnicze" 13.2/2013, pp. 199–201.

71 The text may be interpolated. The basic argument is that in G. 4,182 there is information that the edict did not concern *ignominia* (Gaius uses this term instead of *infamia*) but only the prohibition of *postulatio*. Cf. A. Guarino, *Salvius Iulianus. Profilo bio-bibliografico*, [in:] A. Guarino, *Pagine di diritto romano*, V, Napoli 1994, pp. 224–225.

72 Perhaps even more broadly, the censors may have sanctioned all cases of non-observance of mourning. Cf. A. López Pedreira, *'Tempus lugendi' y 'secundae nuptiae' en derecho romano*, "RIDROM" 11/2013, p. 341.

73 *Leg. reg.* Romulus 9 (FIRA I); cf. G. Franciosi (ed.), *op. cit.*, pp. 48–49.

74 For a detailed discussion of the causes of divorce and the possible reading of the text, see R. Fiori, *'Homo sacer'. Dinamica politico-costituzionale di una sanzione giuridico-religiosa*, Napoli 1996, pp. 236 ff.; J. Zabłocki, *Illeciti delle donne romane*, "Ius Antiquum" 1.8/2001, pp. 78–79; Idem, *The Prohibition on Women Drinking Wine in Ancient Rome*, [in:] J. Zabłocki, *Scripta Gelliana*, Warszawa 2020, pp. 98–99.

75 On the possible evolution of sanctions, from the punishment inflicted within the family structure to the censorial mark, cf. E. Pólay, *Das 'regimen morum' des Zensors und die sogenannte Hausgerichtsbarkeit*, [in:] *Studi in onore di Edoardo Volterra*, III, Milano 1971, pp. 263–317.

76 Cf. T.R.S. Broughton, *op. cit.*, I, p. 165; E. Reigadas Lavandero, *op. cit.*, pp. 153–159.

77 Cf. M. Nowak, *op. cit.*, pp. 11–12.

78 Cf., however, O. Robleda, *Il divorzio a Roma prima di Constantino*, "ANRW" II.14/1982, pp. 358–359, who concluded that Annius divorced without keeping these reasons and therefore needed a *consilium*.

79 On this subject, cf. N. El Beheiri, *Das regimen morum…*, p. 98 ff.; C. Bur, *La citoyenneté dégradée. Une histoire de l'infamie à Rome (312 av. J.-C.-96 apr. J.-C.)*, Rome 2018, p. 62. This episode was not considered true by J. Bleicken, *'Lex publica'. Gesetz und Recht in der römischen Republik*, Berlin 1975, p. 380.

80 Liv. 4,24,7–8.

81 Cf. G. Rotondi, *'Leges publicae populi Romani'. Elenco cronologico con una introduzione sull' attività legislativa dei comizi romani*, Milano 1912, p. 211; D. Flach, *Die Gesetze der frühen römischen Republik. Text und Kommentar*, Darmstadt 1994, pp. 245–246.

82 Cf. C. De Boor, *op. cit.*, p. 3; T.R.S. Broughton, *op. cit.*, I, p. 61; J. Suolahti, *The Roman Censors…*, pp. 171–174.

83 This episode was considered inauthentic by M. Humm, *Il 'regimen morum' dei censori e le identità dei cittadini*, [in:] *'Homo, caput, persona'. La costruzione giuridica dell' identità nell'esperienza romana*, eds. A. Corbino, M. Humbert, G. Negri, Pavia 2010, pp. 287 and 302. A.E. Astin, *'Regimen morum'*, "JRS" 78/1988, p. 16, fn. 12 only recommended caution in interpretation and does not question the reliability of Livy's account. In contrast, J.F. Keseberg, *De censoribus Romanorum commentatio*, Quedlinburg 1829, pp. 7–8, argued that the *regimen morum* had been in the hands of the censors since their appointment in 443 BC and considered Livy's account to be faithful. Cf. F.D. Gerlach, *Die römische Census in ihrem Verhältniß zur Verfassung. Eine historische Untersuchung*, Basel 1842, p. 214.

84 It seems to be Livy's anticipation that he mentioned Mamercus being transferred to the ranks of the *aerarii*. The use of this phrase was intended to clarify for readers the financial nature of the sanction applied. This does not seem to have been a case of acting within the *regimen morum*, which at the time was not yet a specified function of the censors, although Livy did use the term *aerarium facere*. Rather, the action of the censors was, in my view, an expression of revenge, which they could afford to take,

since their power of censorship was discretionary. Therefore, it seems that the event can be considered authentic.

85 Contrarily, M. Humm, *Il 'regimen morum'...*, p. 302, found that the census of the first class was eight times the census of the lowest class, so that the censors multiplied the value of the estate eightfold in order for Mamercus to pay the appropriate tax. The problem of interpretation may arise from the fact that Livy used the terms *tribu movere* and *aerarium facere*, which were unlikely to have been in use at the time. The decision of the censors was probably to charge Mamercus a high tax and to record a false value of his estate.

86 Cf. Gell. 4,3; 17,21,44; Plut., *Comp. Thes. Rom.* 39b; *Comp. Lyc. Num.* 77c; Mor. 267c; 278e; Dion. Hal. 2,25,7; Val. Max. 2,1,4; A. Watson, *The Divorce...*, pp. 38–50; O. Robleda, *Il divorzio...*, pp. 355–365; A. Jacobs, *Carvilius Ruga v Uxor: A Famous Roman divorce*, "Fundamina" 15.2/2009, pp. 92–111.

87 The *iusiurandum* taken during the census took the form, as mentioned, of a sacred oath dedicated to Jupiter, based on the Roman virtue of *fides*, i.e. fidelity in private and public affairs; cf. Cic., *De off.* 3,104.

88 Dion. Hal., *Ant. Rom.* 2,25,7: he was obliged by the censors to swear that he had married for the purpose of having children (transl. E. Cary).

89 Cf. Plaut., *Aulul.* 146–149; *Capt.* 889; Val. Max. 7,7,4.

90 Cf. Cic., *Pro Cluent.* 42.

91 Gell. 17,21,44: Five hundred and nineteen years after the founding of Rome, Spurius Carvilius Ruga, at the advice of his friends, was the first Roman to divorce his wife, on the ground that she was barren and that he had taken oath before the censors that he married for the purpose of having children (transl. J.C. Rolfe).

92 Cf. A. Söllner, *Zur Vorgeschichte und Funktion der 'actio rei uxoriae'*, Köln–Wien 1969, pp. 84–87; C.F. Amunátegui Perelló, *La obligación de restitución de la dote y el nacimiento del divorcio en Roma*, "Revista de Estudios Histórico-Jurídicos" 30/2008, pp. 39–46.

93 Cf. Val. Max. 6,3,10–12; Plut., *Mor.* 267c.

94 In a similar context, another complaint, *actio malae tractationis*, appears in the declamations, which, however, seems rather related to the problem of the return of the dowry. Cf. Ps.-Quint., *Decl. min.* 383; T. Lanfranchi, *Il diritto nei retori romani. Contributo alla storia dello sviluppo del diritto romano*, Milano 1938, pp. 235–238; T. Wycisk, *'Quidquid in foro fieri potest'. Studien zum römischen Recht bei Quintilian*, Berlin 2008, pp. 123–125.

95 Cf. T. Lanfranchi, *op. cit.*, p. 238; T. Wycisk, *op. cit.*, pp. 123–126.

96 From a passage in Ps.-Quint., *Decl. min.* 262,3,1: Nam lex iniusti repudii spectat utramque personam... [For the law of wrongful divorce regards both parties – transl. D.R. Shackleton Bailey], T. Lanfranchi, *op. cit.*, p. 239, drew the conclusion that the husband also could have brought an action against his wife, which does not agree with the context. The declamation informs that the trial examines not only what the husband should have done, but also what the wife should have endured.

97 Ps.-Quint., *Decl. min.* 330 pr.: A man divorced his wife, from whom he had a young son, on a charge of adultery. Cf. Ps.-Quint., *Decl. min.* 327,1,1: she is not taxed with adultery or any license against her husband... (transl. D.R. Shackleton Bailey).

98 It is worth mentioning that according to Pliny, willow seeds could cure infertility (Plin. Mai. 16,110). Aelian wrote that willow fruits deprive men of their fertility (Aelian, *De natura animalium* 4,23).

99 Ps.-Quint., *Decl. min.* 327,5,1: She wanted to escape the stories about stepmothers (transl. D.R. Shackleton Bailey). Cf. P.A. Watson, *Ancient Stepmothers. Myth, Misogyny and Reality*, Leiden–New–York–Köln 1995, pp. 92 ff.

100 Ps.-Quint., *Decl. min.* 327,6,1: She had found a full home, a full will (transl. D.R. Shackleton Bailey).

101 Cf. T. Lanfranchi, *op. cit.*, p. 232.
102 *The lex raptae* is one example of the choice between punishment or *pactio*, under which the offender had to do something to compensate for the damage. An example is the story of the prostitute blinded by her client (Ps.-Quint., *Decl. min.* 297). According to the cited rule, the perpetrator had the choice of incurring the punishment of talion, i.e. being blinded, or becoming a guide for the injured party.
103 Ps.-Quint., *Decl. min.* 251,1,1.
104 Cf. T. Giaro, *'Excusatio necessitatis' nel diritto romano*, Warszawa 1982, pp. 14 ff.
105 Ps.-Quint., *Decl. min.* 262,5–7.
106 Cf. T. Wycisk, *op. cit.*, p. 126.
107 Ps.-Quint., *Decl. min.* 368.
108 Ps.-Quint., *Decl. min.* 368,7,1: She could sue you for wrongful divorce, <if> she wanted to <go back> (transl. D.R. Shackleton Bailey).
109 Dion. Hal., *Ant. Rom.* 20,13,3.
110 The text of the edict should be considered authentic. Cf. G. Bloch, *De l'authenticité de l'édit censorial de 92 av. I. C. contre les rhéteurs latins*, "Klio" 3/1903, pp. 68–73; A. Manfredini, *L'editto 'de coërcendis rhetoribus latinis' del 92 a.C.*, "SDHI" 42/1976, pp. 100–106; E.S. Gruen, *Studies…*, p. 179.
111 Cf. FIRA I no. 52.
112 Cf. Suet., *De rhet.* 25.
113 Suet., *De rhet.* 25; Gell. 15,11,1. Gellius (15,11,3–5) also noted that under Domitian philosophers were removed from Rome and Italy by virtue of the *senatusconsultum*.
114 This issue was addressed by A. Manfredini, *op. cit.*, pp. 99–148.
115 Cf. Liv. 9,30,5.
116 Cic., *De or.* 3,93.
117 E.S. Gruen, *Studies…*, pp. 182–183 questions such political affiliation of the censors.
118 Cf. Cic., *Pro Arch.* 20: Cf. E. Fantham, *op. cit.*, p. 43.
119 A. Manfredini, *op. cit.*, pp. 114–148.
120 E.S. Gruen, *Studies…*, pp. 180–182 challenges the existence of political links between Marius and Plotius, and to this he refutes the view that Marius was opposed to everything Greek and therefore also to Greek teachers. In his view, it was merely an aside.
121 Cf. J.-M. David, *Promotion civique et droit à la parole: L. Licinius Crassus, les accusateurs et les rhéteurs latins*, "MEFRA" 91.1/1979, pp. 169–170.
122 Cf. K. Rupprecht, *Molon (8)*, "RE" XIV.1/1928, p. 12.
123 Cf. Tac., *Dial.* 34; A. Manfredini, *op. cit.*, pp. 144–148.
124 Gell. 4,20,10.
125 Gell. 5,19,15–16: I have observed in a speech of Publius Scipio On Morals, which he made to the people in his censorship, that among the things that he criticized, on the ground that they were done contrary to the usage of our forefathers, he also found fault with this, that an adopted son was of profit to his adoptive father in gaining the rewards for paternity. The passage in that speech is as follows: "A father votes in one tribe, the son in another, an adopted son is of as much advantage as if one had a son of his own; orders are given to take the census of absentees, and hence it is not necessary for anyone to appear in person at the census" (transl. J.C. Rolfe).
126 Scipio considered it reprehensible to accept the census declarations of absent persons. Since deliberate unexcused non-attendance at the census was punishable by confiscation of property and sale into slavery of the *incensus*, it must be assumed that this was a case of allowing declarations to be made in someone else's name, *in absentia*. Since Scipio was against this, it could not have been about people who did not come to the census because of public duties, but about those who did not turn up out of laziness or in order not to catch the eye of the censors and avoid their *nota censoria*.
127 It is likely that a censorial mark could also be imposed in the case of an adoption made to usurp the rights due to fathers. Cf. A. Tarwacka, *Adoption under the Scrutiny of the*

Censors in Republican Rome, [in:] *Family, Law, and Society: From Roman Law to the Present Day*, eds. E. Dawidziuk, P. Panero, A. Tarwacka, Berlin–Bern–Bruxelles–New York–Oxford–Warsaw–Wien 2023, pp. 77–92.

128 Liv. 45,15.

129 Suet., *Div. Iul.* 20,3.

130 Gell. 1,12,8.

131 On the later *ius trium liberorum* cf. M. Zabłocka, *Il 'ius trium liberorum' nel diritto romano*, "BIDR" 30/1992, pp. 361–390.

132 Neither the date nor the circumstances of this speech are known. It is attributed to Cato the Elder, who is supposed to have delivered it after his censorship had already ended. Cf. A.E. Astin, *Cato the Censor*, Oxford 1978, pp. 109–110.

133 Proceedings before censors could take the form of a trial, sometimes referred to as *censorium iudicium* or *iudicium de moribus*. Cf. A. Tarwacka, *Censorial Stigma and the Problem of Guilt*, [in:] *'Culpa'. Facets of Liability in Ancient Legal Theory and Practice. Proceedings of the Seminar Held in Warsaw 17-19 February 2011*, JJP Supplements XIX, ed. J. Urbanik, Warsaw 2012, p. 141 ff.

134 Dion. Hal., *Ant. Rom.* 2,10,3 = *Leg. reg.* Rom. 2 (FIRA I); G. Franciosi (ed.), *op. cit.*, p. 99.

135 Cf. L. Garofalo, *Sulla condizione di 'homo sacer' in età arcaica*, [in:] L. Garofalo, *Studi sulla sacertà*, Padova 2005, pp. 11 ff.; R. Fiori, *op. cit.*, pp. 225 ff.

136 Stat., *Silv.* 4,3,13–15.

137 Suet., *Dom.* 7,1. Cf. Mart., *Ep.* 6,2.

138 Cf. Liv. 39,44; Plut., *Cat. Mai.* 18.

139 Cf. Athen. 6,275a.

140 Cf. R.E.A. Palmer, *The Deconstruction of Mommsen on Festus 462/464 L.*, [in:] *'Imperium Sine Fine'. T. Robert S. Broughton and the Roman Republic*, ed. J. Linderski, Stuttgart 1996, pp. 93 ff.

141 Cf. E. Zanda, *Fighting Hydra-Like Luxury. Sumptuary Regulation in the Roman Republic*, London–New Delhi–New York–Sydney 2013 (reprint), pp. 41 ff.

142 Cf. R. Rodríguez López, *La agricultura como 'officium' en el mundo romano*, "RIDA" 49/2002, p. 187.

143 Cat., *De agr.* pr.

144 Cf. Cic., *De or.* 2,287 discussed above.

145 Cf. Cat., *De agr.* 141; Ovid., *Fast.* 1,669.

146 Cf. Cat., *De agr.* 3,1; Varr., *De re rust.* 1,11; see also Val. Max. 8,1 damn. 7.

147 Cf. Cat., *De agr.* 1.

148 This refers in particular to the senators, who were additionally subject to the regulations introduced in the *lex Claudia de nave senatorum* of 218 BC concerning the prohibition of large-scale maritime trade. Cf. G. Rotondi, *op. cit.*, pp. 249–250; A. Guarino, '*Quaestus omnis patribus indecorus*', "Labeo" 28/1982, pp. 7–16; E. Baltrusch, *Regimen morum. Die Reglamentierung des Privatlebens der Senatoren und Ritter in der römischen Republik und frühen Kaiserzeit*, München 1989, pp. 37–38; N. El Beheiri, *Die 'lex Claudia de nave senatorum'*, "RIDA" 48/2001, pp. 57–63; Eadem, *Das 'regimen morum'...*, pp. 118–120.

149 Liv. 4,8,2. Cf. A. Tarwacka, *The Roman Censors as Protectors of Public Places*, "Diritto@Storia" 12/2014, http://www.dirittoestoria.it/12/tradizione-romana/Tarwacka-Roman-Censors-Protectors-Public-Places.htm.

150 Cf. below.

151 PS. 3,4a,7: A person can be prohibited by the Praetor from receiving an estate on account of his or her morals, in the following terms: "To prevent you from squandering the estate of your father (or grandfather), by your profligacy, and bringing your children to want, I exclude you from the house and from all commercial intercourse" (transl. S.P. Scott).

152 Cf. Cic., *Comm. pet.* 8.

153 Macrob., *Sat.* 2,4,25: As censor Augustus displayed a striking and praiseworthy forbearance. He was upbraiding a Roman knight for having squandered his resources, but the man demonstrated in his presence that he had actually increased them (transl. R.A. Kaster).

154 Cf. G. Aricò Anselmo, *'Societas inseparabilis' o dell'indissolubilità dell'antico consorzio fraterno*, [in:] '*Iuris Vincula'. Studi in onore di Mario Talamanca*, Napoli 2001, p. 149–191; A. Calzada, *'Consortium ercto non cito: consortes qui a communione discedere velint'*, "Iura" 59/2011, pp. 151–176; J. Zabłocki, *'Consortium ercto non cito' in Aulus Gellius' 'Noctes Atticae'*, [in:] J. Zabłocki, *Scripta Gelliana*, Warszawa 2020, pp. 105–117.

V Censorial mark concerning public functions and way of life

1. Preliminary remarks

The forum was the centre of public life in Rome. It was where officials acted, where some assemblies and *contiones* took place, and where key buildings were located: the basilicas, the curia, and the *rostra*. It is worth noting that citizens also gathered in other places, such as the theatres, where opinions were formed and exchanged as well. Therefore, a discussion of the censorial mark in public life will not be limited to issues related to the functioning of state organs but will also cover the issues of spectacle and entertainment. The holding of public office had a military aspect, so this sphere will also be analysed. Besides, the conduct of legal transactions was an important part of the functioning of society, in which the censors had an interest and subjected to scrutiny.

2. Public functions

The role of censors in public life was not insignificant: they influenced the social hierarchy, could control officials during their term of office, and could apply penalties in cases of abuse.

One of the key principles of office during the Republican period was the principle of collegiality, designed to limit excessive usurpation of power and arbitrary decision-making. The censors themselves were, of course, bound by this rule, while they were also tasked with ensuring its application to other magistracies.

> Fronto, *Ad M. Caes.* 5,42: *M. Lucilius tribunus pl(ebis) hominem liberum, civem Romanum, cum collegae mitti iuberent, adversus eorum sententiam ipsius vi in carcerem compegit. Ob eam rem a censoribus notatur.*
>
> *M. Lucilius a tribune of the people, against the decision of his colleagues and with his own hand cast into prison by force a Roman citizen, though they ordered his discharge. For that action he was "marked" by the Censors.*
>
> (Transl. C.R. Haines)

Fronto described an exceptionally interesting case study concerning plebeian tribunes. Although it is a school rhetorical exercise, it seems to be based on a real-life

DOI: 10.4324/9781003486664-6

casus.[1] Tribune M. Lucilius was punished with a censorial mark because he ignored the *intercessio* of his colleagues in office, who had ordered him to release a free Roman citizen. Despite his objections, Lucilius confined this citizen in prison using violence. It should be noted that the tribunes had the right to detain, including imprisoning, a citizen – *ius prendendi.*[2] However, the other tribunes could block such a decision by using *intercessio*, particularly if the citizen sought their assistance taking advantage of the *ius auxilii*. The reason for the censorial mark in this case could therefore be not only ignoring the *intercessio* but also violating the citizen's rights. The *ius auxilii*, alongside the *ius provocationis*, was regarded as a pillar of liberty, a fundamental privilege available to Roman citizens. Both of these powers were applied very widely, so much so that even at the end of the Republic, it was enough to declare *Civis Romanus sum!* and this alone should ensure a person's personal immunity. Lucilius' behaviour therefore not only violated the principle of the collegiality of the office but also infringed on the privileges of the citizen, which could have provided an additional argument for the censors when imposing the mark.

Issues relating to the abuse of office also concern the case of Gaius Gracchus, who was accused by the censors upon his return from his quaestorship in Sardinia and gave a defence speech on the matter. According to Plutarch,[3] Gaius' actions as quaestor troubled the senators. The issue was that Gaius tried to reach an agreement with the inhabitants of the province, negotiating with them for supplies for the army. Thanks to him, the Senate was also approached by deputies of the King of Numidia, who wanted to provide assistance to the governor of Sardinia – a support the Senate rejected. These situations were seen by the *nobilitas* as attempts to secure the favour of the people. Gracchus then returned to Rome, where he was accused before the censors of leaving the province before the governor. He refuted this accusation by arguing that, as quaestor, he could have returned to Rome after a year, while he remained in Sardinia for two years. This may indicate that quaestors, as a rule, were not allowed to leave their appointed province before the end of their term of office.[4] While the governor stayed there by virtue of a *prorogatio imperii*, the length of which was decided by the Senate, the quaestor should have had a one-year term. The case in question, however, suggests that it may have been customary for the quaestor to accompany the governor for longer. The question arises as to the legal basis for such an arrangement and the relationship of such a rule to the length of the term of office. The quaestor assigned to the governor apparently remained in the province until either the governor left it, or another quaestor arrived. On the other hand, the reasoning used by Gaius himself seems to indicate that he could return to Rome at the end of his one-year term.

The application of the mark may also have been prompted by cases of abuse of coercion. One example is the famous case of L. Quinctius Flaminius. Cato condemned him for killing a prisoner at the request of a prostitute during a banquet.[5] The basis of the mark was both excessive lust (*libido*), i.e. abuse of a private nature, and, above all, the tarnishing of an office with an unworthy act, for which Cicero's treatise uses the term *dedecus imperii*. Although the official carried out the death sentence passed, he did so in circumstances that were not in keeping with the dignity of the magistracy, thus dishonouring it.

The censors, who were themselves part of the sacred life of the state through the lustration ceremony, also included in their remit the duties of officials with regard to the relationship between man and the gods. In his treatise *De Divinatione*, Cicero described a very interesting case study related to the auspices[6]: before the unlucky expedition of Crassus to Parthia that ended in the tragic battle of Carrhae, one of the plebeian tribunes, C. Ateius Capito, announced the observation of inauspicious signs by performing an *obnuntiatio*. The censor Appius Claudius Pulcher, who, by the way, held the office of augur, punished him with a mark, stating in the *subscriptio* that the auspices were false, thus exposing the Roman people to a terrible defeat. Cicero, however, emphasised the inconsistency on the part of Appius Claudius, who, as censor, had every right to impose the mark since he found the auspices to be false, but as augur, he should not be claiming that this brought defeat to Rome. The battle's tragic outcome was solely the fault of Crassus, who disregarded the inauspicious signs. In any case, this story allows us to conclude that the abuse of auspices, including the false *obnuntiatio*, could have resulted in the imposition of a censorial mark.

The censors were also supposed to control the works of the Senate.

> Gell. 14,7,8: *Post haec deinceps dicit senatusconsultum ante exortum aut post occasum solem factum ratum non fuisse; opus etiam censorium fecisse existimatos, per quos eo tempore senatusconsultum factum esset.*
>
> *After this he goes on to say that a decree of the senate made before sunrise or after sunset was not valid, and that those through whom a decree of the senate was made at that time were thought to have committed an act deserving censure.*
>
> (Transl. J.C. Rolfe)

Gellius, using the work by Varro called *Εἰσαγωγικόν* written for Pompey when he became consul, informed that the censors should ensure that senate resolutions were not supposed to be passed before sunrise or after sunset. If someone led to the passing of such a *senatus consultum*, it was the duty of the censors to punish him with a mark, i.e. to remove him from the Senate. The need to adjourn after sunset was, moreover, used for obstruction. Gellius read about this in Ateius Capito's work *De officio senatorio*. Cato the Younger, during Caesar's consulship, spoke for an exceptionally long time to stall the deliberations and prevent a resolution from being passed on a matter that, in his opinion, was not in the interests of the Republic. Caesar had him imprisoned, but the whole Senate interceded on his behalf, and the consul, willy-nilly, released him.[7]

In the context of the responsibility of officials, it is still worth examining the passages in Cicero's *De Legibus* concerning censorship.[8] This is, of course, the description of an ideal system modelled on that of Republican Rome. Cicero suggested that censors should guard the laws, by which he meant ensuring that their content was not altered. This solution addressed the problem of auxiliary officials interfering with the content of laws. In creating this function of censorship, Cicero was inspired by the Greek *νομοφύλακες* ('guardians of laws'). Additionally, the censors were to receive reports from retiring officials on their activities during their term of office, with the right to make a preliminary assessment. This is only a draft, but it fits neatly into the socially desirable model of censorship.

Also, judges were subject to censorial control, as mentioned by Cicero in his speech *Pro Cluentio*.[9] However, this part of the speech is very specific and must be treated with caution, as the speaker was trying to undermine the importance of the censorial mark and – moreover – to portray it as a potential tool of tyranny. There is no doubt that judges suspected of corruption could have been punished with the mark. On the other hand, those who had already been stigmatised by the censors were entered in the *iudicium album*. This highlights the lack of lasting effects of censorial sanctions. However, this does not detract at all from the role of censors in shaping the right civic attitudes and eliminating undesirable behaviour. A judge whose integrity was questioned certainly had to face the possibility of a mark being imposed.

3. Army

As a rule, censors had hardly any influence on military matters[10]; they did not command armies. The opinion of Valerius Maximus,[11] who compared the importance of censorship to military discipline and the effects of the censors' efforts to military glory, seems remarkably interesting in this connection.[12] In his view, Rome's power consisted not only of the virtues of the commanders but also of the care of customs in peacetime. Conquests are of no avail if one lives improperly in the state, if one does not prioritise the duties in the forum and the Senate, as well as customs that provide a solid foundation for what one is building. Censorship is referred to in this text as *pacis magistra custosque*, i.e. teacher and guardian of peace. This does not mean that censors were completely removed from military affairs; the very genesis of the office, which originated from the consulate, indicates connections with military matters. First and foremost, the censors were responsible for conducting the census, during which they assigned citizens to property classes and, at the same time, to military centuries. In practice, this meant that the composition of the army depended on them to some extent. As mentioned above, it was also recognized over time that the censorial mark could apply to soldiers, and the competence of the censors in this respect was confirmed by a resolution of the Senate.[13] Military issues were perhaps of particular importance in the context of the *recognitio equitum* described above. The censors applied extremely strict criteria to horsemen so that the elite equestrian centuries included citizens worthy of this honour.

Sometimes censors, using their powers, came to the aid of the consuls. Livy, writing about the events of 169 BC, during the Third Macedonian War when Rome faced trouble with conscription, relayed[14] that the task of conducting conscription was entrusted – in place of the consuls who could not cope with it – to the praetors.[15] The censors decided to assist by issuing an edict. Citizens took an oath (*iusiurandum*) during the census, and in their edict, the censors announced that they would extend it with a new clause for men belonging to the junior centuries,[16] i.e. those under forty-six years of age.[17] They were required to pledge that they would present themselves for any subsequent conscription into the army if they were not enlisted. For soldiers under the authority of their father or grandfather, the censors ordered their names to be given, as *alieni iuris* persons did not present themselves for the census.[18] Additionally, soldiers from legions stationed in Macedonia but residing in Italy were instructed to report for the census within thirty days and then return to the province. Finally, the censors announced that they would reconsider the cases of those dismissed from service; if they decided that they had been discharged too early, those individuals would be reinstated into the army. The provisions concerning soldiers were interpreted by Filippo Cancelli[19] as testifying to the criminal jurisdiction of the censors in *perduellio* cases. Arrigo Manfredini,[20] on the other hand, considered that such an edict of the censors had a right to exist only because of the solemnity of their office and the fear of a censorial mark and deprivation of honour. In my opinion, the censors simply announced that the relevant entries would be made during the census. The list of citizens indicated whether someone was scheduled for military service or was already a reservist. If the censor considered that the honourable discharge (*missio gratiosa*) was premature, he indicated that the person could still be recalled, resulting in re-enlistment in the army.

Frontinus, in turn, reported that the consul Aurelius Cotta asked the censors to punish with a mark the equestrians who refused to do the prescribed work.[21] This excerpt further indicates that cooperation between state authorities may have been of a much broader nature. In this case, additional sanctions for the knights were introduced by the resolution of the Senate and the plebiscite. Incidentally, it is worth noting that this situation fits perfectly with Polybius' portrayal of a Republican system in which different elements could influence and support each other.[22]

Elsewhere, Frontinus cited the decision of the censor Fuvius Flaccus regarding the removal of a military tribune (who happened to be his brother) from the Senate for having discharged a legion without an order from the consul.[23] It seems, therefore, that disobedience to the consul as commander-in-chief of the army could have resulted not only in military penalties but also in a censorial mark.

Other instances of the imposition of a censorial mark may also have been related to the military sphere. The aforementioned censors P. Furius Philus and M. Atilius Regulus applied the mark to Carthaginian captives who had returned to Rome under an oath to come back. The case concerns the violation of the *iusiurandum*, which was a pledge of sacred nature. Cicero emphasised[24] the value of this oath taken in the presence of Jupiter. Its breach was regarded as a betrayal of *fides*, the most important Roman virtue centred on maintaining fidelity (the temple of the personified Fides was located on the Capitol near the sanctuary of Jupiter). Keeping one's word, however, should not stem from fear of the deity, i.e. a negative motivation, but from willingness, i.e. a positive motivation.

The case of the Carthaginian captives took place after the Battle of Cannae in 215 BC. It was described by Cicero,[25] Livy,[26] Gellius,[27] and Nepos. Cicero reported that none of the captives returned to Hannibal, but only one explained that he had retreated to the Punic camp on some pretext and thus absolved himself of his oath. However, although he technically kept his word, he misappropriated the actual content of the pledge, for in the case of *fides*, it is not what you say that matters, but what you feel. As for Nepos' account, it is known about him only thanks to Gellius.[28] The historian wrote about an ongoing discussion in the Senate about the fate of the captives who did not want to return to Hannibal's camp. In the end, the opinion of not surrendering them to the enemy prevailed.

In the case described, the censors punished the captives with a mark for breaking their oaths. Gellius did not specify the exact sanction they applied, but Livy reported that those who belonged to the equestrian centuries were deprived of their horses, and all were transferred to the inferior *tribus* and placed among the *aerarii*.

An additional problem concerns the *ius postliminii* mentioned by Gellius, which refers to the right of return, by virtue of which a returnee from captivity at the hands of the enemy regained his rights, namely liberty, citizenship, *patria potestas*, and property.[29] In the present case, however, the returning captives were bound by an oath, which prevented them from exercising this privilege. Source accounts differ, and it is therefore difficult to determine whether all the captives remained in Rome or only those who claimed to have discharged themselves from the *iusiurandum*, returning to Hannibal's camp for a while on a pretext. This is what Gellius' account indicates. Since there was a discussion in the Senate about the possibility of handing over these men to the Carthaginians, there must have been considerable doubt about the legitimacy of granting them the *ius postliminii*.

There is another example described in Cicero's *De officiis* that may shed some light on the matter. It concerns the case of M. Atilius Regulus, an ancestor of the aforementioned censor, who – captured by the Carthaginians during the First Punic War – was sent to Rome to negotiate the release of Carthaginian captives in exchange for his freedom. Regulus presented his message to the Senate, but refused to participate in the deliberations, acknowledging that as long as he was bound by the *iusiurandum* made to his enemies, he was not a senator. Additionally, he advised against the release of captives and – when the Senate followed his suggestion – he returned to Carthage where he was executed. This case was also analysed by Pomponius, commenting on the work of Quintus Mucius.[30] The jurist concluded that Regulus did not return to Rome by virtue of the *postliminium* because – being bound by an oath (*iusiurandum*) – he did not have the intention to remain in Rome (*animus Romae remanendi*). Following this line of thought, it should be considered that, since the captives mentioned in the *Attic Nights* had the intention to remain in Rome, they could have benefited from the *ius postliminii*. On the other hand, the breaking of the oath (even if they fraudulently seemed to fulfil it) could not have been indifferent to the censors who upheld *fides*.

It can therefore be hypothesised that the intervention of the censors occurred most often when there were no other means to punish those guilty of military negligence constituting behaviour contrary to *mores maiorum*.

Cicero described the decision of the censor Scipio the Younger[31] concerning a centurion who had evaded fighting in the battle of Pydna, claiming that he had remained in camp to protect it.[32] The centurion's behaviour was not a sign of desertion or insubordination. He simply found an excuse that allowed him to stay away from the hostilities. Therefore, the only sanction that could have been imposed was a censorial mark, which in this case consisted of a transfer to another tribe: no rules or orders had been broken. Cicero noted this case because of the witty[33] retort of the censor, who replied to the centurion asking the reason for the sanction that he did not like excessive diligence. Such an explanation could not, of course, be found in the *subscriptio censoria*: Scipio must have given the actual reason for the mark, namely the evasion of battle. This confirms the supposition that the reaction of the censors may have been to fill in the legal loopholes.

It is also worth noting that the increase in the influence of the censors on military issues had to do with the Punic Wars, particularly the defeat at Cannae. There was an obvious need to strengthen the existing means of enforcing obedience, and the censors had effective tools to ensure this.

4. Excessive luxury

The problem of extravagance had been addressed in Roman law since archaic times. The Law of the Twelve Tables regulated funerals, and further regulations were introduced in the so-called *leges sumptuariae*.[34] However, much of the control in this area was exercised by the censors, whose task was to uphold the customs of the ancestors (*regimen morum*). What needs to be analysed are both the cases of imposing a mark for excess, and the relationship between censorial sanctions and other legal regulations.[35]

The first regulations restricting excess appeared, as mentioned, in the provisions of the Twelve Tables concerning the prohibition of excessively grand funerals. This was followed by censorial edicts. The first *lex sumptuaria* is considered to be the *lex Oppia de luxu feminarum* of 215 BC, which restricted the wearing of jewellery and the use of carts by women. It is worth noting that the censors could not regulate this issue, as their *regimen morum* only covered men.

The censors' edicts on the issue of extravagance, the so-called *edicta de moribus* should be discussed first. According to Nepos,[36] Cato the Elder, when he was elected censor with Flaccus in 184 BC,[37] imposed a *nota* on many nobles and added many new provisions to the edict. In this way, the luxury that had begun to spread was stopped. It seems, therefore, that the provisions on customs formed part of the censors' *edictum perpetuum* and that successive officials supplemented its provisions in this regard when necessary.[38]

The new provisions in the edict in question are not known but we can assume that these may have been norms related to curbing excessive luxury, especially for women. According to accounts by Livy and Plutarch,[39] at the time of the census, the censors had inflated the value of women's clothing, ornaments, and vehicles worth more than 15,000 asses tenfold. A tax of three asses per thousand had to be paid for slaves bought after the last *lustrum* for 10,000 asses or more.[40] One can assume that these rules were announced in the edict.[41] It is possible that these strictures were a kind of revenge by Cato for the repeal of the *lex Oppia* in 195 BC,[42] which he strongly opposed.[43]

However, the question can be raised as to why Cato did not use a censorial mark but instead manipulated the values of the declared assets in such an elaborate manner. This doubt is linked to the problem of whose property declarations might have been questioned here. The patriarchal perspective of the Roman census often adopted in the literature, which assumes that only *patres familiarum* appeared to make declarations, can easily be undermined in light of the source texts, which indicate that the subjects of the declarations were also widowed and divorced women and orphans. Against these groups, the application of the *nota* was not possible. The only instrument for sanctioning undesirable behaviour was establishing the property's value. As a rule, such a declaration was made by the citizen himself. In this case the censors seem not to have accepted such a value but imposed a different, inflated one. This was also done, for example, in the famous case of the former dictator Aemilius Mamercus, the *rogator* of the *lex Aemilia de censura minuenda*.[44] Cato, too, used this ploy to punish women who owned luxury goods.

The relationship between the actions of the censors and the *leges sumptuariae* is remarkably interesting. As long as the restrictions on luxury were aimed at men, the censors could introduce them in edicts and quickly sanction them using a mark. However, when the need to restrict women's luxury arose during the Punic Wars, a new method was resorted to – resolutions of popular assemblies – and the role of the censors became apparent only incidentally.

Pliny the Elder described an edict that can be dated to 136 BC.[45] It concerned the sumptuousness of meals: the censors forbade serving dormice[46] and other dishes that Pliny does not mention.[47] It may be that the lex *Aemilia sumptuaria*[48] of 115 BC was enacted as a successor and complement to the norms introduced in that very censorial edict.[49]

The censors' interest in the banqueting menu of citizens may have had a twofold purpose. Firstly, it was to prevent excess that posed a threat to *mores maiorum*. Secondly, it may have been related to politics: banquets were one of the forms of electoral bribery, so edicts and laws may also have affected the *ambitus*.[50]

As for the reasons for imposing the mark, cases of punishment for having too many goods considered luxuries are mentioned very often. For example, the censor Fabricius removed the former consul and dictator Rufinus from the Senate for having ten pounds of silver, even though he had previously supported him as a candidate for the consulship.[51]

It seems that inappropriate dress may also have been grounds for punishment. Gellius noted that it was considered undignified to wear a long-sleeved tunic and quoted a related passage from Publius Africanus' speech against Publius Sulpicius Gallus.[52] Further accusations emerge from the text: of using perfume and tuning up in front of a mirror, of depilating one's eyebrows, chin and thighs, of lying at a feast in a long-sleeved tunic on the sidelines with one's lover, as is usually done by *cinaedi*, i.e. men playing a passive role in homosexual intercourse. The context in which these words were spoken is not known. Gellius made no mention of censorship or *regimen morum* in this passage. However, the charge of extravagance is very characteristic. It can be assumed that this is a fragment of Scipio's censorial speech, in which he justified punishing Gallus with a mark. This thesis is all the more likely because Scipio, during his censorship in 142 BC, delivered a number of speeches condemning the departure from the customs of the ancestors, some of which are also recorded in the pages of the *Attic Nights*.[53]

Some circumstantial evidence may also be provided by the story passed on by Suetonius[54] concerning the Emperor Augustus, who was outraged that there were no citizens wearing togas[55] at the popular assembly; they were all wearing coats. Consequently, the *princeps* asked the aediles to allow only those who were wearing a toga and not a cloak into the forum. This was one element of the policy of a return to *mores maiorum*, which makes it possible to assume that also in the Republican period the censors required citizens to wear dignified attire.

5. Performing disgraceful professions

The practice of certain professions was seen as disgraceful by the Romans, not merely because of the fact of receiving a salary (this was the case with the so-called *munera sordida*) but rather because of the general impropriety of these activities. These professions were seen as violating *mores maiorum*, and therefore a censorial mark can be expected in this case. Acting, performing in the arena, running a gladiatorial school, prostitution, and pimping will be analysed. Such a list of disgraceful professions is supported by the fact that the exercise of some of them was indicated as a reason for exclusion from holding the offices of decurion and senator in local communities in the *Tabula Heracleensis*.[56] The list of reasons indicated in the law seems to overlap to a large extent with the reasons why censors in Rome removed senators from the Senate and represents a transfer of the central model to local conditions.

Theatrical performances were one of the favourite forms of Roman entertainment. As a result of their enormous impact on social life, they interested the censors in at least three respects: the first concerned the censorial mark imposed in connection with the acting profession, the second concerned the construction of theatres, and the third concerned the allocation of audience seats.

According to Livy, *ludi scaenici*, or theatrical performances, were introduced in Rome in 363 BC via the Etruscans, brought in connection with the plague raging in the city.[57] However, it is difficult to assume that this was actually the first contact the Romans had with theatre, especially considering the presence of Greek cities in southern Italy.[58]

There is much to suggest that performances began to be viewed as a sign of luxury and for this reason met with a negative reaction from the censors. This seemed to be related to the efforts during the time of Scipio and Cato the Elder to promote an ethos of true Romans[59]: tough and masculine, not subject to effeminacy. It was a form of defence against the changes associated with conquests and the growth of the state. The historian Lydus, who wrote at the time of Justinian, described censorship in the context of extravagance in his book *De magistratibus*.[60] He first provided general information about the establishment of an office to inventory the estates of citizens because of the costs of wars, then introduced a section on theatre and luxury, and finally discussed the control of customs, clearly indicating the connections between these issues.

The picture that emerges from the source texts thus appears to be inconsistent. On the one hand, it is known that theatrical performances appeared in Rome as a rescue during a terrible epidemic and that they were treated as an element of worship, but on the other hand we learn that they were criticised as a manifestation of decadence. This second aspect is undoubtedly linked to the censorial *regimen morum*.

Plays in Rome were often performed by slaves and freedmen,[61] which generally distinguished Roman theatre from Greek theatre, where actors were, as a rule, free-born citizens. Plautus, for example, was initially a member of an acting troupe and only later became a comedy writer. Terentius' story was similar. Certainly, despite their fame, they were not men of high social standing.[62]

> Cic., *De rep.* 4,10 apud Aug., *De civ. Dei* 2,13,3: *cum artem ludicram scaenamque totam in probro ducerent, genus id hominum non modo honore civium reliquorum carere, sed etiam tribu moveri notatione censoria voluerunt.*
>
> *Since they considered the dramatic art and the theatre in general disgraceful, they desired that all persons connected with such things should not only be deprived of the privileges of other citizens, but should even be removed from their tribes by sentence of the censors.*
>
> (Transl. C.W. Keyes)

St Augustine's treatise *De civitate Dei* preserves a passage from Cicero's work *De re publica*, in which the author attributes words to Scipio regarding the perception of actors: they were not only deprived of the dignity enjoyed by other citizens but also subjected to a censorial mark. The punishment was to consist of *tribu movere*, i.e. the removal of the actor from his own tribe and his reassignment to another, typically from a rural to an urban *tribus*. Such a sanction, of course, only threatened those actors who were citizens (including freedmen, though in their case the social degradation was rather minor).

> Aug., *De civ. Dei* 2,13,4: *Ecce enim recte, quisquis civium Romanorum esse scaenicus elegisset, non solum ei nullus ad honorem dabatur locus, verum etiam censoris nota tribum tenere propriam minime sinebatur.*
>
> *For there you have a model! Any Roman citizen who had chosen a career on the stage was not only barred from any post of honour but was even quite estopped by the censors' stigma from keeping his own tribe.*
>
> (Transl. G.E. McCracken)

Augustine himself commented on the passage quoted from Cicero's work. He found praiseworthy the use of the censorial mark against actors, which not only deprived them of dignity but also removed them from their own *tribus*. Later in the text, however, Augustine condemned the inconsistency of the Romans in their attitude towards the theatre, writing that while they condemned actors, they considered theatrical performances to be the worship of deities. He also made a comparison with Greek communities, where both the performances themselves and the performers were held in high esteem. It is worth adding here that this comparison does not take into account the different social position of the actors. In Rome, they were often slaves, whereas in Greece they never were. This difference must have influenced their reception. Finally, Augustine summarised[63]: The Greeks considered that since the gods were worshipped through theatre performances, there should also be an appreciation of actors; the Romans, by no means, wished to respect such people[64]; and the Christians concluded that such gods who demand performances should not be worshipped at all.

> Tert., *De spect.* 22,2–4: *etenim ipsi auctores et administratores spectaculorum quadrigarios scaenicos xysticos arenarios illos amatissimos, quibus viri animas, feminae autem illis etiam corpora sua substernunt, propter quos se in ea committunt quae reprehendunt, ex eadem arte, qua magnifaciunt, deponunt et deminuunt, immo manifeste damnant ignominia et capitis minutione, arcentes curia rostris senatu equite ceterisque honoribus omnibus simul et ornamentis quibusdam. quanta perversitas! amant quos multant, depretiant quos probant, artem magnificant, artificem notant. quale iudicium est, ut ob ea quis offuscetur, per quae promeretur? immo quanta confessio est malae rei! cuius auctores, cum acceptissimi sint, sine nota non sunt.*
>
> *Take even those who give and who administer the spectacles; look at their attitude to the charioteers, players, athletes, gladiators, most loving of men, to whom men surrender their souls and women their bodies as well, for whose sake they commit the sins they blame; on one and the same account they glorify them and they degrade and diminish them; yes, further, they openly condemn them to disgrace and civil degradation; they keep them religiously excluded from council chamber, rostrum, senate, knighthood, and every other kind of office and a good many distinctions. The perversity of it! They love whom they lower; they despise whom they approve; the art they glorify, the artist they disgrace. What sort of judgement is this—that a man should be blackened for what he shines in? Yes, and what a confession that things are evil, when their authors at the top of their popularity are in disgrace!*
>
> (Transl. T.R. Glover, G.H. Rendall)

Tertullian, too, had already recognised a similar paradox when he wrote of the admiration, even adoration, of people of the stage and their simultaneous condemnation and social degradation. It is clear from the referenced text that those performing on stage, not only actors but also quadriga ushers, athletes, and gladiators, were subject to punishment in the form of loss of good name (*ignominia*). The Christian writer also reported that they suffered *capitis minutio*, a diminution of status in that they were barred from the courts, the rostra, the Senate, the equestrian order, and other dignities. *Capitis minutio*, according to Tertullian, is therefore also a degrading punishment, seemingly coinciding with, but not limited to, the censorial mark. Those performing on stage were to be barred from the courts and the rostra, which corresponds to the provisions of the praetorian edict *De postulando*, by virtue of which such persons could not stand trial on another's behalf. The inability to run for office, on the other hand, is a consequence of permanent exclusion from the senatorial and equestrian orders.

The cited texts therefore indicate that actors were first stigmatised by a censorial mark, imposing *ignominia* on them and transferring them to an inferior *tribus*, and then they were also included in a praetorian edict forbidding *postulare pro aliis*, i.e. appearing in court in someone else's name.[65] These sanctions over time evolved into infamy, which was initially linked only to defamatory complaints but later acquired a broader meaning of social disgrace.

The question arises, however, whether the penalties were linked to the acting profession from the beginning. When theatrical performances came to Rome, the first actors were Etruscans brought for that purpose. Later, the role of actors was taken over by Roman youths, who eventually yielded their place in the new types of performances to professional actors.

> Liv. 7,2,12: *quod genus ludorum (scil. Atellanae) ab Oscis acceptum tenuit iuventus nec ab histrionibus pollui passa est; eo institutum manet, ut actores Atellanarum nec tribu moveantur et stipendia, tamquam expertes artis ludicrae, faciant.*
>
> *The Atellan was a species of comedy acquired from the Oscans, and the young men kept it for themselves and would not allow it to be polluted by the professional actors; that is why it is a fixed tradition that performers of Atellan plays are not disfranchised, but serve in the army as though they had no connexion with the stage.*
>
> (Transl. B.O. Foster)

Livy pointed out that for the Atellana, a type of performance adopted from the Oscans, the youths did not allow professional actors so as not to defile the plays. Therefore, it was accepted that Atellana actors were not transferred to another *tribus* and were allowed to serve in the army.

> Val. Max. 2,4,4: *Atellani autem ab Oscis acciti sunt. quod genus delectationis Italica severitate temperatum ideoque vacuum nota est: nam neque tribu movetur <actor> nec a militaribus stipendiis repellitur.*
>
> *Atellans were introduced from the Oscans. That form of entertainment was tempered with Italian austerity and so it is free from censure, the actor being neither expelled from his tribe nor repulsed from military service.*
>
> (Transl. D.R. Shackleton Bailey)

Valerius Maximus also reported that Atellana actors were not subject to the censorial mark and were not barred from serving in the army. He gave as his reason that this type of performance, having been adopted from the Oscans, was tempered with Italian severity. This information may serve as a starting point for further consideration.

Theatrical performances were adopted by the Romans from the Italic peoples, virtually to the exclusion of the Greeks, although of course in the south of the Apennine peninsula Greek influence was extraordinarily strong. This situation does not seem to be accidental. Hellenistic culture had long been, for the Romans, a symbol of declining manners, its adoption considered contrary to *mores maiorum*. Perhaps for this reason, although the Romans had contacts with the Greek *poleis* and were probably familiar with Greek theatre, they did not adopt it. In contrast, during the plague, when it was recognised that the deities demanded spectacles, envoys were sent to the Etruscans because their customs were closer to those of the Romans. The actors brought from Etruria were replaced by Roman youths.

Over time, new types of plays developed in Rome, roles in which professional actors took over.[66] There is no doubt that these plays were already modelled on the works of Greek tragedians and comedians, which could be seen negatively as contrary to the *mores maiorum*. Additionally, the fact that actors began to be paid a salary was certainly not insignificant; this in a way condemned them to an inferior social status as performers of the *munus sordidum*. Moreover, the employment of slaves as actors, must also have led to the discrediting of this profession.

This evolution also explains the different status of the Atellana actors. Firstly, the performances themselves were of a more familiar nature, which qualified them as being in keeping with ancestral customs. Secondly, the actors were at all times well-born Roman young men who were not paid.

> Fest. 268 L., s.v. *Personata*: *...Atellanos, qui proprie vocantur personati, quia ius est is non cogi in scena ponere personam quod ceteris histrionibus pati necesse est.*
>
> *The Atellans, who are rightly called the masked ones, because they have the right not to be forced to put away a mask that the other actors have to put up with.*
>
> (Transl. AT)

Festus, writing about theatrical masks in the context of a comedy by Nevius entitled *Personata* or 'Masked Comedy,' further reported that the actors of the Atellana were the only ones who were not forced to remove their masks and lay them on the stage after the performance. This privilege was precisely due to their high social position and intact dignity. Since they were not subject to the censorial mark, their identity did not have to be revealed in the theatre.

The task of the censors was to guard the observance of ancestral customs. These officials were therefore sensitive to social and educational innovations, many of which they disapproved of. As long as the theatre had a distinctly Italic flavour, it seemed worthy of acceptance. However, as Greek influence grew and acting became professionalised, the censors took notice. A censorial mark was imposed for parading oneself on stage for money, and this was recorded next to the actors' names on the occasion of each census. The loss of reputation was therefore rather permanent. It can be assumed that it was not the censor himself but the *iurator* who inscribed the mark based on the previous list. Over time, actors also came under the praetorian edict *De postulando*, which appears to have prohibited people of dubious reputation from appearing in court on behalf of others, including all those affected by 'permanent' and repeated censorial marks.

Additional light can be shed on the problem of the application of the censorial mark to actors through two specific, famous cases, namely the case of Rome's most famous actor, Roscius, and that of the poet Laberius.

Quintus Roscius Gallus was an ancient celebrity, enjoying immense popularity not only among the Roman commoners but also among the elite, as evidenced by Cicero. Roscius' acting abilities were certainly outstanding, which translated into an exceedingly high salary. Pliny relayed that it amounted to 500,000 sesterces a year.[67]

According to Macrobius, Roscius received a gold equestrian ring[68] from Sulla.[69] Perhaps up to that point, as an actor, he was subject to the censorial mark; afterwards, this seems unlikely. It must be remembered, moreover, that the office of the censor essentially ceased to exist under Sulla, so the politician probably intended to restore the actor's reputation forever. Roscius is considered to be of free birth, and Claude Nicolet has even suggested that he came from an equestrian family and Sulla restored his birthright status.[70] However, it is difficult to know whether the actor stopped receiving remuneration for his performances after this event in order to avoid a *nota* in the future. He was certainly later treated as a celebrity and admired by his contemporaries.

The case of Roscius was unique for several reasons. Firstly, his extraordinary talent set him apart from his fellow actors; secondly, his social status as a free citizen was superior to that of many others. Roscius managed to win over many influential politicians, including Sulla and Cicero. He himself, did his utmost to ensure that actors began to be seen as public figures with a position akin to speakers. However, while Cicero made no secret of his fascination with the art of acting and admitted to drawing inspiration from it, Romans in general were rather unflattering about likening the art of eloquence to theatre. Acting was viewed negatively, and a speaker who favoured gestures over words, resembling stage performance, often caused indignation rather than admiration. Quintilian's comparison of actor and speaker has a decidedly negative tone and reflects distaste caused by the changes that brought the rostra too close to the theatre stage. Similarly, Macrobius made no secret of his negative attitude towards the theatrical tendencies of orators.[71] It can be assumed that Roscius' extraordinary charisma gave him a unique social position, and the crisis of the office of censor was a guarantee against a censorial mark. However, this does not mean that there was a fundamental change in the perception of actors as a social group.

The case of Decimus Laberius also seems interesting. He belonged to the equestrian state[72] and was an author of mimes, which of course did not qualify him for a censorial mark. According to the sources, he once acted on stage in his own play, not of his own volition, but at the behest of Caesar.[73] Seneca the Rhetorician,[74] Suetonius,[75] and Macrobius[76] relayed that, after playing a role in his mime, Laberius was presented by Caesar with a gold equestrian ring and the sum of 500,000 sesterces.[77] The dictator thus restored him to his status as a knight. His emergence onto the scene therefore meant his removal from the equestrian order, a punishment Caesar subsequently revoked. The issue remains rather puzzling.

The censorial mark was a sanction linked to actions performed by the censors: *lectio senatus*, *recognitio equitum*, and the census itself. How, then, did Laberius' legal position suffer *ipso facto*? Caesar himself played a key role in the whole story. These events took place after he had already seized power (precisely after his triumph in April 46 BC), when he held the office of dictator and when the office of censor had already been in deep crisis for many years with no elections held for it. According to source accounts, Caesar exercised at that time the *praefectura morum*, i.e. the supervision of customs.[78] This was an isolated power allowing Caesar to perform the most important censorial functions without holding the office itself, and therefore without violating the principle of *incompatibilitas*.

> Gell. 8,15: *Quibus modis ignominiatus tractatusque sit a C. Caesare Laberius poeta; atque inibi appositi versus super eadem re eiusdem Laberii.*
>
> *How the poet Laberius was ignominiously treated by Gaius Caesar, with a quotation of Laberius' own words on that subject.*
>
> (Transl. J.C. Rolfe)

Some light is shed on the matter by the title of the unfortunately unpreserved chapter fifteen of the eighth book of Aulus Gellius' *Noctes Atticae*, which suggests that Laberius was deprived of his good name by Caesar. Gellius also quoted verses composed for the occasion by the poet himself, which, although not surviving in the *Attic Nights*, were quoted by Macrobius. It is worth mentioning that both authors often used the same sources, and the information they provided overlapped.

> Macrob., *Sat.* 2,7,3
> *Ego bis tricenis annis actis sine nota*
> *Eques Romanus e Lare egressus meo*
> *Domum revertar mimus: nimirum hoc die*
> *Uno plus vixi mihi quam vivendum fuit.*
>
> *I – who have passed twice thirty years with not a mark against my name – left my household gods a Roman Knight to return to them – a mime.*
>
> (Transl. R.A. Kaster)

These lines, according to the author of the *Saturnalia*, were delivered from the stage in the prologue by Laberius, who was aggrieved by Caesar's treatment of him (which, incidentally, resulted in his defeat in the poets' *agon*). He said that after living sixty years without a *nota* he had left home and was returning to it as a mime, meaning that he had lived one day too many. Since Laberius spoke these words from the stage, he was not yet aware that Caesar would restore his status as a knight, but he knew that his performance had brought him a sanction. What this likely means is that the *praefectura morum* exercised by Caesar was permanent: behaviour subject to the mark was punished immediately, without having to wait for the census of the populace or the *recognitio equitum*. It must be presumed that this primarily referred to members of the social elite and behaviours undoubtedly subject to censorial sanction.

Caesar immediately offered Laberius a gold ring, restoring his equestrian status. This, too, testified to the constant exercise of the custody of customs. The poet therefore returned to his rightful place in the audience, that is, to the first fourteen rows reserved for knights. However, he was met with a negative reaction from the *equites* sitting there, who refused to let him in. This behaviour is indicative, firstly, of a belief that the actor should never regain his good name and, secondly, of resentment towards Caesar's actions, which clearly exceeded traditional censorial powers. Seneca and Macrobius cited on this occasion an anecdotal dialogue between Cicero, who said to Laberius that he would have been happy to let him in, but he had too little room, and Laberius himself, who countered that it was not surprising, since Cicero usually occupied two seats. The former sarcastically referred to the overcrowding in the Senate following the introduction of members of the Gallic elite, while the latter mocked Cicero's political instability and fluctuating sympathies.

Anyway, the Laberius case clearly indicates the formation of a social conviction about the lowly position of actors and their automatic, as it were, subjection to *ignominia*, in principle for life, by the mere fact of appearing on stage. In this case, the type of art heightened the gravity of the matter: mimes were regarded as one of the most despicable forms of performance, which translated into the perception of mime actors and actresses as extremely contemptible.

> Cic., *Ad fam.* 10,32,2: *Sed praeter furta et rapinas et virgis caesos socios haec quoque fecit, ut ipse gloriari solet, eadem, quae C. Caesar: ludis, quos Gadibus fecit, Herennium Gallum histrionem summo ludorum die anulo aureo donatum in XIIII sessum deduxit - tot enim fecerat ordines equestris loci.*
>
> *The following exploits, on the model of C. Caesar as he himself boasts, are in addition to his pilferings and robberies and floggings of provincials: At the games which he gave at Gades he presented a gold ring to an actor, one Herennius Gallus, on the last day of the show, and led him to a seat in the fourteen rows (that being the number he had assigned to the Knights).*
>
> (Transl. D.R. Shackleton Bailey)

Caesar's behaviour was to be emulated by Balbus, as Cicero wrote about in a letter to Asinius Pollio. On the last day of the games, which he organised as a quaestor in the city of Gades in Spain, he gave a gold ring to the actor Herennius Gallus, after which he led him to one of the fourteen rows reserved for the *equites*.

The analysis of these three cases – Roscius, Laberius and Herennius Gallus – may suggest some conclusions. Since the office of the censor began to fall into deep crisis, the censorial mark for actors became more of an individual issue than before.[79] Although, for the public, the mere fact of acting on stage was sufficient reason for a citizen to be considered *ignominiosus*, politicians in power tried to reward actors by moving them into the ranks of the equestrians. It seemed to them that the gift of a gold ring was a sufficient and permanent solution to the problem of status. In the somewhat different case of Laberius, Caesar seems to have used this scheme to taunt the poet, first exposing him to the loss of his reputation, only to restore him to his due honour and social position immediately afterwards. It is worth noting, however, that such actions did not necessarily meet with universal approval and were regarded as an abuse of power.

In Imperial times, references to the loss of one's reputation for acting were associated with the actions of those emperors who assumed the dignity of censor. Suetonius reports that Domitian removed a former quaestor from the Senate for engaging in acting and dancing.[80] As the senator thought he could engage in acting (presumably rather amateurishly), Domitian felt obliged to call him to order, making it clear that his sanctions applied to those who lived contrary to the *mores maiorum*.

The legal position of free female actors, who by virtue of their gender were not subject to the censorial mark, was different. The interference of the censors, on the other hand, is clearly visible in their case when it comes to the issue of marriage. Indeed, in the Republican period, a well-born citizen (a senator or a knight) could be punished with a *nota* for marrying an actress.[81]

The censors usually stigmatised the actors with a mark, but there were also cases of more radical measures, namely the removal of stage performers from the city. Such a situation occurred in 115 BC under the censors L. Metellus Diadematus and Cn. Domitius Ahenobarbus.[82]

> Cassiod., *Chron.* 450: *L. Metellus et Cn. Domitius censores artem ludicram ex urbe removerunt praeter Latinum tibicinem cum cantore et ludum talarium.*
>
> *The censors Lucius Metellus and Cnaeus Domitius banned the performances from the city, except for the Latin flautist with a singer and the dancers.*
>
> (Transl. AT)

According to Cassiodorus, whose source was Livy,[83] the censors removed from the city those engaged in performance (*ars ludicra*) with the exception of *tibicines* or flute players.[84] Probably they also removed the performers of *ludus talarius*, i.e. dance performances combined with singing; this, however, is not certain, as the manuscript version contains the reading *ludum talanum*, which is unintelligible. Leppin[85] adopted the conjecture *talarium*, while Spruit[86] opted for *Atellanum*. The grammatical structure of the text allows two interpretations: this enigmatic *ludus* may have been removed from Rome by the censors, like the *ars ludicra*, or it may have been an exception like the *tibicines*. If we read *ludum talarium*, the first option is more likely, while if *Atellanum*, the second.

The term *ars ludicra* is also questionable in this context. It seems to convey performances of a professional nature.[87] However, it may have more narrowly referred to street performances[88] rather than plays staged at *ludi*, which were ceremonies of a sacred nature.

Perhaps the same case was mentioned by Fronto in his correspondence.

> Fronto, *Ad M. Antoninum de orat.* 157,10: *Laudo censoris factum qui ludos talarios prohibuit, quod semet ipsum diceret quom ea praeteriret, dignitati difficile servire, quin ad modum crotali aut cymbali pedem poneret.*

> *I praise the Censor's act, who shut up the gaming houses because he himself, as he said, when he passed that way could scarce consult his dignity so far as to refrain from dancing to the sound of the castanets or cymbals.*
>
> (Transl. C.R. Haines)

If indeed the same censor's decision is referred to, it can be assumed that Cassiodorus also wrote about the *ludus talarius*. The passage from Fronto's letter explains the reasons for the censor's decision: the banning of the *ludus talarius* was supposedly due to the fact that the official himself, when he passed by, could not stop his feet from submitting to the rhythm of the castanets and cymbals, which did not serve to preserve his dignity. It is worth adding that the dignity of the office of censor was scrupulously protected, and its violation was treated very severely.

In conclusion, it can be assumed that the censors considered the performances in the city as a type of public disorder, simultaneously being behaviour contrary to *mores maiorum*.

The censors' decision was presumably announced in an edict, as this was the primary form of decision-making by officials. However, the question arises as to the effect of such an edict. The removal of actors from the city seems a rather radical measure and can hardly be attributed to the standard powers of the censors. Since the actors were stigmatised with a censorial mark anyway, the threat of its imposition would not be effective. Perhaps, then, the censorial edict banned certain types of performances in the city. In such a situation, actors would have had to travel outside Rome. This type of decision by the censors would have been directed at the organisers, primarily the aediles, on whom the *cura ludorum* rested and who could apply coercive measures.

Problems with performances also arose later, during the Principate period.

> Tac., *Ann.* 11,13: *At Claudius matrimonii sui ignarus et munia censoria usurpans, theatralem populi lasciviam severis edictis increpuit, quod in Publium Pomponium consularem (is carmina scaenae dabat) inque feminas inlustris probra iecerat.*
>
> *Claudius, meanwhile, ignorant of his own matrimonial fortune and engrossed by his censorial functions, reprimanded in austere edicts the licence shown in theatres by the populace, which had directed its ribaldry upon the consular Publius Pomponius (he composed pieces for the stage), and upon several of rank.*
>
> (Transl. J. Jackson)

Tacitus relayed that Claudius, unaware of what was going on in his marriage to Messalina,[89] while holding the office of censor, curbed the swagger of the people in the theatre with harsh edicts, as the spectators were abusive to the former consul Publius Pomponius, who was the author of the play, and to well-born women. The historian explicitly linked the issuing of the edict with censorship, so it can be assumed that it was a censorial edict. The question arises, what could this *theatralis lascivia* consist of? One might be tempted to make an – admittedly hypothetical – reconstruction of events. The audience insulted the playwright and the upper-class women. As far as playwrights were concerned, as a rule they enjoyed an incomparably better reputation than actors and suffered no disgrace. It seems, therefore, that the insults hurled by the audience were in the nature of *iniuria*, for which, however, it was difficult to hold the specific perpetrator responsible. This brings to mind contemporary football hooligans, who also conceal their transgressions by acting in crowds. Claudius' edict was intended to counteract excessive freedom and intemperance in the shouts raised in the theatre. Tacitus called the emperor's edicts harsh, so some kind of sanction, at least a restriction of access to the audience, is to be expected. There is clearly a similarity between the edict of 115 BC and this decision of Claudius in terms of *ratio*. In both cases, there was a disturbance of public order, to which the censors reacted using their *ius edicendi*.

For a long time, the censors blocked the building of permanent theatres, and it was not until 55 BC that Pompey erected the first of these, initially as a temple to Venus (and therefore not directly as a theatre building).

> Tert, *De spect.* 10,3–6: *theatrum proprie sacrarium Veneris est. hoc denique modo id genus operis in saeculo evasit. nam saepe censores nascentia cum maxime theatra destruebant moribus consulentes, quorum scilicet periculum ingens de lascivia providebant, ut iam hinc ethnicis in testimonium cedat sententia ipsorum nobiscum faciens et nobis in exaggerationem disciplinae etiam humana praerogativa. itaque Pompeius Magnus solo theatro suo minor cum illam arcem omnium turpitudinum extruxisset, veritus quandoque memoriae suae censoriam animadversionem Veneris aedem superposuit et ad dedicationem edicto populum vocans non theatrum, sed Veneris templum nuncupavit, cui subiecimus, inquit, gradus spectaculorum.*
>
> *The theatre is, properly speaking, the shrine of Venus; and that was how this kind of structure came to exist in the world. For often the censors would destroy the theatres at their very birth; they did it in the interests of morals, for they foresaw that great danger to morals must arise from the theatre's licentiousness. So here the Gentiles have their own opinion coinciding with ours as evidence, and we have the preliminary judgement of human morality to reinforce Christian law. So when Pompey the Great—and there was nothing except his theatre greater than himself—when Pompey had built that citadel of all uncleanness, he was afraid that some day the censors would condemn his memory; so he built on top of it a chapel to Venus, and, when he summoned the people by edict to its dedication, he called it not a theatre but a temple of Venus, "under which," he said, "we have set seats for viewing the shows."*
>
> (Transl. T.R. Glover, G.H. Rendall)

Tertullian, in his work *De spectaculis*, wrote that the theatre was actually the temple of the goddess of love, Venus. He explained that censors often, citing customary laws, destroyed theatres under construction,[90] because they foresaw that licentiousness would spread in them. The Christian author stressed that the censors' opinion coincided with his own. He went on to report that Pompey, having erected his 'castle of disgrace,' feared a *nota* from the censors when he convened the people by edict to consecrate the building and called it not a theatre but a temple of Venus, to which only a staircase was added[91] to enable performances to be seen.

Certain conclusions can be drawn from the text. Firstly, the person putting up the theatre building may have been subject to a censorial mark. If Pompey feared such a sanction, it must have actually been applied beforehand. Tertullian also used the verb *destruebant*, referring to the demolition of theatres, which of course does not mean that the officials themselves demolished the theatres, but that they ordered their demolition. The latter authority was part of the censor *coërcitio* in relation to the custody of public places by these officials.

The role of the censors is also discernible in the issue of the allocation of audience seats in the theatre. This problem was said to have arisen in 194 BC, a time when stone theatres were not yet built, and only temporary wooden structures were erected.

> Liv. 34,44,5: *(scil. censores) gratiam quoque ingentem apud eum ordinem pepererunt, quod ludis Romanis aedilibus curulibus imperarunt ut loca senatoria secernerent a populo, nam antea in promiscuo spectabant.*
>
> *They (scil. the censors) won enormous gratitude from the senatorial class by ordering the curule aediles to separate senatorial seating from the public at the Roman Games.*
>
> (Transl. J.C. Yardley)

Livy reported that the censors Sextus Aelius Paetus and Gaius Cornelius Cethegus ordered the aediles to separate the seats for the senators in the theatre, thereby winning the gratitude of this social group. The historian added that previously plays had been watched without any division. However, the decision to separate the seats for the senators proved controversial, as alongside the positive reactions there were also negative opinions from those who felt that this showed contempt for the lower classes.[92]

The involvement of the censors in these events is not clear. Some source texts attribute the initiative in the whole affair to Scipio Africanus. Asconius[93] reported that there were two versions of the story, both presented in two different speeches by Cicero: *Pro Cornelio de maiestate* and *De haruspicum responsis*. The first version, according to which the aediles acted on the orders of the censors (*iussu censorum*),[94] and Scipio as consul behaved passively, comes from the history of Antias. The other version, according to which Scipio was the initiator of the idea, is confirmed by Valerius Maximus.[95] Asconius stressed that Cicero treated the issue pragmatically and described the matter as was advantageous to him. It seems that in this case, the decision of the aediles may have been dictated by the wishes of the censors, whose influence on the status of citizens, including the right of sit in the Senate, was unquestionable. The aediles, fearing a mark, would be unlikely to defy the censors.

A little later, under the *lex Roscia theatralis*[96] of 67 BC, fourteen rows in the audience were also reserved for equestrians. Although the censors had nothing to do with this legislation, later sources indicate that it was considered a censorial duty to ensure that these seats were occupied only by the knights. This is particularly evident in the account of the perpetual censorship of Domitian, who restored the equestrian seats in the theatre.[97]

The censors were also concerned with those performing in the arena. However, we only have fairly late accounts of this issue.

> Fronto, *Ad M. Caesarem* 5,37: *res seria est: Consul populi Romani posita praetexta manicam induit, leonem inter juvenes quinquatribus percussit populo Romano spectante. Apud censores expostulatur.*
>
> *The case is a serious one. A consul of the Roman people, laying aside his robes, has donned a coat of mail and among the young men at the feast of Minerval has slain a lion in the sight of the Roman people. He is denounced before the Censors.*
>
> (Transl. C.R. Haines)

In a letter to the future emperor Marcus Aurelius, Fronto proposed a rhetorical exercise concerning the case of a consul of the Roman people who, having laid aside his purple-bordered toga, put on his armour, defeated a lion in the midst of the young men in front of the Roman people, and for this was accused before the censors. The case itself is authentic[98]: the consul of 91 AD, Manius Acilius Glabrio, was forced by the emperor Domitian to take part in a hunting spectacle (*venatio*). The situation took place during the *Iuvenalia* at the emperor's estate in Albanum, and Glabrio handled the lion so brilliantly that he aroused the envy of Domitian, who later sentenced him to death, with one of the charges being this very fight. The fact that Fronto referred in the letter to the office of censor is not necessarily an element invented for educational purposes. Domitian held the office of *censor perpetuus* at the time and was keen to exercise his censorial powers. Some of the charges brought against various individuals during this period appear to have involved *regimen morum*, while the emperor was quick to dispense death sentences and exile. Criminal trials and those *de moribus* seem to be intertwined, as seen in Cassius Dio's account.[99] In the case of Acilius, the fight in the arena was more of a pretext for convicting him of other acts deemed dangerous by Domitian, including perhaps professing Christianity, which was rendered in the source text as a charge of atheism, departing from traditional religion and perhaps from *mores maiorum*.

The *Declamatio minor* 302 concerning the prohibition addressed to gladiators to sit in the theatre in the first fourteen rows intended for the equestrians also seems undoubtedly interesting.[100] From the time of Tiberius onwards, the equestrian order was subject to strict prohibitions related to disgraceful activities, but an interesting passage can be found in the text of the declamation. It refers to a person who performed the act of *auctoratio*, i.e. sold himself to a gladiatorial school to raise funds to bury his father.[101] This man performed in the games and, after a successful fight, was presented with a wooden sword (*rudis*) and then freed, after which he acquired the wealth required for the *equites*. The discussion revolves around the question of the motives driving the person to perform in the arena.

> Ps.-Quint., *Decl. min.* 302,4,1: *Illum ergo maiores prohibuerunt theatro qui vilitate, qui gula se auctorasset.*
>
> *So our ancestors barred from the theatre a person who had hired himself as gladiator out of self-contempt or gluttony.*
>
> (Transl. D.R. Shackleton Bailey)

Particularly noteworthy is the mention of ancestors banning those who became gladiators for low financial motives from the front rows in the theatre. This may indicate that the censorial mark punished only those who performed *auctoratio* for reasons considered reprehensible, to satisfy needs considered low.

The issue of pimping may also have been covered by censorial sanctions. A clue here is provided by the contents of *Declamatio minor* 275, in which a provision appears concerning the imposition of *ignominia* on one who accepted money for adultery.[102] Admittedly, the declamation itself concerns a family situation: one brother caught the other in adultery, forgave him at his father's request, and then, after their father's death, it turned out that he became the sole heir, leading to the conclusion that he had obtained a pecuniary benefit related to the adultery.[103] There are, however, interesting threads in the argument.

> Ps.-Quint., *Decl. min.* 275,1: *Hanc legem adversus eos primum constitutam esse dico qui pecuniam acceperunt ut adulterium committeretur, ideoque ignominiam adiunctam quod viderentur rem fecisse lenonis.*
>
> *I maintain that this law was first enacted against persons taking money in promotion of an adultery and that a stigma was added because they were thought to be doing the job of a pimp.*
>
> (Transl. D.R. Shackleton Bailey)

The genesis of this provision is seen in situations where someone accepted money so that adultery was committed and lost their good name because they behaved like a pimp. It seems, therefore, that the orbit of interest of the censors was both the pimping itself,[104] which resulted in a mark probably imposed at every census,[105] and immoral behaviour comparable to *lenocinium*, in particular the acceptance of money for adultery.

Prostitution in Rome was a very heterogeneous social problem. In many cases, it was an occupation imposed on slaves by their owners, although it was also practised by free persons. It is highly likely that men openly engaged in prostitution were subject to a censorial mark.[106] The majority of practitioners, however, were women, who by virtue of their gender could not be subject to censorial sanctions. This does not change the fact that they did not keep their reputation either, as from Republican times a register of them was created,[107] the maintenance of which was entrusted first to the *tresviri capitales* and then to the aediles. This document, apart from the obvious control aspect, could be seen as a kind of equivalent of a censorial mark.

It is also worth considering whether the *nota* was something that the client of a prostitute might have feared. In his *Pro Caelio*, Cicero stressed that young men were allowed to use the services of harlots and that this was in keeping with ancestral customs. An anecdote concerning Cato the Elder, quoted by the commentator of Horace, may provide additional circumstantial evidence: when Cato saw a young man leaving a lupanar, and when the young man ran away, he summoned him and praised him. However, when he later often saw the same young man leaving the place, he said, "I praised you for being here sometimes, not for living here."[108] The story can be linked to Cato's censorship: when the young man saw the official, he ran away, probably knowing of his severity and fearing sanctions. The censor himself, however, clearly approved of the occasional use of prostitutes. Only the lack of restraint he considered reprehensible.

6. Unreliability in legal transactions

Legal transactions in the archaic period were in many cases based on *fides*. With fiduciary legal transactions, there was a lack of any means of protection for the party taking the risk of transferring ownership to the counterparty, whether in the case of a fiduciary pledge (*fiducia cum creditore contracta*), loan for use (*fiducia cum amico contracta*), or transferring ownership in order to achieve testamentary purposes (*mancipatio familiae*). Similarly, under the *ius civile*, it was not possible to rescind legal acts performed under duress or deception. The only possibility of punishment for breach of equity in this case would have been a censorial mark, as contractual and delictual liability in these cases came much later.

The reason for the imposition of a *nota* in the case of fiduciary actions could be a breach of the given word, whether in the case of a *pactum fiduciae* or *nuncupatio*. Perjury was often the basis for censorial sanctions. A key example is the aforementioned case of Gaius Licinius Sacerdos, whom the censor Scipio accused of perjury at *verba concepta* but did not punish him because no one wanted to testify against him. This case must have been exceptional: since censors could make decisions in a discretionary manner, it would be expected that their conviction of a citizen's guilt should result in a mark. Scipio acted in an unusual way, perhaps reckoning with the opposition of his colleague. In general, however, perjury was an act risking a censorial mark, which allowed the censors to exercise effective control over the contractual sphere when it was primarily based on oaths.[109]

Giving false testimony was also punishable with a mark.[110] This was the reason given, for example, by the censor Livius Salinator when he tried to punish his colleague in office Claudius Nero. This episode certainly did not lead to the actual imposition of the *nota*, as the hostile[111] censors tried to punish each other, but the basis of the sanction should be considered typical.

Censors' attention was also drawn to cases called *iudicium recusare*, i.e. situations involving a refusal to enter a dispute in the proceedings *per legis actiones* under the guise that the plaintiff had failed to state a cause of action.[112] By analogy, it can be assumed that the censors disapproved of the *intestati*, i.e. those who were witnesses at legal actions *per aes et libram* and then refused to testify, and *obvagulatio* was applied to them.[113]

The operation of the censorial mark is also evident in public and private wrongdoings.[114] Censors could punish a person previously convicted in a criminal trial.[115] A sentence handed down by *iudicium populi*, i.e. in a trial held before a popular assembly, involved by its very nature sanction of a criminal nature, including sometimes infamy. The *nota censoria* constituted an additional sanction and allowed for the demotion of the condemned person in the social hierarchy. A similar mechanism can be observed in the case of theft,[116] and perhaps also insult.[117] This last delict – *iniuria* – had a very broad scope of use: it covered both physical violation of integrity, verbal disrespect, or infringement of morality in the case of following a respectful lady. There is some circumstantial evidence that the censors reacted in cases of writing offensive texts: Suetonius wrote[118] that Domitian, while exercising *correctio morum* linked to his perpetual censorship, applied the punishment of *ignominia* to authors of such pamphlets called *scripta famosa*.

It can be hypothesised that private-law defamatory complaints (*actiones famosae*) in both contractual and delictual obligations were associated with the simultaneous threat of a censorial mark. In some cases, censorial sanctions probably preceded the existence of a complaint, as, for example, in the case of *fiducia*; in others, it is difficult – for lack of sources – to examine the temporal correlation. Certainly, however, the censors' reaction could also be expected if the trial ended with the release of the defendant due to too scanty evidence.

The censors' decisions were based on *aequitas*. Therefore, keeping one's word and fidelity were the basic determinants of accepted social behaviour. The activities of the censors resulted in the consolidation of these concepts in the collective consciousness of the Romans, leading to the development of various legal mechanisms for redress in cases of deceit, duress, fraud, or perjury.

Finally, it should be added that the censorial mark probably threatened those who attempted suicide. This may be indicated by Suetonius' reference to the censorship of Claudius, who tried to punish with a mark a person on whom he had received a false report of an attempted suicide.[119]

7. Summary

Public life was the subject to censorial control in many aspects. *Regimen morum* applied to officials performing their duties badly as well as to soldiers. Censorial sanctions were often linked to excessive luxury. In this sphere, it is worth pointing out mechanisms to control women as well: the censors themselves sometimes manipulated the value of luxury goods at the time of the census, and besides – due to the impossibility of punishing a woman with a mark – *leges sumptuariae* were introduced. The censors also punished those who practised disgraceful professions: in particular, acting, arena fighting, pimping, and prostitution.

An interesting area of the censors' activity was the control of fairness in legal transactions. It was thanks to them that principles of equity were respected and that the censorial mark could be applied even in the absence of other means of protection.

Notes

1 The scholars also discuss the problem of the relationship between this letter of Fronto and the letter 5,41, which precedes it in the collection, where the censor Acilius is mentioned. Cf. F.X. Ryan, *The Censorship of Acilius*, [in:] *Politische Kultur und soziale Struktur der Römischen Republik. Bilanzen und Perspektiven. Akten der internationalen Tagung anlässlich des 70. Todestages von Friedrich Münzer (Münster, 18-20. Oktober 2012)*, eds. M. Haake, A.-C. Harders, Stuttgart 2017, pp. 111–134.

2 Cf. Gell. 13,12.

3 Plut., *G. Gracch.* 2.

4 Cf. F. Pina Polo, A. Díaz Fernández, *The Quaestorship in the Roman Republic*, Berlin–Boston, MA 2019, pp. 140–143.

5 Cf. Cic., *De sen.* 12,42; Val. Max. 2,9,3; Liv. 39,42,43; Plut., *Cat. Mai.* 17; *Flam.* 18–19; Sen. Rhet., *Contr.* 9,2,25; cf. P. Fraccaro, *Ricerche storiche e letterarie sulla censura del 184/183 (M. Porcio Catone L. Valerio Flacco)*, [in:] P. Fraccaro, *Opuscula*, I, Pavia 1956, pp. 420–433; F. della Corte, *Catone Censore. La vita e la fortuna*, Torino 1949, pp. 25–26; C. Cascione, *'Lege agere' e 'poena capitis': qualche spunto ricostruttivo*, [in:] *'Iuris Vincula'. Studi in onore di Mario Talamanca*, Napoli 2001, pp. 515–522.

6 Cic., *De div.* 1,29–30: But why cite such ancient instances? We see what happened to Marcus Crassus when he ignored the announcement of unfavourable omens. It was on the charge of having on this occasion falsified the auspices that Gaius Ateius, an honourable man and a distinguished citizen, was, on insufficient evidence, stigmatized by the then censor Appius, who was your associate in the augural college, and an able one too, as I have often heard you say. I grant you that in pursuing the course he did Appius was within his rights as a censor, if, in his judgement, Ateius had announced a fraudulent augury. But he showed no capacity whatever as an augur in holding Ateius responsible for that awful disaster which befell the Roman people. Had this been the cause then the fault would not have been in Ateius, who made the announcement that the augury was unfavourable, but in Crassus, who disobeyed it; for the issue proved that the announcement was true, as this same augur and censor admits. But even if the augury had been false it could not have been the cause of the disaster; for unfavourable auguries – and the same may be said of auspices, omens, and all other signs – are not the causes of what follows: they merely foretell what will occur unless precautions are taken. Therefore Ateius, by his announcement, did not create the cause of the disaster; but having observed the sign he simply advised Crassus what the result would be if the warning was ignored. It follows, then, that the announcement by Ateius of the unfavourable augury had no effect; or if it did, as Appius thinks, then the sin is not in him who gave the warning, but in him who disregarded it (transl. W.A. Falconer).

7 Gell. 4,10,7–8: In the same treatise of Capito is this passage "The consul Gaius Caesar called upon Marcus Cato for his opinion. Cato did not wish to have the motion before the house carried, since he did not think it for the public good. For the purpose of delaying action, he made a long speech and tried to use up the whole day in talking. For it was a senator's right, when asked his opinion, to speak beforehand on any other subject he wished, and as long as he wished. Caesar, in his capacity as consul, summoned an attendant, and since Cato would not stop, ordered him to be arrested in the full tide of his speech and taken to prison. The Senate arose in a body and attended Cato to the prison. But this, he says, "aroused such indignation, that Caesar yielded and ordered Cato's release" (transl. J.C. Rolfe). Cf. Suet., *Div. Iul.* 20,4.

8 Cf. A. Astin, *Cicero and Censorship*, "Classical Philology" 80.3/1985, p. 234; L. Paulson, *A Painted Republic: The Constitutional Innovations of Cicero's 'De legibus'*, "Etica & Politica" 16.2/ 2014, pp. 331–333.

9 Cic., *Pro Cluent.* 117–135; cf. A. Astin, *Cicero and Censorship…*, p. 234.

10 Cf. above, however, Chapter II.

11 Val. Max. 2,9 init.: The binding link of camp discipline and the careful observance of the military system admonish me to press on to the Censorship, mistress and guardian of peace. For as the resources of the Roman people have risen to so high a level through the high qualities of its generals, so uprightness and self-restraint flourish when scrutinized by the Censor's frown, an achievement equal in effect to the glories of war. For what use is good work abroad if life at home is lived amiss? Cities may be stormed, nations snatched up, hands laid on kingdoms, but unless duty and modesty be fittingly established in Forum and Senate house, the skyscraping mass of acquisitions will have no firm foundation. Therefore it is to our purpose to know and, what is more, to record the acts of censorial power (transl. D.R. Shackleton Bailey).

12 Cf. M. Humm, *L'image de la censure chez Valère Maxime: formation et évolution d'un paradigme*, [in:] *Valeurs et mémoire à Rome: Valère Maxime ou la vertu recomposée*, ed. J.-M. David, Paris 1998, pp. 73–93.

13 More in Chapter II.

14 Liv. 43,14,5–10.

15 Liv. 43,14,2–4; cf. T.C. Brennan, *The Praetorship in the Roman Republic*, I, Oxford 2000, p. 123.

16 Cf. Gell. 10,28.

17 From the wording *legem censui censendo dicturos esse*, it should rather be inferred that the edict foreshadowed the issuing of the *lex dicta* by the censors. Cf. A. Magdelain, *La loi à Rome. Histoire d'un concept*, Paris 1978, pp. 72–74.

18 They were registered by *patres familiarum*. Festus noted that one who registered a son was called *duicensus*; cf. Fest. 58 L.

19 F. Cancelli, *Studi sui censores e sull' arbitratus della lex contractus*, Milano 1960, pp. 42–43. However, it is difficult to conclude from Livy's text that anyone was charged with *perduellio* or, as Cancelli argues, desertion. Rather, the soldiers returned to Italy because of the census.

20 A. Manfredini, *L'editto 'de coërcendis rhetoribus latinis' del 92 a.C.*, "SDHI" 42/1976, p. 108, n. 32.

21 Front., *Strat.* 4,1,22: When the consul Aurelius Cotta under pressing necessity ordered the knights to participate in a certain work and a part of them renounced his authority, he made complaint before the censors and had the mutineers degraded. Then from the senators he secured an enactment that arrears of their wages should not be paid. The tribunes of the plebs also carried through a bill with the people on the same matter, so that discipline was maintained by the joint action of all (transl. C.E. Bennett, M.B. McElwain).

22 Polyb. 6,18.

23 Front., *Strat.* 4,1,32: The censor Fulvius Flaccus removed from the Senate his own brother Fulvius, because the latter without the command of the consul had disbanded the legion in which he was tribune of the soldiers (transl. C.E. Bennett, M.B. McElwain).

24 Cic., *De off.* 3,104.

25 Cic., *De off.* 1,40: And again in the Second Punic War, after the Battle of Cannae, Hannibal sent to Rome ten Roman captives bound by an oath to return to him, if they did not succeed in ransoming his prisoners; and as long as any one of them lived, the censors kept them all among the commoners, because they were guilty of perjury in not returning. And they punished in like manner the one who had incurred guilt by an evasion of his oath (transl. W. Miller, adapted).

26 Liv. 24,18.

27 Gell. 6,18,2–10: After the battle of Cannae Hannibal, commander of the Carthaginians, selected ten Roman prisoners and sent them to the city, instructing them and agreeing that, if it seemed good to the Roman people, there should be an exchange of prisoners, and that for each captive that one side should receive in excess of the other side, there should be paid a pound and a half of silver. Before they left, he compelled them to

take oath that they would return to the Punic camp, if the Romans would not agree to an exchange. The ten captives come to Rome. They deliver the message of the Punic commander in the Senate. The Senate refused an exchange. The parents, kinsfolk, and connections of the prisoners amid embraces declared that they had returned to their native land in accordance with the law of postliminium, and that their condition of independence was complete and inviolate; they therefore besought them not to think of returning to the enemy. Then eight of their number rejoined that they had no just right of postliminium, since they were bound by an oath, and they at once went back to Hannibal, as they had sworn to do. The other two remained in Rome, declaring that they had been released and freed from their obligation because, after leaving the enemy's camp, they had returned to it as if for some chance reason, but really with intent to deceive, and having thus kept the letter of the oath, they had come away again unsworn. This dishonourable cleverness of theirs was considered so shameful, that they were generally despised and reprobated; and later the censors punished them with all possible fines and marks of disgrace, on the ground that they had not done what they had sworn to do (transl. J.C. Rolfe).

28 Gell. 6,18,11: Furthermore, Cornelius Nepos, in the fifth book of his *Examples,* has recorded also that many of the senators recommended that those who refused to return should be sent to Hannibal under guard, but that the motion was defeated by a majority of dissentients. He adds that, in spite of this, those who had not returned to Hannibal were so infamous and hated that they became tired of life and committed suicide (transl. J.C. Rolfe).

29 Cf. G. 1,129.

30 D. 49,15,5,3 (Pomp. 37 *ad Q. Mucium*).

31 Cf. C. De Boor, *Fasti censorii*, Berolini 1873, p. 20; T.R.S. Broughton, *The Magistrates of the Roman Republic*, I, Atlanta, GA 1951 (reprint 1986), pp. 474–475; J. Suolahti, *The Roman Censors. A Study on Social Structure*, Helsinki 1963, pp. 393–394.

32 Cic., *De or.* 2,272: A jest very closely resembles this ironical type when something disgraceful is called by an honourable epithet, as happened when Africanus as censor removed from his tribe that centurion who failed to appear at the battle fought under Paulus, though the defaulter pleaded that he had stayed in camp on guard, and sought to know why he was degraded by the censor: 'I am no lover of the over-cautious,' was the answer of Africanus (transl. E.W. Sutton, H. Rackham).

33 In another case, Scipio applied the sanction of taking away a horse to an equestrian. The reason was said to be that during the Third Punic War, this one had given soldiers a cake in the shape of Carthage to conquer. Scipio explained that his decision was due to the fact that the horseman had conquered Carthage before him. Plut., *Mor.* 200 d–e.

34 Cf. Gell. 2,24.

35 Cf. above on the stigmatisation of spendthrifts in Chapter IV.

36 Nep., *Cat. Mai.* 2,3: At Cato, censor cum eodem Flacco factus, severe praefuit ei potestati. Nam et in complures nobiles animadvertit et multas res novas in edictum addidit, qua re luxuria reprimeretur, quae iam tum incipiebat pullulare. [But Cato was chosen censor, once more with Flaccus as his colleague, and administered the office with severity; for he inflicted punishment upon several nobles and added to his edict many new provisions for checking luxury, which even then was beginning to grow in rank. (transl. J.C. Rolfe)].

37 Cf. C. De Boor, *op. cit.*, p. 17; T.R.S. Broughton, *op. cit.*, I, pp. 374–375; J. Suolahti, *The Roman Censors…*, pp. 348–358; A. Astin, *Cato the Censor*, Oxford 1978, pp. 78–103; A. Astin, *Roman Government and Politics, 200-134 B.C.*, CAH 8, *Rome and the Mediterranean to 133 B.C.*, eds. A.E. Astin, F.W. Walbank, M.W. Frederiksen, R.M. Ogilvie, Cambridge 1989, pp. 181–185.

38 Cf. Cic., *In Verr.* 2,1,143; F. Cancelli, *Studi sui censores…*, p. 71.

39 Liv. 39,44; Plut., *Cat. Mai.* 18; cf. T. Mommsen, *Römisches Staatsrecht*^{3}, I, Graz 1952 (reprint), pp. 395–396; D. Kienast, *Cato der Zensor. Seine Persönlichkeit und seine*

Zeit, Darmstadt 1979, pp. 76–77; E. Baltrusch, *Regimen morum. Die Reglamentierung des Privatlebens der Senatoren und Ritter in der römischen Republik und frühen Kaiserzeit*, München 1989, p. 26.

40 It was about young boys being bought for their beauty. Cf. Athen. 6,275 a.

41 Cato also gave a speech *De vestitu et vehiculis*. Cf. E. Schmähling, *Die Sittenaufsicht der Censoren. Ein Beitrag zur Sittengeschichte der römischen Republik*, Stuttgart 1938, pp. 56; P. Fraccaro, *Ricerche*..., pp. 438–440; F. della Corte, *op. cit.*, pp. 128–129; A. Astin, *Cato*..., p. 83.

42 Cf. Val. Max. 9,1,3; G. Rotondi, *'Leges publicae populi Romani'. Elenco cronologico con una introduzione sull'attività legislativa dei comizi romani*, Milano 1912, p. 254; I. Sauerwein, *Die 'leges sumptuariae' als römische Maßname gegen der Sittenverfall*, Hamburg 1970, pp. 40–46; E. Slob, *Luxuria. Regelgeving en maatregelen van censoren ten tijde van de Romeinse Republiek*, Utrecht 1986, pp. 42–47; E. Baltrusch, *op. cit.*, pp. 52–59.

43 Cf. Liv. 34,1–8; cf. A. Astin, *Cato*..., pp. 25–27.

44 Liv. 4,24,7: The censors, in their indignation that Mamercus had abridged a magistracy of the Roman People, removed him from his tribe, and assessing him at eight times his former tax, they transferred him to the ranks of aerarii (transl. B.O. Foster, adapted). More information on this episode in Chapter I.

45 Cf. E. Baltrusch, *op. cit.*, p. 26. The term *leges censoriae* was most commonly used to describe the censors' provisions on public revenue and expenditure. Cf. A. Magdelain, *La loi à Rome*..., pp. 32–38. Here, however, the provision of the censors – by analogy with the others related to customs – was an edict. Similarly, Cicero described the praetor's edict as *lex annua*: *In Verr.* 1,42,108. A. Manfredini, *L'editto*..., pp. 110–111, however, argues that the censors, unable to bring motions for relevant laws, were their originators and that where *leges censoriae* are referred to, what is actually meant is *leges sumptuariae*. It seems more likely, however, that the censors first regulated certain matters in an edict, and then, only, if necessary, did an analogous law or plebiscite get voted.

46 On the subject of dormice, see Varr., *De re rust.* 3,15; Fest. 348 L. s.v. *<r>eglescit*; D.W. Thompson, *The Greek for a Dormouse*, "CP" 40.3/1945, p. 186.

47 This edict must have been a repetition of earlier similar provisions from the censors, for there are already references to forbidden foods in Plautus. Cf. Plautus, *Men.* 208–215; E. Segal, *Roman Laughter. The Comedy of Plautus*[2], Oxford 1987, pp.47–48. Pliny the Elder (8,209) wrote of more censorial edicts: Hence pages of sumptuary laws, and the prohibition of hog's paunches, sweetbreads, testicles, matrix, and cheeks for banquets, although nevertheless no dinner of the pantomime writer Publius after he had obtained his freedom is recorded that did not include paunch-he actually got from this the nickname of Pig's Paunch (transl. H. Rackham). He went on to point out (8,210: As far back as Cato the Censor we find his speeches denouncing boar's meat bacon - transl. H. Rackham) that Cato had already condemned the eating of boar meat in his censorial speeches. It is, therefore, reasonable to assume that such provisions appeared during the Punic Wars.

48 Cf. Gell. 2,24,12; G. Rotondi, *op. cit.*, p. 320; I. Sauerwein, *op. cit.*, pp. 120–127; E. Slob, *op. cit.*, pp. 90–94; E. Baltrusch, *op. cit.*, pp. 86–88; M. Dauster, *Roman Republican Sumptuary Legislation: 182-102*, [in:] *Studies in Latin Literature and Roman History*, ed. C. Deroux, XI, Bruxelles 2003, pp. 65–66.

49 According to Pliny (Plin. Mai. 8, 223) M. Aemilius Scaurus, the long-standing *princeps senatus*, proposed as consul in 115 BC a law restricting excess at feasts. It can therefore be assumed that the provisions of the edict preceded the law and provided, as it were, the impetus for its enactment. Since the content here also refers to the sumptuousness of feasts, above all, the dormice, it could be assumed that the same edict is being referred to. Pliny added that the prohibition also covered serving snails and exotic birds.

50 Cf. M. Dauster, *op. cit.*, pp. 66–93, who points out that the restriction of luxury as far as feasting was concerned may also have made it more difficult for *homines novi* to pursue a political career.
51 Gell. 4,8,7: This Rufinus afterwards, when he had been dictator and twice consul, Fabricius in his censorship expelled from the senat on the charge of extravagance, because he possessed ten pounds weight of silver plate. Gell. 17,21,39: at the same time the censors at Rome, Gaius Fabricius Luscinus and Quintus Aemilius Papus, expelled from the senate Publius Cornelius Rufinus, who had twice been consul and dictator; and they recorded as the reason for that censure the fact that they had learned of his using ten pounds' weight of silverware at a dinner (transl. J.C. Rolfe). Cf. Val. Max. 2,9,4; Liv., *Per.* 14; Dion. Hal., *Ant. Rom.* 20,13,1; Flor. 1,13,22; Zon. 8,6; Plut., *Sull.* 1; Plin. Mai. 18,39; 33,142; Sen., *De vit. beat.* 21; Varr. apud Non. 163; Iuv., *Sat.* 9,141–142.
52 Gell. 6,12.
53 Gell. 4,20,10; 5,19,15–16.
54 Suet., *Aug.* 40,5.
55 Cf. Gell. 13,22.
56 *Tab. Her.* 108–125.
57 Liv. 7,2,3. Cf. E.S. Gruen, *Culture and National Identity in Republican Rome*, New York 1992, pp. 185–188; C. Edwards, *The Politics of Immorality in Ancient Rome*, Cambridge 1993, pp. 100–103.
58 Cf. R. Beacham, *The Roman Theatre and Its Audience*, London 1991, pp. 2 ff.
59 Cf. the very astute reflections of M. Beard, *SPQR. A History of Ancient Rome*, London 2015, pp. 203 ff.
60 Lyd., *De mag.* 1,39–44.
61 Cf. A. Duncan, *Performance and Identity in the Classical World*, Cambridge–New York–Melbourne–Madrid–Cape Town–Singapore–São Paulo 2006, pp. 162–165.
62 Cf. T. Frank, *The Status of Actors at Rome*, "CP" 26.1/1931, pp. 17–18; W.M. Green, *The Status of Actors at Rome*, "CP" 28.4/1933, pp. 303–304; E. Quintana Orive, *Sobre la condición jurídica de los actores en el derecho romano*, "RIDA" 50/2003, pp. 302–303.
63 Aug., *De civ. Dei* 2,13,7: The Greeks lay down the major premise: If such gods must be worshipped, certainly such men should also be honoured. The Romans add the minor: But such men should by no means be honoured. The Christians draw the conclusion: Therefore, such gods are by no means to be worshipped (transl. G.E. McCracken).
64 Cf. Nep. pr. 5: Almost everywhere in Greece it was deemed a high honour to be proclaimed victor at Olympia; even to appear on the stage and exhibit oneself to the people was never regarded as shameful by those nations. With us, however, all those acts are classed either as disgraceful, or as low and unworthy of respectable conduct (transl. J.C. Rolfe).
65 The link between the two issues may be indicated by G. 4,182.
66 The fact that it was doubtful that it was always considered reprehensible to show oneself on stage can also be seen from the discussion between jurists, traces of which can be seen in the texts preserved in the Digest in title D. 3,2 *de his qui notantur infamia*. Ulpian (D. 3,2,4 pr.-1) cited the opinion of Cassius and Sabinus, according to whom athletes who perform on stage to show their bravery should not be punished. This exclusion extended (as Ulpian argued, in common parlance *–ita omnes opinantur*) also to musicians, wrestlers and coachmen, as well as people whose job it was to spray horses and other work needed during the games. Later in the text, Ulpian listed also judges as not subject to punishment, citing Celsus' opinion.
67 Plin. Mai. 7,128: ... already in the time of our ancestors the actor Roscius is said to have earned 500,000 sesterces a year (transl. H. Rackham).
68 It is worth mentioning that during the period of the Principate, the *ius anuli aurei* was granted to certain freedmen who could, after fulfilling a property census, enter the

equestrian order. There were cases of usurpation of status, which were prosecuted under the *lex Visellia*. Cf. C. 9,21,1 pr.-1.

69 Macrob., *Sat.* 3,14,13: The same Roscius was a great favourite of Lucius Sulla, who gave him a gold ring, and he achieved such popularity and renown that all by himself, apart from the ordinary members of his troupe, he received 1,000 denarii a day from public funds (transl. R.A. Kaster).

70 C. Nicolet, *L'ordre équestre à l'époque républicaine (312-43 av. J.-C.)*, II, Paris 1974, pp. 1003–1004. Cf. also A. Duncan, *op. cit.*, pp. 173–174.

71 Macrob., *Sat.* 3,14.

72 Differently, J.F. Gardner, *Being a Roman Citizen*, London 1993, p. 222, fn. 70, who is of the opinion that it was only Caesar who gave Laberius the equestrian rank.

73 Macrob., *Sat.* 2,7,2: But since supreme power has the force of compulsion whether it extends an invitation or even pleads, Laberius too felt Caesar's compulsion, as he bears witness in these verses from the prologue (transl. R.A. Kaster).

74 Sen. Rhet., *Contr.* 7,3,9: The blessed Julius Caesar presented Laberius as a mime at some games of his, then assigned him equestrian rank (transl. M. Winterbottom).

75 Suet., *Div. Iul.* 39,2: During the plays Decimus Laberius, a Roman knight, acted a farce of his own composition, and having been presented with five hundred thousand sesterces and a gold ring, passed from the stage through the orchestra and took his place in the fourteen rows (transl. J.C. Rolfe).

76 Macrob., *Sat.* 2,7,8: Caesar (…) awarded (…) a gold ring with 500,000 sesterces to Laberius (transl. R.A. Kaster).

77 During this period, there was still no formal property threshold for equestrians. A period of civil wars had resulted in the impoverishment of many illustrious families. Caesar's gift was intended as a reward for staging a play, rather than an amount to ensure that Laberius had a proper property censure.

78 Dio Cass. 43,14,4; 44,5,3; Suet., *Div. Iul.* 76,1.See Chapter I.

79 Cf. an inscription from the first century BC, IGR I 975 A from Crete commemorating the actor Lucius Furius, who belonged to the *tribus Falerna*, i.e. a rural tribe, meaning that he was not affected by the sanction of being transferred to the urban tribe. We do not know where this was due to: whether it was due to a crisis of censorship, or to the type of art practiced, or perhaps to the fact that the mark in this case resulted in other sanctions.

80 Suet., *Dom.* 8: Having undertaken the correction of public morals, (…) expelled an exquaestor from the Senate, because he was given to acting and dancing… (transl. J.C. Rolfe).

81 Cf. Chapter IV.

82 Cf. C. De Boor, *op. cit.*, pp. 22–23; T.R.S. Broughton, *op. cit.*, I, pp. 531–532; J. Suolahti, *The Roman Censors…*, pp. 417–420.

83 Cf. C.H. Moore, *The Oxyrhynchus Epitome of Livy in Relation to Obsequens and Cassiodorus*, "AJP" 25/1904, pp. 241–255.

84 *Tibicines* was affected by earlier decisions of the censors in 312 BC, which probably had to do with restricting superfluities at funerals. Reducing the number of flute players in the funeral procession and banning them from feasting in the temple of Jupiter led to the musicians leaving the city. Cf. Liv. 9,30,5; Ovid., *Fast.* 6,663–665.

85 Cf. H. Leppin, *Histrionen. Untersuchungen zur sozialen Stellung von Bühnenkünstlern im Westen des Römischen Reiches zur Zeit der Republik und des Principats*, Bonn 1992, pp. 186–188.

86 Cf. J.E. Spruit, *De juridische en sociale positie der romeinse acteurs*, Assen 1966, p. 61.

87 Cf. E.J. Jory, *'Ars ludicra' and the 'ludus talarius'*, "Bulletin of the Institute of Classical Studies. Supplement" 66/1995, pp. 139–152.

88 Cf. T. Frank, *op. cit.*, pp. 11–12.

89 The historian did not hide the irony: Claudius was unaware that Messalina cuckolded him, and meanwhile took to policing the good manners of the Roman people himself.

Cf. D.W.T.C. Vessey, *Thoughts on Tacitus' Portrayal of Claudius*, "AJP" 92.3/1971, pp. 393–394; M. Griffin, *Claudius in Tacitus*, "CQ" 40.2/1990, p. 485.

90 Cf. Tert., *Apol.* 6,2: the laws which, when theatres first rose for the depravation of morals, at once destroyed them (transl. T.R. Glover, G.H. Rendall).

91 Cf. Gell. 10,1,7.

92 Cf. Liv. 34,54.

93 Ascon., *in Cic. Corn.* 69 C.

94 F. Cancelli, *op. cit.*, pp. 8–9 considers this text as an evidence that the censors were entitled to *imperium*. To me, however, this does not seem convincing. The censors simply had the authority and the corresponding sanction of exclusion from the Senate and so the aediles complied with their requests.

95 Val. Max. 2,4,3. Cf. E. Baltrusch, *op. cit.*, p. 27.

96 Liv., *Per.* 99; Cic., *Pro Mur.* 40; Asc., *In Corn.* 78–79 C.

97 Suet., *Dom.* 8: Having undertaken the correction of public morals, he put an end to the licence at the theatres, where the general public occupied the seats reserved for the knights (transl. J.C. Rolfe). Cf. Mart., *Ep.* 5,8; 5,23; 5,25; 5,41.

98 Cf. Dio Cass. 67,14.

99 Dio Cass. 67,13–14.

100 Ps.-Quint., *Decl. min.* 302 pr.: Do not let a gladiator sit in the fourteen rows (transl. D.R. Shackleton Bailey, adapted).

101 Cf. T. Lanfranchi, *Il diritto nei retori romani. Contributo alla storia dello sviluppo del diritto romano*, Milano 1938, pp. 203–204.

102 Ps.-Quint., *Decl. min.* 275 pr.: Let who so takes money on account of adultery be under stigma (transl. D.R. Shackleton Bailey). Cf. G. Dimatteo, *La 'pena d'infamia' e l'inibizione dello 'ius accusandi'. Le norme e le argomentazioni in tema di 'infamia' delle 'Declamazioni minori' 250,263, 265 e 275*, [in:] *Le 'Declamazioni minori' dello Pseudo-Quintiliano. Discorsi immaginari tra letteratura e diritto*, Berlin–Boston, MA 2016, pp. 54–55.

103 Cf. T. Lanfranchi, *op. cit.*, pp. 456–457.

104 Additional circumstantial evidence here may be provided by the inclusion of the pimps in the edict *de postulando*. Cf. D. 3,2,4,2–3 (Ulp. 6 *ad ed.*).

105 Cf. T.A.J. McGinn, *Prostitution, Sexuality, and the Law in Ancient Rome*, Oxford 2003, pp. 43–44.

106 Cf. D. 3,1,1,6 (Ulp. 6 *ad ed.*).

107 Cf. Plaut., *Asin.* 131–132; C. Cascione, *'Tresviri capitales'. Storia di una magistratura minore*, Napoli 1999, p. 187; T.A.J. McGinn, *Prostitution…*, pp. 211–212.

108 Acr. et. Porph., *In Hor. Serm. comm.* 2,1,31.

109 Cf. C. Masi Doria, *Status and Contract in Ancient Rome: With Some Thoughts on the 'Future of Obligations'*, [in:] *Obligations in Roman Law. Past, Present, and Future*, ed. by T.A.J. McGinn, Ann Arbor, MI 2012, pp. 109–113.

110 Liv. 29,37,10; Plut., *Mar.* 5,4.

111 Cf. D.F. Epstein, *Personal Enmity in Roman Politics 218-43 B.C.*, London–New York 1987 (reprint 1989), p. 17. cf. also M.D. Thomas, *Censure of the Censors: Livy in a 'Comic' Mode*, "Ancient History Bulletin", 8.1/1994, pp. 18–27, on the comic side of this episode.

112 Ascon. 84 C. Cf. J.M. Kelly, *Roman Litigation*, Oxford 1966, pp. 25–27.

113 Tab. 2,3 (FIRA).

114 Cf. C. Cascione, *Roman Delicts and Criminal Law. Theory and Practice*, [in:] *Obligations in Roman Law. Past, Present, and Future*, ed. T.A.J. McGinn, Ann Arbor, MI 2012, pp. 284–286.

115 Liv. 29,37,9.

116 Cic., *Pro Cluent.* 120.

117 This may be indicated by the theme of *Decl. min.* 250: *Qui iniuriarum damnatus fuerit, ignominiosus sit* [Let him who has been found guilty of injuries be under stigma – transl. D.R. Shackleton Bailey]. However, since the loss of a good name is linked in this text to the loss of the right to *postulatio*, it is difficult to determine whether this is a case of *ignominia* or infamy. See also *Decl. min.* 265. Cf. G. Dimatteo, *op. cit.*, pp. 48–50.

118 Suet., *Dom.* 8: Having undertaken the correction of public morals, (…) did away with the prevailing publication of scurrilous lampoons, in which distinguished men and women were attacked, and imposed ignominious penalties on their authors (transl. J.C. Rolfe). Cf. Mart., *Ep.* 1,4.

119 Suet., *Claud.* 16: In fact, one man, who was charged with having stabbed himself, stripped off his clothing and showed a body without a scar (transl. J.C. Rolfe). See also Plin. Mai. 36,107–108; Serv., *In Verg. Aen.* 12,603; A. Wacke, *Der* Selbstmord im römischen Recht und in der *Rechtsentwicklung*, "ZSS" 97/1980, s. 26–77.

Conclusion

The office of censor must be considered one of the most important Republican magistracies. Despite their inconspicuous powers at first sight, it was the censors who were the guarantors of the state's systemic stability. This was the result of an evolution of competences, by virtue of which they gradually started guarding the traditional values behind the general notion of ancestral customs – *mores maiorum*.

Censors were first appointed because of the conflict between plebeians and patricians. Their primary task was to conduct the census and lustration, which had previously been the responsibility of the consuls. It is reasonable to believe that the transfer of these functions to the new patrician officials was intended to limit the influence of the plebeians if they managed to gain access to the consulate. Since the censors were appointed for a specific task, the taking of a census, the length of their term of office was perhaps not initially specified. However, the right to *lustrum condere* was once the prerogative of the king, and this is probably why, in order not to risk usurpation, the term of office was limited to eighteen months by the *lex Aemilia* in 434 BC.

The powers of censors expanded over time, and their status increased markedly. A feature particularly emphasised regarding those exercising censorship was severity. The censors were entitled to the signs of authority characteristic of higher officials: the right to sit in the curule chair, to wear the *toga praetexta*, and *mullei* boots. Special privileges were also granted to former censors, whose position ennobled the entire family from which they descended. They were probably buried in purple togas.

The powers of censors, in addition to the aforementioned census and purification ritual, included drawing up a list of senators (from the *lex Ovinia*), conducting a census of the equestrian centuries, leasing public revenue and expenditure through *locationes censoriae* concluded on behalf of the state, exercising protection of public places, and *regimen morum*. They were counted among the higher and curule officials.

Censors were not held responsible for their official actions (formally based on a Senate resolution of 203 BC), but the arbitrariness of their decisions was sometimes a cause for grief and criticism. Citizens who felt wronged in their own opinion sometimes tried to take revenge by exploiting the opportunities afforded by the exercise of the plebeian tribunate.

DOI: 10.4324/9781003486664-7

The power of the censors was nevertheless subject to certain limitations arising above all from the principle of the collegiality of the office. One censor could always oppose a colleague, with the result that a citizen threatened with a censorial mark could avoid punishment. At the beginning of their term of office, censors also took an oath, pledging to be impartial.

The function for which the censors were appointed was to conduct a census, during which they enrolled citizens into the appropriate property classes, centuries, and tribes. Deliberate failure to attend the census was very severely sanctioned: the property of the *incensus* was subject to confiscation and auction, and he himself was sold into slavery, as a result of which he suffered *capitis deminutio maxima*. In my view, however, these effects were only brought about by a judgment in a criminal trial before the *comitia centuriata*, initiated only after the lustration.

During the census, the censors could also carry out a *manumissio censu*, most often done at the behest of the slave owner. However, the official was not obliged to make an entry. The censor's decision to place a slave on the list was constitutive and therefore conferred citizenship, which was based on the decision of the assembly to confirm the choice of the censor in the *lex centuriata*. The moment of acquisition of citizenship rights, however, was the moment of the lustration, which gave effect to the census. By contrast, it seems that the manumitted slave enjoyed freedom from the moment his declaration was accepted.

It was also the duty of the censors to inspect the equestrian centuries, during which they could punish the knights by depriving them of their horse. If a horseman was no longer fit for service, he was dismissed, but without the penalty of loss of reputation – *ignominia*.

The timing of the granting of the power to the censors to compose the list of senators under the *plebiscitum Ovinium* is an exceptionally controversial subject. However, it seems that the most likely date for its enactment is shortly before or in 318 BC. A clue here is provided by an elogium discovered in Brindisi dedicated to the official who first carried out the *lectio senatus*, and who is hypothesised to have been Gaius Maenius, elected to the office of censor precisely in 318 BC.

The census activities were crowned by a lustration ceremony, for which the censor convened the *exercitus urbanus* as for the *comitia centuriata*. The sacrifice of a boar, ram, and bull (*suovetaurilia*) was performed on the Field of Mars, while the army then followed the official into the city, as on the day of triumph, crossing the *pomerium*. Success for the censor was *lustrum felix* ensuring the prosperity of the state. In the event of a *lustrum infelix* being recognised by the augurs, new censors had to be appointed as the effects of the census depended on the successful performance of this ceremony.

Over time, the censors gradually gained the competence to control customs (*regimen morum*), under which they could punish citizens with a censorial mark, i.e. removal from the senate or equestrian century, transfer to the ranks of the *aerarii*, and to the inferior *tribus*, which entailed loss of reputation (*ignominia*), but did not result in infamy. The application of the mark was quite arbitrary, despite restrictions such as the obligation to act in equity (*ad aequum*), the taking of an oath of impartiality, the possibility of defending oneself or the *intercessio* of a colleague in office. The application of the *nota* may have implicated the conduct of proceedings involving the accuser, witnesses, and defence counsel, but this was at the discretion of the censors. Changes in this regard were brought about by the *lex Clodia de censoria notione* of 58 BC, in force, however, for only six years, which introduced a compulsory adversarial procedure of punishment by censorial mark ending in a formal verdict. In my opinion, by virtue of this plebiscite, it also became necessary for censors to receive and consider all charges brought. Although the *lex Clodia* was repealed, it led to a weakening of the office of the censor. In fact, a crisis of the censorship had already begun earlier, during the dictatorship of Sulla, who introduced a series of regulations resulting in a decline in the importance of the office, and indirectly took over some of its prerogatives. However, Sulla does not seem to have formally abolished censorship. What was evident, however, was an increasing revaluation of the old rules, with *mores maiorum* slowly becoming a relic. Clodius, therefore, hoped that his plebiscite would win him popularity.

Caesar did not exercise censorship, but he was the first to isolate part of its powers, adopting the *praefectura morum*. Augustus, on the other hand, briefly assumed the *censoria potestas*, but then, not wishing to multiply the offices he held, carried out censorial tasks using other powers at his disposal, above all the *tribunicia potestas* and the *imperium proconsulare*. The pair of censors chosen during his reign failed even to carry out the lustration. However, during Augustus's reign, a conviction began to take shape that censorial prerogatives were crucial and that they should be included in the emperor's catalogue of powers. This led to a gradual assimilation of the office of censor with the person of the *princeps*.

Censorship was restored to its former glory first by Claudius, exercising it with Vitellius as his colleague, and then by Vespasian and Titus. However, it was discredited as a separate office by Domitian, who assumed the title of *censor perpetuus*. Subsequent emperors did not embrace the position of censor, and the few later attempts to restore the office met with opposition. Instead, the topos of the emperor as a censor who cares about the morals of citizens, setting the best example for them himself, took shape.

As for the censorial mark itself, its effects could be manifold. The punished person lost his good name, suffering *ignominia*, and was socially degraded: removed from the senate or the centuria of horsemen, transferred to an inferior *tribus*, and placed among the *aerarii*. Initially, it was also possible to place a citizen on the *tabulae Caeritum*, thus depriving him of the right to vote – *ius suffragii*.

The control functions exercised by censors in Republican Rome resulting from their guardianship of morality drove the development of many public and private law institutions. The taint on the name (*ignominia*) imposed on citizens punished by a *nota* was in many cases later transformed into other sanctions, in particular the prohibition of *postulatio*, or the right to represent someone in court. Censorial sanctions may have preceded the protective measures introduced by the praetors in edicts and may have supplemented existing norms of *ius civile*. They also often bridged the regulations of the regal period, which had evolved into custom and were initially part of the functioning of the family with the *pater familias* at the head. The *regimen morum* gave public sanction to these norms.

The issue of the Roman *familia* occupied a special place in the activities of the censors. The enormous, almost unprecedented scope of the power of its superior – the *pater familias* – was initially subject to very few restrictions. On the other hand, the importance of the family for the public interest was so serious that any kind of control had to be ensured. Therefore, the censors dealt with family matters, interfering far into the private lives of citizens.

The institution of marriage was certainly subject to scrutiny, even *ante factum*, namely already at the stage of the engagement (*sponsalia*). Breaking such an agreement could result not only in the payment of a contractual penalty, but also in the imposition of a censorial mark. Marriage itself was not always a free affair: the censors frowned upon unions between men of the equestrian and senatorial families and women of the lower classes. Penalties could be expected if one married a freedwoman or a woman of dubious reputation (e.g. a prostitute). These regulations were later adapted in the marriage legislation of Augustus, with the difference, however, that they only covered senators and their offspring when it came to marriages with freedwomen, while all free-born citizens were affected by the ban on unions with *feminae famosae*.

The roots of Augustus' laws can also be traced to the censor's policy on procreation. The censors urged citizens to marry and have offspring mainly by making speeches on various occasions. In addition, however, they used various forms of pressure: there is a well-known case of imposing a financial penalty on old bachelors, as well as situations of rewarding fathers of numerous offspring.

The censors also tackled the issue of adultery. A man who seduced another man's wife could be liable to a censorial mark. It is worth noting that this was also the prototype for the *lex Iulia de adulteriis*, enacted at Augustus' request. The emperor himself pointed out that he was not the forerunner of the introduced solutions and indicated the decisions of the censors to justify his solutions and convince the citizens.

Another issue subject to censorial control was divorce. The *regimen morum* here was a continuation of archaic law regulations attributed to Romulus, in which the possibility of a wife's repudiation was subject to legal limitations. Crucial in this case was Spurius Carvilius Ruga, who divorced his wife, citing her infertility as the reason and emphasising that he had taken an oath before the censors to marry in order to produce offspring. He thus put the officials in an extremely uncomfortable position. If they had punished him with the mark, they would have acknowledged at the same time that marriage was not necessarily for procreation. Otherwise, they would have allowed the possibility of repudiation without observing the legal prerequisites. Although ancient authors claimed that Carvilius loved his wife, it seems that his behaviour was calculating and cynical. In any case, it can be assumed that one of the censors wanted to punish him, while the other objected, so the mark was ultimately not imposed. The result of this event was certainly a relaxation of the censors' policy on divorce. Divorces became more frequent. On the other hand, however, it seems that in many cases the censors continued to intervene. This can be evidenced by the material collated in the declamations, i.e. rhetorical exercises, of the early Principate. They repeatedly mention the *actio iniusti repudii*, a complaint regarded by scholars as fictitious. Meanwhile, it can be assumed that it represents a non-technical name for proceedings before censors in cases of wrongful divorce, as indicated by the fact that the arguments often cite important grounds for divorce from the regulation of the regal period, as well as infertility evoking the case of Ruga.

It is worth taking this opportunity to state more broadly that the declamations in question constitute a remarkably interesting source that can be used when researching the censorial mark, as the basis of the argumentation is often customary norms identical to *mores maiorum*.

Another area over which the censors exercised control was *patria potestas* as well as guardianship and patronage. Paternal authority was unprecedentedly wide in Rome. However, since the *pater familias* was responsible for the functioning of the family, which in many respects was crucial to the state, his actions were subject to the custody of the censors. Officials checked that the upbringing of offspring, particularly the sons of families from the circle of *nobilitas* predestined for political careers, was based on traditional models to maintain the Republican ethos of power. An example is the edict *de coërcendis rhetoribus Latinis* issued by Gnaeus Domitius Ahenobarbus and Lucius Licinius Crassus in 92 BC. The censors condemned the new type of schools and threatened with a censorial mark not only the teachers but also – and perhaps especially – the fathers sending their sons there. The censors' decision may have had political overtones, but it can be assumed that the officials saw the danger in young people spending their days in Latin rhetorical schools neglecting traditional methods of education, i.e. direct participation in public life as an observer, the so-called *tirocinium fori*.

The censors also paid attention to whether someone was engaging in sham activities to falsely claim to have more offspring than in reality. Fathers could count on certain privileges, thus the issue of adoptions to artificially ensure more children *in potestate* arose. The mere act of adoption itself did not seem to arouse the suspicion of officials, but perhaps its dissolution soon after achieving the benefits did.

A censorial mark could also be issued for breach of duties of patronage and guardianship, with a peculiar hierarchy of duties being observed.

Another issue of interest to the censors was the handling of family inheritance. Punishment could affect a citizen who neglected matters of worship – *sacra*. In addition, the censors paid attention to the cultivation of land. Their objections could be raised both due to the neglect of cultivation and mismanagement of estates by improper proportions between buildings and farmland. It should be noted that particularly in senatorial families, the ideal of a good farmer – *bonus agricola* – was cultivated. This application of the censorial mark involved a clear restriction of property rights: the censors interfered with these rights by requiring landowners to make appropriate efforts.

Finally, at the interface between the *ius civile* and the *regimen morum* was the issue of spendthrifts, which fell into the broader category of luxury subject to strict control by the censors. The narrow legal definition of *prodigus* meant that only in certain cases could the praetor apply *interdictio bonorum*. Censors, on the other hand, were not bound by any restrictions, so that the sanctions they applied could affect citizens who would otherwise go unpunished.

Public life was also subject to censorial control. Officials who violated the rules of office and civil rights, as well as sacred law, were punished with a mark. Censors also kept watch over the deliberations of the senate, ensuring that resolutions were passed between sunrise and sunset. The *nota censoria* was used in the army, particularly to support commanders and as a possible sanction in the absence of other disciplinary measures.

Constant and permanent ignominy was associated with professions considered disgraceful: acting, arena fighting, prostitution and pimping. Regarding the theatre, the censors long blocked the construction of permanent theatre buildings, viewing them as signs of luxury and decadence. Over time, it was on their initiative that seats for senators began to be separated in theatres.

Censorial control generally extended to all manifestations of extravagance, not just spendthrift behaviour. Officials often issued edicts prohibiting the consumption of certain goods. In addition to this, censors guarded the integrity of legal transactions, ensuring that *fides* was adhered to.

In light of the above, it can be concluded that the influence of the censors on the development of the Roman legal order was considerable, impacting both private and public law. The control of the family aimed to ensure the stability of the state's political life, where customary norms known as *mores maiorum* were paramount and constituted an important essence of the Republican ethos. Since the *pater familias* was responsible for those under his authority, he, too, was a subject to censorship. Correspondingly, the husband, who controls his wife's morals (even if she did not remain *in manu*), was himself also a subject to the control of the censors.

Censorial *ignominia* or a blemish on the one's reputation was imposed for both one-off offences and continuous acts. The construction of the praetorian edict introducing the prohibition of *postulatio*, and later the technically conceived *infamia* or loss of honour in many cases continued the tradition of censorial solutions.

Many of the sanctions applied by the praetor coexisted with penalties imposed by the censors, with their scopes not always overlapping. The arbitrary nature of the decisions taken under the *regimen morum* meant that the censors had far-reaching discretion. It is worth noting that they were always guided by the principle of *aequitas*, which also became the basis of the protection measures introduced by the praetor in the edict. Parallels can also be found between the decisions of the censors and the legal norms whose emergence is linked to the *leges regiae*. Even leaving aside the doubts raised by these earliest regulations of Roman law, it is difficult not to see continuity. This continuity is linked to the fact that these regulations later came to be seen as an integral part of customary law.

Despite the crisis and the *de facto* disappearance of the office of censor, its role should also be noted and appreciated from the point of view of the development of the law. In the writings of jurists of the classical period, censorship appeared only incidentally. This does not mean, however, that it was not important. The *regimen morum* formed the basis and model for many legal rules and institutions.

Bibliography

Albanese B., *Brevi studi di diritto romano (II). III. Sui frammenti di 'censoriae tabulae' in Varr., 'De L. Lat.' 6,86-87*, "AUPA" 43/1995, s. 67–102.

Albanese B., *Brevi studi di diritto romano (III). V. Publio Sempronio Sofo, giurista, ed il regime della censura*, "AUPA" 47/2002, s. 55–67.

Albanese B., *'Privilegia', 'maximus comitiatus', "iussum populi' (XII Tab. 9,1–2,12–5)*, "Labeo" 36/1990, pp. 19–35.

Alexander M.C., *Trials in the Late Roman Republic, 149 BC to 50 BC*, Toronto–Buffalo–London 1990.

Amunátegui Perelló C.F., *La obligación de restitución de la dote y el nacimiento del divorcio en Roma*, "Revista de Estudios Histórico-Jurídicos" 30/2008, pp. 37–46.

Amunátegui Perelló C.F., *Origen de los poderes del paterfamilias. El pater familias y la patria potestas*, Madrid 2009.

Ando C., *Census, Censor, Citizenship. Republican Subjectivity in Advance of Monarchy*, [in:] *Citizenship in Antiquity*, eds. J. Filonik, C. Plastow, R. Zelnick-Abramovitz, London 2023, p. 622.

Aricò Anselmo G., *'Societas inseparabilis' o dell'indissolubilità dell'antico consorzio fraterno*, [in:] *'Iuris Vincula'. Studi in onore di Mario Talamanca*, Napoli 2001, pp. 149–191.

Astin A.E., *Augustus and 'Censoria Potestas'*, "Latomus" 22.2/1963, pp. 226–235.

Astin A.E., *Cato the Censor*, Oxford 1978.

Astin A.E., *Censorships in the Late Republic*, "Historia" 34.2/1985, pp. 175–190.

Astin A.E., *Cicero and the Censorship*, "CP" 80.3/1985, pp. 233–239.

Astin A.E., *Livy and the Censors of 214-169 B.C.*, [in:] *Studies in Latin Literature and Roman History*, ed. C. Deroux, IV, Bruxelles 1986, pp. 122–134.

Astin A.E., *Livy's Report of the 'lectio senatus' and the 'recognitio equitum' in the Censorship of 169-8 B.C.*, "Historia" 37.4/1988, pp. 487–490.

Astin A.E., *'Regimen morum'*, "JRS" 78/1988, pp. 14–34.

Astin A.E., *Roman Government and Politics, 200—134 B.C.*, CAH 8, *Rome and the Mediterranean to 133 B.C.*, eds. A.E. Astin, F.W. Walbank, M.W. Frederiksen, R.M. Ogilvie, Cambridge 1989, pp. 163–196.

Astin A.E., *The Censorship of the Roman Republic: Frequency and Regularity*, "Historia" 31/1982, pp. 174–187.

Astin A.E., *The 'Lex Annalis' before Sulla*, Bruxelles 1958.

Astin A.E., *The Role of Censors in Roman Economic Life*, "Latomus" 49.1/1990, pp. 20–36.

Astolfi R., *Il fidanzamento nel diritto romano,* Padova 1987.

Astolfi R., *La 'lex Iulia et Papia'*, Padova 1986.

Badian E., *Publicans and Sinners. Private Enterprise in the Service of the Roman Republic*, Oxford 1972.
Baltrusch E., *Regimen morum. Die Reglamentierung des Privatlebens der Senatoren und Ritter in der römischen Republik und frühen Kaiserzeit*, München 1989.
Banfi A., *Gynaikonomein. Intorno ad una magistratura ateniese del IV secolo ed alla sua presenza nelle fonti teatrali greche e romane*, [in:] *Diritto e teatro in Grecia e Roma*, eds. E. Cantarella, L. Gagliardi, Milano 2007, pp. 17–29.
Bartošek M., *Variazioni metodologiche su tema ciceroniano ('Lex Voconia', 'ius novum', retroattività)*, [in:] *Studi in onore di Gaetano Scherillo*, II, Milano 1972, pp. 648–679.
Barzanò A., *Catone il Vecchio e il processo contro Manio Acilio Glabrione candidato alla censura (189 a.C.)*, [in:] *Processi e politica nel mondo antico*, ed. M. Sordi, Milano 1996, pp. 129–144.
Baudy D., *Römische Umgangsriten. Eine ethologische Untersuchung der Funktion von Wiederholung für religiöses Verhalten*, Berlin–New York 1998.
Bauman R.A., *Lawyers in Roman Transitional Politics. A Study of the Roman Jurists in Their Political Setting in the Late Republic and Triumvirate*, München 1985.
Bauman R.A., *Women and Politics in Ancient Rome*, London 1992 (reprint 2003).
Beacham R., *The Roman Theatre and its Audience*, London 1991.
Beard M., *SPQR. A History of Ancient Rome*, London 2015.
Beck H., *Karriere und Hierarchie. Die römische Aristokratie und die Anfänge des 'cursus honorum' in der mittleren Republik*, Berlin 2005.
Beloch K.J., *Römische Geschichte bis zum Beginn der punischen Kriege*, Berlin–Leipzig 1926.
Benner H., *Die Politik des P. Clodius Pulcher. Untersuchungen zur Denaturierung des Clientelwesens in der ausgehenden römischen Republik*, Stuttgart 1987.
Berger A., *Note on Gellius, N.A., I,6*, "AJP" 67.4/1946, pp. 323–328.
Biondi B., *La legislazione di Augusto*, [in:] *Scritti giuridici*, II, ed. T. Perassi, Milano 1965, pp. 77–188.
Biscardi A., *'Auctoritas patrum'. Problemi di storia del diritto pubblico romano*, Napoli 1987.
Bleicken J., *Das Volkstribunat der klassischen Republik*, München 1955.
Bleicken J., *'Lex publica'. Gesetz und Recht in der römischen Republik*, Berlin 1975.
Bleicken J., *Zum Begriff der römischen Amtsgewalt. Auspicium – potestas – imperium*, Göttingen 1981.
Bloch G., *De l'authenticité de l'édit censorial de 92 av. I. C. contre les rhéteurs latins*, "Klio" 3/1903, pp. 68–73.
Blumenthal F., *Zur zensorischen Tätigkeit des Augustus*, "Klio" 9/1909, pp. 493–500.
Bonnefond-Coudry M., *Le 'princeps senatus': vie et mort d'une institution républicaine*, "MEFRA" 105/1993, pp. 103–134.
Bosworth A.B., *Vespasian and the Provinces: Some Problems of the Early 70's A.D.*, "Athenaeum" 51.1–2/1973, pp. 49–78.
Botsford G.W., *The Roman Assemblies from Their Origin to the End of the Republic*, New York 1909 (reprint New Jersey 2001).
Bottiglieri A., *La legislazione sul lusso nella Roma repubblicana*, Napoli 2002.
Bramante M.V., *'Patres', 'filii' e 'filiae' nelle commedie di Plauto. Note sul diritto nel teatro*, [in:] *Diritto e teatro in Grecia e a Roma*, eds. E. Cantarella, L. Gagliardi, Milano 2007, pp. 108–113.
Brennan T.C., *The Praetorship in the Roman Republic*, I–II, Oxford 2000.
Broughton T.R.S., *The Magistrates of the Roman Republic*, I, Atlanta 1951 (reprint 1986); II, New York 1952.

Brunt P.A., *Italian Manpower 225 B.C.-A.D. 14*, Oxford 1971.

Bruun C., *Il funzionamento degli acquedotti romani*, [in:] *Roma imperiale. Una metropoli antica*, ed. E. Lo Cascio, Roma 2010.

Buckland W.W., *The Roman Law of Slavery. The Condition of the Slave in Private Law from Augustus to Justinian*, Cambridge 1908.

Bunse R., *Die frühe Zensur und die Entstehung der Kollegialität*, "Historia" 50.2/2001, pp. 145–162.

Buongiorno P., *'Senatus consulta Claudianis temporibus facta'. Una palingenesi delle deliberazioni senatorie dell'età di Claudio (41-54 D.C.)*, Napoli 2010.

Buongiorno P., *Sui fondamenti della dittatura di Marco Fabio Buteone (216 a.C.)*, [in:] *La dittatura romana*, red. L. Garofalo, III, Napoli 2022, pp. 255–277.

Bur C., *'Auctoritas' et 'mos maiorum'*, [in:] *L'auctoritas à Rome. Une notion constitutive de la culture politique*, eds. J.-M. David, F. Hurlet, Bordeaux 2020, pp. 65–90.

Bur C., *La citoyenneté dégradée. Une histoire de l'infamie à Rome (312 av. J.-C.-96 apr. J.-C.)*, Rome 2018.

Bur C., *Les censeurs privaient-ils du droit de vote? Retour sur l'aerarium facere et le tribu mouere*, "MEFRA" 128.2/2016, pp. 419–437.

Bur C., *Le spectacle du cens. Relecture du déroulement de la professio sous la République romaine*, "Athenaeum" 105.2/2017, pp. 520–550.

Burdese A., *Manuale di diritto pubblico romano*[3], Torino 2005.

Busacca C., *Qualche riflessione sull'attribuzione della 'lectio senatus' ai censori*, [in:] *Scritti in onore di G. Silvestri*, ed. A. Ruggeri, I, Torino 2016, pp. 333–346.

Busacca C., *Sulla datazione del 'plebiscitum Ovinium'*, [in:] *Scritti per Alessandro Corbino*, ed. I. Piro, I, Tricase 2016, pp. 429–452.

Buttrey T.V., *Domitian's Perpetual Censorship and the Numismatic Evidence*, "CJ" 71/1975, s. 26–34.

Calzada A., *'Consortium ercto non cito: consortes qui a communione discedere velint'*, "Iura" 59/2011, pp. 151–176.

Camodeca G., *Il 'censorium' di Beneventum: un nuovo vocabolo del lessico latino*, [in:] *'Voce concordi'. Scritti per Claudio Zaccaria*, ed. F. Mainardis, Trieste 2016, pp. 119–126.

Cancelli F., *Studi sui censores e sull'arbitratus della lex contractus*, Milano 1960.

Cañas Navarro P., *Aspectos jurídicos del censo romano (II)*, "Revista de Derecho UNED", 4/2009, pp. 103–138.

Carcaterra A., *La 'pignoris capio' nel diritto pubblico romano*, "Ann. Bari" 5/1942, pp. 59–79.

Cascione C., *'Lege agere' e 'poena capitis': qualche spunto ricostruttivo*, [in:] *'Iuris Vincula'. Studi in onore di Mario Talamanca*, Napoli 2001, pp. 515–522.

Cascione C., *'Quodcumque postremum populus iussisset, id ius ratumque esset': spunti per un'interpretazione politica del versetto*, [in:] *Scritti in onore di Michele Scudiero*, I, Napoli 2008, pp. 421–425.

Cascione C., *Roman Delicts and Criminal Law. Theory and Practice*, [in:] *Obligations in Roman Law. Past, Present, and Future*, ed. T.A.J. McGinn, Ann Arbor, MI 2012, pp. 267–295.

Cascione C., *'Tresviri capitales'. Storia di una magistratura minore*, Napoli 1999.

Casinos Mora F.J., *La restricción del lujo en la Roma Republicana. El lujo indumentario*, Madrid 2015.

Cassisi S., *L'editto di Verre e la 'lex Voconia'*, "Annali del Seminario Guiridico Università di Catania" 3/1948–1949, pp. 490–505.

Cássola F., *Ancora sull'elogio di Brindisi*, "Labeo" 8.3/1962, pp. 307–316.

Cássola F., Labruna L., *I censori*, [in:] *Lineamenti di storia del dirtto romano*², ed. M. Talamanca, Milano 1989, pp. 167–172.

Cássola F., Labruna L., *Linee di una storia delle istituzioni repubblicane*², Napoli 1979.

Catalano P., *Contributi allo studio del diritto augurale*, Torino 1960.

Cenderelli A., *Varroniana. Istituti e terminologia giuridica nelle opere di M. Terenzio Varrone*, Milano 1973.

Chantraine H., *Zur Entstehung der Freilassung mit Bürgerrechtserwerb in Rom*, "ANRW" I.2/1972, pp. 59–67.

Cimma M.R., *Ricerche sulle società di publicani*, Milano 1981.

Clemente G., *Cicerone, Clodio e la censura: la politica e l'ideale*, [in:] *'Munuscula'. Scritti in ricordo di Luigi Amirante*, ed. E. Dovere, Napoli 2010, pp. 51–73.

Clemente G., *I censori e il senato. I mores e la legge*, "Athenaeum" 104.2/2016, pp. 446–500.

Clemente G., *When the Senators Became 'The Best'*, [in:] *Institutions and Ideology in Republican Rome. Speech, Audience and Decision*, eds. H van der Blom, C. Gray, C. Steel, Cambridge 2018, p. 206–221.

Coli U., *Sui limiti di durata delle magistrature romane*, [in:] *Studi in onore di Vincenzo Arangio-Ruiz nel XLV anno del suo insegnamento*, Napoli 1953, pp. 395–418.

Cooley A.E., *'Res gestae Divi Augusti'. Text, Translation, and Commentary*, Cambridge 2009.

Cornell T.J., *The 'Lex Ovinia' and the Emancipation of the Senate*, [in:] *The Roman Middle Republic. Politics, Religion and Historiography*, ed. C. Bruun, Rome 2000, pp. 69–89.

Cosentini C., *Studi sui liberti*, I, Catania 1948.

Coudry M., *Denys d'Halicarnasse, Plutarque, Dion Cassius: trois visions grecques de la censure?*, [in] *Visions grecques de Rome. Griechische Blicke auf Rom*, eds. M.L. Freyburger, D. Meyer, Paris 2007, pp. 31–72.

Cram R.V., *The Roman Censors*, "HSCP" 51/1940, pp. 71–110.

Crawford M.H., *The Roman Republic*², Harvard University Press, Cambridge, MA, 1992.

Crawford M.H., Coleman R.G., (Galsterer H.), *'Lex Osca Tabulae Bantinae'*, [in:] *The Roman Statutes*, ed. M.H. Crawford, I, London 1996, pp. 271–292.

Crifò G., *Sul caso di C. Ostilio Mancino*, [in:] *Studies in Roman Law in Memory of A. Arthur Schiller*, eds. R.S. Bagnall, W.V. Harris, New York 1986, pp. 19–32.

Cursi M.F., *'Captivitas' e 'capitis deminutio'. La posizione del 'servus hostium' tra 'ius civile' e 'ius gentium'*, [in:] *'Iuris vincula'. Studi in onore di Mario Talamanca*, II, Napoli 2001, pp. 295–340.

Cursi M.F., *La struttura del 'postliminium' nella repubblica e nel principato*, Napoli 1996.

Danieli R., *Contributi alla storia delle manomissioni romane*, Milano 1953.

Daube D., *Two Early Patterns of Manumission*, "JRS" 36/1946, pp. 57–75.

Dauster M., *Roman Republican Sumptuary Legislation: 182-102*, [in:] *Studies in Latin Literature and Roman History*, ed. C. Deroux, XI, Bruxelles 2003, pp. 65–93.

David J.-M., *Promotion civique et droit à la parole: L. Licinius Crassus, les accusateurs et les rhéteurs latins*, "MEFRA" 91.1/1979, pp. 135–181.

De Boor C., *Fasti censorii*, Berolini 1873.

De Francisci P., *Arcana imperii*, III.1, Milano 1948.

De Francisci P., *Primordia civitatis*, Roma 1959.

de Kleijn G., *The Water Supply of Ancient Rome. City Area, Water and Population*, Amsterdam 2001.

de las Heras Sánchez G., Polo Toribio G., *Plus quam annua ac semestris*, "AFDUDC", 11/2007, pp. 169–175.

della Corte F., *Catone Censore. La vita e la fortuna*, Torino 1949.

De Martino F., *Intorno all'origine della schiavitù a Roma*, "Labeo" 20/1974, pp. 163–193.

De Martino F., *Storia della costituzione romana*², I–V, Napoli 1973.

De Martino F., *Sulla storia dell'equitatus romano*, [in:] *Diritto, economia e società nel mondo romano. II. Diritto pubblico*, eds. F. De Martino, F. D'Ippolito, Napoli 1996, pp. 281–298.

Deniaux E., *Rome, de la Cité - État à l'Empire. Institutions et vie politique aux Iie et ie siècle av. J.-C.*, Paris 2001.

De Ruggiero E., *Dizionario epigrafico di antichità romane*, Roma 1900.

Dessau H., *A Roman Senator under Domitian and Trajan*, "JRS" 3.2/1913, pp. 301–309.

Desserteaux F., *Études sur la formation historique de la 'capitis deminutio'*, I, Dijon 1919.

Dettenhofer M.H., *Herrschaft und Widerstand im augusteischen Prinzipat*, Stuttgart 2000.

de Vaan M., *Etymological Dictionary of Latin and the Other Italic Languages*, Leiden–Boston, MA 2008.

Develin R., *Appius Claudius Caecus and the Brindisi 'elogium'*, "Historia" 25/1976, pp. 484–487.

De Visscher F., *De l'acquisition du droit de cité romaine par l'affranchissement*, "SDHI" 12/1946, pp. 69–85.

Dimatteo G., *La 'pena d'infamia' e l'inibizione dello 'ius accusandi'. Le norme e le argomentazioni in tema di 'infamia' delle 'Declamazioni minori' 250,263, 265 e 275*, [in:] *Le 'Declamazioni minori' dello Pseudo-Quintiliano. Discorsi immaginari tra letteratura e diritto*, eds. A. Casamento, D.V. Mal-Maeder, L. Pasetti, Berlin–Boston, MA 2016, pp. 47–62.

Dixon S., *Breaking the Law to Do the Right Thing: The Gradual Erosion of the Voconian Law in Ancient Rome*, "Adelaide Law Review" 9/1985, pp. 519–534.

Ducos M., *Les Romains et la loi. Recherches sur les rapports de la philosophie grecque et de la tradition romaine à la fin de la République*, Paris 1984.

Duff A.M., *Freedmen in the Early Roman Empire*, Cambridge 1958.

Dumézil G., *Servius et Essaila Fortune. sur la fonction sociale de Louange et de Blâme et sur les élément indo-européens du cens romain*, Paris 1943.

Dumont J.-C., *'Servus'. Rome et l'esclavage sous la république*, Rome 1987.

Duncan A., *Performance and Identity in the Classical World*, Cambridge–New York–Melbourne–Madrid–Cape Town–Singapore–São Paulo 2006.

Edwards C., *The Politics of Immorality in Ancient Rome*, Cambridge 1993.

El Beheiri N., *Das regimen morum der Zensoren. Die Konstruktion des römischen Gemeinwesens*, Berlin 2012.

El Beheiri N., *Das regimen morum zwischen Institution und Geschichte*, [in:] *Ad geographiam historico-iuridicam ope iuris Romani colendam. Studia in honorem Gábor Hamza*, ed. D. Ceccarelli Morolli, Budapest 2015, pp. 149–160.

El Beheiri N., *Die 'lex Claudia de nave senatorum'*, "RIDA" 48/2001, pp. 57–63.

Epstein D.F., *Personal Enmity in Roman Politics 218-43 B.C.*, London–New York 1987 (reprint 1989).

Ernout A., Meillet A., *Dictionnaire étymologique de la langue latine*, Paris 1951.

Evans R.J., *The Augustan Purge of the Senate and the Census of 86 BC*, "Acta Classica" 40/1997, pp. 77–86.

Fantham E., *Censorship. Roman Style*, "Echos du Monde Classique" 21/1977, pp. 41–53.

Fayer C., *La familia romana. Aspetti giuridici ed antiquari. Sponsalia. Matrimonio. Dote. Parte seconda*, Roma 2005.

Ferenczy E., *The Censorship of Appius Claudius Caecus*, "AAH" 15/1967, pp. 38–50.

Fernández Baquero M.E., *La actividad de los censores en la Administración de la República romana*, "e-Legal History Review" 15/2013, https://www.iustel.com/v2/revistas/detalle_revista.asp?id_noticia=412967.
Fernández de Buján A., *Derecho público romano*[26], Madrid 2023.
Fiori R., *'Homo sacer'. Dinamica politico-costituzionale di una sanzione giuridico-religiosa*, Napoli 1996.
Fiske G.C., *The Politics of the Patrician Claudii*, "HSCP" 13/1902, pp. 1–59.
Flach D., *Die Gesetze der frühen römischen Republik. Text und Kommentar*, Darmstadt 1994.
Flower H.I., *Disgrace and Oblivion in Roman Political Culture*, Chapel Hill 2006.
Forcellini A. (ed.), *Totius Latinitatis Lexicon*, Patavii 1805.
Fotheringham L., *Repetition and Unity in a Civil Law Speech: The 'Pro Caecina'*, [in:] *Cicero the Advocate*, eds. J. Powell, J. Paterson, Oxford 2004, pp. 253–276.
Fraccaro P., *'Accensi'*, [in:] P. Fraccaro, *Opuscula*, II, Pavia 1957, pp. 315–326.
Fraccaro P., *Ricerche storiche e letterarie sulla censura del 184/183 (M. Porcio Catone L. Valerio Flacco)*, [in:] P. Fraccaro, *Opuscula*, I, Pavia 1956, pp. 417–508.
Fraccaro P., *'Tribules' ed 'aerarii'. Una ricerca di diritto pubblico romano*, [in:] P. Fraccaro, *Opuscula*, II, Pavia 1957, pp. 149–170.
Franciosi G. (ed.), *'Leges regiae'*, Napoli 2003.
Frank T., *The Status of Actors at Rome*, "CP" 26.1/1931, pp. 11–20.
Frezza P., *Note esegetiche di diritto pubblico romano*, [in:] *Studi in onore di Pietro De Francisci*, I, Milano 1956, pp. 199–211.
Frolov R., *Public Meetings in Ancient Rome. Definitions of the 'contiones' in the Sources*, "Graeco-Latina Brunensia" 18/2013, pp. 75–84.
Fronda M.P., *Privata hospica, beneficia publica? Consul(ar)s, Local Elite and Roman Rule in Italy*, [in:] *Consuls and Res Publica. Holding High Office in the Roman Republic*, eds. H. Beck, A. Duplá, M. Jehne, F. Pina Polo, Cambridge 2011, pp. 232–255.
Fuhrmann M., *Cicero und die römische Republik*, Düsseldorf 2006.
Gabba E., Crawford M.H., '*Lex Cornelia de XX quaestoribus*', [in:] *The Roman Statutes*, ed. M.H. Crawford, I, London 1996, pp. 293–300.
Gabba E., *Il ceto equestre e il senato di Silla*, "Athenaeum" 34.3–4/1956, pp. 124–138.
Gabba E., *L'elogio di Brindisi*, "Athenaeum" 36.1–2/1958, pp. 90–105.
Gabba E., *Un documento censorio in Dionigi d'Alicarnasso 1.74.5*, [in:] *Synteleia Arangio-Ruiz*, I, Napoli 1974, pp. 486–493.
Gagé J., *Les rites anciens de lustration du Populus et les attributs "triomphaux" des censeurs*, "MEFRA" 82.1/1970, pp. 43–71.
Gagliardi L., *I censimenti romani della tarda repubblica e il caso dei 'proletarii'*, "BIDR" 117/2023, pp. 81–89.
Gagliardi L., *'Romam commigrare'. I Romani, I Latini e l'immigrazione*, Milano 2023.
García Morcillo M., *Staging Power and Authority at Roman Auctions*, "Ancient Society" 38/2008, pp. 153–181.
Garcia Sanchez J., *Algunas consideraciones sobre el 'tempus lugendi'*, "RIDA", 23/1976, pp. 141–151.
Gardner J.F., *Being a Roman Citizen*, London 1993.
Gardner J.F., *Women in Roman Society and Law*, London 1986 (reprint 1995).
Garofalo L., *Sulla condizione di 'homo sacer' in età arcaica*, [in:] L. Garofalo, *Studi sulla sacertà*, Padova 2005, pp. 11–50.
Gerlach F.D., *Die römische Censur in ihrem Verhältniß zur Verfassung. Eine historische Untersuchung*, Basel 1842.

Giangrieco Pessi M.V., *Brevi riflessioni sul ruolo della censura nella dialettica costituzionale della prima repubblica*, [in:] *'Societas – ius'. 'Munuscula' di allievi a Feliciano Serrao*, Napoli 1999, pp. 159–170.
Giangrieco Pessi M.V., *Dalla 'lex Aemilia' al plebiscito Ovinio: Problemi e riflessioni*, [in:] *Leggi e società nella repubblica romana*, ed. F. Serrao, II, Napoli 2000, pp. 299–307.
Giaro T., *'Excusatio necessitatis' nel diritto romano*, Warszawa 1982.
Gibbon E., *The History of the Decline and Fall of the Roman Empire*, I, Oxford 1827 (reprint).
Gintowt E., *Le changement du caractère de la 'tribus' romaine, attribué à Appius Claudius Caecus*, "Eos" 43.1/1949, pp. 198–210.
Giovannini A., *Cheval public et ordre équestre à la fin de la République*, "Athenaeum" 98.2/2010, pp. 353–364.
Gizewski C., *Incensus*, [in:] *Brill's New Pauly. Encyclopedia of the Ancient World. Antiquity*, eds. H. Schneider, M. Landfester, H. Cancik, VI, Leiden–Boston, MA 2005, p. 753.
Greco G., *Census. Profili storico-giuridici delle attività di censimento a Roma*, Torino 2022.
Green E.C., Lewis A.D.E., Crawford M.H., *'Lex Iulia de maritandis ordinibus. Lex Papia Poppaea'*, [w:] *The Roman Statutes*, red. M.H. Crawford, II, London 1996, pp. 801–809.
Green W.M., *The Status of Actors at Rome*, "CP" 28.4/1933, pp. 301–304.
Greenidge A.H.J., *Infamia. Its Place in Roman Public and Private Law*, Oxford 1894.
Grelle F., *La 'correctio morum' nella legislazione flavia*, "ANRW" II.13/1980, pp. 340–365.
Grenade P., *Essai sur les origines du principat. Investiturenet renouvellement des pouvoirs impériaux*, Paris 1961.
Griffin M., *Claudius in Tacitus*, "CQ" 40.2/1990, pp. 482–501.
Gruen E.S., *Culture and National Identity in Republican Rome*, New York 1992.
Gruen E.S., *Studies in Greek Culture and Roman Policy*, Leiden 1990.
Guarino A., *Il dubbio contenuto pubblicistico delle XII tavole*, "Labeo" 34/1988, pp. 323–335.
Guarino A., *L' 'exaequatio legibus' dei 'plebisscita'*, [in:] *Festschrift Fritz Schulz*, I, Weimar 1951, pp. 458–465.
Guarino A., *'Quaestus omnis patribus indecorus'*, "Labeo" 28/1982, pp. 7–16.
Guarino A., *Salvius Iulianus. Profilo bio-bibliografico*, [in:] A. Guarino, *Pagine di diritto romano*, V, Napoli 1994, pp. 183–255.
Guizzi F., *Censores*, "NNDI" 3/1964, pp. 101–104.
Hahn G., *De censorum locationibus*, Lipsiae 1879.
Hantos T., *'Res publica constituta'. Die Verfassung des Dictators Sulla*, Stuttgart 1988.
Hardy E.G., *'Lectio Senatus' and 'Census' under Augustus*, "CQ" 13.1/1919, pp. 43–49.
Harries J., *Cicero and the Jurists. From Citizen's Law to the Lawful State*, Bodmin 2006.
Henderson M.I., *The Establishment of the 'Equester Ordo'*, "JRS" 53/1963, s. 51–62.
Hill H., *Livy's Account of the 'Equites'*, "CP" 25.3/1930, pp. 244–249.
Hill H., *Sulla's New Senators in 81 B.C.*, "CQ" 26.3–4/1932, pp. 170–177.
Hoffmann E., *Das Gesetz der Zwölf-Tafeln von der Forcten und Sanaten*, "Zeitschrift für die österreichischen Gymnasien" 17/1866, pp. 547–611.
Holford-Strevens L., *Aulus Gellius. An Antonine Scholar and His Achievement*, Oxford 2003.
Honoré A.M., *The 'Fragmentum Dositheanum'*, "RIDA" 12/1965, s. 301–323.
Houston G.W., *The Duration of the Censorship of Vespasian and Titus*, "Emerita" 44/1976, pp. 397–402.
Hölkeskamp K.-J., *Die Entstehung der Nobilität*, Stuttgart 1987.
Humbert M., *Hispala Faecenia et l'endogamie des affranchis sous la Republique*, "Index" 15/1987, pp. 131–140.

Humm M., *Appius Claudius Caecus et la construction de la via Appia*, "MEFRA" 108.2/1996, pp. 693–746.
Humm M., *Appius Claudius Caecus. La république accomplie*, Rome 2005.
Humm M., *Il 'regimen morum' dei censori e le identità dei cittadini*, [in:] *'Homo, caput, persona'. La costruzione giuridica dell'identità nel'esperienza romana*, eds. A. Corbino, M. Humbert, G. Negri, Pavia 2010, pp. 283–314.
Humm M., *La figure d'Appius Claudius Caecus chez Tite-Live*, [in:] *Le censeur et les Samnites sur Tite-Live, livre IX*, eds. D. Briquel, J.-P. Thuillier, Paris 2001, pp. 65–96.
Humm M., *L'image de la censure chez Valère Maxime: formation et évolution d'un paradigme*, [in:] *Valeurs et mémoire à Rome: Valère Maxime ou la vertu recomposée*, ed. J.-M. David, Paris 1998, pp. 73–93.
Humm M., *Le Comitium du forum romain et la réforme des tribus d'Appius Claudius Caecus*, "MEFRA" 111.2/1999, pp. 625–694.
Humm M., *Servius Tullius et la censure: élaboration d'un modèle institutionnel*, [in:] *Invention des grands hommes de la Rome antique*, eds. M. Coudry, T. Späth, Paris 2001, pp. 221–247.
Huzar E.G., *Mark Antony. Marriages vs. Careers*, "*CJ*" 81.2/1986, pp. 97–111.
Jacobs A., *Carvilius Ruga v Uxor: A Famous Roman Divorce*, "Fundamina" 15.2/2009, pp. 92–111.
Jarcke C.E., *Versuch einer Darstellung des censorischen Strafrechts der Römer: ein Beytrag zur Geschichte des Criminalrechts*, Bonn 1824.
Jehne M., *The Rise of the Consular as a Social Type*, [in:] *Consuls and 'Res Publica'. Holding High Office in the Roman Republic*, eds. H. Beck, A. Duplá, M. Jehne, F. Pina Polo, Cambridge 2011, pp. 211–231.
Jones A.H.M., *The Censorial Powers of Augustus*, [in:] A.H.M. Jones, *Studies in Roman Government and Law*, Oxford 1960 (reprint 1968), pp. 19–26.
Jones A.H.M., *The 'Imperium' of Augustus*, "JRS" 41.1–2/1951, pp. 112–119.
Jones B.W., *A Note on the Flavians' Attitude to the Censorship*, "Historia" 21.1/1972, p. 128.
Jones B.W., *Some Thoughts on Domitian's Perpetual Censorship*, "CJ" 68/1973, pp. 276–277.
Jory E.J., *'Ars ludicra' and the 'ludus talarius'*, "Bulletin of the Institute of Classical Studies. Supplement" 66/1995, pp. 139–152.
Jörs P., *'Dositheanum fragmentum'*, "RE" 10/1905, pp. 1603–1605.
Kacprzak A., *The Senatusconsultum Claudianum and the Mysterious Lex Concerning the Status of Children Born to Free Women Cohabiting with Slaves (G. 1,86)*, "Zeszyty Prawnicze" 20.4/2020, pp. 53–89.
Karlowa O., *Römische Rechtsgeschichte. I. Staatsrecht und Rechtsquellen*, Leipzig 1885; II, Leipzig 1901.
Kaser M., *Die Anfänge der 'manumissio' und das fiduziarisch gebundene Eigentum*, "ZSS" 61/1941, pp. 153–186.
Kaser M., *Infamia und ignominia in den römischen Rechtsquellen*, "ZSS" 73/1956, pp. 220–278.
Keaveney A., *The Last Republican Sulla*², London–New York 2005.
Kelly J.M., *Roman Litigation*, Oxford 1966.
Keseberg J.F., *De censoribus Romanorum commentatio*, Quedlinburg 1829.
Keyes C.W., *Original Elements in Cicero's Ideal Constitution*, "AJP" 42.4/1921, pp. 309–323.
Kienast D., *Cato der Zensor. Seine Persönlichkeit und seine Zeit*, Darmstadt 1979.
Klotz A., *Zur Geschichte der römischen Zensur*, "RhM" 88/1939, pp. 27–36.

Kornhardt H., *'Postliminium' in republikanischer Zeit*, "SDHI" 19/1953, pp. 1–37.
Kremer D., *Il censo nelle colonie latine prima della guerra sociale*, [in:] *Gli statuti municipali*, eds. L. Capogrossi Colognesi, E. Gabba, Pavia 2006, pp. 627–645.
Kron G., *The Augustan Census Figures and the Population of Italy*, "Athenaeum" 93.2/2005, pp. 441–495.
Krüger H., Kaser M., *'Fraus'*, "ZSS" 63/1943, pp. 117–174.
Kubitschek W., *Censores*, "RE" 3/1899, pp. 1902–1908.
Kunkel W., Wittmann R., *Staatsordnung und Staatspraxis der römischen Republik. Zweiter Abschnitt. Die Magistratur*, München 1995.
Kupiszewski H., *Das Verlöbnis im altrömischen Recht*, "ZSS" 77/1960, pp. 125–159.
Laffi U., *Le funzioni giudiziarie dei senati locali nel mondo romano*, [in:] U. Laffi, *Studi di storia romana e di diritto*, Roma 2001.
Lanfranchi T., *Il diritto nei retori romani. Contributo alla storia dello sviluppo del diritto romano*, Milano 1938.
Lange L., *De plebiscitis Ovinio et Atinio Disputatio*, Lipsiae 1879 (reprint).
Lange L., *Römische Alterthümer*[2], Berlin 1863.
Last H., *The Servian Reforms*, "JRS" 35/1945, pp. 30–48.
Lemmenais N., *Censeurs et mos maiorum dans la construction de l'ethos républicain*, "Revue historique" 706.2/2023, pp. 259–279.
Lemosse M., *L'affranchisement par le cens*, "RHD" 27/1949, pp. 161–203.
Lemosse M., *Mort e 'lustratio'. Á propos de Dio Cass. 54,28,4*, "TR" 36/1968, pp. 519–524.
Lenel O., *Palingenesia iuris civilis*, Graz 1960.
Lenschau T., *Hannibal*, "RE" VII,2/1912, pp. 2318–2351.
Leppin H., *Histrionen. Untersuchungen zur sozialen Stellung von Bühnenkünstlern im Westen des Römischen Reiches zur Zeit der Republik und des Principats*, Bonn 1992.
Leuze O., *Zur Geschichte der römischen Censur*, Halle 1912.
Levi M.A., *Augusto e il suo tempo*, Milano 1994.
Levick B., *Claudius*, London 1990 (reprint 2001).
Levy E., *Die römische Kapitalstrafe*, [in:] E. Levy, *Gesamelte Schriften*, II, Köln–Graz 1963, pp. 327–332.
Levy E., *'Libertas' und 'civitas'*, [in:] E. Levy, *Gesamelte Schriften*, II, Köln–Graz 1963, pp. 3–24.
Licandro O., *In magistratu damnari. Ricerche sulla responsabilità dei magistrati romani durante l'esercizio delle funzioni*, Torino 1999.
Linderski J., *The Augural Law*, "ANRW" II.16.3/1986, pp. 2146–2312.
Lindholmer M.O., *Digressions and the Fall of the Republic in Cassius Dio*, [in:] *Digressions in Classical Historiography*, eds. M. Baumann, V. Liotsakis, Berlin–Boston, MA 2024, pp. 241–272.
Lintott A.W., *The Constitution of the Roman Republic*, Oxford 1999.
Little D., *Politics in Augustan Poetry*, "ANRW" II.30.1/1983, pp. 254–370.
Lo Cascio E., *Il census a Roma e la sua evoluzione dall'età "serviana" alla prima età imperiale*, "MEFRA" 113.2/2001, pp. 565–603.
Lo Cascio E., *La popolazione*, [in:] *Roma imperiale. Una metropoli antica*, ed. E. Lo Cascio, Roma 2010, pp. 17–69.
Lo Cascio E., *Le procedure di recensus dalla tarda repubblica al. Tardo antico e il calcolo della popolazione di Roma*, [in:] *La Rome impériale: démographie et logistique*, ed. C. Virlouvet, Roma 1997, 3–76.
Lo Cascio E., *The Size of the Roman Population: Beloch and the Meaning of the Augustan Census Figures*, "JRS" 84/1994, pp. 23–40.

López Barja de Quiroga P., *Historia de la manumisión en Roma. De los orígenes a los Severos*, Madrid 2007.
López Barja de Quiroga P., *La fundación de Carteya y la 'manumissio cens'*, "Latomus" 56.1/1997, pp. 83–93.
López Pedreira A., *'Tempus lugendi' y 'secundae nuptiae' en derecho romano*, "RIDROM" 11/2013, pp. 332–377.
Lotti Faravelli A., *Origine della censura romana*, Como 1937.
Macbain B., *Appius Claudius and the Via Appia*, "CQ" 30.2/1980, pp. 356–372.
Mac Cormack G., *'Partes secanto'*, "TR" 36/1968, pp. 511–515.
Maffi A., *Ricerche sul 'postliminium'*, Milano 1992.
Magdelain A., *La loi à Rome. Histoire d'un concept*, Paris 1978.
Magdelain A., *Recherches sur l''imperium'. La loi curiate et les auspices d'investiture*, Paris 1968.
Manfredini A., *L'editto 'de coërcendis rhetoribus latinis' del 92 a.C.*, SDHI 42/1976, pp. 99–148.
Manzo A., *'Lustratio' e divieto del 'suffectus': due aspetti sacerdotali del censore?*, "Teoria e Storia del Diritto Privato" 12/2019, pp. 1–22.
Markowski H., *On Censuses during the Reign of Emperor Augustus*, "Classical Quarterly" 5.1/1931, pp. 13–20.
Maschek D., *Not Census But Deductio: Reconsidering the 'Ara of Domitius Ahenobarbus'*, "JRS" 108/2018, pp. 27–52.
Masi Doria C., *'Civitas, operae, obsequium'. Tre studi sulla codizione giuridica dei liberti*, Napoli 1999.
Masi Doria C., *'Exemplum pessimum: Quinto Mucio e il 'testimonium' in Val. Max. 4.1.11*, "Index" 38/2010, pp. 70–88.
Masi Doria C., *In margine a PS. 2,21A,11*, [in:] *Au-delà des fontierès. Mélanges de droit romain offers à Witold Wołodkiewicz*, I, eds. M. Zabłocka, J. Krzynówek, Z. Służewska, J. Urbanik, Varsovie 2000, pp. 507–519.
Masi Doria C., *La denuntiatio nel senatusconsultum Claudianum: i legittimati e la struttura del procedimento*, [in:] *Parti e giudici nel processo: dai diritti antichi all'attualità*, eds. C. Cascione, E. Germino, C. Masi Doria, Napoli 2006, pp. 125–156.
Masi Doria C., *Status and Contract in Ancient Rome: With Some Thoughts on the 'Future of Obligations'*, [in:] *Obligations in Roman Law. Past, Present, and Future*, ed. by T.A.J. McGinn, Ann Arbor, MI 2012, pp. 102–130.
McDonnell M., *The Speech of Numidicus at Gellius, N.A.1.6*, "AJP" 108.1/1987, pp. 81–94.
McGinn T.A.J., *Prostitution, Sexuality, and the Law in Ancient Rome*, Oxford 2003.
Melničuk J.V., *'Lustrum' en su aspecto marcial*, "Diritto@Storia" 4/2005, http://www.dirittoestoria.it/4/Tradizione-Romana/Melniciuk-Lustrum.htm.
Melničuk J.V., *Некоторые аспекты римского сакрального ритуала 'lustrum'*, "Ius Antiquum" 1.11/2003, pp. 54–64.
Melničuk J.V., *Ответственность цензоров перед 'civitas' в середине V – середине II вв. до н.э.*, "Ius Antiquum" 1.9/2002, pp. 113–125.
Melničuk J.V., *Римские цензоры и характер государственных подрядов ('cura operum locandarum')*, "Ius Antiquum" 1.6/2000, pp. 32–42.
Melničuk J.V., *Законодательное оформление института цензуры (V-IV вв. до н.э.)*, "Ius Antiquum" 1.8/2001, pp. 62–65.
Meyer E.A., *Legitimacy and Law in the Roman World. 'Tabulae' in Roman Belief and Practice*, Cambridge 2004.

Milazzo F., *La realizzazione delle opere pubbliche in Roma arcaica e repubblicana. Munera e ultro tributa*, Napoli 1993.

Millar F., *The 'Aerarium' and Its Officials under the Empire*, "JRS" 54/1964, pp. 33–40.

Momigliano A., *An Interim Report on the Origins of Rome*, "JRS" 53/1963, pp. 95–121.

Mommsen T., *Römisches Staatsrecht*[3], II.1, Graz 1952 (reprint).

Mommsen T., *Römisches Strafrecht*, Leipzig 1899.

Moore C.H., *The Oxyrhynchus Epitome of Livy in Relation to Obsequens and Cassiodorus*, "AJP" 25/1904, pp. 241–255.

Mora F., *La scelta del 'princeps senatus'*, "Historia" 52.4/2003, pp. 502–504.

Muccigrosso J.D., *The Brindisi 'Elogium' and the Rejected 'lectio senatus' of Appius Claudius Caecus*, "Historia" 52.4/2003, pp. 496–501.

Münzer F., *C. Maenius (9)*, "RE" XIV.1/1928, pp. 152–155.

Münzer F., *Zu den Fasti censorii*, "RhM" 61/1906, pp. 19–27.

Nicolet C., *Censeurs et publicains. Économie et fiscalité dans la Rome antique*, Paris 2000.

Nicolet C., *Les listes des centuries: La prétendue centurie 'Niquis scivit'*, "MEFRA" 113.2/2001, pp. 723–734.

Nicolet C., *L'ordre équestre à l'époque républicaine*, I, Paris 1966; II, Paris 1974.

Nicolet C., *The World of the Citizen in Republican Rome*, transl. P.S. Falla, Berkely–Los Angeles, CA 1980.

Nicolet C., Crawford M.H., *'Tabula Heracleensis'*, [in:] *The Roman Statutes*, ed. M.H. Crawford, I, London 1996, pp. 355–391.

Nowak M., *Die Strafverhängungen der Censoren*, Breslau 1909.

Ogilvie R.M., *Lustrum Condere*, "JRS" 51.1–2/1961, pp. 31–39.

Osgood J., *Claudius Caesar. Image and Power in the Early Roman Empire*, Cambridge 2011.

Otto W.F., *Lustrum*, "RhM" 71/1916, pp. 17–40.

Palmer R.E.A., *The Deconstruction of Mommsen on Festus 462/464 L.*, [in:] *'Imperium Sine Fine'. T. Robert S. Broughton and the Roman Republic*, ed. J. Linderski, Stuttgart 1996, pp. 75–101.

Paulson L., *A Painted Republic: The Constitutional Innovations of Cicero's 'De legibus'*, "Etica & Politica", 16.2/ 2014, pp. 307–340.

Peachin M., *Frontinus and the 'curae' of the 'curator aquarum'*, Stuttgart 2004.

Perry M.J., *Gender, Manumission, and the Roman Freedwoman*, Cambridge 2014.

Pfaff I., *'Incensus'*, "RE" IX.2/1916, pp. 1245–1246.

Pfeilschifter R., *Die Brüchigkeit der Rituale. Bemerkungen zum Niedergang der römischen Zensur*, "Klio" 84.2/2002, pp. 440–464.

Pieri G., *L'histoire du cens jusqu'à la fin de la République romaine*, Paris 1968.

Pina Polo F., *Las 'contiones' civiles y militares en Roma*, Zaragoza 1989.

Pina Polo F., Díaz Fernández A., *The Quaestorship in the Roman Republic*, Berlin–Boston, MA 2019.

Pólay E., *Das 'regimen morum' des Zensors und die sogenannte Hausgerichtsbarkeit*, [in:] *Studi in onore di Edoardo Volterra*, III, Milano 1971, pp. 263–317.

Polo G., *Idoneidad de las tabulae censoriae como instrumentos de publicidad de los miembros de la comunidad*, "RIDROM" 5/2010, pp. 126–177, http://www.ridrom.uclm.es/documentos5/Polo_pub.pdf.

Polo Toribio G., *Algunas puntualizaciones entorno a la figura jurídica del incensus*, "RGDR" 12/2009.

Polo Toribio G., *Finalidad probatoria de la professio censualis*, "RIDROM" 8/2012, pp. 118–142.

Polo Toribio G., *La pretendida prueba material en la defensa del poeta Arquías*, "Diritto@ Storia" 8/2009, http://www.dirittoestoria.it/8/Tradizione-Romana/PoloToribio-Defensa-poeta-Arquias.htm.

Polo Toribio G., *La prorogatio en la magistratura censoria*, "RGDR" 13/2009.

Polo Toribio G., *Lex de censoribus creandis*, [in:] *Homenaje al Profesor Armando Torrent*, eds. A. Murillo Villar, M. Aránzazu Calzada González, S.C. Pérez-Gómez, A.J. Torrent Ruiz, Madrid 2016, pp. 717–730.

Polo Toribio G., *Manumissio. Libertas. Census. Civis. Incensus*, Madrid 2023.

Polverini L., '*Alius et idem*'. *Il tribunato della plebe nel corso della storia romana*, "Diritto@ Storia" 7/2008, http://www.dirittoestoria.it/7/Memorie/Polverini-Tribunato-plebe-storia-romana.htm#_ftn23.

Poma G., *Dionigi d'Alicarnasso e la cittadinanza romana*, "MEFRA" 101.1/1989, pp. 187–205.

Poma G., *Provvedimenti legislativi e attività censoria di Claudio verso gli schiavi e i liberti*, "Rivista storica dell' antichità" 12/1982, pp. 143–174.

Purcell N., '*Atrium Libertatis*', "PBSR" 61/1993, pp. 125–155.

Posner E., *Archives in the Ancient World*, Cambridge, MA 1972 (reprint 2003).

Quintana Orive E., *Sobre la condición jurídica de los actores en el derecho romano*, "RIDA" 50/2003, pp. 301–315.

Raditsa L.F., *Augustus' Legislation Concerning Marriage, Procreation, Love Affairs and Adultery*, "ANRW" II.13/1980, pp. 278–339.

Ramage E.S., *Juvenal and the Establishment: Denigration of Predecessor in the 'Satires'*, "ANRW" II.33.1/1989, pp. 640–707.

Rampazzo N., *Quasi praetor non fuerit. Studi sulle elezioni magistratuali in Roma repubblicana tra regola ed eccezione*, Napoli 2008.

Razzini C.S., *Il diritto romano nelle satire di Giovenale*, Torino 1913.

Reduzzi Merola F., *'Abrogare, derogare, obrogare' in Cicerone*, [in:] *Au-delà des frontierès. Mélanges de droit romain offers à Witold Wołodkiewicz*, II, Varsovie 2000, pp. 739–742.

Reduzzi Merola F., '*Aliquid de legibus statuere*'. *Poteri del senato e sovranità del popolo nella Roma tardorepubblicana*, Napoli 2007, pp. 11–14.

Reduzzi Merola F., *'Servo parere'. Studi sulla condizione degli schiavi vicari e dei sottoposti a schiavi nelle esperienze greca e romana*, Napoli 1990.

Reigadas Lavandero E., *Censura y res publica: aportación constitucional y protagonismo político*, Madrid 2000.

Robinson O.F., *Ancient Rome. City Planning and Administration*, London–New York 1992.

Robinson O.F., *The Sources of Roman Law. Problems and Methods for Ancient Historians*, London–New York 1997.

Robleda O., *Il diritto degli schiavi nella Roma antica*, Roma 1976.

Robleda O., *Il divorzio a Roma prima di Constantino*, ANRW II.14/1982, pp. 347–390.

R. Rodríguez López, *La agricultura como 'officium' en el mundo romano*, "RIDA" 49/2002, pp. 185–202.

Rodríguez Neila J.F., *Cuestiones en torno a la censura municipal romana*, "Gerion" 4/1986, pp. 61–99.

Roncati S., *'Censor legibus scribundis'?*, [in:] *Studi in onore di Franca De Marini Avonzo*, eds. M. Bianchini, G. Viarengo, Torino 1999, pp. 321–327.

Rotondi G., *'Leges publicae populi Romani'. Elenco cronologico con una introduzione sull' attività legislativa dei comizi romani*, Milano 1912.

Rupprecht K., *Molon (8)*, "RE" XIV.1/1928, p. 12.

Ryan F.X., *Rank and Participation in the Republican Senate*, Stuttgart 1998.

Ryan F.X., *The Censorship of Acilius*, [in:] *Politische Kultur und soziale Struktur der Römischen Republik. Bilanzen und Perspektiven. Akten der internationalen Tagung anlässlich des 70. Todestages von Friedrich Münzer (Münster, 18-20. Oktober 2012)*, eds. M. Haake, A.-C. Harders, Stuttgart 2017, pp. 111–134.
Ryan F.X., *The 'lectio senatus' after Sulla*, "RhM" 139/1996, pp. 189–191.
Sabbatucci G., *La censura: istituzione rivoluzionaria dell'antica Roma*, "Index" 3/1972, pp. 192–202.
Salerno F., *Dalla consecratio alla publicatio bonorum*, Napoli 1990.
Santalucia B., *Alle origini del processo penale romano*, "Iura" 35/1984, s. 47–72.
Santalucia B., *I tribuni e le centurie*, [in:] B. Santalucia, *Studi di diritto penale romano*, Roma 1994, pp. 49–64.
Santalucia B., *Osservazioni sulla giustizia penale nei 'municipia'*, [in:] B. Santalucia, *Altri studi di diritto penale romano*, Padova 2009, pp. 329–355.
Santalucia B., *Processo penale*, [in:] B. Santalucia, *Studi di diritto penale romano*, Roma 1994, pp. 145–231.
Sauerwein I., *Die 'leges sumptuariae' als römische Maßname gegen der Sittenverfall*, Hamburg 1970.
Schanz M., Hosius C., *Geschichte der römischen Literatur bis zum Gesetzgebungswerk des Kaisers Justinian*, IV.2, München 1971.
Shaw B.D., *Raising and Killing Children. Two Roman Myths*, "Mnemosyne" 54.1/2001, pp. 31–77.
Scherillo G., *Appunti sulla 'sectio bonorum'*, "Iura" 4/1953, pp. 197–205.
Schmähling E., *Die Sittenaufsicht der Censoren. Ein Beitrag zur Sittengeschichte der römischen Republik*, Stuttgart 1938.
Schönberger O., *Der glückliche Cato*, "RhM" 112/1969, p. 190.
Segal E., *Roman Laughter. The Comedy of Plautus*², Oxford 1987.
Siber H., *Cäsars Diktatur und das Prinzipat des Augustus*, "ZSS" 55/1935, pp. 99–158.
Siber H., *Die plebeischen Magistraturen bis zur 'lex Hortensia'*, Leipzig 1936.
Siber H, *Römisches Verfassungsrecht in geschichtlicher Entwicklung*, Lahr 1952.
Siber H., *Zur Kollegialität der römischen Zensoren*, [in:] *Festschrift Fritz Schulz*, I, ed. W. Flume, Weimar 1951, pp. 466–474.
Simshäuser W., *'Iuridici' und Munizipalgerichtsbarkeit in Italien*, München 1973.
Slob E., *Luxuria. Regelgeving en maatregelen van censoren ten tijde van de Romeinse Republiek*, Utrecht 1986.
Solazzi S., *'Manumissio ex mancipatione'*, [in:] S. Solazzi, *Scritti di diritto romano*, III, Napoli 1960, pp. 199–218.
Soltau W., *Zur römischen Verfassungsgeschichte. Zur 'lex centuriata de imperio'*, "Philologus" 75/1918, pp. 232–237.
Söllner A., *Zur Vorgeschichte und Funktion der 'actio rei uxoriae'*, Köln–Wien 1969.
Spagnuolo Vigorita T., *'Casta domus'. Un seminario sulla legislazione matrimoniale augustea*², Napoli 2002.
Spruit J.E., *De juridische en sociale positie der romeinse acteurs*, Assen 1966.
Stark R., *Catos Rede 'de lustri sui felicitate'*, "RhM" 96/1953, pp. 184–187.
Staveley E.S., *The Political Aims of Appius Claudius Caecus*, "Historia" 8.4/1959, pp. 410–433.
Staveley E.S., *The Significance of the Consular Tribunate*, "JRS" 43/1953, pp. 30–36.
Stella Maranca F., *Il tribunato della plebe dalla 'lex Hortensia' alla 'lex Cornelia'*, Lanciano 1901 (reprint Napoli 1982).
Stewart R., *Domitian and Roman Religion: Juvenal, Satires Two and Four*, "TAPA" 124/1994, pp. 309–332.

Stobart J.C., *The Senate under Augustus*, "CQ" 2.4/1908, pp. 296–303.
Stockton D., *Cicero: A Political Biography*, Oxford 1971.
Stockton D., *The Gracchi*, Oxford 1979 (reprint 2002).
Suolahti J., '*Princeps senatus*', "Arctos" 7/1972, pp. 207–218.
Suolahti J., *The Roman Censors. A Study on Social Structure*, Helsinki 1963.
Syme R., *Paullus the Censor*, "Athenaeum" 65.1–2/1987, pp. 7–24.
Syme R., *The Roman Revolution*, Oxford 1939 (reprint 2002).
Tansey P., *The 'Princeps Senatus' in the Last Decades of the Republic*, "Chiron" 30/2000, pp. 15–30.
Tarwacka A., *A Censor and a Woman. Censorial Reproach of Clodia in Cicero's 'Pro Caelio'*, [in:] *Women, Society and Law. From Roman Law to Digital Age*, eds. M. Eysymontt, C. Lázaro Guillamón, Warsaw 2022, pp. 171–182.
Tarwacka A., *Adoption under the Scrutiny of the Censors in Republican Rome*, [in:] *Family, Law, and Society: from Roman Law to the Present Day*, eds. E. Dawidziuk, P. Panero, A. Tarwacka, Berlin–Lausanne–Bruxelles–Chennai–New York–Oxford 2023, pp. 77–91.
Tarwacka A., *Cenzor w sypialni. Urzędnicza kontrola moralności w życiu rodzinnym Rzymian okresu republiki*, Warszawa 2021.
Tarwacka A., *Come vendicarsi dei censori? Scontri politici e responsabilità penale dei guardiani della morale*, "Diritto@Storia" 14/2016, http://www.dirittoestoria.it/14/tradizione/Tarwacka-Come-vendicarsi-dei-censori.htm.
Tarwacka A., *'Dictator senatui legendo'. The Unusual Dictatorship of M. Fabius Buteo*, "Zeszyty Prawnicze" 13.1/2013, pp. 185–196.
Tarwacka A., *Prawne aspekty urzędu cenzora w starożytnym Rzymie*, Warszawa 2012.
Tarwacka A., *Romans and Pirates. Legal Perspective*, Warszawa 2009.
Tarwacka A., *The Censorial Mark in Ancient Roman Marital Matters*, "Zeszyty Prawnicze" 19.1/2019, pp. 241–255.
Tarwacka A., *The Censors and Their Duties in the Comedies of Plautus*, "RGDR" 23/2014, http://www.iustel.com/v2/revistas/detalle_revista.asp?id_noticia=415488.
Tarwacka A., *The Censors' Influence on Marriage in Republican Rome*, "Zeszyty Prawnicze" 18.1/2018, pp. 173–191.
Tarwacka A., *The Roman Censors as Protectors of Public Places*, "Diritto@Storia" 12/2014, http://www.dirittoestoria.it/12/tradizione-romana/Tarwacka-Roman-Censors-Protectors-Public-Places.htm.
Tarwacka A., *Vir cum divortium fecit mulieri iudex pro censore est. Were the woman's morals examined and assessed during or out of a lawsuit?*, [in:] *Alternative Dispute Resolution: From Roman Law to Contemporary Regulations*, eds. B. Sitek, J. Szczerbowski, K. Ciućkowska-Leszczewicz, C. Lázaro Guillamón, S. Kursa, A. Bauknecht, Warsaw 2016, pp. 181–188.
Tassi Scandone E., *'Leges Valeriae de provocatione'. Repressione criminale e garanzie costituzionali nella Roma repubblicana*, Napoli 2008.
Tatum W.J., *The 'lex Clodia de censoria notione'*,"CQ" 85.1/1990, pp. 34–43.
Tatum W.J., *The Patrician Tribune Publius Clodius Pulcher*, Chapel Hill 1999.
Taylor L.R., *Republican and Augustan Writers Enrolled in the Equestrian Centuries*, "TAPA" 99/1968, pp. 469–486.
Taylor L.R., *Roman Voting Assemblies. From the Hannibalic War to the Dictatorship of Caesar*, Ann Arbor, MI 1966 (reprint 2003).
Thomas M.D., *Censure of the Censors: Livy in a 'Comic' Mode*, "Ancient History Bulletin", 8.1/1994, pp. 18–27.
Thompson D.W., *The Greek for a Dormouse*, "CP" 40.3/1945, pp. 185–186.

Tomulescu C.S., *Quelques petites études de droit romain*, "BIDR" 82/1979, pp. 95–117.

Torelli M., *Typology & Structure of Roman Historical Reliefs*, Ann Arbor, MI 1982.

Torrent A., *Para una interpretacion de la 'potestas censoria' en los emperadores flavios*, "Emerita" 36/1968, pp. 213–229.

Toynbee J.M.C., *Death and Burial in the Roman World*, London 1971 (reprint 1996).

Treggiari S., *Roman Marriage. 'Iusti coniuges' from the Time of Cicero to the Time of Ulpian*, Oxford 1993.

Treggiari S., *Roman Freedmen during the Late Republic*, Oxford 1969 (reprint London 2000).

Trisciuoglio A., *Sarta tecta, ultrotributa, opus publicum faciendum locare. Sugli appalti relativi alle opere pubbliche nell'età repubblicana e augustea*, Napoli 1998.

Tuori K., *Breaking Chairs. Sella Curulis in Roman Law, Identity and Memory*, "Arctos" 54/2020, pp. 257–284.

Tuori K., Heikonen J., *Spaces of Citizenship. The Census in Roman Republican Topography and Ideology*, "MEFRA" 134.2/2022, pp. 335–360.

Urbanik J., *Husband and Wife*, [in:] *The Oxford Handbook of Roman Law and Society*, eds. P.J. du Plessis, C. Ando, K. Tuori, Oxford 2016, pp. 473–486.

Urbanik J., *'Tuas res tibi habeto': la funzione delle 'parole approvate' nel divorzio*, [in:] *Dire le droit: normes, juges, jurisconsultes*, ed. B. Anagnostou-Canas, Paris 2006, pp. 87–98.

Urso G., *Cassio Dione e i magistrati. Le origini della repubblica nei frammenti della 'Storia romana'*, Milano 2005.

Vessey D.W.T.C., *Thoughts on Tacitus' Portrayal of Claudius*, "AJP" 92.3/1971, pp. 385–409.

Villers L., *Le mariage envisagé comme institution d'État dans le droit classique de Rome*, "ANRW" II.14/1982, pp. 285–301.

Vitucci G., *Intorno a un nuovo frammento di 'elogium'*, "Rivista di Filologia e di Istruzione Classica" 81/1953, pp. 43–61.

Vollmer F., *De funere publico Romanorum*, Leipzig 1892.

Volterra E., *Manomissione e cittadinanza*, [in:] *Studi in onore di Ugo Enrico Paoli*, Firenze 1956, pp. 695–699.

Volterra E., *Ricerche intorno agli sponsali in diritto romano*, [in:] E. Volterra, *Scritti giuridici*, I, Napoli 1991, pp. 339–420.

Volterra E., *Sull' 'incensus' in diritto romano*, [in:] E. Volterra, *Scritti giuridici*, II, Napoli 1991, pp. 433–447.

Von Premerstein A., *Vom Werden und Wesen des Prinzipats*, München 1937.

Wacke A., *Der Selbstmord im römischen Recht und in der Rechtsentwicklung*, "ZSS" 97/1980, s. 26–77.

Watson A., *The Divorce of Carvilius Ruga*, "TR" 33/1965, pp. 38–50.

Watson A., *'Gentis enuptio'*, [in:] A. Watson, *Studies in Roman Private Law*, London–Rio Grande 1991, pp. 3–13.

Watson A., *Roman Slave Law*, Baltimore, MD–London 1987.

Watson A., *The Law of Persons in the Later Roman Republic*, Oxford 1967.

Watson P.A., *Ancient Stepmothers. Myth, Misogyny and Reality*, Leiden–New–York–Köln 1995.

Weiss E., *'Manumissio'*, "RE" 14.2/1930, pp. 1366–1377.

Welwei K.W., *Piraterie und Sklaverei in der frühen römischen Republik*, [in:] *Fünfzig Jahre Forschungen zur Antiken Sklaverei an der Mainzer Akademie 1950-2000. Miscellanea zum Iubiläum*, Stuttgart 2001, pp. 73–81.

Wenger L., *Die Quellen des römischen Rechts*, Wien 1953.
Wesch-Klein G., '*Funus publicum*'. *Eine Studie zur öffentlichen Beisetzung und Gewährung von Ehrengräbern in Rom und den Westprovinzen*, Stuttgart 1993.
Willems P., *Le sénat de la république romaine*, I, 1878 (reprint Aalen 1968).
Wiseman T.P., *The Census in the First Century B.C.*, "JRS" 59.1–2/1969, pp. 59–75.
Wlosok A., *'Nihil nisi ruborem' – über die Rolle der Scham in der römischen Rechtskultur*, "Grazer Beiträge" 9/1980, pp. 155–172.
Wolf J.G., *Das Stigma ignominia*, "ZSS" 126/2009, pp. 55–113.
Wolf J.G., *Lo stigma dell'ignominia*, [in:] *Homo, caput, persona. La costruzione giuridica dell' identità nell'esperienza romana*, eds. A. Corbino, M. Humbert, G. Negri, Pavia 2010, pp. 491–550.
Wright A., *Velleius Paterculus and L. Munatius Plancus*, "CP" 97.2/2002, pp. 178–184.
Wycisk T., '*Quidquid in foro fieri potest*'. *Studien zum römischen Recht bei Quintilian*, Berlin 2008.
Yaron R., *Minutiae on Roman Divorce*, "TR" 28/1960, pp. 1–12.
Zabłocka M., *Il 'ius trium liberorum' nel diritto romano*, "BIDR" 30/1992, pp. 361–390.
Zabłocka M., *Le XII Tavole – fonte dei principi del diritto contemporaneo*, "Iura" 53/2002, pp. 1–16.
Zabłocki J., *Appunti sull''officium iudicis' nella 'Noctes Atticae'*, [in:] *Au-delà des fontierès. Mélanges de droit romain offers à Witold Wołodkiewicz*, II, eds. M. Zabłocka, J. Krzynówek, J. Urbanik, Z. Służewska, Varsovie 2000, pp. 1115–1126.
Zabłocki J., *'Consortium ercto non cito' in Aulus Gellius' 'Noctes Atticae'*, [in:] J. Zabłocki, *Scripta Gelliana*, Warszawa 2020, pp. 105–117.
Zabłocki J., *Illeciti delle donne romane*, "Ius Antiquum" 1.8/2001, pp. 75–80.
Zabłocki J., *Il segreto nel diritto romano*, [in:] *Scritti per Alessandro Corbino*, ed. I. Piro, VII, Tricase 2016, pp. 589–599.
Zabłocki J., *'Iudex qui iuravit rem sibi non liquere'*, [in:] J. Zabłocki, *Scripta Gelliana*, Warszawa 2020, pp. 241–255.
Zabłocki J., *'Leges de plebiscitis'. Equiparazione dei 'plebiscita' alle 'leges'*, [in:] *'Forum Romanum'. Doklady III miezhdunarodnoj konferencji. 'Rimskoe czastnoe i publicznoe pravo*, Moskva 2003, pp. 15–18.
Zabłocki J., *'Leges votatae' nelle assemblee popolari*, "Diritto@Storia" 10–11/2011/2012, https://www.dirittoestoria.it/10/Tradizione-Romana/Zablocki-Leges-voto-assemblee-popolari.htm.
Zabłocki J., *Procedura esecutiva nella legge delle XII Tavole*, [in:] *Studi in onore di Antonino Metro*, ed. C. Russo Ruggeri, VI, Milano 2010, pp. 513–534.
Zabłocki J., *The Image of a Roman Family in 'Noctes Atticae' by Aulus Gellius*, "Pomoerium" 2/1996, pp. 35–44.
Zabłocki J., *The Picture of a Roman Family in 'Noctes Atticae' by Aulus Gellius*, [in:] J. Zabłocki, *Scripta Gelliana*, Warszawa 2020, pp. 45–61.
Zabłocki J., *The Prohibition on Women Drinking Wine in Anient Rome*, [in:] J. Zabłocki, *Scripta Gelliana*, Warszawa 2020, pp. 93–104.
Zanda E., *Fighting Hydra-Like Luxury. Sumptuary Regulation in the Roman Republic*, London–New Delhi–New York–Sydney 2013 (reprint).
Zanker P., *The Power of Images in the Age of Augustus*, transl. A. Shapiro, Ann Arbor, MI 1990.
Zevi F., *Catone e i cavalieri grassi. Il culto di Vulcano ad Ostia: una proposta di lettura storica*, "MEFRA" 121.2/2009, pp. 505–513.
Ziółkowski A., *Storia di Roma*, Milano 2010.

General Index

Index of Sources Cited

Note: Page numbers followed by "n" denote endnotes.